The Presidency and the Rhetoric of Foreign Crisis

Studies in Rhetoric/Communication
Thomas W. Benson, General Editor

The Presidency and the Rhetoric of Foreign Crisis

Denise M. Bostdorff

University of South Carolina Press

Copyright © 1994 University of South Carolina

Published in Columbia, South Carolina, by the
University of South Carolina Press

Manufactured in the United States of America

Library of Congress Cataloging-in-Publication Data

Bostdorff, Denise M., 1959–
    The presidency and the rhetoric of foreign crisis / Denise M.
Bostdorff.
        p.   cm.
    Includes bibliographical references and index.
    ISBN 0–87249–968–5 (hard cover : acid-free)
    1. United States—Foreign relations—1945–1989.   2. Rhetoric—
Political aspects—United States—History—20th century.
3. Presidents—United States—History—20th century.
4. Communication in politics—United States—History—20th century.
I. Title.
E840.B66   1994
327.73′009′045—dc20   93-21561
                                                            CIP

CONTENTS

PREFACE

In this book I examine the phenomenon of crisis promotion and management—how presidents have convinced the public that foreign crises exist and that the presidents have handled these crises most admirably. I take the perspective that foreign crises are linguistic constructions, for it is largely through presidential communication that foreign crises become real for American citizens. Presidents do not concoct all foreign crises out of thin air, but American citizens' distance from foreign locales and lack of knowledge about other countries mean that presidents must persuasively advance claims of crisis in order to prompt public support for their crisis policies. Nonetheless, presidential discourse frequently heightens the significance of base events that otherwise would attract little public attention—for example, a coup on the tiny Caribbean island of Grenada—and thereby persuasively implores citizens to support U.S. military intervention there and to view the president's policy as a great victory. Indeed, my analysis indicates that presidents gain substantial political benefits from successful crisis promotion and management.

I also argue that presidents have used crisis rhetoric to accrue more power over foreign affairs and have, in turn, relied on public and congressional acceptance of power usurpation to promote more crises. This is not to say that crisis promotion and management infallibly result in advantages for commanders-in-chief. Presidential efforts to define political reality have backfired when the president found he was unable to resolve the crisis he had promoted or discovered he was trapped by his earlier words into a particular course of action. Potential drawbacks notwithstanding, presidents have frequently found crisis promotion to be an alluring issue management option.

I begin with an explanation of the communication perspective and method this study adopts and an examination of what previous research has said about presidential crisis rhetoric. The chapters that follow consist of six case studies of crisis promotion and management, each taken from a different administration, beginning with John Kennedy and the 1962 Cuban missile crisis. Because Kennedy served as a catalyst for structural/legal changes and sophisticated news management techniques, he created a context in which crisis promotion and management could occur on a regular basis. The other cases analyzed here include Johnson and the Gulf of Tonkin, Nixon and Cambodia, Ford and the *Mayaguez,* Carter and Iran, Reagan and Grenada, and, along with my conclusions in chapter 8, Bush and Panama.

In each of these cases, I focus on three key components of the presidents' rhetoric: how they portrayed the crisis *situation,* the *style,* or attitude, their discourse typically exhibited, and the *identificational appeals* they employed to encourage citizen identification with and support for presidential policies. I attempt to illumine *how* presidents promote and manage crises through their language. Finally, I raise some disturbing questions about the implications presidential crisis promotion has for the American polity.

ACKNOWLEDGMENTS

Like crises, books simultaneously connote for their authors both threat and opportunity: the threat that the study will never be completed and the opportunity to focus one's energies and attentions upon a single research project. Although I cannot possibly thank all the individuals who aided me with this book, a number deserve special mention.

First, I acknowledge my doctoral committee at Purdue University, where this book took its initial form as a dissertation. David M. Berg, Richard E. Crable, and Myron Q. Hale all made contributions to this project. In particular, I thank my advisor, Steven L. Vibbert, for his invaluable insights. As a mentor and colleague, he has been without equal.

Second, I thank the staffs of the John F. Kennedy Library in Boston, the Lyndon Baines Johnson Library in Austin, the Nixon Presidential Materials in Alexandria, Virginia, the Gerald Ford Library in Ann Arbor, and the Jimmy Carter Library in Atlanta for their assistance in my research. I am especially grateful to Joan Howard who provided me with invaluable aid and to Bill Joyner who shared generously of his help and humor. I appreciate the vital monetary support of the David Ross Foundation, the Lyndon Baines Johnson Foundation, the Purdue Research Foundation, and the Purdue University Library Scholars Grant Program, which made my study of presidential archives possible.

Next, I mention others who made this a better book than it otherwise would be. My students at Purdue University—particularly Kirt Wilson, Mary Keehner, Lisa Goodnight, and Bill Elwood—read early drafts and made helpful suggestions. In addition, Kenneth Burke, David Zarefsky, and Kathleen Turner provided me with constructive criticism on early versions of particular chapters. Kathie merits special thanks for her continued encouragement and support as my academic "big sister." Moreover, I thank Kurt Ritter for his recommendations on the penultimate draft of this book and acknowledge Tom Benson who showed a remarkable ability simultaneously to guide, to challenge, and to provide me with the independence that I needed.

I thank my parents, brother, sisters, and grandparents for their love and continuing interest in my work. I also express my deep love and appreciation for Dan, my best friend and companion for life. His insightful comments improved the quality of this book, and his humor served as a constant source of encouragement. Finally, I would be remiss if I did not mention Morgan Bostdorff O'Rourke, for he has proven without a doubt that "the Germans and the Irish really are good for one another."

The Presidency and
the Rhetoric of
Foreign Crisis

Chapter One

PRESIDENTS AND THE PROMOTION
OF FOREIGN CRISES
An Introduction

In the early morning of Wednesday, December 20, 1989, President George Bush appeared on nationwide television: "My fellow citizens, last night I ordered U.S. military forces to Panama. No President takes such action lightly. This morning, I want to tell you what I did and why I did it."[1] The commander-in-chief went on to detail how "the dictator of Panama, General Manuel Noriega, an indicted drug trafficker," had declared Panama to be at war with the United States the previous week. According to Bush, he decided to take action against Noriega after Panamanian forces killed one American serviceman, attacked two others, and threatened the wife of a serviceman with sexual abuse. The president said he had ordered Operation Just Cause, the U.S. invasion of Panama, to combat the illegal drug trade, to protect the integrity of the Panama Canal treaty, to protect American lives, and to restore democracy to Panama.[2]

In the days that followed, heavy fighting resulted in the deaths of at least twenty-four American soldiers and hundreds of Panamanian civilians.[3] Noriega found temporary refuge at the Vatican embassy, but eventually turned himself in to U.S. authorities, who took him to Miami to face charges of drug trafficking.[4] In the streets of Panama, citizens cheered American troops. The Panamanian crisis also proved to be a tremendous political boon at home: Bush's management of the crisis had won him widespread public and congressional support and laid to rest questions about his "toughness."[5] According to journalist R. W. Apple, Jr., Bush had undergone a presidential rite of passage. Apple observed that contemporary U.S. leaders frequently "have felt a need to demonstrate their willingness to shed blood to protect or advance what they construe as the national interest."[6]

This book is about *how* American presidents have invoked this rite, or how they have convinced the public that foreign crises exist and that they have handled these crises admirably. Contemporary commanders-in-chief have promoted foreign crises by explicitly advancing a claim of crisis or implicitly treating an event as a crisis in their public discourse. The choice of the term *promote* to describe this type of communication activity is most appropriate. "To promote" means to advance a claim and bring it to the attention of others. Because foreign locales are so distant and knowledge of them is far removed from most Americans' daily lives, presidents must persuasively advance claims of crisis in order to prompt public support for their crisis policies. Presidents do

1

not concoct all foreign crises out of thin air; rather, they have information about foreign affairs that ordinary citizens do not—unless presidents choose to share that information. Thus presidents promote a sense of crisis whether they believe such an assertion is justified or whether they simply believe such an allegation is politically expedient. Of course another meaning of "to promote" is to advance a person to a higher position of honor. Whatever the reasons for a president's crisis promotion, good or ill, he may advance his career through the political benefits that a crisis terminology can offer. To what degree this occurs rests largely—albeit not exclusively—with the president's management abilities, for commanders-in-chief must not only establish the existence of a crisis, but also manage the crisis by attempting to resolve it through military or other means. And they must attempt to persuade citizens that the resolution was the most appropriate one available. In this book, I examine six case studies and explain how presidents have used language to promote and manage foreign crises from 1962 through the present.

Beyond a primary concern with the characteristics and strategies of presidential crisis rhetoric, I explore the relationship between crisis promotion and management and the gradual accumulation of power over foreign affairs by contemporary commanders-in-chief. Although the founding fathers split the nation's war powers between the legislative and executive branches, we now have what historian Arthur Schlesinger has described as an "imperial presidency," where power has shifted significantly to the White House.[7] In this book, I examine how presidents have used foreign crises to accrue more power and, in turn, have relied on public and congressional acceptance of power usurpation to promote more crises. Despite efforts to reassert congressional authority, presidents today involve the nation in military intervention in other countries almost at will. The presidential pattern of crisis promotion and management not only perpetuates such behavior, but also has grave implications for our political system because of the disturbing way it encourages Americans to perceive their political world.

In this chapter, I first explain the integral role of rhetoric in foreign crises and provide a basic framework for understanding crisis promotion and management. I then discuss what is known about presidential crisis rhetoric and describe why and how this analysis was conducted.

PRESIDENTS, CRISES, AND RHETORIC

Shortly after the invasion of Panama, President Bush told reporters at a press conference that he would not comment on Noriega's legal case or "any matters that could even inadvertently affect the outcome" of his trial. Lesley Stahl of CBS News then asked the president if he had not prejudiced the case already with his recent descriptions of Noriega as a thug and a drug trafficker. Bush replied that such characterizations of Noriega had come from all quarters, including "the press, columnists, even commentators, Presidents, Members of the United States Congress. He is now in custody. [The] time for rhetoric is over."[8] The president's statement reaffirmed the commonplace cry of "mere rhetoric!" that disparages political language as just so many alluring shadows, which may distract us from the political realities that lie outside Plato's cave. Although Bush acknowledged that even he had partaken of rhetoric from time to time, he treated it as if it were somewhat unseemly and emotional, quite distinct from the facts of political substance.

The president's claim notwithstanding, the time for rhetoric had barely begun. Bush's statement that he would not comment on Noriega's case helped portray the commander-in-chief as a fair and law-abiding leader, in stark contrast to the villainous drug-running fugitive from whom we had saved Panama. By refusing to speak about possibly prejudicial matters, Bush also gained a measure of control over public portrayals of U.S. intervention in Panama. He could talk about aspects of the invasion that supported his depiction of events and legitimately avoid the discussion of troublesome questions. He did just that when a reporter in the same news conference asked about his contacts with General Noriega during the Reagan administration and whether he had been aware of the general's drug activities at that time. Bush told the reporter that he had answered these questions in the past, "so punch it in the computer," which implied that the president had previously been forthright about such inquiries and that his answers were a matter of public record. Furthermore, Bush reminded the journalist that "I'll have nothing more to say about it because I do not want, even inadvertently, to prejudice this case."[9] The reporter pursued the question no further. George Bush was employing rhetoric, or persuasive speech, and his words did much to construct a particular political reality that was presented to millions as a result of the media audience the president had chosen to address.

In *Verbal Behavior and Politics,* Doris Graber reports that citizens today learn almost everything they know about the political world not from direct experience, but from the words of others.[10] The most prominent speakers today, American presidents, use words to shape our view of what matters and what does not. Sometimes they direct our attention away from an "economic downturn" and point self-servingly to "opportunities for growth." Presidents also have their more selfless moments when they create national goals such as the Great Society and racial equality and encourage citizens to reach them. Rhetoric is sometimes cynical and manipulative, sometimes high-minded and admirable, but it is always persuasive discourse that, especially when uttered by presidents, helps construct our political realities.

According to Jeffrey Tulis, presidents speak much more frequently to citizens today than they have at any time in the past. Tulis claims that a "rhetorical presidency" now exists and that the mass media have facilitated this development "by giving the president the means to communicate directly and instantaneously to a large national audience, and by reinforcing . . . verbal dramatic performance."[11] With the help of the mass media, presidential rhetoric—not bombast, but public talk—has encouraged Americans to reach the moon, forgive Richard Nixon, declare a war on drugs, return the Panama Canal, beware the evil empire, and later accept the Soviet Union as a worthy adversary with whom we could negotiate. These attempts at persuasion met with varying degrees of success, but they underscore the importance of presidential communication in our society.

Indeed, political scientist Mary Stuckey goes so far as to describe the president as the nation's "interpreter-in-chief."[12] Communication scholar Rod Hart similarly observes that rhetoric is so important to the office today that no mute could serve as president. Congress, citizens, political parties, and the media would not know what to do "when confronted with a president who could reason, decide, and act, but who could not utter words."[13] For all of these reasons, the present study takes presidential rhetoric seriously. It recognizes, in Murray Edelman's terms, that "political language *is* political reality."[14]

Because of the symbolic nature of our political world, the issues that presidents discuss are not objective, independent entities, but linguistic constructions. Cities, weapons, the elderly, wildlife, and oil fields certainly exist; meaning, however, does not lie in these entities themselves, but in the language used to interpret them and the events in which they are involved. Richard Crable and Steven Vibbert explain that issues come to life only when an individual or organization attaches importance to a perceived problem and gives voice to that concern; in other words, they "make an issue" out of some situation.[15]

Whether a particular issue becomes a *public* issue depends on the degree to which an advocate can convince others to attach importance to the problem. The attention the general public pays to the issue of hunger, for example, has less to do with changes in the numbers of hungry citizens or other conditions than with the significance attached to those conditions.[16] Most Americans do not lack for sustenance, but they sometimes argue that the poverty in our country is a national disgrace and at other times scarcely pay attention to it at all.

Presidents find that, because of their legitimacy, access to the media, and other resources, they are especially efficacious issue managers. According to political scientist Richard Neustadt, presidential power is "the power to persuade."[17] Chief executives can use language to give birth to an issue, to encourage us to believe that no issue exists, and to convince us that some issues are more urgent and deserving of our attention than others. Furthermore, presidential rhetors recognize that the way they define issues is also important, for a definition establishes the *stasis,* or central point, on which an issue turns.[18] Citizens will evaluate the desirability of expensive weapons projects, for instance, differently depending on whether their president persuasively argues that the weapons are essential for our "national defense" or whether he claims they are an example of "pork barrel politics." Likewise, the call for censorship of government-funded works of art may be deemed necessary if the issue at hand is one of "pornography," but dangerous if the issue is "freedom of speech." Wise presidential rhetors name an issue in such a way that their proposed policy appears to be the best possible resolution. As David Zarefsky aptly observes, "to choose a definition is to plead a cause."[19]

Despite the institutional and other advantages that presidents possess, they frequently find that public persuasion can be a source of frustration. For example, Hermann Stelzner claims that Gerald Ford had to retreat from his war against inflation in part because media definitions of the nation's economic woes were at odds with his own.[20] Similarly, Jimmy Carter tried to legitimize the issue of energy, but failed to enlighten citizens as to its importance. Nor did John Kennedy's eloquent appeals on behalf of civil rights convince significant numbers of southern citizens that integration was in the public's best interest. At other times, a president's initial definition of an issue may work well, but later pose major problems. According to Zarefsky, Lyndon Johnson's declaration of an unconditional war against poverty served to unite Americans against a common enemy and to ensure passage of his Great Society programs. The definition also contained "the seeds of its own destruction" when Americans eventually felt that the war could not be won.[21] Presidents may have strategic advantages when it comes to public persuasion, but they also meet with their share of defeats.

Perhaps because of this, presidents find the language of crisis alluring, especially when applied to the realm of foreign affairs. According to the *Oxford English Dictionary,* the word *crisis* refers to "the turning-point of a disease for better or worse" and the "vitally important or decisive stage in the progress of anything." Crisis derives from the Greek word κρίσις, which means a choosing, a dispute, an issue, or a decision.[22] One may think of crisis as the critical moment of decision in the life of an issue or dispute.

Because a crisis terminology has particular implications, rhetors can use it to their persuasive advantage. The word *crisis,* for instance, defines an issue as especially threatening, which helps an advocate focus the attention of citizens and government officials on a problem. Additionally, the urgency implied by *crisis* legitimizes the issue, the need for quick action, and any sacrifices citizens may be asked to make.[23] A crisis terminology provides the simple, appealing polarization of "threat" versus "the threatened" and thereby offers rich drama for media coverage. The ominous character of crisis also encourages auditors to unite in support of a policy that will bring the crisis to an end. Like the related term *war,* crisis implies urgency. Unlike war, crisis connotes a short-term issue, something that will be resolved fairly quickly and with limited sacrifice.[24] This can pose problems when crises become protracted or seem to expend too many resources. This disadvantage is countered, however, because crisis does not suggest the elusive goal of complete victory, as war does. Rhetors also may attach the term *crisis* to issues for which they have ready solutions. According to Edelman, "Those who favor a particular course of governmental action are likely to cast about for a widely feared problem to which to attach it in order to maximize its support."[25] The language of crisis imbues any problem or issue with fear; hence, rhetors can use this terminology to gain passage of proposed policies and to portray themselves as efficacious.

If the terminology of crisis possesses inherent advantages, these advantages rapidly multiply when the rhetor is a president who uses the role of commander-in-chief to expound upon a foreign crisis. Presidents function as symbols of national unity, and a greater reverence exists for them than for other government officials. Citizens tend to believe presidents, especially when the topic is foreign affairs. Many Americans have limited knowledge in this area and believe the president has superior information.[26] Consequently, presidents legitimize the definition of a situation as a foreign crisis the moment they publicly give voice to it. Chief executives, as caretakers of the nation's highest office, can also easily draw on traditional American values and historical examples to provide additional legitimation.

This relationship between definition and legitimation is especially important in crisis promotion because a president with a high degree of personal credibility will find it easier to convince citizens that a crisis exists. Furthermore, a president bolstered by both institutional and personal legitimacy has more credibility to draw upon should the crisis not end as successfully as the president wishes; popular presidents can afford untidy crises and policy resolutions because they can lend their personal credibility to more positive interpretations of those events. John Kennedy, for instance, suffered a military defeat at the Bay of Pigs, but did not suffer fatal political repercussions. The legitimacy of his office and Kennedy's personal popularity allowed his administration to redefine the failed invasion as part of Kennedy's presidential education. Only later, when citizens perceived that Kennedy had also floundered in Vienna and acceded to the construction of the Berlin Wall, did serious questions arise about his competence. Personal popularity, then, provides presidents with a special resource to legitimize their definitions of crisis situations. This resource is not without its limits, for low personal credibility may actually mitigate against the institutional legitimacy of the presidential office. At the time the hostage seizure began, Jimmy Carter already had low credibility, which hindered his long-term attempts to persuade Americans to accept his interpretation of the hostage crisis and the desirable policy resolutions to that crisis.

In addition to the benefits that institutional legitimacy and high personal credibility may provide, chief executives possess a second advantage for crisis promotion: their ability to exert a great deal of influence over media coverage of foreign crises. When presidents claim that foreign crises exist, they immediately gain media attention. Moreover, the commander-in-chief can easily control information about foreign crises. Not only do such crises occur in regions that are remote for most Americans, but the president can, in the name of national security, withhold information or place curbs on news coverage. In so doing, the president puts constraints on the public dissemination of information that might contradict his depiction of crisis. Because foreign crises involve a conflict between our nation and some threatening nation or philosophy, foreign crises are also conducive to classic hero vs. villain polarizations, which make for dramatic journalistic accounts and positive portrayals of the president as our country's chief hero.

Another advantage the commander-in-chief can rely on for crisis promotion is that citizens usually support their president's chosen policy resolution. As opinion-tracking studies clearly indicate, citizens consistently rally around their leaders when the leaders (and therefore the nation) are threatened from abroad.[27] Aiding and abetting such support is the president's control over foreign policy. Today a president can enact policy *before* announcing the existence of a crisis; the issue definition then serves to rationalize the president's course of action. Because crises imply threat and the urgent need for resolution, many citizens enthusiastically jump aboard the president's crisis bandwagon.

Even if a president announces a foreign crisis and *then* decides to pursue a particular policy, whether military or otherwise, his critics typically find the task of opposition difficult. Communication analyst Theodore Windt explains that presumption is against the president's opponents: they must attack the president's definition of the issue before they can attack his policy.[28] To do so is a complicated task. To criticize the commander-in-chief in the midst of an apparent crisis may appear downright unpatriotic. Therefore opponents discover that arguments against the president's assertions quickly garner them opponents of their own.

The conceptual framework developed here is not meant to imply that presidents need only claim that a crisis exists for citizens to believe it is so. Richard Nixon, for example, warned Americans of the crisis in Cambodia with rhetoric that seemed similar to that of Kennedy about the Cuban missiles, Johnson about the Gulf of Tonkin, and Reagan about Grenada. Nonetheless, Nixon failed to gain the strong and widespread public support for his actions that these other commanders-in-chief did. Gallup found that although Nixon won the approval of 50 percent of Americans polled, 39 percent disapproved of his policy decision.[29] College campuses exploded with antiwar protests, and Nixon faced considerable criticism on Capitol Hill. Several factors contributed to Nixon's problems, but two are of particular interest here.

Americans had a high awareness of Vietnam and Cambodia, and they held established opinions on what should be done there—and these opinions frequently clashed with Nixon's actions. Although citizens were highly aware of Cuba in the fall of 1962, a majority of Americans wanted Kennedy to "do something" about Cuba, especially after the Bay of Pigs fiasco. In contrast, the relative obscurity of the Gulf of Tonkin and Grenada at the time these crises were promoted worked in the favor of the commanders-in-chief in charge; few Americans knew enough about these places to question what the president said.

Beyond the problem of public awareness and opinion, Nixon's crisis lacked cohesive public support because Nixon, despite all his efforts, could not control media information, which led to the extensive circulation of criticisms of his policy. Kennedy and Reagan, in particular, skillfully managed the news during their crises, which seems to have contributed to their triumphs.

As Nixon's example demonstrates, crisis promotion does not guarantee commanders-in-chief persuasive success, for a president's crisis rhetoric will never convince everyone, and at times a president may even fail to persuade a majority of Americans that a crisis exists or that his policies are the best way to resolve that crisis. The contribution of the Iranian hostage crisis to Jimmy Carter's downfall stands as testimony of this point. Nevertheless, presidents clearly possess resources that give them a decided advantage over those who articulate competing views.

If the commander-in-chief can persuade citizens to accept his preferred interpretation of a crisis and its resolution, he has much to gain. Successful crisis promotion allows the president to increase his personal credibility or supply of public goodwill, which he can draw upon during future policy decisions.[30] The Cuban missile crisis, for instance, symbolized an increase in substantive power for Americans and verified that their country was still proud and secure. Kennedy accordingly procured a large amount of goodwill during the crisis. With its resolution, the president's approval rating increased greatly, and Democrats won a historic, off-year congressional victory.[31]

Presidents can also use crisis promotion to accrue valuable symbolic reserves. Long after the successful resolution of a crisis, the crisis may continue to serve as a powerful reminder of the nation's triumph—what Edelman and Graber call a condensation symbol.[32] The president may refer to this symbol of victory in the future as a means to distribute symbolic reassurance. Two months after the Gulf of Tonkin crisis, for example, Lyndon Johnson still referred to his "limited and fitting response" to that crisis to reassure voters about his intentions in Vietnam. In his election bid against Barry Goldwater, Johnson cast himself as a man of peace. He told an Iowa campaign crowd, "We used our power [in the Gulf of Tonkin] with judgment and restraint, and I want you to know that if I am continued as your Commander in Chief, I am willing to go anywhere, I am willing to talk to anyone, I am anxious to sit down and get the advice of men in both parties."[33] Through the promotion and management of a crisis in the Gulf of Tonkin, Johnson replenished his symbolic reserves for future use.

Communication studies by Windt, Richard Cherwitz, Cherwitz and Kenneth Zagacki, Jeff Bass, and Bonnie Dow point out that presidents may also use the threat of crisis to justify policies they have already enacted or to legitimize policies they want.[34] In May 1986, for instance, Ronald Reagan gave one of his weekly radio chats in which he discussed how the House of Representatives had passed a military budget that was "wholly inadequate." The president went on to praise the heroes of the Libyan crisis, "men like Captain Lorence and Captain Ribas-Dominicci, Air Force pilots who recently lost their lives in the raid on Libyan terrorists." According to Reagan, "We honor them today and all the members of freedom's honor guard. And we say thank you to you, our Armed Forces, and pledge our support for adequate military expenditures, a strong defense, and the dream of world freedom and peace."[35] By invoking the Libyan crisis and the names of those who had sacrificed their lives, the president made his insistence on a larger military budget seem justified, if not essential.

Yet another benefit for commanders-in-chief is that successful crisis promotion and management may divert public attention from other issues. The crisis in Grenada, for example, focused attention on the Reagan administration's successful "rescue mission" in the Caribbean and away from the deaths of more than two hundred Marines that the White House had sent to Beirut. In this way, crises serve to mask issues a president finds troublesome and to highlight his successes instead.[36]

Related to this is a fifth and final benefit: successful crisis promotion and management can make the president appear especially presidential. Jeff Bass and Gerard Hauser argue that crises give presidents an opportunity, given their control over foreign policy and over interpretations of that policy's success, to portray themselves as efficient and indispensable heads of state.[37] For many Americans, Gerald Ford's management of the *Mayaguez* crisis in 1975 made his presidential bid viable in 1976. The crisis seemed to prove that Ford possessed the necessary qualities for presidential leadership. Because the president could announce that the entire *Mayaguez* crew had been rescued through his efforts, few paid attention to the number of casualties the operation incurred. Crisis promotion and management prove that in politics "nothing succeeds like success."

When presidents talk about a foreign crisis, they treat the crisis like a completely objective, factual state of affairs that has occurred as a result of some other party's actions. A closer look reveals that crises have a different origin. According to Windt, "Situations do not create crises. Rather, the president's perception of the situation and the rhetoric he uses to describe it mark an event as a crisis."[38] What else can explain why U.S. missiles in Turkey near the

Soviet border were defensive, whereas the Soviets' missiles in Cuba were offensive and highly threatening? Why did Ronald Reagan call the incident in which the Soviets shot down a Korean airliner a "tragedy," rather than a crisis? What made Manuel Noriega a threatening drug trafficker who had to be brought to justice when earlier he had been an ally and worked closely with George Bush? Why did the holding of our hostages in Iran constitute a "crisis," whereas a U.S. diplomat and other Americans held hostage in Colombia in 1980 warranted not a single White House statement?[39]

For each question, the answer is that the president made a decision about what was a crisis and what was not, then used his public language accordingly. Commanders-in-chief may believe that a crisis truly exists to which we must respond; they may feel that to call an event a crisis—or to refrain from doing so—is the politically expedient course of action; or they may simply add their voices to those of other individuals who have already named an event a crisis. Regardless of how or why the crisis is initiated, presidents who talk about foreign crises are engaged in an intensive communication effort, or as Wayne Brockriede and Robert Scott describe the Cuban missile crisis, "a complex persuasive campaign."[40] To illumine how presidents engage in such public persuasion is not the only way to understand foreign crises. To study these events rhetorically, however, is to understand foreign crises as most Americans experience them.

CRISIS RHETORIC RESEARCH: A REVIEW AND RATIONALE

A number of scholars, such as psychologists, historians, and political scientists, have demonstrated an interest in foreign crises.[41] Included among these researchers are rhetorical critics who come from the field of communication. Rhetorical critics are not critics in the usual sense of the term. They do not, for example, listen to George Bush's televised announcement about Panama and then vote thumbs-up or thumbs-down with regard to his communication skills. Nor do rhetorical critics claim "President Bush's speech moved me. I liked it." Such a response would not be criticism but—to paraphrase Edwin Black—the expression of the state of their glands.[42] According to the *Oxford English Dictionary*, one meaning of *criticism* is "the art of estimating the qualities and character of literary or artistic work."[43] This definition broadly describes the work of rhetorical critics, for rhetorical critics are scholars who analyze communication. They may be interested in its characteristics, its functions, its ethics, its antecedents, its descendants, or some other related element. In all of these cases, though, rhetorical critics are primarily concerned with the *explanation* of discourse that occurs when that discourse is analyzed in relation to other discourse and in the context of communication theory.

A rhetorical critic interested in Bush's address on Panama, for instance, would situate the speech among previous presidential crisis speeches and among relevant communication concepts and research. On the basis of such analysis, rhetorical critics make judgments about the identifying characteristics of a piece of discourse, its key persuasive functions, the ethicality of its appeals, its linguistic roots in earlier rhetoric, its relationship to rhetoric that followed, or some other aspect of the talk. Furthermore, rhetorical critics make judgments about how their analysis impacts communication theory: Does it corroborate earlier findings? Does it suggest the refinement of a communication concept? Does it call an established communication concept into question? Does it contribute something completely new? Like scholars in other fields, rhetorical critics make decisions about how their research affects theory.

Since 1970, rhetorical critics have published eighteen studies that examine presidential foreign crisis talk.[44] The scope of these studies has been far-reaching, and a number of them have been especially insightful. Beyond their explication of the linguistic nature of crisis and some of the ways in which foreign crises function, many of the scholars reached similar conclusions about the characteristics of presidential crisis rhetoric.

One finding that appears in a number of crisis studies is that commanders-in-chief typically depict the United States as a passive nation interested "in maintaining world peace and enhancing the welfare of other nations." Nonetheless, Cherwitz and Zagacki report that "when culprit nations strike, the U.S., the hero, transforms into an active, retaliatory party." Such characterizations justify U.S. policy by portraying the United States as a country that takes action against others only as a last resort for its own defense or for the defense of other goodwilled nations that are under siege.[45] At the same time, these depictions make clear that the United States has both the capability and the determination to act when needed.

A second discovery of previous research is that presidents often elevate crises into tests of national will. In Windt's comparison of Kennedy's announcement of the Cuban missile crisis with Nixon's announcement of the Cambodian invasion, he claims that "even as each President announced his policy, he also attempted to shift the issue from its obvious military and political context to an ethical context; that is, from the consequences of war to a question of American character."[46] The pragmatic goals of removing missiles or capturing enemy supplies become less important than our nation's desire and ability to prove its toughness. For these reasons, international crises sometimes evolve into dangerous games of chicken.

Two recent studies argue that commanders-in-chief make appeals to progress in their crisis rhetoric. Although a benefit of crisis promotion is that it allows commanders-in-chief to strike a presidential pose, case studies by Bass and David Klope suggest that one of the ways in which presidents do so is by using arguments based on efficiency. Bass, in his study of Johnson and the Dominican Republic crisis, argues that "while critics continued to doubt the existence of a

Communist threat and the legality of the intervention, the President simply asked the American public to evaluate his performance on the grounds that he accomplished what he set out to do." American citizens obliged—and supported Johnson. Similarly, Klope contends that Reagan's televised address on Lebanon and Grenada provided the public with a sense of progress as his talk proceeded from disorder (Lebanon) to order (Grenada).[47] Perceptions of efficacy, in turn, contribute to perceptions of leadership.

Of all the conclusions that previous research has reached, the one that has perhaps been affirmed and reaffirmed most often is that presidential crisis rhetoric engages in victimage through scapegoating. Commanders-in-chief describe an enemy responsible for the crisis and rally the nation to unite against that enemy. This strategy helps presidents gain popular support for their policies; and by shifting the blame to someone else, it allows Americans and their leaders to escape culpability for any U.S. actions that may have contributed to a crisis. According to Cherwitz and Zagacki, presidential crisis discourse is a type of epideictic oratory "where the ritual of identifying and blaming adversaries is performed." Many other studies point to how particular presidents have constructed a "diabolical enemy image," portrayed the nation as "confronting the enemy," made use of "victimage," or concentrated on foes such as Communism in the attempt to rally support for their crisis management.[48] Despite the apparent unanimity, the conclusion that victimage necessarily characterizes presidential crisis rhetoric is *not* one supported by this book.

Because scholarly work in the area of crisis discourse has been plentiful, as well as percipient, the need for yet another examination of presidential crisis rhetoric may not be immediately clear. But I believe this study builds upon the foundations laid by earlier scholars in a useful way.

This book goes beyond the analysis of televised crisis announcement speeches, which have been the focus of most studies to this point, and examines subsequent public messages, as well. For instance, the approach taken in this study would regard Reagan's announcement of the bombing of Libya as important, but would also examine his strategic remarks at a White House correspondents dinner. At that social event, the president talked about the Libyan crisis and thanked reporters for their "vigorous, probing, and unbiased" account of "one of the most important stories of this decade."[49] By equating accurate and independent journalism with coverage of the Libyan crisis, the president gave greater credence to news reports and also encouraged journalists to provide him with the same type of accurate, independent—and positive— stories in the future. Reagan recognized that glowing media coverage should not go unrewarded, for there always will be a "next time," nor could he pass up the opportunity to emphasize the significance of his administration's actions under the guise of appreciating their newsworthiness.

Similarly, this approach would account more fully for Lyndon Johnson who, never comfortable with televised speeches and never a fan of journalists or press conferences, searched for a more congenial live audience when academics and reporters continued to criticize U.S. intervention in the Dominican Republic. The president found sympathetic listeners at a gathering of AFL-CIO members, whom he told with great drama about the "Communist seizure" in the Dominican Republic and how "American blood" would have run in the streets if he had not sent in the marines.[50] Johnson's remarks met with a favorable response, both his message and the audience response received media attention, and the president's speech thereby served to legitimize his management of the Dominican crisis. As these examples demonstrate, a president's televised national address about a foreign crisis does not reveal everything about how the commander-in-chief developed a crisis as a public issue and attempted to manage it.

The findings discussed in this book are based on an examination of the many public statements that commanders-in-chief made about their foreign crises. By including more than televised announcements, I attempt not only to confirm or disconfirm earlier findings about how presidents announce foreign crises, but also to enlarge the understanding of each president's crisis rhetoric. More specifically, I provide the reader with a glimpse of the big picture: how the president's numerous discrete pieces of discourse coalesced to promote a crisis and to persuade citizens that the president was resolving the crisis in the best way possible. As a result of this approach, my research suggests how crisis talk worked to the president's political and rhetorical advantage—or failed to do so—not only when the president first spoke about the crisis but after the crisis was resolved.

In this study, I treat the president's words as his own, despite the fact that most presidential rhetoric is written in full or in part by a staff of speechwriters and presidential aides. The presidency is, in Hart's words, *"a corporate entity"*[51] but the president nonetheless must take responsibility for the words he utters just as other corporate entities like Mobil Oil and Planned Parenthood must take responsibility for their public words. Therefore, I examine presidential persuasion recognizing that the president does not write all of his discourse, but also knowing that authorship does not matter to citizens when they listen to the president make public pronouncements.

A second rationale for this study is that it incorporates a greater number of case studies than previous critics have examined: Kennedy and the Cuban missile crisis, Johnson and the Gulf of Tonkin, Nixon and Cambodia, Ford and the *Mayaguez,* Carter and Iran, and Reagan and Grenada. The discussion of an additional case study, George Bush and Panama, appears in chapter 8.

These particular crises were chosen for several reasons. One factor was that they represented six different White House administrations, three Democratic presidents and three Republicans. The crises spanned two decades of contemporary U.S. history and represented political turning points where presidents marshaled massive American resources, often including military force, to meet some threat from abroad. Such episodes are of special rhetorical interest because the commanders-in-chief turned to public discourse to convince citizens that a crisis existed and to encourage them to support the deployment of resources to resolve it. In addition to their scope and rhetorical significance, these crises marked pivotal moments within each administration when the president expanded his control—and the control of his office—beyond constitutional war powers shared by the executive and legislative branches.

Presidents have gradually appropriated more power during times of crisis, and the examination of these cases allowed investigation of whether presidential crisis rhetoric had evolved as well. As succeeding chapters will reveal, the characteristics of presidential crisis discourse have stayed fairly constant since Kennedy's time, but commanders-in-chief have employed crisis promotion to accrue more power, and then used accumulated power to promote more crises.

By analyzing six different cases, I attempt to reveal important commonalties that presidential crisis promotion tends to share and thereby to extend knowledge about crisis rhetoric beyond the typical single crisis study. At the same time, I recognize the integrity of individual rhetors' persuasive efforts by providing a portrait of each president's rhetoric and imparting a better understanding of his particular crisis event.

To sift through and make sense of multiple pieces of discourse, I employ a method of rhetorical criticism that provides a systematic means by which to compare different presidents' talk. This method derives from the work of Kenneth Burke, a theorist who has long maintained a special interest in the uniquely human ability to create, use, and misuse symbols.[52]

PRESIDENTS AND FOREIGN CRISES:
AN EXPLANATION OF THE METHOD

According to Burke, all human beings have a particular framework of interpretation that derives from the language of the culture into which they were born and that may evolve with exposure to the vocabularies of other social groups. Through their linguistic framework, people ascribe meaning to the world they encounter.[53] Burkean scholar Barry Brummett points out that unlike Freud, who believes language reflects the motives of human thought, Burke claims that motives originate with the terms that people use to describe situations and that these terms provide people with the motives for their actions.[54] Burke refers to motives, for example, as "distinctly linguistic products" and explains that "our words for motive are in reality words for situation."[55]

Because interpretive frameworks or orientations vary somewhat, different people will pick different aspects of a situation as particularly meaningful.

Burke explains that the relationships people find significant "are not *realities,* they are *interpretations* of reality—hence different frameworks of interpretation will lead to different conclusions as to what reality is" and, correspondingly, to different conclusions as to how one should deal with that reality. The rhetorical analyst's job is to shed light on the motives of discourse by analyzing the way in which rhetors talk about or interpret the world around them.[56] Burke developed his theory of dramatism to perform just such a task.

Burke says that dramatism is not a metaphor, but a theory of terminology that literally considers language a mode of action or drama; furthermore, dramatism provides a means by which researchers may study symbolic action. As Burke explains it, "dramatism is a method of analysis and a corresponding critique of terminology designed to show that the most direct route to the study of human relations and human motives is via a methodical inquiry into cycles or clusters of terms and their functions."[57] Burke's method is language-centered. It involves the detailed examination of rhetoric in order to illumine the most important terms of a speaker's talk, the relationships among those terms, and the persuasive appeals upon which the speaker draws. In this book, Burke's method is used to answer three questions about each president's crisis rhetoric: (1) How did the president portray the crisis situation? (2) What style did the president exhibit in his promotion and management of the crisis? (3) How did the president encourage citizens to identify with him and his policies?

Situation

In our everyday lives, we seem to realize, implicitly, that to understand a particular event, we must appreciate the situation out of which that event arose. For example, a neighbor may tell us that her uncle recently suffocated his wife with a pillow, and we will almost certainly react with horror. If the neighbor then explains that the wife was terminally ill and in a great deal of pain, although we may not applaud the uncle's actions, we will probably feel some sympathy for his plight. We had to understand the situation, as we frequently say to one another, in order to comprehend the event more completely. In a similar fashion, scholarly disciplines have realized that they must account for situations in their research.

A psychologist interested in Nazi Germany, for instance, might examine the drives and psychoses that led Hitler to persecute minority groups. In historical research, on the other hand, a scholar might explore how the peace settlement of World War I contributed to the rise of fascism and World War II. A political scientist might detail the governmental structure of Germany in the 1930s and how Hitler used and altered this structure to his advantage. In these cases, researchers have accounted for the psychological, historical, or political situation of Nazi Germany in order to explain a particular event. Just like scholars in the disciplines of psychology, history, and political science, scholars of communication believe an elucidation of situation is essential for their work. And like these other researchers, rhetorical critics' conception of situation is rooted firmly in the subject matter they study. This analysis of presidents and crises therefore accounts for situations through the examination of *how presidential rhetors portrayed those situations.*

According to Burke, situation may be equated with the motives of a speaker's discourse or linguistic choice-making; a rhetor's words sum up both how the rhetor explains a situation and the strategy the rhetor has taken to deal with that situation. A stockbroker who succumbs to insider trading, for instance, might tell his family, "I was so anxious to provide for you that I made some mistakes." Such a statement not only indicates how that broker interprets his situation, but also the linguistic form that his motives or strategies for managing the situation take. To illumine the rhetorical situation, Burke says that critics must ascertain the representative anecdote or dramatic structure of a rhetor's talk, which consists of the key terms the rhetor uses to describe a particular situation and the significant relationships among those descriptive terms. According to Burke, any "rounded statement about motives" must account for five questions or anecdotal principles: (1) what took place? (terms for act); (2) who performed the deed? (terms for actor); (3) what was the background of the act or where did it take place? (terms for scene); (4) by what avenue was the act performed? (terms for means); and (5) what was the goal of the act? (terms for purpose).[58] The answers to these questions provide a synopsis of how speakers interpret a particular situation and choose to deal with it in their language.

In the case of our hypothetical stockbroker, we might examine more extensive amounts of his discourse and find that the relationship between terms for purpose and terms for act comprised the major motive of his talk. The stockbroker may have claimed that the goal of providing for his family compelled him to engage in insider trading. In this way, his discourse provided motives: the stockbroker excused his actions as mistakes—rather than willful, illegal behavior—and explained that they resulted from a noble purpose, rather than from his own greed and arrogance.

To explain Burke's pentadic method further, a brief demonstration of its application is in order. An analysis of Kennedy's 1961 address about the Bay of Pigs before the American Society of Newspaper Editors, for example, might construct the following representative anecdote from Kennedy's version of events: because of the relentless worldwide struggle between freedom and Communism (scene), we (actor) must recognize the danger and reexamine our tactics (act) through the lessons learned at the Bay of Pigs (means) in order to ensure the survival of our free system (purpose).

According to the president, the scene was one of "a relentless struggle in every corner of the globe that goes far beyond the clash of armies or even nuclear armaments." Kennedy claimed the Communists were "picking off vulnerable areas one by one." Because of this danger, "we"—the United States and other representatives of the free world—must "determine the real nature of our struggle" with Communism and pick new strategies in light of the "facts" and "useful lessons" of the Bay of Pigs. The purpose of this reexamination and renewed determination was to ensure "our system's survival and success" and to avoid being "swept away with the debris of history."[59] These anecdotal principles exemplify Kennedy's interpretation of the crisis situation.

After identifying and explaining the key terms that correspond to the five anecdotal principles, the rhetorical critic looks for special relationships, or ratios, between terms.[60] These terminological ratios allow communication analysts to interpret the motivational grammar of a president's rhetoric or to understand the linguistic form his choices about a situation took. In Kennedy's speech, the key terminological relationship was scene-act: the president's rhetoric portrayed the crisis situation as one in which a highly threatening scene dictated what actions must be taken. At one point, for instance, Kennedy told journalists that the Bay of Pigs was "not the first time that Communist tanks have rolled over gallant men and women fighting to redeem the independence of their homeland" and that it also was not "the final episode in the eternal struggle of liberty against tyranny, anywhere on the face of the globe, including Cuba itself." As the president described it, the scene of crisis was not limited to Cuba; the Bay of Pigs was simply symptomatic of the larger "peril to freedom" and threat from "Communist penetration." According to Kennedy, this struggle had recently assumed a new and even more treacherous character, for weapons no longer were the primary means of Communist advancement. Instead, armaments now served "primarily as the shield behind which subversion, infiltration, and a host of other tactics steadily advance." The president asserted that "this struggle is taking place every day, without fanfare, in thousands of villages and markets—day and night—and in classrooms all over the globe." Kennedy warned that as a result of this quiet Communist infusion, countries might fall without the firing of a single shot.[61]

This extremely dangerous scene in the president's talk mandated what actions must be taken. According to Kennedy, the United States and other free nations "must take an ever closer and more realistic look at the menace of external Communist intervention and domination." The commander-in-chief explained to his audience that the United States could no longer afford to underestimate the forces of Communism. "We dare not fail to see," he said, "the insidious nature of this new and deeper struggle. We dare not fail to grasp the new concepts, the new tools, the new sense of urgency we will need to combat it—whether in Cuba or South Viet-Nam." In addition to recognizing the threat, our nation, Kennedy said, must "reorient our forces of all kinds—our tactics and our institutions here in this community" if we were to win the struggle for freedom.[62] The United States needed to adapt to the new challenges that Communism now posed.

Overall, Kennedy argued that the crisis scene called for particular acts. Episodes like the Bay of Pigs intervention were, in his speech, simply battles in the larger conflict between Communism and freedom. Kennedy escalated the importance of every interaction, whether between soldiers and guerrillas in South Vietnam or between teachers and students in every school around the world. Not surprisingly, the president's description of the crisis in such dangerous and far-reaching terms pointed to the need for urgent actions. Americans and other free people needed to face the fact that they were in horrendous danger, and they needed to retool completely if they hoped to survive. As if to underscore the importance of the stakes involved, Kennedy concluded that as president of the United States, he was determined that we would win, "regardless of the cost and regardless of the peril!"[63] The president's words seemed to presage the apocalypse.

Through pentadic analysis, the rhetorical analyst can not only situate a president's discourse or understand how he described the crisis situation, but also illumine the linguistic form that his strategies for dealing with that situation assumed. By reducing a president's crisis talk to five anecdotal principles and discovering relationships among these key terms, the rhetorical critic can make sense of huge amounts of discourse, for the tool allows the communication researcher to interpret motive or situation as it is depicted in a president's rhetoric.

More importantly, this method provides critics with a way to compare the rhetorical situation of a specific president in a specific body of discourse with that of another. We can discover, then, how individual presidents portrayed particular crisis situations and whether various presidents' portrayals were similar in any way. Reductions, of course, always have the potential to result in superficial analysis, but I believe the case studies in this book demonstrate that the method described here does justice to the richness and uniqueness of particular presidents' discourse at the same time that it provides clarification and the possibility of comparison. In the chapters ahead, readers may judge for themselves.

If presidents engage in campaigns for terminological control, then the focus on words for situation in this study is most appropriate. The term *campaign* derives from the French word, *campagne,* which originally referred to an open landscape that was amenable to military maneuvers.[64] Hence, *campaign* contains within its etymological roots a sense of place. To study a terminological, as opposed to military, campaign, one must comprehend its place through an analysis of the rhetor's terms for situation, which consist of more than just words for scene. Burke points out that a situation also involves terms for actors, actions, means, and purposes, and the relationships among these words. Situation is not the only aspect of discourse for which Burke provides a means for examination; he also indicates how the rhetorical critic might study a speaker's style.

Style

In everyday encounters, listeners attribute style to the speaker who seems particularly eloquent. For their part, rhetoricians historically have written about style as the management of language, decoration, schemes and tropes, ornamentation, or embellishment.[65] Embedded in both of these conceptions of style is the idea of patterns or the notion that speakers have style because they *consistently* talk with great eloquence. Thus, perhaps a better way to think of style is *how a rhetor typically speaks,* regardless of how elegant that may be. In *Verbal Style and the Presidency: A Computer-Based Analysis,* Hart develops this concept when he refers to style as the "persuasive habits," or "language patterns," that communication researchers discern in a speaker's talk.[66] Because particular speakers develop particular patterns, style appears to be related to the character of the individual rhetor.

Burke claims that style is the way in which rhetors adhere to personal values in their discourse.[67] A speaker who prizes reason above all else, for instance, consistently might make appeals based on logic and employ the language of rationality. In this case, Burke would say that the speaker's style is the speaker's attitude, for the speaker's style reveals how she is predisposed to act. Burke writes that attitude, or style, is related to words for actor in any piece of discourse, which means that rhetorical critics can easily identify and study it.[68] To explain the stylistic component of rhetoric, researchers would identify the terms that correspond to actor; examine adjectives that describe the actor and words that depict the manner of the actor, or how the actor acted;[69] and identify the dominant ratio, or relationship, in which terms for actor are involved.

An examination of Reagan's nationwide address on the Libyan crisis demonstrates how the rhetorical critic might apply such principles. First, the researcher would identify "we" or "America" as the central actor. Then the analyst would note the adjectives Reagan used to describe this actor. The president said, for instance, that we had perseverance, kept our promises, and were free. We also were patient people who desired peace above all else. Nonetheless, Reagan claimed that our patience had its limits and that Libyan leader Mu'ammar Qadhafi had finally exceeded them. The president explained that "we Americans are slow to anger. We always seek peaceful avenues before resorting to the use of force—and we did. We tried quiet diplomacy, public condemnation, economic sanctions, and demonstrations of military force. None succeeded. Despite our repeated warnings, Qadhafi continued his reckless pursuit of terror. He counted on America to be passive. He counted wrong."

Although Reagan emphasized that we were aggressive when provoked, he also quickly made clear that America was not a bully that simply had grasped at any excuse to attack. He said evidence linking Libya to recent terrorist acts against Americans was "solid," "precise," and "irrefutable."[70] We were most reasonable and acted militarily only when a clear culprit gave us no other choice.

To ascertain the manner of the actor, the researcher would examine words that describe how the act is or will be performed. Reagan used very few such terms in his speech about Libya, perhaps because he employed so many words to describe what the actor was like. America was reasonable, for instance; therefore, one could infer that we had not acted hastily but with great deliberation. Likewise, because the actor kept its promises, Reagan implied that America had acted faithfully. One "how" word that the president mentioned explicitly was the term "carefully." According to the commander-in-chief, we had acted cautiously to "minimize casualties among the Libyan people with whom we have no quarrel."[71] This term also minimized the violence of America's action by indicating that, as much as possible, innocent people would be spared.

As a final step in stylistic analysis, the rhetorical critic would reveal the dominant terminological relationships that involved actor. In Reagan's case, these ratios consisted of terms for scene-actor and terms for actor-scene: the president described a terrible scene of terrorism that called for the United States to intervene and then claimed that the United States had altered that scene. Reagan told his audience that Colonel Qadhafi was an "enemy of the United States" and had a "record of subversion and aggression against the neighboring States in Africa. . . . He has sanctioned acts of terror in Africa, Europe and the Middle East, as well as the Western Hemisphere." Because of these dangerous crimes, the president said, "we have done what we had to do. If necessary, we shall do it again."[72] The latter sentence was most telling. The Libyan crisis and our response to it were important in Reagan's discourse as an indicator of what observers could expect in the future. "When our citizens are abused or attacked anywhere in the world on the direct orders of a hostile regime, we will," he warned, "respond so long as I'm in this Oval Office."[73] Whenever terrorism struck, America would come to the rescue.

The second stylistic ratio, terms for actor-scene, indicated that the United States' retaliation against Qadhafi had been worth the effort. According to Reagan, "I said that we would act with others, if possible, and alone if necessary to ensure that terrorists have no sanctuary anywhere. Tonight, we have."[74] America had eliminated a terrorist refuge. In his speech, the president gave hope that we would have additional impact, as well. Reagan explained that we would "not only diminish Colonel Qadhafi's capacity to export terror" but also "provide him with incentives and reasons to alter his criminal behavior." As a result, America would "bring closer a safer and more secure world for decent men and women."[75] The United States—with the guidance of Ronald Reagan—was an effective agent of change.

As a whole, the linguistic actor arising from Reagan's style, or attitude, might be described as determined and efficacious. If terrorism occurred, the president said, the United States would act, and according to Reagan, America was efficient because our actions resulted in the elimination of terrorist sanctuaries. Reagan's style also embodied a streak of romanticism; it portrayed the United States as a heroic nation that was called to battle global terrorism and did so successfully. Furthermore, the president countered the violent nature of America's actions with descriptions of our desire for peace, our patience, and our efforts to prevent harm to innocents.

The equating of style with attitude, a property of the linguistic actor, finds corroboration in the work of writers other than Burke. According to Hugh Blair, for instance, "style has always some reference to an author's manner of thinking." In *The Presidential Character,* Barber also observes this connection. He writes that style is "how the President goes about doing what the office requires him to do," whereas character is the way the president "*orients himself toward life*—not for the moment, but enduringly." Hence, Barber would argue that the styles of various presidents reveal their characters. Buffon summed up the deep connection between a person and his or her style when he said that "style is the man himself."[76] This does not mean a rhetor's linguistic style remains exactly the same in every situation; nevertheless, the researcher who studies extensive amounts of a particular rhetor's discourse may discover that rhetor's "character-istic" style or attitude.

Burke provides a way to ascertain the style or attitude exhibited by presidential language about foreign crises. The application of this macroscopic approach reveals the degree to which contemporary presidents invoked similar styles and whether those styles corresponded with particular portrayals of the crisis situation. Beyond the explication of situation and style in crisis discourse, I also account for presidential attempts to persuade citizens to support them and their policies. Here, too, Burke's theory proves informative.

Identificational Appeals

To examine foreign crises from a rhetorical perspective, researchers must recognize that a president's public messages are addressed to someone, that his discourse persuasively appeals, overtly or covertly, to some audience. To discover how a president attempts to persuade others, Burke asserts that analysts must study how a president's talk makes use of identification. Indeed, Burke claims identification is synonymous with persuasion. He says rhetors persuade audiences only insofar as their language identifies the ways of the rhetor with the ways of the audience. More simply put, speakers must convince the audience that they share the audience's interests. Burke places identification at the core of his theory because he says that rhetoric would not exist if humans were in complete agreement and identified with one another.[77] Because people are not inherently unified, rhetoric is necessary in order to convince citizens to view a foreign crisis and its corresponding White House policy from the president's point of view.

Beyond this general explanation of identification, Burke also details three basic ways in which identification functions: explicitly, antithetically, and implicitly. Explicit identification occurs when rhetors clearly and obviously identify their ways with those of their audience.[78] When Kennedy addressed the nation about the 1961 Berlin crisis, for example, he said, "I, as president and commander-in-chief, and all of us as Americans, are moving through serious days."[79] The president's discourse here made overt connections between the problems the crisis posed for him in his official role and the danger it posed for all citizens. Likewise, Kennedy said, "In meeting my responsibilities in these coming months as president, I need your goodwill, and your support—and above all, your prayers."[80] Through such discourse, Kennedy explicitly linked the success of his foreign policy with the support that American citizens were ready to lend him.

A second type of identification, antithetical, occurs when speakers encourage their audience to unite with them against some shared enemy.[81] In a 1986 address to the nation, for instance, Reagan claimed the Sandinista government had made Nicaragua a Soviet "beachhead in North America" where Cuban and Soviet military advisors and "all of the elements of international terror—from the PLO to Italy's Red Brigades" were welcome. According to Reagan, the Sandinistas were responsible for the torture and attempted murder of Pastor Baltodano, as well as "black lists," "secret prisons," and "mob violence."[82] The president's language cast the Sandinistas as enemies who embodied values that were the very opposite of those that Americans held dear. In his speech, Reagan asked, "Will we permit the Soviet Union to put a second Cuba, a second Libya, right on the doorstep of the United States?"[83] The president's language exemplified antithetical principles, for he constructed an evil enemy and encouraged Americans to unite with him against that enemy by supporting U.S. funds for the Contras, who were fighting to overthrow the Sandinistas.

The third way identification may function is implicitly. Burke says the most common implicit identification is "the word 'we,' as when the statement that 'we' are at war includes under the same head soldiers who are getting killed and speculators who hope to make a killing in war stocks."[84] Johnson made use of this principle in his discourse after the Dominican crisis. In a speech to the legislative conference of the AFL-CIO, the president told members that "we have two purposes: we want to evacuate our citizens and we want to preserve, to see that a plan is worked out where the people themselves can select their own government."[85]

The use of "we" in this statement subtly identified American citizens with their commander-in-chief and the goals he articulated. A different form of implicit identification can be observed in Reagan's speech about Nicaragua before a joint session of Congress in 1983. At one point, the president observed that "for several years now, under two administrations, the United States has been increasing its defense of freedom in the Caribbean Basin."[86] Here the reference to "the United States" quietly linked all Americans with the leader of their country. Because implicit identification is subtle, it often goes unnoticed. Burke claims it is the most powerful form of identification.[87]

Burke's work provides a way for the rhetorical critic to ascertain the characteristic identificational appeals of a president's crisis discourse. Such appeals are crucial, for the commander-in-chief must forge a consensus of public opinion behind him and his policy resolution if his crisis promotion is to succeed. The explicit, antithetical, and/or implicit characteristics of a president's identificational strategy reveal a great deal about the specific crisis rhetoric under examination. This approach also pinpoints any identificational appeals that tend to appear consistently in presidential crisis talk as a whole.

Through the dramatistic approach overviewed here, I ascertain how each president portrayed the situation in his crisis talk, what style each commander-in-chief exhibited in his crisis promotion and management, and what kinds of identificational appeals each president used to encourage citizen support for him and his policies. This approach also reveals how presidents who *appear* to talk similarly about foreign crises often talk quite differently and how presidents who *seem* to speak quite differently about international conflicts frequently speak in ways that are much alike. The approach employed in this study, it is hoped, not only sheds light on particular presidents' crisis discourse, but also leads to a greater understanding of all presidential crisis promotion.

THE PRESIDENTIAL PODIUM: WORDS TO REMEMBER

A president is, perhaps, best remembered by his words. When presidents enter office, they do not do so silently. Instead, they take the occasion to extol particular values and set the tone for their administrative actions. Chief executives also address their fellow Americans to appraise the state of the union, to argue vigorously for domestic policy initiatives, to comfort gently in the face of national tragedy, and most importantly for this study, to announce foreign crises and expound upon their resolutions. In contemporary times, the president's voice has carried further and been heard more often than in the past. This is due in large part to the electronic mass media that also preserve presidential speechmaking for posterity and periodically resurrect it. A president's voice may grow weaker over the years, but its echoes never die. When Americans think of their presidents, they recall not the policy details of the White House, but the rhetoric of the man who lived there. A contemporary president's words characterize his presidency, from the elegant summons of John Kennedy ("ask not what your country can do for you") to the folksy aphorisms of the Great Communicator ("I know there's a pony in here somewhere.")

Of all the issues that presidents address in their discourse, however, perhaps the one they show the most fondness for is crisis. Rhetorical critic Dan Hahn goes so far as to argue that *"all non-ceremonial national presidential speeches are crisis speeches"* because, aside from ceremonies, our chief executives talk to us only when they believe something is wrong.[88] Whatever their reason for speaking, presidents regularly expound upon crises, particularly those that deal with international affairs.

In this book, I explore foreign crises in an effort to illustrate how commanders-in-chief convince citizens that a crisis exists and that presidential policy will lead to its successful conclusion. I analyze presidents' words during six crises to understand better the situation, style, and identificational appeals of their discourse. A comparison of these cases then reveals the important commonalties and differences that exist among them and illumines crisis promotion and management as a whole. Along the way, I will also make some observations about the evolution of the structural/legal framework that encourages crisis promotion and the dangers that the presidential fondness for foreign crises poses to our political system. Presidential words about foreign crises may gradually fade from the public arena, but their reverberations continue to be felt in troubling ways.

Chapter Two

THE RHETORIC OF DEFLECTION
John F. Kennedy and the Cuban Missile Crisis of 1962

In October 1962, the world came perilously close to nuclear war. President John F. Kennedy appeared on nationwide television on Monday the 22d and announced that the Soviet Union was building "offensive missile sites" in Cuba. In response to this threat, the president ordered a quarantine of all ships carrying offensive military equipment to the island. Kennedy also proclaimed that "it shall be the policy of this Nation to regard any nuclear missile launched from Cuba against any nation in the Western Hemisphere as an attack by the Soviet Union on the United States, requiring a full retaliatory response upon the Soviet Union."[1] For nearly a week the world watched and waited as the two super-powers challenged each other "eyeball to eyeball."[2] The Cold War, many feared, was teetering dangerously close to full-scale nuclear war.

Finally, on Sunday, October 28, Nikita Khrushchev capitulated. The premier maintained that the missiles had been intended purely for defensive purposes. Because the United States had assured him that it would not invade Cuba, Khrushchev agreed to dismantle the weapons.[3] Kennedy's most famous crisis had passed. The president's special counsel, Theodore Sorensen, would write that Kennedy "had been engaged in a personal as well as national contest for world leadership and he had won."[4]

Kennedy's promotion and management of the Cuban missile crisis represents the pinnacle for an administration that dealt with an exceptional number of foreign crises. The missile crisis, which was a political success for the Kennedy administration, is an important part of this study. Kennedy was the catalyst for structural/legal changes and news management techniques that created a context in which crisis promotion and management could continue on a regular basis. Only by understanding how these changes coalesced during the Cuban missile crisis can one fully appreciate the crisis promotion of the presidents who came after Kennedy.

My analysis confirms and amplifies the findings of previous rhetorical studies. Critics Wayne Brockriede and Robert Scott, Theodore Windt, and James Pratt are in agreement that Kennedy emphasized devil-angel appeals, an accusatorial strategy, or the theme of deception in his talk. Furthermore, Windt observed that Kennedy portrayed the crisis as a test of character.[5] The present analysis corroborates these findings and provides them with additional support, for I examine statements other than Kennedy's October 22 address, the only presidential text examined in previous rhetorical criticisms.

This study also draws on Kennedy White House documents that relate to message construction—including transcripts released in the 1980s of meetings between the president and his advisers—in order to shed additional light on how Kennedy's rhetoric functioned in its political context. Whether presidents believe that a crisis exists or whether they simply think a crisis would be politically expedient, these documents about the Cuban missile crisis demonstrate that presidents and their advisers are intimately aware of how they must use public persuasion to promote a sense of crisis and to encourage citizens to support their policy resolutions.

My analysis reveals that Kennedy's public discourse about Cuba prior to the discovery of the missiles boxed him in politically and led him to demand their removal. With this decision, Kennedy faced another problem: how to justify his ultimatum against "offensive" weapons to a world audience when the United States had recently activated intermediate-range missiles along the Turkish-Soviet border and had attempted to invade Cuba through the CIA-sponsored Bay of Pigs operation. In this chapter, I argue that Kennedy's discourse deflected attention from the United States by focusing on the threat of the crisis scene and the evil of the Soviet villains who were part of that scene. According to the president, this crisis scene had forced the United States to aim for particular goals and to take particular actions. Kennedy portrayed the United States as peaceful, but made it clear that the nation would willingly face nuclear war in order to prove its character and to defeat its Communist foes. Through his crisis rhetoric, Kennedy placed the burden of responsibility for the crisis, as well as for its resolution, on the shoulders of the Soviet Union. The vehement anti-Communism of Kennedy's crisis discourse may have appeared more persistently in his presidential rhetoric as a whole than his liberal admirers would like to remember.

In this chapter, I look at the structural/legal foundations of crisis promotion; the news management techniques of the Kennedy administration; the rhetorical context of the missile crisis; and the situation, style, and identificational appeals of Kennedy's discourse and how they deflected questions of scruples from the United States to the Soviet Union.

STRUCTURAL AND LEGAL FOUNDATIONS OF CRISIS PROMOTION

In the *Federalist Papers,* Alexander Hamilton wrote, "Of all the cares or concerns of government, the direction of war most peculiarly demands those qualities which distinguish the exercise of power by a single hand."[6] Hamilton, as well as other founding fathers, worried that Congress would prove too large and unwieldy to command the military efficiently in the event of armed conflict. Because of this concern, the U.S. Constitution declares that the president "shall be Commander in Chief of the Army and Navy of the United States, and of the

Militia of the several states, when called into the actual Service of the United States." Nevertheless, the Constitution also says that only Congress has the power to declare war. The meaning of this constitutional arrangement is that the legislative branch has the authority to declare hostilities and that the president, once Congress has announced hostilities, will direct U.S. forces.

To offset the greater power of the legislative branch, the Constitution gives the president the right to administer foreign policy in coordination with Congress: for example, to make treaties, appoint envoys, and so on. Congress alone may have the power to *declare* war, but the powers related to foreign policy and the conduct of armed conflict are split between the legislative and executive branches.[7]

In the latter half of the twentieth century, this balance of power changed. Today contemporary presidents do not merely administer foreign policy, they also create it. Furthermore, commanders-in-chief routinely commit troops to armed conflict without the advice or permission of Congress. Chief executives therefore promote and manage crises with greater ease than they once did. The gradual transferral of these war powers from one branch to another can be traced through the foreign policy making of the senior White House staff and through presidential claims of power in the realm of foreign affairs. The 1962 Cuban missile crisis marked a significant milestone in these changes.

The Decline of the National Security Council and the Rise of the Senior White House Staff

In 1947, Congress approved the National Security Act, which instituted the National Security Council, or NSC.[8] According to the enabling legislation, "the function of the Council shall be to advise the President with respect to the integration of domestic, foreign, and military policies relating to the national security so as to enable the military services and the other departments and agencies of the Government to cooperate more effectively in matters involving the national security."[9] The goal of the council was to stabilize and integrate national security policy; cabinet members who sat on the NSC would serve as links between the president and permanent government agencies.[10] During the Korean War, the NSC functioned as a neutral advisory body; Truman ordered that all major proposals on national security policy come to him through that forum.[11]

President Dwight D. Eisenhower formalized the NSC's advisory role further when he formed two subsidiary committees, the Planning Board and the Operations Coordinating Board (OCB), to handle particular elements of the NSC's work. The Planning Board dealt solely with the formulation, revision, and clarification of policy. The OCB translated policies into operational guidelines and supervised the implementation and coordination of policies.[12] In

1953, Eisenhower created the position of special assistant for national security affairs to preside over the NSC and its related bureaucracy.[13]

Although Eisenhower firmly institutionalized the NSC in his administration, he did not attempt to control the council. In a report from the Institute for Defense Analyses, Keith Clark and Laurence Legere explain that departments and agencies influenced the policy agenda through the staff work they provided, and the special assistant did not serve as the president's advocate, but as a facilitator and coordinator for the various board and council members.[14] The NSC support staff, "a permanent, career oriented cadre of professionals charged with preserving continuity," functioned as a neutral body during the Eisenhower years.[15] This situation changed irretrievably with the presidency of John F. Kennedy.

As Kennedy prepared to take office in 1961, Sen. Henry Jackson and his Subcommittee on National Policy Machinery released a report that attacked the NSC as a morass of bureaucracy and paperwork. Jackson suggested that the council be transformed into "an intimate forum" where the chief executive and his advisers could discuss policy decisions. The president-elect concurred and publicly praised Jackson's recommendations.[16] In February 1961, Kennedy abolished the Operations Coordinating Board that Eisenhower had established.[17] The demise of the OCB, which had coordinated policy implementation in a structurally disinterested way, signified the demise of the NSC as a neutral advisory body.

After the attempted invasion of Cuba at the Bay of Pigs, Kennedy changed the NSC system further to give White House senior staff members more direct control over foreign policy making. The president blamed the disastrous Cuban operation, in part, on the bad advice he had received from the National Security Council and, particularly, the CIA. According to Schlesinger, Kennedy realized that these groups were not committed to the success of his administration. He thereafter relied on the advice of appointees and staffers who had entered the executive branch at his behest and with whom Kennedy had a trusted relationship.[18]

After the Bay of Pigs, Attorney General Robert Kennedy and Special Counsel Theodore Sorensen, two men with great personal loyalties to Kennedy, took part in all major national security decisions. Unlike Eisenhower's special assistant for national security affairs, Robert Cutler, McGeorge Bundy did not focus on neutral planning and the coordination of national security policy among various departments and agencies. Rather, he concerned himself with the "management of the president's personal, day-to-day foreign and defense business." With this personalization of the national security system, Kennedy had, to quote Bundy, "deliberately rubbed out the distinction between planning and operation."[19] The importance of the National Security Council decreased, but presidential control over national security policy grew.

The new role of senior administration officials became most evident in October 1962. In the face of the Cuban missile crisis, Kennedy did not gather NSC members for consultation. Instead, he called together what was later known as Ex Comm, or the Executive Committee of the National Security Council, a group of hand-picked experts and advisers to whom Kennedy would turn for advice throughout the crisis. The national security staff had become a presidential staff.[20]

As a result of Kennedy's innovations, contemporary presidents have obtained greater personal control over national security policy. I. M. Destler, scholar of congressional-executive relations in foreign affairs, claims that this evolution presents dangers because it "changes the role of staff from *mediating* between the president and senior officialdom to that of *substituting* for officialdom, reducing the president's perceived need to work with and through established institutions [such as the State Department] at all."[21] This structural change in the national security system encourages chief executives and senior administration officials to take policy into their own hands and to protect presidential interests. Because this change confers more power on the president, it also provides a strong foundation for crisis promotion. If presidents can create and implement policy in accordance with their perceptions of a situation or their personal needs—without disinterested institutional interference—they have important resources upon which to draw for crisis promotion.

Through his reliance on personal advisers and ad hoc meetings, John Kennedy initiated a trend toward unilateral White House foreign policy making. This structural change took on even greater importance once the Kennedy administration firmly established the legal precedent for crisis promotion and management: the commander-in-chief's power to commit troops to battle.

Presidential Claims of Prerogative Power

According to political scientist Richard Pious, U.S. presidents from the very start have periodically made claims of prerogative power; that is, presidents have argued that they had the constitutional authority to institute domestic and national security policies in a unilateral fashion.[22] Presidential claims of prerogative power in the realm of foreign affairs have special significance as legal precedents for the promotion and management of crises. Although the founding fathers gave Congress the power to declare war, Schlesinger argues that they did not wish to deny the president the right to repel surprise attacks when Congress was not in session. A number of presidents made use of this fact to involve the nation in armed conflict, ostensibly for defensive purposes. In Schlesinger's words, commanders-in-chief implied that they held the "unilateral authority to conduct defense so aggressively that those on the receiving end might well be pardoned if they mistook it for aggression." Men such as Andrew Jackson,

Abraham Lincoln, and others greatly enlarged the president's legal powers in military affairs through their interpretations of the Constitution.[23] These changes paled, however, in comparison to those that occurred after World War II.

On June 25, 1950, North Korean troops invaded South Korea. In response, the United States introduced a resolution at the United Nations Security Council that demanded that the North Koreans withdraw and that member nations "render every assistance" to implement the resolution. The measure passed. That night President Harry Truman conferred with top military and State Department officials and resolved to provide the South Koreans with air and naval support, but did not meet with congressional leaders to inform them of this action until June 27, two days later.[24]

That same day, the U.N. Security Council met for a second time and called on members to "furnish such assistance to the Republic of Korea as may be necessary to repel the armed attack and to restore international peace and security in the area." The Security Council approved the measure just before midnight. Three days later, on June 30, Truman ordered that two American divisions be sent to South Korea and that the navy institute a blockade of North Korea. The president met with congressional leaders only after the fact. Although Congress approved of Truman's decision, several senators—Robert Taft, H. Alexander Smith, and Kenneth Wherry—argued that the president should have sought congressional authorization for his actions. Smith recommended that Truman request a joint resolution to fulfill this function. The president agreed to look into the matter, but after consultation with Secretary of State Dean Acheson, a former law clerk for Justice Brandeis and a distinguished lawyer in his own right, Truman decided to justify his decision on the basis of his "prerogative" power as commander-in-chief.[25]

For the first time in history, a president of the United States had committed the nation to ongoing military action without a formal declaration from Congress. Francis Wormuth and Edwin Firmage, scholars of constitutional law, write that until the Korean War, "no judge, no President, no legislator, no commentator ever suggested that the President had legal authority to initiate war."[26] Under the Eisenhower administration, evermore expansive claims of presidential power continued.

In January 1955, Chinese Communist troops attacked the Tachens, a group of islands two hundred miles from Formosa that were occupied by Chinese Nationalists. Mainland forces captured Ichiang, which was only a few miles north of the Tachens, one week later. At the same time, Communist China had begun to improve its airfields directly across from Formosa. Chiang Kai-shek and his fellow Nationalists understandably felt threatened. Only one month earlier, in December 1954, President Eisenhower had made treaty arrangements with Nationalist China in which the United States agreed to defend Formosa and the Pescadores, a group of islands near Formosa.[27]

Nonetheless, Eisenhower still felt he needed to make clear to Communist China that the United States *would* defend Formosa. He later explained, "I believed the Korean War had resulted, partially at least, from the mistaken Communist notion that under no circumstances would the United States move to the assistance of the Korean Republic." This time the president wanted "no uncertainty" about our resolve and, as a result, requested a joint congressional resolution that would give him the authority to initiate military action.[28] According to the resolution, known as the Formosa Doctrine, the president was "authorized to employ the Armed Forces of the United States as he deems necessary for the specific purpose of securing and protecting Formosa and the Pescadores against armed attack."[29] Both the House and the Senate passed the measure by large majorities.

According to historian Stephen Ambrose, "for the first time in American history, the Congress had authorized the President in advance to engage in a war at a time and under circumstances of his own choosing."[30] Not only had Congress given the president a "blank check," but Eisenhower also insisted that he held the prerogative power claimed by Truman during the Korean War. Eisenhower maintained that "authority for some of the actions which might be required [by the Chinese situation] would be inherent in the authority of the Commander-in-Chief" and that the resolution would publicly serve to reinforce this authority. Later the president wrote that "in asking for the resolution I did not imply that I lacked constitutional authority to act." Eisenhower simply wanted to make his intentions known to the Chinese Communists.[31]

In March 1957, the Eisenhower administration followed a similar path when it sought and gained congressional passage of the Middle East Resolution. The statute stipulated that "if the President determines the necessity thereof," he could employ U.S. troops in support of Middle East nations "requesting assistance against armed aggression from any country controlled by international communism."[32] Once again, Congress delegated its war powers to the occupant of the Oval Office.

During the Cuban missile crisis, Kennedy reinforced presidential claims of prerogative power and brought about their widespread acceptance so that congressional approval became a politically strategic, rather than legal, touchstone.

In September and October 1962, Republican senators Kenneth Keating and Homer Capehart warned Americans about a "Soviet buildup" of technicians and weapons in Cuba. Keating claimed, in fact, that offensive, intermediate-range ballistic missile sites were under construction on the island, although he refused to divulge the source of his information, and both senators attacked

Kennedy for his inaction.[33] According to the president, no action was needed. He explained that the military buildup in Cuba was "under our most careful surveillance" and that the weapons did "not constitute a serious threat" to the hemisphere. Furthermore, Kennedy added that if the Communist buildup ever included offensive weapons "then this country will do whatever must be done."[34]

In response to the tensions that had arisen over the buildup, Congress began to prepare a joint resolution, not unlike that accorded to Eisenhower. Kennedy insisted that the resolution was not needed because "as President and Commander in Chief I have full authority now to take . . . action."[35] A document from the administration's National Security Files, penned by an anonymous author, seems to reflect the views of the Kennedy White House quite well:

> President Eisenhower was apparently uncertain of his constitutional authority and wanted Congress to uphold his hand. Democrats were glad to give him the support which *he* felt he needed. President Kennedy is not uncertain of his responsibilities under the Constitution and has not asked Congress to uphold his hand. . . .
>
> It is not the responsible course to authorize the President to do by Congressional resolution what he is already authorized to do by the Constitution: to command the armed forces of the United States and to conduct its foreign relations.[36]

The State Department suggested that if Congress insisted on a resolution, the statute should claim that the president "possesses all necessary authority" to use military action in the situation, but several senators opposed this phraseology as a delegation of war powers. Because of their objections, the resolution merely restated U.S. policy toward Cuba. Congress approved the measure on October 3, 1962.[37] This resolution seemed to constitute a backlash against the presidential usurpation of congressional war powers, but Kennedy's claims and the way in which he later took action without congressional consent had quite the opposite effect.

In three important ways, Kennedy's promotion and management of the Cuban missile crisis firmly established prerogative power for the presidents who came after him. First, from the beginning Kennedy talked about prerogative power as though it were an established fact. Second, the president took offensive military action against Cuba based on his claims of prerogative power. He failed to discuss with the legislative branch his intention to blockade Cuba; instead, he merely briefed congressional leaders prior to his televised announcement of the crisis.[38] In that address, Kennedy said he had taken action "under the authority entrusted to me by the Constitution" that was merely "endorsed" by the congressional resolution.[39] Third, Kennedy's promotion and management of the Cuban missile crisis were a great political and personal success. As Schlesinger, a Kennedy confidant, later observed, "The very brilliance of Kennedy's performance appeared to vindicate the idea that the President must take unto himself the final judgments of war and peace."[40] Not surprisingly, later presidents followed Kennedy's example; in particular, Lyndon Johnson and Richard Nixon would compare their unilateral crisis decision-making with that of Kennedy during the Cuban missile crisis.

Since the 1940s, the executive branch gradually has subsumed the majority of power over foreign policy and the conduct of armed conflict. The Kennedy administration, particularly during the Cuban missile crisis, contributed significantly to this shift in power through the role the president gave senior White House staff in foreign policy-making and through the claims of prerogative power that he made. These structural and legal changes provided the foundation for crisis promotion and management because they gave the commander-in-chief greater control over foreign affairs. Beyond these precedents, Kennedy's promotion of the Cuban missile crisis also refined extensive news management techniques, which forced or encouraged the media to present the administration's view of the crisis. Other presidents, most notably Ronald Reagan, would employ these techniques when they promoted crises of their own.

THE KENNEDY ADMINISTRATION AND NEWS MANAGEMENT

According to journalism scholars John Tebbel and Sarah Miles Watts, all U.S. presidents have attempted to manage news coverage to some degree because of the key role that the media play in the public discussion and resolution of issues.[41] If a president hopes to convince citizens to support his positions, he would be foolish not to encourage journalists to accept and disseminate his preferred issue definitions and policy arguments. Nonetheless, the media strategies of twentieth-century chief executives sometimes have crossed the fine line between persuasion and manipulation. President Calvin Coolidge, for instance, invented "the White House spokesman," the nonexistent person to whom reporters were to attribute presidential statements that otherwise might prompt negative public reactions, and Franklin Roosevelt proved quite adept at planting stories that benefited him and defamed his enemies.[42]

Compared to previous presidencies, however, the Kennedy administration's practices constituted a significant expansion in news management techniques. *New York Times* columnist Arthur Krock, a Pulitzer Prize winner with nearly fifty years of reporting experience, pronounced in March 1963 that "a news management policy not only exists but, in the form of *direct and deliberate* action, has been enforced more cynically and boldly than by any previous Administration in a period when the U.S. was not in a war or without visible means of regression from the verge of war."[43] Like other presidents, Kennedy attempted to shape media perceptions from the day he entered the White House, but many of his techniques were more sophisticated than those of his predecessors and, during the Cuban missile crisis, were extreme. Kennedy's political success also demonstrated the importance of news management in crisis promotion and justified the practice in the name of national security.

Kennedy understood how the media worked, and he used his knowledge to further the aims of the New Frontier. Journalists found that they had direct access to Kennedy's advisers and could discuss issues with them in their White House offices or over lunch. The president wooed reporters with social events, exclusive interviews, and numerous background or not-for-attribution briefings on a much larger scale than previous presidents.[44] Through these efforts, the administration satisfied journalists' desire for information and simultaneously ensured that the administration's views received wide dissemination.

In addition to these more subtle attempts at news management, Kennedy took overt action as well, beginning with the Bay of Pigs invasion in April 1961. Kennedy convinced the *New York Times* and the *New Republic* that month to drop or to censor their stories on the upcoming operation.[45] During the invasion, news management attempts continued when government officials lied about the number of invaders involved; journalists, in turn, criticized the administration for its lack of forthrightness.[46]

After the Bay of Pigs, Kennedy further increased tensions between the White House and the press when he blamed the disaster, at least in part, on the conduct of the media. Only ten days after the covert operation, the president addressed members of the American Newspaper Publishers Association. Although the United States had not officially declared war, Kennedy warned journalists that the American way of life was under attack by "a monolithic and ruthless conspiracy" that was bent upon world domination. The president stated, "Every newspaper now asks itself, with respect to every story: 'Is it news?' All I suggest is that you add the question: 'Is it in the interest of the national security?' "[47]

In May, the president invited several of the nation's top editors, publishers, and press association executives to the White House where he told his visitors that although he had no intention of placing official restrictions on newsgathering, he believed that the dangerous nature of the times dictated that the press show more self-discipline. The news executives disagreed.[48] The president remained convinced that the media posed a threat to his management of foreign policy, and during the 1962 Cuban missile crisis, he took offensive control in this arena for his advantage.

By Press Secretary Pierre Salinger's own account, the administration repeatedly lied to the media prior to the president's announcement of the missile crisis, and Kennedy personally interceded the night before his speech to prevent the *New York Times* and the *Washington Post* from publishing the story.[49] Once

Kennedy announced the presence of the missiles, the media became almost wholly dependent on the government for information. This attempt at control was, in some ways, unremarkable given the complete censorship enforced during World War II and the censored information that military officials gave reporters during Korea. Unlike presidents during those two wars, however, Kennedy would not allow journalists to witness events firsthand from blockade ships or Guantanamo naval base. According to Salinger, eyewitness accounts would have deprived Kennedy of "a certain amount of flexibility" and publicized facts that were "helpful to the enemy."[50]

The administration attempted to control the information that the press received in other ways as well. When Kennedy first became president, he issued a directive that called for more centralization of information dissemination. Press Secretary Salinger, as a result, cleared the policy statements of major government departments.[51] In the midst of the missile crisis, Salinger illustrated this point when he told journalists that "to avoid having two press conferences tonight, and have everybody run over town" to the Pentagon, he would provide reporters with the desired information as long as they, in turn, attributed the statement to a Defense Department spokesperson.[52]

The White House also took steps to provide reporters with information that would support the president's preferred interpretation of events in Cuba. According to an administration history of the Cuban missile crisis, Kennedy himself told his advisers that "for public purposes at least" they must "sing one song."[53] Secretary of Defense Robert McNamara's initial backgrounder with the press, Secretary of State Dean Rusk's presentation before the OAS, and Ambassador Adlai Stevenson's speech before the U.N. exemplified this unity of purpose. All three men, for example, emphasized Soviet aggression.[54]

In a memo to the United States Information Agency and other government media outlets, Thomas Sorensen, Deputy Director of Policy and Plans for the USIA, encouraged government information personnel to stress similar themes in their messages and to remain consistent with the president's public statements. "It is imperative," he said, "that we obtain maximum public support for our policies and actions with respect to Cuba."[55] To enhance this support, the White House released intelligence photos of missile sites to American reporters, after their release in Great Britain served to document Kennedy's claims and resulted in favorable media coverage for him there.[56]

To complement these efforts at consistency during the missile crisis, the administration issued information directives for the Pentagon and State Department and thereby decreased the likelihood that individuals within the government might offer the press points of view that differed from the president's. According to Krock, the State Department policy, for example, dictated that personnel could talk to the press only if the administration deemed them "authorized" to do so. Furthermore, even an authorized person could meet with a journalist only if "an official colleague was also present" or if the office of the Assistant Secretary for Public Information was informed about the details of the interview. These directives allowed the Kennedy White House to authorize spokespersons who would be supportive of the president's official line and to create a climate in which few individuals would be likely to raise their voices in dissent. Eventually, the White House withdrew the State Department directive, but only after reporters vehemently protested its continued use after the crisis had been resolved.[57]

In addition to centralizing its communication and censoring information at the source, the Kennedy administration also attempted to shape the way in which journalists reported the news that they actually received. Salinger issued a memorandum to the press that suggested that some types of information, such as the degree of alert of U.S. forces, should not be published for national security reasons.[58] Beyond understandable guidelines such as these, the White House tried to tailor news coverage in other ways as well. The press secretary, for instance, held regular briefings, but he frequently stipulated that journalists could quote him "on background" only; reporters could use his statements as long as they attributed them to a "White House official" or similar such figure rather than the specific source. The president and other members of his inner circle also used this procedure to publicize their perceptions of the crisis, to cast Kennedy as a heroic figure in now-it-can-be-told articles after the crisis had ended, and to plant stories that portrayed U.N. Ambassador Stevenson as an appeaser who had advocated weak diplomatic solutions to the crisis during Ex Comm meetings.

According to journalism professor James Pollard, this practice was not new with the Kennedy administration, but Kennedy used it much more extensively than his predecessors had.[59] "On background" served the interests of the White House because reporters were likely to use the coveted inside information they received. This meant that the media propagated the administration's preferred portrayals of the crisis, yet the ambiguous attribution of "top White House officials" allowed Kennedy and his representatives to escape accountability for what they said. Although journalists grumbled about what seemed like an excessive use of "on background," their need for information, and perhaps the flattery they felt when figures like Kennedy or McNamara confided in them, convinced them to follow the procedure. Journalists simply inquired, as one did of Salinger, about what "literary devices" the official in question preferred.[60]

Through extensive, well-coordinated news management techniques, Kennedy controlled media portrayals of the Cuban missile crisis and virtually eliminated coverage that countered the view of reality he posited in his public statements. Kennedy's constraints on news coverage cast criticisms of his foreign policy as speculations at best and personal vendetta at worst. To a large extent, administration officials seemed to regard the press as a tool to be used for governmental purposes. Brig. Gen. Chester Clifton, Kennedy's military aide, wrote a memo that asked: "Is there a plan to brief and brainwash the key press within twelve hours or so?—N.Y. Times—Lippmann—Childs—Alsop—Key Bureau Chiefs?"[61] Assistant Secretary of Defense for Public Affairs Arthur Sylvester even went so far as to call the news media part of "the arsenal of weaponry" in the Cold War and to assert "the inherent right of the government to lie . . . to save itself when faced with nuclear disaster."[62]

In their analysis of Kennedy's use of the mass media, Montague Kern, Patricia Levering, and Ralph Levering conclude that the media's need for news, dependence on official sources for that news, and sensitivity to domestic opinion make it an easily manipulated tool during national emergencies.[63] Kennedy was not the first president to employ news management techniques, but he exploited the media's vulnerabilities to exert a theretofore unrivaled degree of presidential control over news coverage. The fact that "an often trusting, usually uncritical press"[64] cooperated with Kennedy only proved that the political benefits of news management were large and its drawbacks few.

During his administration, John Kennedy served as a catalyst for changes that, in turn, created a favorable context for the promotion and management of foreign crises. Kennedy stripped the NSC of its neutrality as an advisory board and simultaneously conferred power on partisan White House senior staff members to make policy unilaterally. During the Cuban missile crisis, his political appointees and advisers were the ones who largely determined how the United States would respond. Moreover, the president took military action against Cuba based on his authority as commander-in-chief and treated prerogative power in his public discourse as if it were an established right. According to Arthur Schlesinger, the shift in power over war and peace from Congress to the White House during contemporary times has resulted in what he refers to as the "imperial presidency."[65] Kennedy's contributions to the imperial presidency were great. More pertinent to my purposes here, the structural/legal changes that Kennedy wrought during the Cuban missile crisis made it easier for the presidents who followed him to promote and manage crises of their own. Kennedy also instituted news management techniques in a more expansive and sophisticated fashion than had been previously employed. Through the political success of the missile crisis, the president demonstrated to government officials the pragmatic needs that news management could fulfill and, at the same time, legitimized the practice in the eyes of most American citizens. The 1962 Cuban missile crisis not only represented a personal triumph for John Kennedy, it also established the structural/legal foundations for crisis promotion and the news management techniques essential to its success. In many ways, the missile crisis was a harbinger of presidential rhetoric yet to come.

THE RHETORICAL CONTEXT OF THE CUBAN MISSILE CRISIS

On Tuesday, October 16, National Security Adviser McGeorge Bundy informed Kennedy of the news: U-2 reconnaissance photos showed that the Soviets were installing intermediate-range nuclear missiles in Cuba. The president reacted angrily. Repeatedly, the Soviets had assured him that they would provide only defensive weapons to the island; now Kennedy realized he had been deceived. He began to discuss with Ex Comm how the missiles might be removed.[66]

For Kennedy, the news was especially inauspicious. In November, midterm congressional elections would be held, and Cuba was considered a primary issue.[67] Republican senators Keating and Capehart had publicly sounded the alarm against a Soviet military buildup in Cuba, while Kennedy had publicly maintained that the weapons posed no danger to the United States. Worse yet, Kennedy had flatly denied Keating's charge that the Soviets were shipping intermediate-range missiles to Castro. Given the president's record in foreign affairs, the Cuban issue was particularly salient.

During his first year in office, Kennedy had found himself in a seemingly endless series of confrontations with Khrushchev from which the Soviet premier always seemed to emerge on top: Kennedy had been bullied by Khrushchev at the summit in Vienna, embarrassed by the failure of U.S.-sponsored guerrillas to depose Khrushchev's protege, Fidel Castro, and unable, short of all-out war, to prevent construction of the Berlin Wall. These were particularly troublesome turns of events for a vocal anti-Communist like Kennedy. When Elie Abel visited him after these foreign policy debacles had occurred, he asked the president if he could write a book about the administration's first year in office. "Who would want to read a book about disasters?" Kennedy morosely replied.[68]

On discovery of the missiles, the president and his advisers feared, quite justifiably, that the news would spell political disaster for the Democrats in November. The president told adviser Kenneth O'Donnell, "We've just elected Capehart in Indiana, and Ken Keating will probably be the next President of the United States."[69] The missiles may not have altered the strategic balance of military power, but they wielded great political strength because of the fear they induced. A recently released transcript of an Ex Comm meeting on October 16 shows that Kennedy was highly cognizant of the political problem before him. According to the transcript, he asked his advisers, "What difference does it make? They've got enough to blow us up now anyway." Kennedy claimed the real problem of the missiles was that he had told the American people quite explicitly that he and his administration were not about to allow the Soviets to place offensive weapons in Cuba. When one of the Ex Comm members insisted that the administration could handle the discrepancy, Kennedy responded,

"*Last month* I said we weren't going to." The president's advisers laughed.[70] In the somber atmosphere of the Ex Comm meetings, this bit of gallows humor may have helped relieve tensions, but it also demonstrated vividly how Kennedy's earlier rhetoric had boxed him in and now compelled him to deal with a political quandary he was loathe to face.

Kennedy had drawn a line—no offensive missiles were to be placed in Cuba—and publicly told the Soviets not to cross it. But the Soviets had done just that. Even without Kennedy's earlier discourse, the American people in 1962 would have had little tolerance for nuclear weapons on Cuban soil. The potential political repercussions were even greater, however, because of Kennedy's less than glowing record in dealing with Khrushchev, his strong condemnation of Communist expansion, his repeated assurances about the missiles, and the apparent audacity of the Soviets. These factors established a context in which Kennedy believed he had to respond.

For nearly a week, the president continued to discuss with Ex Comm the secret missiles and how they should be removed.[71] Kennedy's advisers were well aware that their public presentation of the situation not only would affect how the Soviets reacted, but also how American citizens and people in other countries responded. In one meeting, Robert Kennedy apparently was concerned that an unannounced air strike against the missiles would not have enough legitimacy in the eyes of public opinion. He wondered aloud about the possibility of some other justification, inquiring whether "there is some *other* way we can get involved in this through, uh, Guantanamo Bay, or something, er, or whether there's some ship that, you know, sink the *Maine* again or something."[72] After several days of intensive meetings, Ex Comm decided on an option that Secretary of State Rusk had offered at one of its first meetings: "build up the crisis to the point where the other side has to consider very seriously about giving in."[73] The president agreed.

He and Ex Comm realized that this course of action would be difficult to implement successfully. One potential obstacle was that the United States had provided Turkey with intermediate-range Jupiter missiles that had become operational in 1962.[74] According to presidential aides Kenneth O'Donnell and Dave Powers, the Jupiters were of little military value, but they held great symbolic import for Turkey. Kennedy suspected that Khrushchev would point to their location so close to the Soviet border and demand that the United States remove them in exchange for the removal of the Soviet missiles from Cuba. Equally as troublesome, Kennedy feared that other countries would see no difference between the U.S. missiles in Turkey and the Soviet missiles in Cuba.[75]

In light of these potential problems, the president and his advisers made several strategic decisions about his communication during the crisis. To avoid the perception that the conflict was between the United States and the tiny island of Cuba, Kennedy referred to the missiles as Soviet weapons. The transcript of an Ex Comm meeting indicates that a discussion of whether the missiles should be considered Cuban or Soviet took place and Bundy asserted, "what we say for political purposes and what we think are not identical here."[76]

According to presidential speechwriter Ted Sorensen, another decision was to emphasize the suddenness and deceptiveness of the Soviet deployment in order to legitimize U.S. actions.[77] An examination of Kennedy White House documents supports Sorensen's recollection. Instructions and drafts indicate that at least two messages underwent revision to correspond to these themes and also to emphasize the danger that the missiles posed.[78] During an October 16 discussion, an Ex Comm member, unidentified in the meeting transcript, suggested that Kennedy keep his appointment with Soviet Foreign Minister Andrei Gromyko that Thursday and that he ask Gromyko about the nature of the weapons the Soviets were sending to Cuba. According to the Ex Comm member, the president's "public presentation" would be strengthened if he could say that "the Soviets have, uh, lied to you, either privately or in public."[79] Kennedy followed this advice, and his account of the meeting with Gromyko appeared in his major address on the crisis as yet another example of Soviet deceit.

On Monday, October 22, Kennedy appeared on nationwide television to tell the country and the world about the existence of the missiles and what his administration planned to do. According to Richard Walton, Kennedy's speech was "probably the most dramatic and most frightening presidential address in the history of the republic."[80] The Cuban missile crisis had begun.

THE RHETORIC OF DEFLECTION:
KENNEDY'S DISCOURSE ON THE CUBAN MISSILE CRISIS

In 1955, John Kennedy published a Pulitzer Prize–winning book, *Profiles in Courage.* This book detailed the stories of eight U.S. senators who had faced difficult choices with, in Kennedy's words, "that most admirable of human virtues—courage." According to Kennedy, courage remained especially important during the dangerous Cold War era. He explained that "in the days ahead, only the very courageous will be able to take the hard and unpopular decisions necessary for our survival in the struggle with a powerful enemy."[81] Senator Kennedy's literary tribute to courage and tests of character presaged President Kennedy's 1962 discourse on the Cuban missile crisis. In *Profiles in Courage,* Kennedy warned readers of the worldwide Soviet threat; in his Cuban missile rhetoric, he depicted a specific scene of crisis in which Soviet Communists and their weapons threatened the Western Hemisphere. This crisis was, according to Kennedy's discourse, a test of American character—and, perhaps, of his character, as well.

Although most Americans in 1962 would agree that the missiles posed a danger, Kennedy had reason to worry that other countries might listen to his arguments with indifference. The Soviets may have placed intermediate-range nuclear missiles in Cuba, but the United States had installed similar weapons in Turkey near the Soviet border and had overtly threatened Cuba with its bungled invasion attempt at the Bay of Pigs. Kennedy's announcement of the crisis would also include the declaration of a U.S. naval blockade of Cuba, which was an act of war.

To sway both domestic and international public opinion, the president turned to rhetoric. Kennedy's discourse portrayed a highly threatening scene of crisis that dictated U.S. goals and actions, which meant that the scene and the Soviets who were part of that scene, rather than the United States or its leader, had the highest degree of accountability. Through this focus, Kennedy deflected attention from questions about his own and U.S. scruples. At the same time, Kennedy lent moral legitimacy to U.S. efforts when he maintained that the United States' actions were consistent with its national character and that the United States should take particular actions in order to prove its character. The president also appealed to audiences to unite with him in the fight against the common foes of the Soviet Union and Communism. In this section, I examine Kennedy's promotion and management of the Cuban missile crisis through the framework established in chapter 1. The analysis of the situation, style, and identificational appeals of his rhetoric reveals the way in which Kennedy constructed a particular view of reality and convinced others not only to accept that interpretation, but also to embrace the policy resolutions that he set forth.

Situation

As explained in chapter 1, in this book I examine the rhetorical situation of crisis talk by ascertaining the representative anecdote of each president's discourse or how that president described the situation. This method recognizes that commanders-in-chief do not discuss objective reality in their crisis rhetoric; they provide instead an interpretation of reality. Through this type of analysis, the critic can explain how a president portrayed the crisis situation and the linguistic strategies he used to deal with it. In the case of the Cuban missile crisis, the president's representative anecdote might be summarized as:

Because the Soviets duplicitously placed offensive nuclear missiles in Cuba (scene), the United States—or "we"—and Kennedy—or "I"—(coactors), through the authority given to Kennedy by the Constitution and validated by Congress (means), have initiated a quarantine, increased Cuban surveillance, announced a policy on nuclear missiles launched from Cuba, reinforced Guantanamo military base, called for a meeting of the OAS Organ of Consultation, asked for an emergency U.N. Security Council meeting, and told Khrushchev to halt the buildup (acts), in order to prevent the use of the missiles, to secure their withdrawal, and to protect freedom and peace (purposes).

Kennedy's rhetoric about the crisis conveyed a scene of great danger. The president told Americans that "unmistakable evidence has established the fact that a series of offensive missile sites is now in preparation" in Cuba.[82] Kennedy asserted that "the Soviets are rapidly continuing their construction of missile support and launch facilities," which would give the Soviet Union the ability to launch a nuclear attack against the Western Hemisphere.[83] According to the president, this threat indicated what our purposes should be: the elimination of the missiles and, hence, the protection of freedom and peace. Kennedy also delineated the many actions the United States had taken—such as the institution of a blockade—in order to reach these goals.[84]

In Kennedy's discourse, the dominant term for actor was "we," which the president usually employed interchangeably with the "United States" or "this nation." The other term for actor, which Kennedy used nearly as often, was "I." Through his terms for means, the president also indicated that this second actor, "I," held the power needed to carry out U.S. actions. Kennedy claimed to act "under the authority entrusted to me by the Constitution as endorsed by the resolution of Congress."[85] By referring to the Constitution, a sacred text in American society, Kennedy legitimized his actions. By mentioning the statute, the president paid his respects to Congress, while making clear that the resolution had been irrelevant since he already possessed the necessary prerogative powers.

A second step in situational analysis, as conducted in this study, is the examination of key ratios, or relationships, among the rhetor's terms for situation. In Kennedy's overall discourse about the Cuban missile crisis, two terminological ratios played an important role: scene-purpose and purpose-act. The scene-purpose ratio was particularly important in the president's televised address about the crisis, but it also appeared in his other crisis discourse. According to Kennedy, the United States and its allies faced an extremely ominous crisis scene in which the Soviet Union had deceptively shipped offensive nuclear weapons to Cuba. Kennedy's October 22 speech described the "urgent transformation of Cuba into an important strategic base—by the presence of these large, long-range, and clearly offensive weapons of sudden mass destruction." In addition, the president emphasized that the buildup "contradicts the repeated assurances of Soviet spokesmen, both publicly and privately delivered, that the arms buildup in Cuba would retain its original defensive character." These weapons were "so destructive" and "so swift,"

Kennedy claimed, their installation posed a "clandestine, reckless, and provocative threat to world peace."

To make the threat more concrete, Kennedy explained that the Soviets were installing medium-range ballistic missiles, which would be "capable of striking Washington, D.C., the Panama Canal, Cape Canaveral, Mexico City, or any other city in the southeastern part of the United States, in Central America, or in the Caribbean area." Kennedy also pointed out the even more frightening information that the Soviets were building sites for intermediate-range ballistic missiles, "capable of traveling more than twice as far—and thus capable of striking most of the major cities in the Western Hemisphere, ranging as far north as Hudson Bay, Canada, and as far south as Lima, Peru."[86] The president's terms for scene emphasized the international setting of the scene, its causes, and its dangers.

At first glance, to consider terms that describe actors (the Soviets) and actions (giving false assurances, transforming Cuba) as part of a scene may seem odd. Burke, however, encourages rhetorical critics to look beyond the face value of a term to the principle it represents (scene, act, actor, purpose, means) in the rhetor's discourse. For example, a mayor might describe his morning walk through the city with terms in which street vendors selling their wares, cops walking their beat, and children playing in water from a fire hydrant constitute the scene, or context, in which his constitutional took place. Similarly, a social activist could depict the history of humanity—consisting of various places, events, people, goals, and policies—as the scene, or backdrop, for her own acts in the present.

In Kennedy's case, his crisis rhetoric delineated a scene of peril in which Soviet Communists had secretly, deliberately, and defiantly placed offensive weapons in Cuba. In fact, the first half of the president's speech accentuated the danger of the crisis scene and thus encouraged fear in listeners that, in turn, prepared them to embrace the goals and policies that Kennedy proceeded to provide.

Specifically, terms for scene were directly related to terms for purpose. For example, Kennedy paralleled the particular scene of crisis the world faced with one from several decades earlier and indicated how the characteristics of these comparable scenes dictated what our goals must be. According to the president, "the 1930's taught us a clear lesson: aggressive conduct, if allowed to go unchecked and unchallenged, ultimately leads to war. . . . Our unswerving objective, therefore, must be to prevent the use of these missiles against this or any other country, and to secure their withdrawal or elimination from the Western Hemisphere."

The crisis scene of the president's October 22 talk pointed to a second purpose beyond the removal of the missiles: "Our goal is not the victory of might, but the vindication of right—not peace at the expense of freedom, but both peace *and* freedom, here in this hemisphere, and, we hope, around the world."[87] Through this and related statements, Kennedy legitimized his actions with respect to Cuba. He described the goal as "ours," rather than as a politically expedient objective that was his alone. Moreover, Kennedy said that our purpose was to attain peace and freedom, two highly revered values in American society in principle if not always in practice, and that our purpose was morally right.

The use of inversion ("not") clarified that we did not intend to bully, nor did we plan to appease the Soviets by settling for a peace that would threaten our security, and ultimately, our freedom. Through rhyme ("might" and "right") and alliteration ("victory," "vindication"), Kennedy gave the statement a poetic sound that imbued the goals with romance and legitimacy.

The second situational ratio in Kennedy's televised speech consisted of terms for purpose-act. Just as the president maintained that the scene directed what the United States' purposes must be, he asserted that our purposes would be fulfilled through particular actions. He said, for example, "to halt this offensive buildup, a strict quarantine on all offensive military equipment under shipment to Cuba is being initiated."[88] Through the linguistic choice of "quarantine"—a phrase suggested by Richard Nixon[89]—rather than "blockade," Kennedy simultaneously sidestepped questions of legal propriety and portrayed U.S. actions as defensive rather than offensive. A September 10 memo from Bundy to Abram Chayes, legal adviser for the State Department, reflected concerns about such matters when it inquired into the legalities of a "pacific blockade."[90] By the time the president spoke on October 22, the word "quarantine" had been adopted, a term that historically had referred to preventive isolation intended to stave off epidemic. Kennedy's terminological choice described U.S. actions not as a blockade, or act of war, but as a defensive step that would prevent the contagion of nuclear missiles in Cuba from spreading. He also reinforced this perception through the use of passive voice and his description of how the quarantine would be carried out. According to Kennedy, the quarantine "is being initiated," and ships that carried offensive weapons would "be turned back." He did not explicitly state that the United States had implemented the quarantine, although he used active voice to accentuate the key role of the United States and himself in carrying out other policy actions, nor did he say that U.S. military forces would shoot at other ships to enforce the policy. These alternative linguistic choices would have suggested that the United States bore at least some responsibility for the crisis, a perception that Kennedy did not want to perpetuate and that his emphasis on a dangerous, Soviet-created crisis scene did much to avoid.

Moments after Kennedy had portrayed U.S. actions as defensive and restrained, he employed a purpose-act ordering of terms that contained an implied threat of war. The president claimed that he acted "in the defense of our own security and the entire Western Hemisphere." In accordance with this goal, Kennedy announced a new policy: that the United States would respond to "any nuclear missile launched from Cuba against any nation in the Western Hemisphere as an attack by the Soviet Union on the United States."[91] Kennedy may have described the initial U.S. military response as a peaceful "quarantine," but his articulation of U.S. nuclear policy also sent the unmistakable message that he and his country were willing to go to war over the issue at hand. The president's statement demonstrated the importance that he attached to the issue and served to warn—as well as to threaten—Soviet adversaries about possible U.S. responses.

In addition to the implementation of a quarantine and the announcement of a new nuclear policy, Kennedy discussed other acts he and the United States had taken in order to eradicate the missiles. He said, for instance, "I have directed the continued and increased close surveillance of Cuba and its military buildup" and "we are calling tonight for an immediate meeting of the Organ of Consultation under the Organization of American States, to consider this threat to hemispheric security." Furthermore, Kennedy added, "I call upon Chairman Khrushchev to halt and eliminate this clandestine, reckless, and provocative threat to world peace."[92] This latter remark had the force of a command and therefore portrayed Kennedy's action in response to the crisis as quite strong. The assertion again placed culpability for the crisis on the Soviet Union and also gave that nation the responsibility for crisis resolution.

Because of the importance of his televised speech and because Kennedy made a relatively limited number of other public statements about the crisis, I have focused thus far almost exclusively on his October 22 address, just as other critics have done. The same scene-purpose and purpose-act ordering of terms that were important in this speech, however, appeared in many of his other public comments. In a statement on October 27, for instance, Kennedy described how Soviet "offensive weapons" in Cuba menaced "Western Hemisphere countries and they alone." This dangerous scene meant that the United States' "first imperative" must be "to deal with this immediate threat" or to end "the present Soviet-created threat." In order to achieve this goal, Kennedy said that "work on the Cuban bases must stop; offensive weapons must be rendered inoperable; and further shipment of offensive weapons to Cuba must cease."[93] The October 22 speech commanded Khrushchev to remove the missiles; the October 27 statement iterated the same.

The terminological ratios of scene-purpose and purpose-act also played a role in the president's news conference of November 20. In remarks to reporters, Kennedy said:

> I have today been informed by Chairman Khrushchev that all of the IL-28 bombers now in Cuba will be withdrawn in 30 days. He also

agrees that these planes can be observed and counted as they leave (scene). Inasmuch as this goes a long way towards reducing the danger which faced this hemisphere 4 weeks ago (fulfillment of purpose), I have this afternoon instructed the Secretary of Defense to lift our naval quarantine (act).[94]

With an alteration in the scene, much of the United States' goal had been achieved, which meant, consequently, that particular actions could be taken.

Likewise, a statement on October 28 described how the Soviets had stopped building bases in Cuba and had agreed to remove the missiles. Kennedy noted, "It is my earnest hope that the governments of the world can, with a solution of the Cuban crisis, turn their urgent attention to the compelling necessity for ending the arms race and reducing world tensions."[95] Once the scene had changed, Kennedy claimed that the United States—as well as other nations— could attend to new goals. These new goals, the president implied, would require new types of action.

Throughout Kennedy's discourse about the Cuban missile crisis, he depicted a situation in which the scene dictated that particular purposes be fulfilled and in which those purposes mandated that specific actions be taken. Burke notes that rhetors can deflect criticism of their actions if they describe their acts as determined by the nature of the scene in which the acts took place.[96] More so than any other president in this study, Kennedy used fear-arousing language to construct a ghastly crisis scene that dominated his discourse. His language preempted alternative interpretations of the scene in which Jupiter missiles threatened Soviet borders and in which U.S.-sponsored insurgents had attempted to invade Cuba at the Bay of Pigs.

Equally important, the crisis scene of Kennedy's talk focused attention on the Soviets' secret missile buildup and away from questions about Kennedy's own inflammatory acts of instituting a naval blockade and issuing ultimatums. The situation of the president's discourse argued, in effect, that the United States had been forced to take particular actions because of Soviet aggression. Nonetheless, Kennedy took pains not to portray the United States as a weak and passive actor who scrambled to respond to emergencies, but was incapable of assertive action of its own. An analysis of the president's style demonstrates that he provided instead a profile of the United States as a courageous nation that would willingly face great risk in order to prove its character.

Style

In this study, I take a macroscopic approach to illumine Kennedy's style and assume, following the tenets of Burke, that style or attitude is the way in which rhetors adhere to personal values in their talk. Burke explains that style deals most directly with terms for actor and with terms that describe how the actor acts. To analyze Kennedy's style, I first ascertain his key terms for actor, then how the president described this actor and how the actor acted, and finally, the dominant ratio or ratios in which terms for actor were involved. The latter step is an adaptation of pentadic analysis and examines only terminological ratios that involve actor. If terms for actor play a major role in the portrayal of the situation, stylistic examination traces the secondary relationships in which terms for actor also are involved.

In Kennedy's discourse, the most typical terms for the actor were "we"— used interchangeably with references to the United States—and "I." Of these two terms, "we" more importantly reflected Kennedy's attitude or style because the president described what "we" were like and how "we" would act. Conversely, Kennedy employed almost no descriptive terms in relation to "I." His rhetoric allowed "I" to bask in the reflected nobility of the "we" of whom Kennedy was a part.

In his discourse about the Cuban missile crisis, Kennedy portrayed a heroic actor who had a number of laudable characteristics. "We" were peaceful, principled, rational, courageous, and resolved. The president told listeners in his October 22 address, for example, that "We have no wish to war with the Soviet Union—for we are a peaceful people who desire to live in peace with all other peoples." Similarly, he noted that "this nation is opposed to war. We are also true to our word." Despite these noble intentions, the United States felt compelled to respond to the Soviet missile buildup in Cuba, but Kennedy made it clear that the United States had not reacted irrationally. He said, "We have been determined not to be diverted by mere irritants and fanatics."[97]

Months after the crisis had passed, Kennedy reinforced this depiction when rumors that the missiles were still in Cuba came up at a press conference. The president said that for the United States to take action against Soviet missiles in Cuba, "we have to move with hard intelligence. We have to know what we're talking about."[98] In other words, the United States was not a nation that acted precipitously. Beyond these descriptions of a peaceful and reasonable actor, Kennedy's discourse about the crisis provided hints about the United States' nerve and resolve. He talked, for instance, about the United States' willingness to take action during dangerous times, its courage, and its intention to meet all threats "with determination."[99]

Perhaps the statement that best summed up Kennedy's characterization of the key actor is this one from his televised address: "We will not prematurely or unnecessarily risk the costs of worldwide nuclear war in which even the fruits of victory would be ashes in our mouth—but neither will we shrink from that risk at any time it must be faced."[100] The actor of Kennedy's discourse may have been cautious and desirous of peace, but that actor also would act boldly and face great danger if it were necessary to achieve national goals.

A further stylistic analysis reveals that Kennedy's terms for actor were involved in two dominant ratios: actor-act and act-actor. For example, he said, "The path we have chosen for the present is full of hazards, as all paths are—but it is the one most consistent with our character and courage as a nation." Kennedy reasoned that the quality of the actor determined the quality of the act. In a kindred fashion, the president observed, "Our policy has been one of patience and restraint, as befits a peaceful and powerful nation, which leads a worldwide alliance." In his major address on the missile crisis, Kennedy also indicated that "we" were prepared "to discuss new proposals for the removal of tensions on both sides . . . for we are a peaceful people."[101]

Although terms for actor-act played a major role in Kennedy's style, terms for act-actor were even more significant. The commander-in-chief told Americans, for instance, that we could not allow the missiles to remain in Cuba "if our courage and our commitments are ever to be trusted again by either friend or foe." According to Kennedy, our acts reflected upon our character as a nation. He claimed that the United States had never engaged in deception by secretly sending missiles to other countries, nor had we imposed our rule upon other nations; the president maintained that these actions indicated the purity of our intentions.[102]

After the crisis was over, Kennedy told members of the Economic Club of New York, "Less than a month ago this Nation reminded the world that it possessed both the will and the weapons to meet any threat to the security of free men."[103] Likewise, the president spoke to reporters in February 1963 about the crisis and about the continued presence of Soviet military personnel in Cuba: "I think the actions the United States has taken over the last four months indicate that we do not view the threat lightly."[104] Our action during the crisis was proof of our resolve, preparedness, and concern.

In Kennedy's discourse, the key stylistic actor was peaceful, patient, and reasonable. This actor produced acts that naturally reflected such admirable characteristics (actor-act). At the same time, the actor felt impelled to take particular actions so that others would associate the actor with these positive qualities, and Kennedy also pointed to past actions as indications of the actor's worthy character (act-actor).

In the situation of Kennedy's rhetoric, he described a grave crisis scene that dictated U.S. purposes and actions and, hence, placed responsibility for those goals and acts upon the Soviet-created crisis scene. The president's style also indicated that blame for the crisis situation must lie with someone else, for a moral and prudent actor like "we" surely could not be at fault. Nevertheless, Kennedy was careful not to portray the United States as a completely passive actor who would be easily overcome by an adversary, and he ascribed traits like courage, commitment, and fortitude to "we." Through his style, Kennedy supported his situational explanations and, at the same time, implored Americans to endorse his policies in order to prove the nation's character. The president's portrait of a nation that would willingly face nuclear peril to uphold its commitments served as a warning to the Soviet Union about the seriousness of the United States' position.

Kennedy invoked identificational appeals that worked in unison with the situation and style of his talk. The president's chief identification strategy focused on the Soviet Union and exhorted listeners to unite with Kennedy to defeat this evil foe.

Identificational Appeals

Identification is synonymous with persuasion in Burke's theory of dramatism. That is, rhetors who hope to persuade must convince their audience that they share the audience's interests in some way. In the case of presidential discourse, that audience is typically composed of American citizens who listen to their leader's nationally broadcast messages or hear what he said secondhand through the news. Windt points out, however, that allies and adversaries also listen attentively to foreign policy speeches for information about U.S. positions.[105]

Much more so than the other presidents examined in this book, Kennedy overtly aimed his identificational appeals at an international audience. His October 22 speech openly addressed not only American citizens, but also countries of the "Western Hemisphere," "the world community of nations," and "peoples to whom we are committed."[106] A number of Kennedy's other statements about the crisis also seemed to have international, as well as domestic, listeners in mind.

Regardless of the audience, Kennedy's chief identificational strategy was antithetical in character; he attempted to convince listeners that they should join forces with him to combat a shared enemy. This analysis reaffirms Windt's finding that Kennedy in his October 22 speech "elevated his particular policy to a struggle between the Free World and the Communist World, one in which ideological angels do mortal and moral combat with ideological devils."[107] Kennedy's other talk about the missile crisis also tended to rely upon an antithetical strategy.

The president treated the Soviet Union and the Communist philosophy it embodied as scapegoats for the current crisis and for many other ills in the world. For instance, on October 22 Kennedy referred to Communist leaders as the "puppets and agents of an international conspiracy."[108] Similarly, on October 27, the president emphasized that "the action of the Soviet Government in secretly introducing offensive weapons into Cuba" was the cause of "the current crisis."[109]

Kennedy's discourse not only placed blamed for the crisis on the Soviets, but also depicted their behavior as deceitful, threatening, and rash. In his announcement of the crisis, the president explained that

> this secret, swift, and extraordinary buildup of Communist missiles—in an area well known to have a special and historical relationship to the United States and the nations of the Western Hemisphere, in violation of Soviet assurances, and in defiance of American and hemispheric policy—this sudden, clandestine decision to station strategic weapons for the first time outside of Soviet soil—is a deliberately provocative and unjustified change in the status quo which cannot be accepted.[110]

The president's antithetical appeals created an enemy against whom Americans and citizens of the world should unite. Kennedy described the weapons in Cuba as "Communist," a word choice that linked the missiles with the more frightening, overarching devil of Communism rather than simply with the Soviet Union. Moreover, the president sandwiched an interjection of where the missiles were and how the Soviets had lied and violated the law between repetitive phrases that emphasized the deception ("secret," "clandestine") and quickness ("swift," "sudden") of the buildup. The staccato clip of the passage also conveyed a sense of urgency about the threat the Soviets posed. In a White House statement on October 26, Kennedy underscored this urgency, as well as the treachery of the enemy, when he described the Soviets as "rapidly continuing their construction of missile support and launch facilities" and commented on Soviet attempts to "camouflage their efforts."[111] Kennedy's State of the Union message in 1963 similarly looked back at the shock that nations felt over "the Soviets' sudden and secret attempt to transform Cuba into a nuclear striking base."[112]

Beyond these negative portrayals, Kennedy's October 22 speech further encouraged his listeners to rally behind him in opposition to the Soviets and Communism when he compared the evil of these enemies with the goodness of the United States in the contexts of law and morality. The president argued, for instance, that the missiles were "in flagrant and deliberate defiance of the Rio Pact of 1947, the traditions of this Nation and hemisphere, the joint resolution of the 87th Congress, [and] the Charter of the United Nations." In contrast, Kennedy portrayed his own actions and those of the United States as well within the boundaries established by U.S. and international law. The president claimed he had acted legally in accordance with the Constitution and a congressional resolution.

When the United States asked for an emergency meeting of the U.N. Security

Council, Kennedy claimed it did so based on "the Charter of the United Nations." Similarly, the president did not call upon the OAS simply to take action, but rather "to invoke articles 6 and 8 of the Rio Treaty."[113] By placing the crisis within a legal context, Kennedy demonstrated that the Soviets were at odds with the canons of international responsibility, whereas the United States abided by established legal principles.

The president also compared the Soviets to Americans within the context of morals. He emphasized, for example, the Soviets' "deliberate deception" in regard to the missiles as opposed to U.S. openness about what it would accept or not accept and about its own installation of missiles in other countries. Kennedy told Americans:

> only last month, after I had made clear the distinction between any introduction of ground-to-ground missiles and the existence of defensive antiaircraft missiles, the Soviet Government publicly stated on September 11 that, and I quote, "the armaments and military equipment sent to Cuba are designed exclusively for defensive purposes," that, and I quote the Soviet Government, "there is no need for the Soviet Government to shift its weapons . . . for a retaliatory blow to any other country, for instance Cuba," and that, and I quote their government, "the Soviet Union has so powerful rockets to carry these nuclear warheads that there is no need to search for sites for them beyond the boundaries of the Soviet Union." That statement was false.[114]

Kennedy went on to testify how Soviet Foreign Minister Gromyko, too, had lied to him, even after the president knew the truth about the missiles' offensive applications. By quoting the Soviet government and foreign minister, Kennedy used the Soviets' own words against them, thereby providing proof for his charge that the Soviets were bald-faced liars. The United States, by comparison, seemed honest and forthright. According to Kennedy, "our own strategic missiles have never been transferred to the territory of any other nation under a cloak of secrecy and deception."[115]

Related to this quality of character, the president argued that our country was more humane than the Soviet Union. Kennedy acidly observed that "our history—unlike that of the Soviets since the end of World War II—demonstrates that we have no desire to dominate or conquer any other nation or impose our system upon its people." Additionally, the commander-in-chief explained that in response to the Soviets' aggressive installation of missiles, the United States had implemented a peaceful and compassionate "quarantine." Kennedy added, "We are not at this time . . . denying the necessities of life as the Soviets attempted to do in their Berlin blockade of 1948."[116] Just as the style of the president's discourse equated the key actors of the United States and Kennedy with their acts, the antithetical appeals of his crisis talk appeared to equate the Soviets with the evil of their actions. In this way, Kennedy seemed to say, "you need not accept my word about the wickedness of the Soviets. Examine their actions and decide for yourself." Through his descriptions of present and past Soviet behavior, Kennedy provided his listeners with the evidence from which they could draw the conclusions he wanted them to draw.

Most typically, then, Kennedy's crisis discourse employed a simplistic strategy of antithetical identificational appeals. Even when Kennedy referred to "I," his discourse frequently pitted "I" against an enemy, such as Khrushchev, or treated "I" as a representative of the larger United States, which was opposed to the Soviet Union. Although implicit and explicit appeals appeared, antithetical appeals overwhelmingly characterized Kennedy's rhetoric. The president described the Soviet Union in negative ways, compared the evil of its acts with the goodness of U.S. acts, and thereby encouraged listeners to unite against the Soviet villain.

Kennedy's rhetoric treated the Cuban missile crisis as if it were one more test of character in the larger Cold War. At a press conference in February 1963, for example, the president expressed fears over potential schisms among Western allies. He said, "I think it would be a disaster if we should divide. The forces in the world hostile to us are powerful. We went through a very difficult and dangerous experience this fall in Cuba. I have seen no real evidence that the policy of the Communist world towards us is basically changed."[117] The crisis had been resolved successfully, but Kennedy's antithetical appeals maintained that the Communist threat was far from finished.

The president's rhetoric about the Cuban missile crisis consisted of a situation dominated by terms for scene-purpose and purpose-act, a style characterized by terms for actor-act and act-actor, and identificational appeals that were strongly antithetical. The ways in which these elements interacted in Kennedy's talk invite two summary observations.

First, Kennedy discussed the Cuban missiles in terms of a broader context. The president insisted that the weapons not only posed a physical threat, but also an even greater political danger in regard to the global struggle between the United States and the Soviet Union. Because of this, when Kennedy held that actions consistent with the character of the United States were demanded—or that the United States would lose credibility if it did not act in a particular way—this president vowed to do whatever was necessary. Hence, Kennedy's discourse portrayed the Cuban crisis in terms of something else: a test of character. Sorensen writes that Ex Comm developed five possible theories that could explain the Soviet Union's actions. He claims that Kennedy leaned most strongly to one called "Cold War Politics." According to this theory,

Khrushchev believed that the American people were too timid to risk nuclear war and too concerned with legalisms to justify any distinction between our overseas missile bases and his—that once we were actually confronted with the missiles we would do nothing but protest—that we would thereby appear weak and irresolute to the world, causing our allies to doubt our word and to seek accommodations with the Soviets, and permitting increased Communist sway in Latin America in particular. This [the missile installation] was a probe, a test of America's will to resist.[118]

According to Walton, the tendency to jump from particular incidents to broader contexts is characteristic of Cold War politics.[119] The examination of Kennedy's crisis discourse indicates that it also may be a characteristic of Cold War rhetoric.[120] For Kennedy, the Cuban missiles could be understood only through their relationship to other contexts: political, legal, moral, and—especially—tests of character, national and, perhaps, personal.

A second insight that can be gleaned from this analysis is an explanation for the pessimism of Kennedy's talk. Although the president's rhetoric on Cuba understandably sounded glum, Rod Hart maintains that Kennedy's presidential discourse as a whole displayed less optimism than that of any other post–World War II president.[121] One reason for this may lie in the relationships among style, identificational appeals, and situation in Kennedy's rhetoric.

Stylistically, Kennedy portrayed acts that reflected actors and actors that determined acts. Similarly, his identificational appeals implied that the Soviet Union was consubstantial with the quality of its acts, acts that Kennedy described as devious, reckless, illegal, and inhumane. Because the Soviet Union performed evil acts, Kennedy insinuated that it was by necessity an evil nation. This premise in Kennedy's rhetoric also explained why threatening scenes occurred. The Soviets, acting in accordance with their character, created scenes of crisis. Kennedy depicted the Soviet Union as evil; therefore, he reasoned that it would continue to perform evil deeds that, in turn, would produce dangerous scenes, which would dictate particular U.S. purposes and actions. Kennedy could not help but sound pessimistic.

Kennedy's rhetoric seemed to presage a never-ending conflict between the acts of a good actor and those of a dialectically opposed villain, both of whom were bound up in a shared scene of crisis. In Kennedy's discourse, the Cold War lived on indefinitely.

This theme may not have been unique to the president's Cuban rhetoric. In their examinations, both Hart and Carol Berthold found that "Communism" was a key devil term in much of Kennedy's presidential communication as a whole, and in *Presidents and Protesters,* Windt observed the theme of anti-Communism in several of Kennedy's crisis speeches.[122] Even the president's conciliatory foreign policy addresses seem to reflect remnants of the Cold War ideology that permeated his Cuban missile rhetoric. At American University on June 10, 1963, Kennedy asserted, "The Communist drive to impose their political and economic system on others is the primary cause of world tension today."[123] Similarly, on July 26, 1963, he appealed for citizen support of the Test Ban Treaty, but emphasized that, "at many points around the globe the Communists are continuing their efforts to exploit weakness and poverty. Their concentration of nuclear and conventional arms must still be deterred."[124]

In these remarks and others like them, Kennedy described the Soviets as evil foes who performed evil acts and, therefore, created world tensions or crises. In contrast, the United States was a weary, but stalwart, soldier, grimly determined to prevent world domination by the Soviets. According to Hart, "this is the John Kennedy who makes his liberal admirers squeamish."[125] The president's predilection for discussing foreign affairs as tests of character between the United States and the Soviet Union also *may* explain why so many foreign crises occurred during Kennedy's brief tenure in office. In retrospect, the president who set the standard for contemporary crisis promotion may have tended to see world events in crisis terms.

THE LEGACY OF THE CUBAN MISSILE CRISIS

On October 28, 1962, Nikita Khrushchev announced that the missiles in Cuba would be removed. In response, the president said he welcomed this "statesmanlike decision" and called it "an important and constructive contribution to peace."[126] He could afford to be gracious. The Cuban missile crisis had made Kennedy a national hero, and it would sweep Democrats to a historic, off-year victory in Congress.[127] In the euphoria of America's triumph, however, few took the time to examine the more troubling aspects of this episode.

Indeed, the missile crisis left a less glorious legacy, as well. According to historian Barton J. Bernstein, Khrushchev's public humiliation contributed to the arms race because the Soviets never wanted to find themselves in such a position of weakness again.[128] Other critics, such as Kennedy revisionists Richard Walton and Garry Wills, argue that the president's bold military moves and public ultimatums, while politically advantageous, only added to the atmosphere of crisis.[129] This criticism rings especially true in light of a 1989 Soviet revelation. According to Sergei Khrushchev, son of the former Soviet premier, nuclear warheads were already in Cuba when Kennedy announced the crisis and could have been attached to the missiles in a matter of hours for deployment against American cities.[130] The military situation in Cuba was, therefore, much more dangerous than Americans realized in 1962.

Beyond this, the Kennedy administration itself must bear at least part of the blame for the missile installation. Cables from Khrushchev to Kennedy during the crisis argued that the Soviets considered the missiles to be defensive weapons in light of the U.S.-sponsored coup attempt at the Bay of Pigs. In a memorandum written during the missile crisis, the CIA also reported that the Soviets had provided arms to the Cubans to prevent "the US from 'liquidating' the Castro regime."[131] Khrushchev's actions may have been reckless, but they were not without provocation.

Today some citizens recall the Cuban missile crisis as a rash show of profile; others remember it as an act of political courage. Regardless of which position one takes, Kennedy used rhetoric to extricate himself from a difficult political circumstance. He deflected questions of hypocrisy and responsibility from the United States and focused them instead squarely on the Soviet Union through discourse that emphasized a threatening crisis scene and that encouraged listeners to unite to defeat an evil Soviet foe. At the same time, Kennedy reassured Americans and U.S. allies that the United States remained strong, using stylistic terms that tempered his portrayals of the United States as patient and forced to respond with depictions of the nation as courageous and willing to face whatever risks were necessary.

The Cuban missile crisis also marked the culmination of structural and legal changes that paved the way for later crisis promotion and management. With the Cuban crisis, Kennedy transferred power over foreign policy-making from other governmental bodies to the senior White House staff and relied on his prerogative power as commander-in-chief as if it were a well-established right. Kennedy refined news management techniques, as well, which forced or encouraged the media to propagate the administration's views. Through these actions, Kennedy greatly expanded presidential power over foreign affairs and thereby increased the commander-in-chief's ability to promote and manage crises. Lyndon Johnson, the president's successor, exploited these presidential powers to promote and manage a crisis in an obscure little place called the Gulf of Tonkin.

Chapter Three

LBJ BALANCES STRENGTH AND RESTRAINT
The 1964 Gulf of Tonkin Crisis
and the Danger of the Middle Ground

On August 4, 1964, President Lyndon Baines Johnson interrupted nation-wide television with news that North Vietnamese vessels had attacked "United States ships on the high seas in the Gulf of Tonkin." In retaliation, the commander-in-chief had ordered air raids against North Vietnamese gunboats and support facilities. Lest citizens fear that the United States had gone to war, Johnson also added, "our response, for the present, will be limited and fitting. We Americans know, although others appear to forget, the risks of spreading conflict. We still seek no wider war."[1] So began what journalist Murrey Marder called "the greatest military confrontation since the Cuban missile crisis of 1962."[2]

The Gulf of Tonkin crisis marked a turning point in the conduct of U.S. foreign policy in Southeast Asia. For the first time, American planes bombed targets in North Vietnam.[3] In addition, the Gulf of Tonkin crisis brought about congressional passage of the Southeast Asia Resolution, which gave the president nearly unlimited power to conduct military operations against North Vietnam. Johnson claimed that the events of the Gulf of Tonkin constituted a crisis; they also presaged America's deeper involvement in the Vietnam war.

According to rhetorical critic Richard Cherwitz, Johnson's creation of a crisis in the Gulf of Tonkin allowed him to implement his private plans for expanding the war without losing public support. Cherwitz explains that Johnson portrayed the crisis as a circumstance beyond his control that had forced him to take stronger military action than he would have preferred. The Gulf of Tonkin thereby allowed Johnson to continue to appear restrained even as he escalated American involvement in Vietnam.[4]

Others argue that the Gulf of Tonkin had more immediate political rewards. In *Lyndon B. Johnson: The Exercise of Power,* Rowland Evans and Robert Novak write that Johnson's use of the Gulf of Tonkin to obtain passage of the Southeast Asia Resolution was "a shrewd political act, shoring up Johnson against the Republican campaign charge that he was 'soft on Vietnam.'" Political scientist Bruce Altschuler concurs when he says that the Gulf of Tonkin crisis defused Goldwater's criticism that the president and his policies in Southeast Asia were not tough enough.[5]

In this chapter I corroborate much of what Cherwitz, Evans and Novak, Altschuler, and others have written about the Gulf of Tonkin, but I also offer an explanation of the symbolic import of the crisis and Johnson's rhetoric about it that is somewhat more complex. I agree, for example, that the Gulf of Tonkin and the passage of the Southeast Asia Resolution allowed the president to increase the strength of U.S. military involvement in Vietnam even as he depicted U.S. retaliation as an unavoidable and restrained response. Nevertheless, I argue that peace and the military defense of freedom did not start out as contrary policies in Johnson's discourse. Instead, these concepts were compatible because peace, Johnson maintained, could only exist if we preserved and defended freedom.

Through his rhetoric about the Gulf of Tonkin, the president defined his actions as moderate—both strong and restrained—and argued that moderate policies, rather than withdrawal or all-out war, were consistent with the goals of peace and defense of freedom. Withdrawal, Johnson argued, would mean the end of freedom in Vietnam, and escalation might lead to the end of world peace. The president maintained the compatibility of peace and the defense of freedom by redefining them as commensurate with moderate military involvement. But Johnson's discourse also raised the possibility that peace and the defense of freedom, as well as strength and restraint, might actually be at odds, as a policy of strength (escalation) would threaten peace and a policy of restraint (withdrawal) would threaten freedom. Johnson's inadvertent dissociation, or splitting, of these concepts would assume greater significance once the Vietnam war was underway.

An analysis of administration documents and the president's crisis discourse suggests how his rhetoric provided benefits for Johnson in the summer and fall of 1964 and the factors that may have influenced it. First, Johnson and his advisers recognized that the Gulf of Tonkin provided a golden political campaign opportunity. The president used the crisis to negate Goldwater's charges that Johnson was weak and, simultaneously, to pound away at his rival's chief weakness: the perception that Goldwater was trigger happy. In his crisis discourse, Johnson portrayed himself as an advocate of moderate policies who would engage neither in pacifism nor in warmongering, a depiction that nonetheless implied that peace and the defense of freedom might be opposed.

Second, as Cherwitz argues, White House officials in 1964 were preparing for possible military escalation. Administration documents indicate officials urged the president to emphasize peace in order to win the support of congressional doves for what would become the Southeast Asia Resolution and to emphasize the need for force so that citizens would not feel they had been misled if the administration later escalated the war. Johnson's discourse consequently situated him on the middle ground as a moderate of strength and restraint, a leader who would be responsible on issues of war and peace, in Vietnam and elsewhere. Again, though, his talk suggested that peace and the defense of freedom were not compatible, nor were restraint and strength.

In the long run, Johnson's moderate lines of argument left him vulnerable to attacks from both the left and the right. According to Kathleen Turner, author of *Lyndon Johnson's Dual War: Vietnam and the Press,* Johnson's later rhetoric about the Vietnam war dissatisfied most of the population because many believed that the president was not doing enough to help South Vietnam, whereas another large group thought he was doing too much.[6] Johnson's indirect dissociation of peace and the defense of freedom in his Gulf of Tonkin discourse, I suggest, helped trap the president in a moderate Vietnam policy and corresponding rhetoric that made him vulnerable to attack for a number of reasons. His moderate policy did not appear to be successful in upholding the goals he had articulated; he found it politically difficult to adopt different policies once he had rejected them as inconsistent with either peace or the defense of freedom; and critics on the left and the right, picking up on the inadvertent dissociation of his crisis talk, argued that these goals simply were not compatible.

In this chapter, I discuss the rhetorical context of the Gulf of Tonkin crisis; the situation, style, and identificational appeals of Johnson's discourse about the Gulf of Tonkin and how the latter two elements served to dissociate peace and the defense of freedom; and finally, how Johnson's terminological choices, which worked in the short term, had implications that led to the persuasive failure of his later rhetoric about limited war.

THE RHETORICAL CONTEXT OF THE GULF OF TONKIN CRISIS

In August 1964, Americans remained largely unaware of events in Vietnam; opinion polls found that more than two-thirds of the population claimed to pay little or no attention to what was going on there.[7] One reason for this inattention was that U.S. involvement remained limited. Although Americans served as advisers and helicopter crew members for the South Vietnamese, U.S. ground troops had not yet arrived in Vietnam, and American casualties remained low.

Nevertheless, Vietnam loomed as a potential problem for Lyndon Johnson in the 1964 presidential election. In July, the Republican leaders of the House and the Senate, Representative Charles Halleck and Senator Everett Dirksen, announced jointly that Vietnam would be a major campaign issue that year because "President Johnson's indecision has made it one." According to Halleck, "contradictions, confusion, and vacillation" characterized the administration's policy.[8] The Republican presidential nominee, Barry Goldwater, attacked Johnson both for his ambiguous position on Vietnam and for his refusal "to say . . . whether or not the objective over there is victory." Senator Goldwater told Americans that "failures infest the jungles of Vietnam" and that if he were elected president, the United States would pursue a "win policy" there.[9]

Presidential communication scholar Kathleen Hall Jamieson notes that at the time of the Republican convention, research showed that twice as many Americans planned to vote for Johnson as planned to vote for Goldwater.[10] Despite this comfortable lead, Johnson, the first U.S. president to retain a private polling firm on a continuing basis, remained highly attuned to the potentially shifting tides of public opinion. According to Altschuler, Johnson's polls showed that Goldwater's attacks on his Vietnam policy were making an impact, albeit a small one.[11]

At the same time that Goldwater was attacking Johnson as weak, Goldwater himself had to battle the public perception that he might be inclined toward impulsive and reckless action. Goldwater pollster Thomas Benham found that 26 percent of Americans surveyed after the Republican convention thought Goldwater "acts without thinking." According to Benham, this later was successfully translated by the opposition into "the notion that he would be likely to involve the country in nuclear war."[12]

In July 1964, Johnson found himself in a situation where accusations of weakness had the potential to hurt his campaign and where his opponent seemed susceptible to allegations of overeagerness on the matter of war. A few weeks later, the perfect opportunity to put charges against Johnson to rest and to exploit Goldwater's vulnerability presented itself.

On August 2, 1964, three North Vietnamese torpedo boats attacked the U.S. destroyer *Maddox* in the Gulf of Tonkin, a body of water that separates North Vietnam's east coast from the southwestern tip of China's Hainan island. According to official government reports, the *Maddox* was "on routine patrol in international waters" and was the victim of an "unprovoked attack." With air support from the U.S.S. *Ticonderoga,* the *Maddox* was able to fend off the North Vietnamese boats. President Johnson's response to the incident was to send another destroyer, the *Turner Joy,* to patrol with the *Maddox.* In addition, the commander-in-chief announced that he had ordered the ships "to attack any force which attacks them in international waters, and . . . to attack with the objective not only of driving off the force but of destroying it."[13]

Two days after the attack, the administration claimed that the North Vietnamese had struck again; this time, both the *Maddox* and the *Turner Joy* were targets. Johnson held that the United States must make "a sharp but limited response" to the attacks. He ordered American fighter-bombers from aircraft carriers to attack four North Vietnamese patrol-boat bases and a large oil depot.[14] Prior to his televised speech about the retaliation, Johnson briefed Goldwater, who then issued a statement of approval before Johnson had publicly announced the crisis. The Republican nominee asserted, "I am sure that every American will subscribe to the action outlined in the President's statement. I believe it is the only thing that he can do under the circumstances."[15] Johnson also informed congressional leaders of his decision and read to them a statement that he planned to make on nationwide television.

In the draft of this statement, Johnson balanced the forcefulness of U.S.

actions with three different references to their "limited" scope. Senators Leverett Saltonstall, Everett Dirksen, Bourke Hickenlooper, and Congresswoman Frances Bolton argued that the statement should be stronger. According to notes taken at the meeting, Dirksen said that "If I had it to do I would put our references to the word 'limited' in deep freeze. It connotes we would be like sitting ducks. We should make it clear that we would meet every enemy threat." Johnson obliged with a slight revision of the original statement.[16]

At 11:36 P.M. on August 4, the president appeared on television and informed citizens of the North Vietnamese attack and how he had ordered a United States "reply." Johnson's choice of the term "reply," rather than "attack" or "retaliation" or "revenge," served to portray the president as decisive (as "reply" suggested an immediate response) and also as a leader who had taken defensive, as opposed to offensive, action (as "reply" suggested that the enemy had initiated the crisis and Johnson had merely responded). Johnson described U.S. actions as strong and insisted that Americans now were even more determined to help South Vietnam. Despite the concerns congressional leaders had raised, the president also maintained at two points in his speech that our nation's military actions had been "limited." Even the timing of Johnson's speech underscored his dual message of strength and restraint. The dramatic late-night announcement made the president appear resolute; it also ensured that many people would not see his address but simply read about the United States' response in the morning paper. Johnson's initial message treated strength and restraint as compatible qualities, rather than as contrary characteristics.

In addition to his announcement of the crisis, Johnson stated that he would seek the passage of a congressional resolution, which would make "it clear that our Government is united in its determination to take all necessary measures in support of freedom and in defense of peace in southeast Asia."[17] After Johnson's speech, Secretary of Defense Robert McNamara appeared on television, surrounded by maps of Southeast Asia, to provide additional information about the crisis.[18]

In the days that followed the U.S. raid, the Johnson administration waged a campaign to gain congressional passage of the Southeast Asia Resolution. On August 5, McNamara gave press briefings and numerous television interviews in which he encouraged support for the administration's actions with his testimony of how U.S. attacks successfully had destroyed enemy boats and oil storage facilities. The Secretary of Defense also reinforced Johnson's portrayal of U.S. actions as firm and limited. Perhaps McNamara's concern for this official interpretation showed itself best when the fatigued Secretary of Defense told Peter Hackes of NBC News that he had "slept all too limited last night."[19]

On the day following the night of crisis, the president also devoted himself to the campaign for a congressional resolution. Johnson recounted the crisis in his remarks at the dedication of the Newhouse Communications Center at Syracuse

University and later that day delivered a special message to Congress about the proposed Southeast Asia Resolution. He said the legislation could be based on similar resolutions of the past, such as those enacted to deal with Formosa in 1955, the Middle East in 1957, and Cuba in 1962.[20] Both McNamara and Secretary of State Dean Rusk appeared before congressional committees to advocate the Southeast Asia Resolution; Rusk, like Johnson, pointed to the Formosa Doctrine of 1955 and the Cuban Resolution of 1962 as established precedents for such legislative action.[21]

In the House of Representatives, members discussed the resolution for only forty minutes and then voted unanimously in its favor. In the Senate, debate consumed just eight hours. According to historian Eric Goldman, the discussion "had the weird quality of being thoroughly troubled while its result was preordained. Senator after senator, of many different types, took the floor to announce a vote for the resolution and to add worried questions or statements." In the end, only two senators voted against the measure: Wayne Morse of Oregon and Ernest Gruening of Alaska.[22] President Johnson signed the legislation on the same day it was approved—August 7—just three days after the second Gulf of Tonkin attack.

As it was passed into law, the Southeast Asia Resolution gave the president enormous power over the conduct of military operations in Vietnam. More specifically, the measure stated that:

> Congress approves and supports the determination of the President, as Commander in Chief, to take all necessary measures to repel any armed attack against the forces of the United States and to prevent further aggression.
>
> Sec. 2. The United States . . . is, therefore, prepared, as the President determines, to take all necessary steps, including the use of armed force, to assist any member or protocol state of the Southeast Asia Collective Defense Treaty requesting assistance in defense of its freedom.
>
> Sec. 3. This resolution shall expire when the President shall determine that the peace and security of the area are reasonably assured by international conditions created by action of the United Nations or otherwise, except that it may be terminated earlier by concurrent resolution of the Congress.[23]

Through such sweeping language and by its own hand, Congress formally surrendered its war powers to the commander-in-chief. Johnson later described the resolution as "like grandma's nightgown; it covered everything."[24]

The Gulf of Tonkin crisis represented a significant victory for Lyndon Johnson. According to McNamara, the American air strike had inflicted heavy damage on North Vietnam and had cost the United States only two casualties.[25] Across the country, citizens applauded the president's actions. A Louis Harris poll revealed that 72 percent of Americans supported Johnson's handling of Vietnam, compared to only 42 percent before the crisis.[26] Congress also approved of the president's decisions and immediately gave him a legislative blank check for future military operations in the region. Even the president's political rival, Barry Goldwater, expressed his public support for the commander-in-chief, as did the Republican leadership in the Senate and the House. Johnson speechwriter Richard Goodwin later noted that Goldwater's response did much to nullify Vietnam as a problematic election-year issue for the president.[27]

According to Anthony Austin, much of Johnson's success can be attributed to his public statements that framed the crisis. Austin claims that Johnson's discourse was that "of a President who had punched the Commies in the nose when they challenged him but who wasn't about to be rattled into any foolishness."[28] Indeed, Johnson's rhetoric negated Republican charges of weakness by discussing the Gulf of Tonkin crisis as a representative example of how he would deal moderately and reasonably with matters of war and peace. Simultaneously, Johnson used the crisis to reinforce perceptions that Goldwater might be dangerous. The president discussed the Gulf of Tonkin on the campaign trail in the context of responsibility in matters of war and peace, particularly the use of nuclear weapons, occasionally drawing an explicit comparison between himself and Goldwater, but more often making implicit comparisons that did not mention his opponent by name.

The president balanced depictions of strength and restraint with ease largely because of how his crisis talk intertwined two related, but higher order concepts: peace and the defense of freedom. This terminological merger was a natural one for Johnson; to him and many others who came of age in the 1930s and 1940s, defense and peace *were* intertwined. In *The Vantage Point,* Johnson observed that "like most men and women of my generation, I felt strongly that World War II might have been avoided if the United States in the 1930s had not given such an uncertain signal of its likely response to aggression in Europe and Asia."[29] Had the United States and other nations defended freedom immediately in the face of early fascist aggression, Johnson believed peace, rather than world war, would have been the outcome.

He also claimed that Americans had taken these lessons to heart. In a 1964 New Hampshire campaign speech, the president noted, "that policy—strength and firmness matched to restraint and patience—has been the same basic foreign policy of both political parties for the past 20 years. Our hand has always been out, but our guard has always been up."[30] This same doctrine had application to the Gulf of Tonkin. Upon signing the Southeast Asia Resolution, Johnson said that when the enemy attacked U.S. ships, the "cause of peace clearly required that we respond with a prompt and unmistakable reply." Similarly, he told his audience at Syracuse University that the world must always remember "that aggression unchallenged is aggression unleashed." Because of this, Johnson insisted that the United States must respond to North Vietnamese attacks.[31] The president also connected the defense of freedom to resoluteness, strength, and forcefulness, even as he aligned peace with restraint, self-control, and responsibility. Because defense and peace were linked, Johnson was able to intertwine these various characteristics, as well. The two sets of terms were not necessarily opposed, and the president portrayed himself as the champion of both.

A closer examination of Johnson's crisis discourse, however, reveals that his terminological mergers were not as complete as they at first appeared. In the president's attempt to present his actions as neither too strong nor too restrained, he redefined the concepts of defense and peace and gave them more moderate meanings. This strategy aided Johnson in the short term, but raised the possibility that defense and peace and their related concepts of strength and restraint might be opposed, rather than compatible. In remarks before the American Bar Association, for instance, the president said U.S. retaliation in the Gulf of Tonkin showed that our nation would continue to combine restraint and firmness in its Vietnamese policy. Johnson then commented:

> Some say we should withdraw from South Viet-Nam, that we have lost almost 200 lives there in the last 4 years, and we should come home. But the United States cannot and must not and will not turn aside and allow the freedom of a brave people to be handed over to Communist tyranny. This alternative is strategically unwise, we think, and it is morally unthinkable.
>
> Some others are eager to enlarge the conflict. They call upon us to supply the American boys to do the job that Asian boys should do. They ask us to take reckless action which might risk the lives of millions and engulf much of Asia and certainly threaten the peace of the entire world. Moreover, such action would offer no solution at all to the real problem of Viet-Nam.[32]

Johnson altered the meaning of peace and defense so that both constituted moderate military involvement. In this way, the president demonstrated that his moderate retaliatory action in the Gulf of Tonkin was still consistent with the principles of peace through strength. Moreover, his discourse refuted Goldwater's claims that Johnson was soft on Communism, at the same time that it portrayed Goldwater—one of the "others" eager to enlarge the conflict—as trigger happy. Unfortunately for Johnson, though, his redefinition also included what Chaim Perelman and L. Olbrechts-Tyteca would call an indirect dissociation: his rhetoric inadvertently split a unitary concept[33]—in this case, peace and the defense of freedom, and the related conceptual pair of restraint and strength. Johnson's redefinition of these terms as moderate military action may have maintained their consistency, but his rhetoric also dissociated these concepts in a way that served to verbalize very different possibilities: that real peace was withdrawal or the absence of war (restraint), not military intervention, and that the real defense of freedom demanded a complete military commitment (strength), not a half-hearted effort. Through his words, Johnson suggested that peace and defense, as well as restraint and strength, were not as intertwined as most Americans had once thought.

Documents from the Johnson White House during this time period indicate that the president's unintended dissociation may have had its roots in behind-the-scenes policy-making. These documents make it hard not to be cynical about the administration's motives, for whereas Johnson publicly attended first to the crisis in the Gulf of Tonkin and passage of the Southeast Asia Resolution, and then to adoring campaign crowds, he and his advisers on Vietnam privately discussed an escalation in U.S. involvement in Southeast Asia.

As early as June 3, the Assistant Secretary of State for Public Affairs, James L. Greenfield, circulated a memo in which he warned that the administration needed to address Americans' concerns about Vietnam "as soon as the crisis moves visibly to the front burner—if not before."[34] Four months later, National Security Adviser McGeorge Bundy wrote Johnson that there was "a better than even chance that we will be undertaking some air and land action in the Laotian corridor and even in North Vietnam within the next two months."[35] William Bundy, the Assistant Secretary of State for Far Eastern Affairs and McGeorge's brother, had drafted a recommendation in September that the president strengthen U.S. advisory efforts in Vietnam, introduce major new U.S. units for pacification work in "specified areas," and increase the combat use of American soldiers already in Vietnam.[36]

William Bundy had also made the case within the administration for a congressional resolution two months prior to the Gulf of Tonkin. His recommendation treated the military defense of freedom in Vietnam as different from peace when he suggested that a draft resolution place "maximum stress on our peaceful objectives" in order to win the support of as many congressional doves as possible. At the same time, Bundy noted that Johnson might find it hard to get approval for such a resolution because he could point to no drastic change in the Vietnam situation. Bundy added, "The opposing argument is that we might well not have such *drastic* change even later in the summer and yet conclude . . . that we had to act."[37] The attacks in the Gulf of Tonkin, which many now argue either never took place or were provoked by U.S.–South Vietnamese intelligence operations,[38] provided, as Cherwitz points out, a dramatic crisis that served to legitimize the president's request for a resolution. Johnson's emphasis on peaceful intentions helped persuade congressional members (with the exception of Morse and Gruening) who previously had misgivings about his Vietnam policy.

At the same time that the administration began to discuss plans for escalation in Vietnam, campaign advance man Frank Gibney and presidential aide Bill Moyers further encouraged the inadvertent dissociation of peace and the defense of freedom when they suggested that Johnson and his speechwriters emphasize the president's great commitment to peace, a strategic campaign move in view of Goldwater's image of recklessness.[39] McGeorge Bundy, meanwhile, warned the president in October that he might want to "give a hint of firmness" in his public statements on Vietnam, as well, because "we do not want the record to suggest even remotely that we campaigned on peace in order to start a war in November."[40]

In actuality, the U.S. ground troops would begin to arrive in March. Bundy himself had helped craft earlier Johnson messages about the crisis that relied on the firmness-and-restraint theme, perhaps as part of his personal effort to build the "appropriate" public record.[41] Although Gibney and Moyers probably had little or no knowledge of the escalation plans, one is struck with how the overall administration began to treat the military defense of freedom in Vietnam and peace there as two distinct and perhaps contrary concepts.

An uncharitable reading of White House records would lead one to believe that the administration had already decided to increase U.S. involvement in Vietnam, as Cherwitz argues, and therefore intentionally exploited the Gulf of Tonkin in order to gain passage of the Southeast Asia Resolution and to secure Johnson an overwhelming victory as a leader of strength and restraint. A more charitable reader might argue that all administrations make contingency plans, many of which are never enacted, or that arguments for escalation had been made in the summer and fall of 1964, but the president had not made up his mind, and the Gulf of Tonkin simply served as a warning message to North Vietnam. Yet a third interpretation might encompass the other two: that Johnson felt he had to escalate in Vietnam in order to defend freedom and to keep peace; that, nevertheless, he had great ambivalence about doing so and postponed a final decision; and finally, that the president knew how to make political hay when he saw the opportunity.

In 1970, Johnson told Doris Kearns that "everything I knew about history told me that if I got out of Vietnam and let Ho Chi Minh run through the streets of Saigon, then I'd be doing exactly what Chamberlain did in World War II. I'd be giving a big fat reward to aggression." He added that the demonstration of U.S. weakness would have led to Soviet and Chinese aggression.[42]

Although Johnson felt he had to escalate U.S. involvement in Vietnam, he clearly had misgivings about it, because of the impact the war would have on his poverty programs and because of the pressures that might develop to use the atomic bomb, something he refused to do.[43] The president told Kearns that he knew "If I left the woman I really loved—the Great Society—in order to get involved with that bitch of a war on the other side of the world, then I would lose everything at home. All my programs."[44] The way in which Johnson inadvertently dissociated defense and peace so that they were opposed may have had its origins in the dilemma he faced. To keep the peace and prevent further aggression, the president's experience and that of his advisers told him that he had to do whatever was necessary to defend freedom in Southeast Asia. Two of Johnson's speech drafts on the Gulf of Tonkin, in fact, included references to how the United States would not repeat the "timidity of the Thirties . . . the folly of the Forties" and how we had "learned the lessons of Munich."[45] These lines, however, were deleted in the final versions.

Despite the dictum of peace through strength, Johnson also seemed to realize that military intervention in Vietnam would mean bloodshed and the diversion of valuable resources and that the ultimate defense of freedom—the bomb— would mean the end of peace. The president therefore attempted to remain loyal to his world view, in which defense and peace were linked, but he frequently acted and talked in a way that indicated their possible opposition. Johnson's recognition of the short-term political rewards of the Gulf of Tonkin in his campaign against Barry Goldwater similarly encouraged this indirect dissociation. By contrasting his crisis management with the policy extremes of withdrawal and all-out war, Johnson defused charges that he was weak and pummeled Goldwater as an irresponsible warmonger. What Johnson did not realize was that the stratagem that worked in the immediacy of the campaign had set up the very argumentative weapons that eventually would destroy him.

LBJ'S BALANCING ACT:
STRENGTH, RESTRAINT, AND INDIRECT DISSOCIATION IN JOHNSON'S RHETORIC ABOUT THE GULF OF TONKIN

As noted in chapter 1, previous research found that contemporary crisis rhetoric tended to blend depictions of U.S. strength with portrayals of U.S. restraint. Brockriede and Scott, Cherwitz and Zagacki, Heisey, and Klope claim that presidents described the United States as a passive nation that was uninterested in military conflict, but would actively retaliate if forced to do so.[46] In the case studies of crisis promotion examined in this book, I also found that depictions of power and self-control were frequently part of presidential discourse.

Discussion of the nation's strength served as a signal that the United States had the capability and determination to fight if pushed too far. At the same time, talk of the country's restraint placed blame for the crisis elsewhere, for a peaceful, self-controlled actor like the United States certainly could not have started the conflict. This also justified the righteous fury with which our nation pursued military retaliation once it decided to act. Commanders-in-chief have not treated strength and restraint as exactly the same in their crisis discourse, but they have discussed these traits as compatible, as one can exemplify both in a complementary fashion. Nonetheless, a tension also has existed between the poles of strength and restraint in contemporary crisis rhetoric. The source of this tension is the nuclear age.

With the advent of the atomic bomb, Turner points out, presidents could no longer wage all-out war without facing the possibility of nuclear destruction.[47] World War II had taught Americans that peace and the defense of freedom went hand in hand, but the existence of nuclear weapons created complications. If a president involved the United States in an international conflict, he had to reassure citizens—as well as his international audience—that he would not rashly start a nuclear war. Simultaneously, he needed to convince his listeners that he was acting forcefully enough or would act forcefully enough to defend freedom and keep the peace.

During the Cuban missile crisis, for instance, Kennedy declared, "We will not prematurely or unnecessarily risk the costs of worldwide nuclear war in which even the fruits of victory would be ashes in our mouth—but neither will we shrink from that risk at any time it must be faced."[48] Kennedy's statement reflected the need for reassurance at the same time that it sent a message about our—and his—forcefulness and determination. He treated restraint and strength as compatible qualities, but his statement still exemplified the tension between them.

Vietnam in 1964 posed the same problems of strength and restraint for Lyndon Johnson. His experience told him that the United States must defend freedom there or Communist aggression would continue to expand; but he also recognized that an all-out military effort might lead to the use of the atomic bomb, something he wished to avoid, and bring an end to world peace. According to Turner, Harry Truman had dealt with this dilemma during the Korean War, but Lyndon Johnson faced even greater problems because of the pervasiveness of television. At the time that Johnson first began to grapple with U.S. policy in Southeast Asia, the television networks had just started to expand the length of their news programs, the size of their news budgets, and, accordingly, their need for news. In 1950, Turner points out "only 2 percent of American homes owned a set . . . and newscasts were primitive, underfinanced, fifteen-minute operations."[49]

Johnson, who closely monitored network coverage,[50] may have realized that through the medium of television American citizens would be able to see the brutality and gore of a war in Vietnam. This, in turn, might prompt appeals for two very different policies, a withdrawal of U.S. troops or the use of nuclear weapons, in an attempt to resolve the conflagration quickly. The president also recognized that a withdrawal would herald the end of freedom in South Vietnam, nuclear weapons would threaten world peace, and escalation even of a less extreme nature would harm his domestic programs. The problem for Johnson was how to rectify the conflict between the lessons of World War II and the realities of war in an age of nuclear weapons and television.

In many ways, the Gulf of Tonkin seemed like an ideal solution. The president warned North Vietnam of the United States' and his determination, assured Americans that he would be loyal to the goals of peace and defense of freedom, and calmed any fears that he might unnecessarily escalate U.S. military involvement in Vietnam. The Gulf of Tonkin also allowed Johnson to attend to political matters, for he was able to put Goldwater's charges of weakness to rest and simultaneously portray his opponent as reckless.

Despite the advantages that Johnson's crisis discourse gained him, his attempts to deal with these myriad issues led him to increase the tension between strength and restraint, rather than lessen it. Administration encouragement to emphasize one or the other of these qualities further tightened the strained relationship between the concepts. In the situation of his crisis talk, Johnson depicted the Gulf of Tonkin as if it were just like other situations where the United States had faced aggression and that had necessitated the goals of peace and defense of freedom. The style and identificational appeals of his discourse, though, were in conflict with the situation. On the surface, these two elements of Johnson's rhetoric appeared to treat strength and restraint as compatible concepts. The style of his talk focused repetitively on how the key actors embodied both strength and restraint. However, Johnson's style also treated the concepts as separate entities by contrasting one with the other and by using conjunctions and qualifiers that suggested their distinctiveness.

In a similar fashion, the president's identificational appeals frequently expounded upon exactly what constituted action that was too strong and action that was too restrained. Johnson then placed the response to the Gulf of Tonkin crisis squarely between these poles. Through such explanation, Johnson clearly defined his and U.S. actions in the Gulf of Tonkin as moderate and, because the actions were successful, he showed listeners how moderation was consistent with the tenets of peace and defense of freedom. Unfortunately, the president's explanations also indirectly dissociated strength and restraint by opposing them and provided standards of moderation by which Americans could evaluate and condemn his Vietnam policy in the future. Johnson's rhetoric increased the tension between strength and restraint—and the related concepts of defense and peace—until the relationship between them snapped, and Johnson, the rhetorical tightrope walker, came crashing to the ground.

Situation

Pentadic analysis of Johnson's crisis discourse provides the following representative anecdote:

> Because hostile North Vietnamese vessels attacked U.S. ships on the high seas in the Gulf of Tonkin (scene), "we" and "I" (coactors) took retaliatory action and legislative action (acts), through an air attack and request to Congress (means), to maintain and to demonstrate our commitment to peace and the defense of freedom (purpose).

Johnson described a scene of grave danger where U.S. ships had been victims of "open aggression on the high seas." He told a nationwide television audience on August 4, for example that "the initial attack on the destroyer *Maddox*, on August 2, was repeated today by a number of hostile vessels attacking two U.S. destroyers with torpedoes."[51] Because of this scene, Johnson claimed that the United States must strive to uphold two purposes: "to defend freedom and preserve peace in southeast Asia."[52] The actions needed to sustain these goals were (1) retaliatory action, carried out through air strikes, and (2) legislative action, carried out through congressional approval.

In the president's rhetoric, the actor who performed the needed actions was "we" and, less often, "I," although Johnson also referred to "America," "the United States," and "the Government." At first glance, Johnson's actors appear to parallel the actors of Kennedy's talk, but closer examination reveals that Johnson's "we" was much more ambiguous. Although "we" most often seemed to allude to the nation, Johnson frequently used the term in such a way that it could represent any of a number of groups. Johnson also employed "we" and "I" interchangeably, which meant he had a more important personal role in his rhetoric than Kennedy had in his Cuban missile discourse. Johnson's talk, consequently, reflected more directly upon his portrayal of himself.

In Kennedy's discourse about the Cuban missile crisis, the ratios of terms for scene-purpose and terms for purpose-act dominated the president's talk. These same terminological ratios prevailed in Johnson's crisis rhetoric about the Gulf of Tonkin. Of importance in pentadic analysis, however, are not only the key relationships among pentadic principles, but also the emphasis that the rhetor places upon the components of each of those relationships.

Kennedy's crisis discourse, for example, deflected attention from the United States'—and his own—goals and actions by emphasizing terms for a terrifying crisis scene. Johnson, like his predecessor, also portrayed a scene that dictated American purposes and acts. But unlike Kennedy, Johnson paid relatively little attention to the scene, focusing instead on the aims and acts of "we" and "I."

The scene simply provided an opportunity for the nation and the president who led it to uphold and demonstrate their characteristic goals and behavior in response to a foreign policy crisis.

According to Johnson, the crisis scene or backdrop for U.S. goals and acts consisted of an incident of renewed enemy aggression against U.S. forces in a particular global locale. The president told listeners at Syracuse University the day after U.S. retaliation, "On August 2 the United States destroyer *Maddox* was attacked on the high seas in the Gulf of Tonkin by hostile vessels of the Government of North Viet-Nam. On August 4 that attack was repeated in those same waters against two United States destroyers." Johnson painted a picture in which innocent U.S. ships in the neutrality of "the high seas" had been the victims not simply of one episode, but of recurrent episodes of enemy aggression.

In addition, Johnson claimed the attacks were "deliberate" and "un-provoked."[53] In a special message to Congress that same day, he repeated this theme when he said that "the North Vietnamese regime" had "conducted further deliberate attacks against U.S. naval vessels operating in international wa-ters."[54] Johnson often did not bother to mention the enemy by name, simply discussing the crisis scene in terms of the assault that had taken place. He explained to reporters on August 8, for example, that the crisis was "created by unprovoked aggression against our naval forces on the high seas."[55]

In the president's rhetoric, the immediate scene of crisis was related to two larger scenes. Johnson's televised speech of August 4 claimed "aggression by terror against the peaceful villagers of South Viet-Nam has now been joined by open aggression on the high seas against the United States of America."[56] Furthermore, he made connections between the contemporary scene of aggres-sion in Vietnam and an older, more historic scene.

Although Johnson did not specifically mention World War II, he conjured up images of that earlier time when he said about the Gulf of Tonkin: "Aggression—deliberate, willful, and systematic aggression—has unmasked its face to the entire world. The world remembers—the world must never forget—that aggression unchallenged is aggression unleashed."[57] In a nation-wide televised address in October and in several other public appearances, Johnson talked about the Gulf of Tonkin and provided a litany of other places and times where aggression had challenged the United States, such as Greece, Turkey, and Korea under the Truman administration; the Formosa straits during the Eisenhower years; and Cuba under Kennedy's watch. Before campaign crowds in El Paso on September 25, Johnson likewise compared the Gulf of Tonkin to other places "where freedom has been under attack."[58] Like Ken-nedy, Johnson had the Cold War penchant for jumping from particular scenes to broader contexts. He did not talk about the Gulf of Tonkin as a particular circumstance. Instead, he treated it as symptomatic of the larger scene of aggression that the United States historically had faced and continued to face worldwide.

Because of the crisis scene he described, Johnson insisted that two particular goals must be fulfilled: peace and the defense of freedom. These ends were so important, in fact, that the president mentioned the objective of peace at least three dozen times in his rhetoric about the Gulf of Tonkin and referred to the defense of freedom, along with statements of how the United States would not allow aggression to go unchallenged, nearly as often. Whereas Kennedy had emphasized terms for scene, Johnson focused on terms for purpose.

In Johnson's discourse, the scene served as the impetus for particular purposes by reminding the United States and others of what our nation's goals were. Johnson made the connection between the multiple scenes he had described and the key actors' purposes quite clear. For instance, in an August 11 speech to members of the National Association of Counties, Johnson referred to how "we were faced with the challenge of a direct, deliberate, and unprovoked act of aggression" in the Gulf of Tonkin. Shortly afterward, he noted, that "the world understands that the United States' only purpose is peace. . . . Our resources are committed, our sacrifices are made, our vigil is maintained so that there shall be no win for aggression in our times."[59] In this statement, Johnson indicated that the scene of crisis in the Gulf of Tonkin reminded the world of the United States' dual purposes. Simultaneously, the phrase "no win for aggression in our times" conjured up Neville Chamberlain's infamous words about "peace in our time" after he had signed the Munich accords with Hitler before World War II.

The president's discourse implied that the Gulf of Tonkin was similar to other scenes of deliberate enemy aggression, but the key actor of "we" in his discourse—and "I" who was part of that "we"—recognized that peace could only come if aggression were not tolerated. Hence, peace and the defense of freedom were compatible in the situation of Johnson's crisis talk.

Speaking before the nation on August 4, the president discussed a scene where the "initial attack on the destroyer *Maddox*" had been "repeated today by a number of hostile vessels attacking two U.S. destroyers with torpedoes." He related this crisis scene to our larger purposes in Vietnam when he asserted, "The determination of all Americans to carry out our full commitment to the people and to the government of South Viet-Nam will be redoubled by this outrage."[60]

The second crucial ratio of Johnson's discourse consisted of terms for purpose-act. According to Johnson, the scene of crisis in the Gulf of Tonkin dictated that the United States maintain and demonstrate its commitment to peace and the defense of freedom; in turn, the purpose-act ordering of terms in his rhetoric argued that these goals must guide our actions. The president told citizens on August 4, for instance, "I shall immediately request the Congress to pass a resolution making it clear that our Government is united in its determination to take all necessary measures in support of freedom and in defense of peace in southeast Asia."[61] To show that we were committed to our goals, a congressional resolution was needed.

Johnson's discourse also exemplified a purpose-act ratio when he told journalists that our "actions this week" had allowed the United States to "make clear not only our determination to give a clear and positive reply to aggression at sea, but our general determination to resist and repel aggression in the area as a whole."[62] On other occasions, the president referred to a comparable goal that shepherded U.S. policy, as he did when he related the following account to guests at a Texas barbecue on August 29: "It was an act [military retaliation] that I realized was a very serious act. But I felt that it was in the best interest of this Nation and it was the only course I could follow if I really wanted peace, to let them know that we meant what we said and said what we meant, and we were prepared to back it up. And we did that."[63]

In this case, Johnson talked about the crisis from his perspective as president and how he wanted peace, which had led him to order military retaliation against enemy aggression in the Gulf of Tonkin. Johnson indicated that "we" and "I" held congruent purposes when he stated that peace was in "the best interest" of the United States and when he said that "we" had to "let them know that we meant what we said and said what we meant." In this statement, the president also implied that peace and the defense of freedom were compatible goals, for the decision not to tolerate aggression was described as a necessary policy "if I really wanted peace."

Johnson was not content merely to state the purposes that guided the actions of "we" and "I" in the immediate context of the Gulf of Tonkin. Rather, on a number of occasions he explained the purposes that guided our Vietnam policy as a whole. In a message before Congress, the president described the purposes and acts that had transpired as a result of the crisis scene in the Gulf of Tonkin. He then went on to describe the "propositions" of our policy in Vietnam. According to Johnson, "*Our purpose is peace.* We have no military, political or territorial ambitions in the area. . . . Our military and economic assistance to South Vietnam and Laos in particular has the purpose of helping these countries to repel aggression and strengthen their independence."[64] Just as Johnson's terms for scene suggested that the immediate scene of crisis in the Gulf of Tonkin was representative of scenes of aggression elsewhere, his terms for purpose-act indicated that the key actors' goals in the Gulf of Tonkin and in Vietnam were the same.

The situation of Johnson's Gulf of Tonkin discourse typically portrayed a scene of crisis that indicated that the purposes of peace and the defense of freedom must be fulfilled; these purposes then piloted U.S. and presidential actions. As an indication of how these two terminological ratios worked in tandem, one can look to the president's remarks at Syracuse University.

Johnson discussed the "aggression" that had taken place "on the high seas" against U.S. forces and declared that as a result of that scene, there must be "no doubt about the purpose" of the United States and other "nations that are devoted to peace." According to the president, "Peace requires that we and all our friends stand firm against the present aggressions of the government of North Viet-Nam."[65] The situation of Johnson's crisis discourse emphasized terms for purpose as central to understanding U.S. policy and treated the goals of peace and the defense of freedom as interchangeable.

The president's style and identificational appeals, however, worked against the consistency of his terms for situation. In his attempts to distinguish his leadership from that of Barry Goldwater and to encourage citizens to identify with him and his policies, Johnson inadvertently dissociated peace and the defense of freedom—along with the concepts of restraint and strength—such that they were opposed, rather than compatible.

Style

Throughout his presidency, Johnson suffered from comparisons with John Kennedy. Johnson was colloquial—often coarse—and hailed from rural Texas; Kennedy had been a sophisticated, witty, urbane northeasterner, a persona particularly appealing to journalists, who were highly literate and most of whom, as Turner points out, were "oriented toward the eastern-based style of the institutions" where they worked.[66] Journalists' complaints about Johnson's lack of style notwithstanding, *Washington Post* editor and Kennedy confidant Ben Bradlee once offered a different perspective. "If you read the dictionary about style," he said, "the fact is that Johnson had more style than Kennedy. If style is individuality—that individuality by which one distinguishes a person— he was just a goddamn bank vault of style."[67]

The examination of Johnson's crisis discourse reveals that it, too, in many ways had more style than Kennedy's talk about the Cuban missile crisis. To a much greater degree than Kennedy, Johnson described the central actors of his rhetoric, how they behaved, and the key terminological relationships in which terms for actor were involved. Furthermore, the style of Johnson's discourse reflected more personally upon the "I" of his talk than the style of Kennedy's discourse did.

The most consistent term for actor in Johnson's rhetoric was "we" used interchangeably with "America" or "the United States," but equally as often the referent for "we" was ambiguous. Also of significance was a secondary actor of "I." The president's talk about the crisis remained highly personal because both "we" and "I" subsumed Johnson and made him an integral part of his discourse.

This also meant that language that described "we" necessarily depicted the president, as well.

Of these two key actors, Johnson lavished the most attention on "we." He portrayed "we" as an actor who aspired only to defend freedom and to achieve peace. On the day he signed the Southeast Asia Resolution, Johnson stated:

> To any in southeast Asia who ask our help in defending their freedom, we shall give it.
>
> In that region there is nothing we covet, nothing we seek—no territory, no military position, no political ambition.
>
> Our one desire—our one determination—is that the people of southeast Asia be left in peace to work out their own destinies in their own way.[68]

The president's comments here described an ambiguous and selfless "we" for whom peace could only exist if freedom, or the ability to choose one's destiny, also were preserved. In other public remarks, Johnson was more specific about who the key actor was. He told one audience that "peace is the only purpose of the course that America pursues" and said to another that "for 20 years our country has been the guardian at the gate of freedom."[69] As with his terms for situation, Johnson's terms for style treated peace and the defense of freedom as compatible aims—at least on the surface; his style also implied that these ends were extremely important for understanding what the key actor was like.

Johnson seemed to underscore the compatibility of defense and peace when he described the ambiguous "we" and the nation through words that clustered around strength and words that clustered around restraint. Strength and restraint, like the defense of freedom and peace, were not necessarily opposed, and Johnson's crisis rhetoric revealed a key actor who exemplified both qualities.

The first cluster of descriptive terms portrayed "we" and the United States as determined and strong. In his special message before Congress, for example, Johnson reminded his audience that *"America keeps her word"* and that "we must and shall honor our commitments." Likewise, he spoke of our "national determination" to preserve peace and defend freedom in Vietnam.[70] Related to this determination was the characteristic of strength.

In an August 11 speech, Johnson discussed the firmness of the United States' response to the Gulf of Tonkin. He then remarked on the strength of the nation and added, "We have . . . worked to strengthen our preparedness, for only the strong can be brave in the pursuit of peace."[71] Johnson's statement ascribed strength to "we" and underscored the positive relationship among strength, defense, and peace in his talk. In an October speech at Johns Hopkins University, Johnson explained that U.S. strength came, in part, from our possession of nuclear weapons. He said, "We are possessed of great power in America—power to destroy all human life or to make human life sublime."[72] Because he chose to make periodic references to America's nuclear power, the president risked the chance that he might unintentionally depict "we" as belligerent and aggressive. Perhaps because of this, Johnson balanced these descriptive terms of strength with terms that clustered around restraint.

According to the president, the primary actor of his talk exhibited not only strength, but also traits related to restraint: composure, wisdom, and morality. Johnson told reporters on August 8 that we had "steadiness and stability and straightforwardness."[73] The attribution of these characteristics to "we" did not contradict Johnson's assertions about the actor's strength and determination. His ascription of steadiness, stability, and straightforwardness served to sketch a moderate and more complex actor who would not use power unthinkingly or dishonestly.

In El Paso on September 25, the president underscored this notion; he claimed that the United States had displayed "wisdom" in its use of strength to defend freedom in the Gulf of Tonkin and elsewhere. According to Johnson, we had stood firm against aggression, but we had not "pressed our adversaries to the point where nuclear assault was their only alternative."[74] Johnson's comments again served to disclose a moderate actor who blended the attributes of determination and power with those of stability and wisdom. Before the American Bar Association, the president added another dimension to "we" when he reflected upon how our foreign policy in the Gulf of Tonkin and the world at large derived "from moral purpose." As Johnson explained, we had attempted to protect peace and defend freedom "for a reason that is often difficult for others to understand. We have done it because it is right that we should."[75] This statement modified his portrayal of U.S. strength by inferring that the nation exerted its power only when it was morally right to do so.

Finally, Johnson attributed restraint itself to the United States or an ambiguous "we" on several occasions and showed how this trait was compatible with and complementary to the characteristic of strength. He told a nationwide audience, for example, that the U.S. response in the Gulf of Tonkin had been "limited and fitting," which served to describe U.S. retaliation as restrained, rather than extreme, and yet severe enough to match the crime that had been committed against American forces. In the conclusion of his address, Johnson blended the attributes of strength and restraint with his observation that "firmness in the right is indispensable today for peace; that firmness will always be measured."[76] Johnson's descriptive terms for the nation and ambiguous "we," and the frequency with which he used these terms, portrayed a moderate actor who would put an end to enemy aggression in a reasonable way that did not involve excessive force.

Because "we" and the United States necessarily subsumed Johnson himself, the president's attributions of strength and self-control to the primary actor of his discourse reflected on the qualities of the secondary coactor, or "I," as well. Johnson also took the opportunity at various times to discuss "I" as a responsible actor in two senses: first, because of his constitutional duties, and second, because of the moral obligations he had and the rational manner in which he fulfilled those obligations.

On August 10, for example, Johnson signed the Southeast Asia Resolution into law. He asserted that as commander-in-chief he had the constitutional responsibility for ordering the retaliation in the Gulf of Tonkin and as president he had the duty to bring his policy before Congress in the form of the Southeast Asia Resolution for the legislature to confirm or deny.[77] Through these titles, the president reminded the audience of his legal responsibilities and indicated that he had fulfilled them satisfactorily, especially since the attack had been a success and Congress obviously had endorsed his policies.

On other occasions, however, Johnson talked about responsibility in a slightly different way, as a moral obligation that he had fulfilled by behaving in a rational manner. In his first public speech about the crisis, Johnson referred to the "solemn responsibility" he had felt when ordering "even limited military action," but claimed the counterattack had been necessary in order to preserve peace.[78] The president depicted himself as a sober actor who would send troops to battle when needed, but who also recognized the gravity of even a restrained military response.

Given his emphasis on the vast nuclear powers the United States wielded and his own legal authority over American military might, Johnson's attention to how he carried out his obligations portrayed him not just as a president who held constitutional responsibility, but as a president who was responsible—able to think and act rationally. In this way, the president's style contrasted how "I" behaved with public perceptions of how rival Barry Goldwater might act.

Johnson made this comparison extremely clear in an August 15 news conference, where he refuted Goldwater's assertion that he had ordered commanders in the Gulf of Tonkin to use "any weapons." According to Johnson, the charge was false and Secretary of State Rusk and Secretary of Defense McNamara had been proper in calling "the Republican candidate's interpretation 'unjustified and irresponsible.'" The president then connected, albeit subtly, the immediate issue to the larger question of how Goldwater would handle questions of war and peace: "The control of nuclear weapons is one of the gravest of all the responsibilities of the Commander in Chief, the President of the United States. Loose charges on nuclear weapons without any shadow of justification by any candidate for office, let alone the Presidency, are a disservice to our national security, a disservice to peace, and, as for that matter, a great disservice to the entire free world." Johnson described Goldwater, a candidate who made "loose charges," as a loose cannon who posed a threat to peace and the defense of freedom. In contrast, he referred to his administration as "responsible" and assured "the people of my own country and the people of the world . . . that we speak and act with responsibility."[79]

This episode notwithstanding, Johnson typically did not draw overt comparisons between himself and Goldwater. He emphasized instead the way in which he handled the powers of his office and let his listeners draw their own conclusions. On a campaign swing through California, for instance, Johnson told one audience that in the Gulf of Tonkin and similar circumstances, "I have had this awesome responsibility" but "so far as I am concerned, I am one President that had rather reason and talk than fight. Fight I will, if fight I must, or if fight I need to, but I just won't do it as a Sunday afternoon exercise just to entertain somebody."[80]

A few days later, in San Diego, Johnson described how his heart went up into his throat when he had to send soldiers into action. He explained, "you know they are some mother's son, and except for the grace of God it might be my mother's son. I try to keep that in mind."[81] Through these comments, Johnson gave the impression of a leader who recognized the human cost of military engagement and who did not take decisions about such matters lightly. He was not only rational, but also sensitive.

Throughout the president's discourse, both sets of terms for actor were involved in one dominant stylistic ratio: act-actor. Johnson's rhetoric argued that words for act indicated what kind of actors the ambiguous "we," or America, and "I" were. On August 7, for example, Johnson claimed that the passage of the Southeast Asia Resolution and the huge vote margin by which Congress enacted it "prove our determination to defend our own forces, to prevent aggression, and to work firmly and steadily for peace and security in the area."[82] A particular act demonstrated the qualities of the actor (determination), how the actor acted (firmly and steadily), and the goals that the actor held dear (the defense of American forces, the prevention of aggression, the attainment of peace and security).

Like John Kennedy, Johnson also indicated on several occasions that U.S. actions were of great symbolic significance because of the message that they sent to other countries about our nation's character. The president told reporters that because of U.S. military retaliation in the Gulf of Tonkin and the passage of the Southeast Asia Resolution, "Today, both adversaries and allies have the basis for new respect and understanding of America's resoluteness."[83] At the East Room ceremony where he signed the Southeast Asia Resolution into law, Johnson similarly remarked, "Thus, today, our course is clearly known in every land. There can be no mistake—no miscalculation—of where America stands or what this generation of Americans stands for."[84]

Unlike Kennedy, Johnson frequently spelled out the relationship between the actors and the actors' actions, rather than allowing listeners to infer the connection themselves. Perhaps the best example of this came in the president's address before members of the American Bar Association where he said that the response to the Gulf of Tonkin proved that

> we will continue to meet aggression with firmness and unprovoked attack with measured reply.
>
> That is the meaning of the prompt reaction of our destroyers to unprovoked attack. That is the meaning of the positive reply of our aircraft to a repetition of that attack. That is the meaning of the resolution passed by your Congress with 502 votes in favor and only 2 opposed. That is the meaning of the national unity that we have shown to all the world last week.[85]

Through the use of simple sentence structure and repetition, Johnson seemed to harken back to his days as a schoolteacher in order to make the significance of our actions clear. The same techniques exemplified the act-actor terminological relationship in other instances of Johnson's crisis discourse, as well. In the style of the president's talk, the primary actor's actions were important for what they revealed to other countries about our national character. Johnson's overt, repetitive efforts to explicate the act-actor terminological ratio, however, indicated that he was also concerned with the conclusions that Americans drew. Moreover, the fact that he referred to the chief actor not only as the United States, but also as "we," suggested that the character of Johnson and his administration also had been demonstrated through the response to the Gulf of Tonkin incident, particularly since he often used "we" and "I" interchangeably.

Throughout his Gulf of Tonkin discourse, Johnson's typical attitude, or style, projected the image of actors who were committed to peace and the defense of freedom, who exemplified the characteristics of self-control and strength, and whose actions revealed the kind of actors they were. The president's style thus overtly treated peace and the defense of freedom as compatible and depicted restraint and strength as complementary attributes. He portrayed the United States—and himself—as an actor who engaged in armed conflict only when necessary, but who would fight resolutely if circumstances demanded it. Through inadvertent dissociation, however, Johnson also suggested that peace and the defense of freedom, as well as restraint and strength, were not completely compatible after all.

Perelman and Olbrechts-Tyteca explain that rhetors may indirectly dissociate or split the meaning of a concept through statements that oppose "a word and what is ordinarily regarded as a synonym for it."[86] Examples of this include, "I would like my job if it were not for the work"; "He is highly virtuous for a religious man"; "She always invites my opinion, but she always dislikes my advice." Each of these statements uses words usually considered synonymous and indicates that they really do not mean the same thing. In his stylistic talk about the key actors of his discourse, Johnson encouraged indirect dissociation through the way he used conjunctions and qualifiers to discuss defense and peace—and the related concepts of strength and restraint—as if they were separate entities.

In his address before members of the American Bar Association, for example, Johnson indirectly dissociated the defense of freedom and peace when he said that Americans valued "freedom" and believed that "the strong should help the weak defend their freedom." He then added, "There is *another* value which guides America's course . . . the deep American belief in the peaceful process of orderly settlement."[87] Johnson did not treat peace and the defense of freedom as synonymous here but as two different values that America held.

Likewise, he detailed for New Hampshire newspaper editors the responses of previous presidents to aggression and then recounted his own administration's retaliation in the Gulf of Tonkin. According to Johnson, "These consistent actions contain *two* great lessons: We must stand firm when the vital interests of freedom are under attack. *And* we must use our overwhelming power with calm restraint."[88] On August 10, the president gave a speech that reflected the same method of indirect dissociation: "It is everlastingly right that we should be resolute in reply to aggression and steadfast in support of our friends. *But* it is everlastingly necessary that our actions should be careful and should be measured. We are the most powerful of all nations—we must strive *also* to be the most responsible of nations."[89]

Johnson's use of "but" portrayed defense and peace not as concepts roughly equated with one another, but as distinct ideas that should be acted upon. His employment of "also" in reference to power and responsibility had the same effect.

The president further fostered the indirect dissociation of strength and restraint—and peace and defense—when he played these concepts against one another. In a campaign address at Johns Hopkins University, Johnson described the actions of an ambiguous "we," apparently his administration, who had made a "prompt and adequate response" to the Gulf of Tonkin crisis by destroying only the PT fleet that had attacked U.S. ships, rather than targeting civilian populations. He explained, "I use these illustrations to show you that it could have been easy in one wave to wipe out women and children and to drop bombs on North Viet-Nam and on China. . . . But government must be restrained in the pursuit as well as the use of power itself. And government must be moderate in the belief of its own infallibility."[90]

Johnson's statement portrayed his administration's actions as moderate, but the way he aligned the possibility of civilian bombing with "power" and contrasted these with the concept of restraint indicated that strength and restraint were not necessarily compatible and might actually be opposed. Similarly, in a public speech on August 12, Johnson discussed how the response to the Gulf of Tonkin demonstrated the larger policy of "we" in Vietnam: "No one should think for a moment that we will be worn down, nor will we be driven out, and we will not be provoked into rashness. But we will continue to meet aggression with firmness and unprovoked attack with measured reply."[91] The president portrayed the key actor as essentially peaceful when he described "we" as an agent who was cautious, rather than reckless, and who responded defensively to the aggression of others, rather than acting offensively.

The fact that we responded and remained determined served to convey the actor's fortitude. Johnson's description of how we acted with "firmness" and with "measured reply" also mixed the attributes of strength and self-control. To be firm means to be resolute and to reply implies a quick response. On the other hand, "firmness" connotes a limited use of power, just as a parent would be firm but not harsh with a child, and "measured" means calculated, deliberate, and restrained. In short, Johnson once again seemed to have taken pains to define the primary actor as the epitome of moderation.

Nonetheless, his initial assertion implied a dichotomy: we would not be worn down or driven out (the actor would be strong), and we would not act rashly (the actor would be restrained). Because withdrawal and escalation are contrary policies, Johnson suggested that strength and restraint might be contrary, too. The president's August 15 attack on Goldwater likewise insinuated that an all-out military effort (Goldwater's "loose charges on nuclear weapons") was at odds with the concept of wise moderation (Johnson's "responsible" administration).

The ways in which Johnson contrasted defense and peace, as well as strength and restraint, might have had little impact had he merely indulged in such explanations from time to time. After all, John Kennedy told the American people during the Cuban missile crisis that our goal was "not peace at the expense of freedom, but both peace *and* freedom."[92] The difference was that Kennedy made this comment once, whereas Johnson frequently played these concepts against one another in his efforts to describe the key actors as wisely moderate and to explain how their actions in the Gulf of Tonkin reflected their moderate characters. As a result of this repetition, the style of Johnson's discourse encouraged the dissociation of the concepts represented by each of these pairs.

Johnson reinforced this inadvertent dissociation through the identificational appeals of his crisis rhetoric. By constantly explaining what constituted moderate—and thus desirable—policies, the president encouraged citizens to identify with him. He also, however, dissociated peace and the defense of freedom by explaining how policies that were too restrained and policies that were too strong were both undesirable and contrary to one another.

Identificational Appeals

Because crises usually involve enemies, one might expect Johnson's talk to corroborate earlier crisis research, which found that presidents typically employed antithetical appeals, or appeals to unite against a shared enemy. On the contrary, Johnson relied on a strategy of identification through antithesis infrequently in his Gulf of Tonkin rhetoric. Pratt notes, for instance, that in the president's initial announcement of the crisis, he seemed "to go out of his way to avoid identifying the parties responsible for the direct attack on United States ships."[93] Close examination reveals that Johnson named the enemy as "North Viet-Nam" only once in this major address. The president employed antithetical appeals in his later crisis talk, sometimes against North Vietnam and occasionally against Barry Goldwater, but this kind of appeal certainly did not typify his discourse.

Overall, Johnson's rhetoric can best be characterized by its preponderance of implicit appeals that emphasized national oneness and that united citizens under the rubric of "we." In his message to Congress on August 5, for example, the president stated that "the United States is united in its determination to bring about the end of Communist subversion and aggression in the area."[94] Similarly, he told an audience at Syracuse University that in times of crisis like the Gulf of Tonkin, "We are one nation united and indivisible. And united and indivisible we shall remain."[95] Through these appeals to national solidarity, Johnson encouraged citizens to accept the goals that he articulated and to rally around their president in the midst of crisis, rather than to question him.

The second and more frequent type of implicit appeals in Johnson's discourse was his invocation of an ambiguous "we," which automatically incorporated any of a number of groups under its heading. He told reporters on August 8 that the Gulf of Tonkin situation remained serious, but that there had "been no further incidents in the last 24 hours. We, of course, remain fully alert against any attempt to renew or widen the attacks from any source."[96] "We" here plausibly could have referred to the United States, the Johnson administration, or the U.S. government as a whole.

The president also invoked the ambiguous "we" when he discussed the strength and restraint of this key actor. At a fall political rally in Des Moines, Johnson recalled, "Recently near Viet-Nam, in the Gulf of Tonkin, when they fired on our flag, we retaliated in kind." He then reassured Iowans that we had acted strongly by destroying "the nests" that housed the North Vietnamese boats involved in the attack against U.S. forces, yet we had been restrained since we "didn't drop a bunch of bombs on civilian women and children in an act of desperation or in a thoughtless moment."[97]

Likewise, Johnson told attendants at a Texas barbecue that our retaliation against North Vietnamese military installations had been strong. He explained that we had also exerted self-control since "we didn't bomb any cities" and "we didn't kill any women and children"; in fact, he said, "we carefully refrained from doing that."[98] Because the ambiguous "we" automatically incorporated members of the audience under its heading, it prompted audience identification in a more compelling fashion than "I" or "my administration" could. "We" had carried out the moderate actions of strength and restraint in the Gulf of Tonkin; consequently, Johnson's implicit appeals portrayed listeners as consubstantial with him, which encouraged them to support the president and his policies.

This is not to say that explicit appeals, specifically self-references, were unimportant in Johnson's discourse. These appeals were not only present, but quite prominent in his talk, a finding that would not be surprising to rhetorical critic Rod Hart or journalist Frank Cormier. In *Verbal Style and the Presidency,* Hart's computer analysis revealed that Johnson's rhetoric during his White House years tended to contain a large number of self-references, especially in comparison to the discourse of Truman, Eisenhower, and Kennedy.

Cormier observed that Johnson had a tendency to personalize everything about which he spoke; Cormier claimed that the president "even talked in one speech about the 'State of *My* Union Address,' which we recorded as a Freudian slip."[99] In his Gulf of Tonkin rhetoric, the president's personal involvement manifested itself through numerous explicit appeals, which tended first, to emphasize Johnson's authority and responsibilities, and second, to link him with endorsement figures, particularly past presidents.

In his analysis of Johnson's crisis talk from August 4 and 5, Cherwitz argues that the president "made frequent references to his official sanction and authority as president."[100] My own examination confirms Cherwitz's finding. From the evening of the Gulf of Tonkin retaliation through the fall 1964 campaign, Johnson often relied on explicit identificational appeals that emphasized his presidential authority and responsibility. For example, Johnson opened his televised address on August 4 with: "As President and Commander in Chief, it is my duty to the American people to report that renewed hostile actions against United States ships . . . have today required me to order the military forces of the United States to take action in reply."[101] In this statement and others like it, Johnson lent greater credibility to his message by reminding citizens of his official titles and, hence, of the authority and expert knowledge on foreign affairs that are presumed to come with those roles.

The president went even further in his public remarks upon signing the Southeast Asia Resolution into law. In his comments, Johnson recalled North Vietnamese attacks, U.S. retaliatory raids, and his own role in the Gulf of Tonkin crisis.

> As Commander in Chief the responsibility was mine—and mine alone. I gave the orders for that reply, and it has been given.

But, as President, there rested upon me still another responsibility—the responsibility of submitting our course to the representatives of the people, for them to verify it or veto it. . . .

This resolution confirms and reinforces powers of the Presidency. I pledge to all Americans to use those powers with all the wisdom and judgment God grants to me.[102]

In this passage, Johnson appealed to the authority of his constitutional roles and described himself as a selfless leader who took full responsibility for his actions. Additionally, he depicted the resolution as a test of public support for U.S. policy and also of support for him personally. Indeed, the president treated approval of the legislation as a trial run for the November election; his last sentence in this passage could as well be a line from a presidential inaugural address. In this way, Johnson focused on the power and credibility of his office and pointed toward public support of the president—in this case, Lyndon Johnson.

A second type of explicit identificational appeal also appeared in the president's crisis rhetoric on a regular basis: the use of endorsement figures, particularly past presidents, to lend credibility to Johnson's actions. In his initial televised address on the crisis, Johnson told citizens that the "leaders of both parties" had assured him that the Southeast Asia Resolution would be quickly introduced, discussed, and passed. Moreover, he added, "just a few minutes ago I was able to reach Senator Goldwater and I am glad to say that he has expressed his support of the statement that I am making to you tonight."[103] Through these remarks, Johnson circumvented partisan criticism by showing that Democrats and Republicans alike, including the Republican presidential nominee, approved of his actions. Goldwater's own public expression of support, in addition to congressional praise for the president, reinforced Johnson's statement and further legitimized him and his Gulf of Tonkin policies.

His use of Goldwater notwithstanding, past presidents remained Johnson's favorite endorsement figures. In an August 5 speech, for example, he noted that

For 10 years three American Presidents—President Eisenhower, President Kennedy, and your present President—and the American people have been actively concerned with threats to the peace and security of southeast Asia from the Communist government of North Viet-Nam.

President Eisenhower sought—and President Kennedy sought—the same objectives that I still seek.[104]

Through this form of explicit appeal, Johnson linked himself to the institution of the presidency (a strategic move given the means by which he had ascended to the office and the short period of time that he had served) and to his primary audience, "the American people." Johnson also demonstrated that his goals and concerns were consistent with those of a popular Republican president and a popular, recently martyred Democratic president.

On other occasions, Johnson argued that the strength and restraint demonstrated by his administration were consistent with the foreign policy of his predecessors. The president told members of the American Bar Association on August 12 about the retaliation he had ordered in the Gulf of Tonkin and then observed, "No one who commands the power of nuclear weapons can escape his responsibility for the life of our people and the life of your children." Through this comment, Johnson showed the similarity between his concerns ("the life of your children") and those of his audience, at the same time that he brought up the issue on which Goldwater was most vulnerable.   The president continued,

> It has never been the policy of any American President to sympathetically or systematically place in hazard the life of this Nation by threatening nuclear war. . . . Our firmness at moments of crisis has always been matched by restraint—our determination by care. It was so under President Truman at Berlin, under President Eisenhower in the Formosa Straits, under President Kennedy in the Cuba missile crisis. And I pledge you that it will be so as long as I am your President.[105]

Johnson's discourse here aligned him and his policies with the presidential office, past presidents of both parties, and successful crisis resolutions in our nation's history. Rather than make a direct attack against Goldwater, Johnson used explicit appeals to legitimize himself as a responsible leader who was consistent with foreign policy principles of the past and left his audience to wonder whether Goldwater deviated from those principles. The president linked his Gulf of Tonkin policy of "strength and firmness matched to restraint and patience"[106] to his predecessors in four other speaking engagements, as well.

Although Johnson's discourse can be characterized by implicit appeals, undergirded by explicit appeals, perhaps the most interesting aspect of his rhetoric was how these two types of persuasive appeals interacted. An excerpt from Johnson's address in Manchester, New Hampshire, serves to demonstrate this pattern:

> So just for the moment I have not thought that we were ready for American boys to do the fighting for Asian boys. What I have been trying to do, with the situation that I found, was to get the boys in

Viet-Nam to do their own fighting with our advice and with our equipment. That is the course we are following. So we are not going north and drop bombs at this stage of the game, and we are not going south and run out and leave it for the Communists to take over.[107]

According to rhetorical critic Thomas Benson, "Speakers and writers, acting rhetorically, create not only themselves, but their audiences."[108] That is, rhetors use language to construct an image of themselves and also an image of the audience and how the audience should react to the message it hears. Through explicit appeals, Lyndon Johnson distinguished himself from his audience, whether through the simple use of "I" or through his overt attempts to portray himself as a responsible, legitimate leader whom citizens should obey. Nonetheless, his reliance on implicit appeals served to depict him as one with his listeners.

In the above excerpt, the president's transition from explicit appeals to implicit appeals portrayed him first as different from the audience (the "I" who had been making policy decisions) and then as part of it (the "we" who was carrying out the policy). Through this shift, Johnson made his actions and characteristics indistinguishable from those of his listeners. If the president were powerful and restrained, then so were the American people; if the United States were forceful and self-controlled, then so was Johnson. The net result was to make the president appear to be an especially fitting leader for our nation and to encourage citizens to support him.

Johnson's interchangeable use of explicit and implicit appeals also demonstrates how the commander-in-chief strategically exploited the ambiguity of "we." The word "we," in and of itself, does not clearly refer to any particular group. In Johnson's rhetoric, the president continually drew connections between himself, "I," and an equivocal "we," so that he linked himself with any of a number of desirable parties that his listeners might have in mind:

> I am proud to be a Democrat, and I want to make that clear. But I am humble, I am humble in the belief that on the issue of war, when you take your boy down to the depot to say goodby, maybe never to see him again, on the issue of war and peace I share the view of the Presidents of both parties who have preceded me, and I share the view of what I think is the overwhelming majority of Americans today.
>
> We believe that the courage of the age is demonstrated only by handling carefully—never carelessly—any test which may arise. There are many of them, and there is no way to prevent them. We must be ready to handle them when they come. We must do it with care and with coolness and with courage. This we have done.[109]

In this passage, "we" could have represented any of a variety of groups: Democrats, presidents of both parties, the majority of Americans, even the Johnson administration. The benefit of this ambiguity was that almost all listeners conceivably could identify with "we." In this way, Johnson's rhetoric gave the impression that "I" was part of whatever "we" with whom listeners identified.

Through his identificational appeals, Johnson encouraged the public to support his actions in the Gulf of Tonkin and to support him as a presidential candidate. The president relied primarily on a strategy of implicit appeals that emphasized national oneness in times of crisis and that united Johnson and his audience under the rubric of an ambiguous "we," who had acted with strength and restraint to uphold peace and the defense of freedom.

As a secondary strategy, Johnson employed extensive explicit appeals that emphasized his authority and presidential office. Johnson's explicit appeals also legitimized his foreign policy of strength and restraint as a responsible one through the use of endorsement figures, particularly past presidents, and subtly raised questions about whether Goldwater would be equally as trustworthy on matters of war and peace.

Finally, Johnson often shifted from explicit appeals to implicit appeals, such that "I" became consubstantial with the ambiguous "we." In other words, Johnson transformed himself—the responsible, legitimate president of strength and restraint—into the "we" who had acted with strength and restraint in the Gulf of Tonkin. Johnson's identificational appeals as a whole urged citizens not only to unite behind his crisis management, but also to unite behind him for the presidency in the 1964 campaign.

Despite the compelling nature of Johnson's identificational strategy, it posed major problems for the president over time. Johnson's appeals defined his and "our" actions in the Gulf of Tonkin as moderate ones, in keeping with what he claimed was the moderate foreign policy of previous presidents, and showed how moderation was consistent with the nation's goals of peace and defense. Nevertheless, the president's attempts to encourage identification with his audience also served to dissociate strength and restraint indirectly, such that these concepts no longer seemed compatible, but actually appeared to be in conflict with one another. This unintended dissociation, in turn, reflected upon the related conceptual pair of peace and defense of freedom.

Johnson's identificational appeals invoked what Perelman and Olbrechts-Tyteca refer to as "the indirect introduction of a dissociative definition," or "the statement that something falls or does not fall within a given concept."[110] On a number of occasions, Johnson told Americans what his moderate policies of strength and restraint did *not* include. These statements defined his policies as desirably moderate—and thus worthy of citizen support—but also suggested that strength and restraint might be mutually exclusive.

In a September 28 speech before members of the New Hampshire Weekly Newspaper Editors Association, for instance, the president first discussed how previous administrations had displayed firmness and calm restraint during foreign crises and noted that "the Johnson administration" had remained true to this tradition in its response to the Gulf of Tonkin. He then went on to discuss illusions that "if believed and followed, would put our freedom and the peace of the world in mortal peril." According to Johnson, "Mr. Goldwater" and others apparently held "the illusion that force, or the threat of force, can solve all problems." A related illusion in "this nuclear age" was that "the United States can demand resolution of all the world's problems and mash a button and get the job done."[111]

Although he did not mention Goldwater in regard to this particular illusion, Johnson's discussion of his opponent in reference to the excessive use of force linked Goldwater to overeagerness in the use of nuclear weapons. The president claimed that he rejected such illusions and instead desired "to be very cautious and careful." He warned of a third illusion, as well, the desire to have the United States "retire from the world." If we abandoned our commitments abroad, Johnson warned that we "would endanger freedom everywhere. And I think it would end the hope for peace."[112] Through his discussion of these three illusions, Johnson defined himself and his policies as moderate by describing principles that he did *not* embrace: a reliance upon excessive force, including nuclear weapons, and a desire to withdraw from foreign involvement altogether.

The president also made clear that moderate policies were commensurate with the goals of peace and defense of freedom. Moreover, Johnson connected these ideas to his policy in Vietnam when he said, "we are not going north and we are not going south; we are going to continue to try to get them to save their own freedom with their own men, with our leadership, and our officer direction, and such equipment as we can furnish them."[113] Exactly who "we" was, Johnson did not say. Johnson's speech associated him with the wise policies of strength and restraint that past presidents had followed and encouraged citizens to become part of the "we" pursuing such policies in Vietnam. The problem was that the president's remarks also suggested that strength and restraint might be opposed because the policy extremes he rejected were the escalation of military force by moving north (strength) and the withdrawal from involvement by moving south (restraint).

In a similar fashion, Johnson discussed the Gulf of Tonkin crisis and Vietnam with members of the American Bar Association. He told them that "the United States cannot and must not and will not" withdraw from Vietnam because such an action would bring an end to freedom there. He also maintained that the nation should not "enlarge the conflict" or engage in "reckless" military action because such a policy would threaten world peace.[114] Once again, the president defined his policy as desirably moderate by locating it squarely between the poles of restraint (withdrawal) and strength (escalation). Since withdrawal would end freedom and escalation would threaten peace, Johnson implied that restraint and strength, as well as peace and defense of freedom, were in conflict rather than in harmony.

On August 29 in Texas, the president likewise discussed how "we" had not attacked civilians in our response to the Gulf of Tonkin. He followed this observation with the assertion that he had chosen not to enlarge the war in Vietnam because it would involve "committing a good many American boys to fighting a war that I think ought to be fought by the boys of Asia."[115] In a campaign speech in Oklahoma, Johnson repeated this theme when he said that bombing North Vietnamese supply lines would escalate the conflict and, in words that no doubt would come back to haunt him, the last thing the United States wanted to do was to "get tied down in a land war in Asia."[116]

The president's exhortations about what his policy did and did not include helped him define actions of strength and restraint as moderate actions and allowed Johnson to argue that moderate policies were consistent with the valued goals of defense and peace. Simultaneously, his repeated efforts to detail exactly what made up a moderate policy and what did not led to the indirect dissociation of restraint and strength, as well as the higher order concepts of peace and the defense of freedom. Johnson's explanations, which drew clear connections between the Gulf of Tonkin and Vietnam, also set up the criteria by which citizens could evaluate his Vietnam policy in the future.

The president's difficulties would begin when Americans who at first accepted Johnson's preferred meanings learned the awful truth: that his restrained yet strong actions included a barrage of U.S. bombs on Vietnamese cities, the deaths of innocent civilians, and the deployment in ever larger numbers of American soldiers, many of whom would never come home. Johnson had sometimes qualified his policy statements by saying that "just for the moment" he had decided not to send more American soldiers or that "at this stage" we would not bomb North Vietnam,[117] but often he did not qualify his assertions at all. In the end, citizens did not remember his qualifications. They recalled instead how Johnson had defined strength/restraint and peace/defense in moderate terms and had established that his policies fulfilled those criteria, and how he later violated the principles on which he had expounded. Small wonder that so many citizens came to question his veracity.

Through his crisis discourse in the summer and fall of 1964, Lyndon Johnson managed his partisan political affairs by putting Goldwater's charges that he was too restrained in Vietnam to rest and by raising questions about his opponent's responsibility on matters of war and peace, particularly nuclear weapons. Once the 1964 race was well underway, Johnson's campaign staff would further reinforce the notion that Goldwater was trigger happy through the infamous daisy commercial and other advertisements. In fact, Theodore White later argued that millions of Americans voted against Goldwater because Johnson succeeded in framing the campaign as a choice "between peace and *risk* of war," in which Goldwater constituted the risk.[118] The foundation for this framework can be observed in Johnson's Gulf of Tonkin discourse. At the same time that the president attended to campaign concerns, his crisis rhetoric also dealt with the conflict that existed between historic lessons about peace and defense and the new realities of a nuclear and television age. His discourse equated his strong and restrained policies with moderation and redefined the goals of peace and the defense of freedom so that they were consistent with moderate means. As Goldwater pollster Thomas Benham later observed, "Johnson managed to pre-empt the middle of the road in the minds of voters."[119]

Despite the astuteness with which Johnson handled these issues, his rhetoric posed long-term problems for him. The situation of his crisis talk depicted the Gulf of Tonkin—and Vietnam—as similar to other situations where the United States had defended freedom and protected peace. However, the style and identificational appeals of his discourse were in conflict with the situation, for they indirectly dissociated defense and peace—and strength and restraint—and thereby suggested that these concepts were not compatible with one another. Just as Johnson's talk forged a framework for the 1964 campaign, his rhetoric also created a framework through which Americans could examine and evaluate his Vietnam policy in the future. Unfortunately for Johnson, the terminological boundaries he established would not serve him well.

THE DANGER OF THE MIDDLE GROUND

In *Lyndon Johnson's Dual War: Vietnam and the Press,* Kathleen Turner writes that Johnson dared not employ rhetoric about Vietnam that was too inflammatory for fear it would lead to public pressure to use atomic weapons in order to win. Johnson, therefore, could not draw on the appeal of heroes, villains, and moral imperatives in his discourse; but he still faced the "rhetorical hazards of a wartime situation" in the form of lost lives and depleted national resources.[120]

During the summer and fall of 1964, before the arrival of American ground troops in Vietnam, Johnson redefined restraint and strength—as well as peace and defense—so that they were compatible with the moderate military actions he had taken in the Gulf of Tonkin. This deft rhetorical maneuver helped the president secure his landslide election and the passage of his much-desired congressional resolution, but also had the unintended effect of dissociating the elements in each of these conceptual pairs so that they became opposed. Johnson particularly tended to encourage this indirect dissociation in his lengthy ad-libs on the campaign trail, for whatever his misgivings about overall U.S. involvement in Vietnam, he could not resist the temptation to use the Gulf of Tonkin to his immediate advantage.

In a White House memo, exasperated aide Horace Busby complained that Johnson ad-libbed to elicit applause from the audience when his prepared texts failed to do so.[121] One pictures the president on the stump, in what Douglas Cater would describe as Johnson in "a good speechifying mood,"[122] enthralled with the enthusiastic crowds that so often greeted him and ad-libbing lines about his latest success in order to prompt more cheers. Later when Johnson used this rhetorical posture to talk about the limited war in Vietnam, rather than the crisis in the Gulf of Tonkin, he would find that the appeal of his talk, like the applause of campaign crowds, was fleeting and that many Americans had come to reject the assertion that he was pursuing both peace and defense.

Perelman and Olbrechts-Tyteca warn that rhetors who do not order two values hierarchically eventually run into trouble; they explain that "simultaneous pursuit of these values leads to incompatibilities, obliges one to make choices."[123] In Johnson's case, he found himself pursuing policies that were no longer commensurate with his earlier definitions, and many citizens felt betrayed. Turner claims that the president's rhetoric on the Vietnam war resulted in "an inability to convince a large portion of the population that America was doing enough for Vietnam, coupled with an inability to convince another large element that America was not doing too much—ultimately leaving only a relative few who were not dissatisfied in some way."[124]

Zarefsky points out that once a president situates himself on the middle ground, he opens himself up to attacks from both the left and the right.[125] In Johnson's Gulf of Tonkin rhetoric, the inadvertent dissociation of peace and defense as contrary terms offered an alternative view that his opponents embraced. This is not to say, of course, that critics argued "Peace now!" or "Win in Vietnam!" only because the president suggested these arguments to them. On the other hand, there is a difference between one who is dragged unwillingly to the gallows and one who places the noose around his own neck. Johnson offered arguments that, at the time of the Gulf of Tonkin, only relatively small groups of people had articulated, but which large segments of the public later would use to hang him.

Perhaps former Johnson Press Secretary George Reedy summed it up best when he observed that the president "was probably the most gifted political tactician that the country has ever had, but he was not a strategist. His great weakness was that he really could not look down the road. He could not put things in historical perspective."[126] In Johnson's Gulf of Tonkin discourse, one can discern the seeds of his Vietnam despair.

Johnson's balance between strength and restraint in his crisis rhetoric demonstrates, on one level, the tension that has existed between these two concepts for all post–World War II presidents. A commander-in-chief who involves the nation in military conflict must convince an international audience that he is acting forcefully enough to defend freedom and to keep the peace. At the same time, he must reassure Americans and allies alike that he will not recklessly engage in nuclear war. Johnson was not content merely to depict himself and the nation as strong but self-controlled. In his efforts to manage competing issues, the president increased the tension between these concepts to the point where the relationship between them eventually snapped.

Johnson also illustrates why presidents should be wary of the tempting political dividends that crisis promotion can offer. What is rhetorically appealing in the short term may not remain so over time. Johnson's discourse about the Gulf of Tonkin may have coerced Congress to acquiesce to his desire for the Southeast Asia Resolution as Cherwitz argues, but in the long run his rhetoric also limited his own alternatives by trapping him into a moderate policy that showed no sign of success or by forcing him to face condemnation if he embraced a policy that he formerly had rejected.

When Johnson left office, the political polarizations that plagued him did not disappear. His successor, Richard Nixon, also faced a nation bitterly divided over U.S. policy in Vietnam. Unlike Johnson, Nixon seemed to welcome public controversy; his presidential discourse even encouraged it. Six years after the Gulf of Tonkin, Nixon announced to Americans that a crisis existed in Cambodia. His crisis rhetoric unleashed a firestorm of public reaction.

Chapter Four

RICHARD M. NIXON AND THE GROTESQUE
The 1970 Invasion of Cambodia

On April 20, 1970, President Richard M. Nixon announced that 150,000 U.S. troops would be withdrawn from Vietnam within the next year. Because enemy attacks in Cambodia and Laos still continued to escalate, Nixon warned Americans that such a policy involved "risks." Nonetheless, the president maintained that "we finally have in sight the just peace we are seeking."[1] At long last, the end to American involvement in Vietnam seemed near.

A mere ten days after this speech, Nixon appeared on television with a very different announcement: the president had taken it upon himself to expand the war. According to Nixon, South Vietnamese and U.S. forces had invaded neutral Cambodia to destroy enemy sanctuaries there. He explained that such an operation was necessary to "protect our men who are in Vietnam and to guarantee the continued success of our withdrawal and Vietnamization programs."[2] The war that had been on the wane only ten days earlier had widened to include another country.

Despite the apparent contradiction, a majority of Americans rallied around the president.[3] Others did not. Across the country, tensions rose as university and college campuses erupted with renewed antiwar protests. Disturbances resulted in the deaths of students at Kent State and at Jackson State. On Capitol Hill, Senators Frank Church and John Sherman Cooper proposed an amendment that would eliminate funding for the Cambodian incursion, and Senators Mike Mansfield, J. W. Fulbright, Edward Kennedy, and others denounced the president. Nixon reassured Americans that the operation had been a success, but he faced a deeply divided nation. *Newsweek* noted that "the Republican President who had once promised to bring Americans together had, by word and deed, pulled them further apart."[4]

Nixon's discourse on Cambodia poses an intriguing case of crisis promotion and management, for the president received far less public support during Cambodia than Kennedy did during the Cuban missile crisis or than Johnson did during the Gulf of Tonkin crisis. Several factors contributed to Nixon's lack of cohesive support. In 1970, Americans had a high awareness of Vietnam and Cambodia; they had strong beliefs about what should be done there; and these beliefs frequently clashed with Nixon's policies. And try though he might, the president could not control media information about the invasion, which led to the widespread coverage and criticism of his policy.

Another reason for these negative reactions may have had to do with Nixon's discourse itself. In reference to the president's talk during the crisis, observers have used words like "paradoxical," "erratic and irrational," and "surreal."[5] Both journalist Stanley Karnow and rhetorical analyst Robert Newman claim that Nixon's April 30 speech stirred up unnecessary controversy. In Newman's words, the address was "a clear case of rhetorical overkill" as Nixon could have quietly ordered raids on the Cambodian sanctuaries without a bellicose call to arms and thus avoided the public turmoil that his discourse generated.[6]

Communication scholars Richard Gregg and Gerard Hauser locate one source of the speech's controversy in its resemblance to "classical models of manhood—*arete, virtue, machismo.* All require external validation and engaging in acts of reckless daring and might to secure the awe of fellows and rivals alike." Gregg and Hauser argue that just as Indian chiefs in potlatch ceremonies confronted rivals in order to bestow credibility upon themselves and their tribes, Nixon encouraged Americans to support him in his display of manhood in order to prove the nation's worth. This intended identification, the authors contend, was a major factor in the negative response the president's announcement received.[7] Theodore Windt similarly observes that Nixon portrayed the Cambodian crisis as a test of American character.[8]

In this chapter, I provide yet another analysis of Nixon's April 30 speech and include an examination of his other discourse about the Cambodian crisis as well. Although I build upon earlier findings, I also attempt to provide a more inclusive explanation for the disquieting nature of the president's talk. Specifically, I argue that Nixon's rhetoric resembled an ancient, poetic structure called "the grotesque." He employed recognizable themes and appeals in unrecognizable combinations; that is, his discourse consisted of constant, unresolved incongruities, in which no transcendent meaning existed. The grotesque explains the puzzling inconsistencies in Nixon's portrayal of the crisis situation, the way in which the personal focus of his style contradicted his claims of selfless concern for the nation, and the discordant manner in which he attempted both to identify with and to repel particular segments of the American public.

Furthermore, the grotesque may shed light on the fierce response that Nixon's discourse garnered, for art scholar Philip Thomson claims that the grotesque triggers alienation in those who recognize its inconsistencies.[9] To explain the chaotic character of Nixon's talk, I first examine the rhetorical context of the Cambodian crisis and then turn to the grotesque incongruities of the situation, style, and identificational appeals in the president's discourse.

THE RHETORICAL CONTEXT OF THE CAMBODIAN CRISIS

In January 1970, the Vietnam War still raged and the nation of Cambodia continued to maintain an official neutrality toward the conflict. Cambodia's leader, Prince Norodom Sihanouk, protected his country with what Noam Chomsky called "a delicate balancing act," in which Sihanouk played the

Communists and the Americans against one another.[10] Despite Cambodia's historic distrust of the Vietnamese, Sihanouk in 1965 allowed the North Vietnamese and Vietcong to set up base camps along Cambodia's border with South Vietnam. When the United States instituted a coastal blockade of Vietnam a short time later, the Communists needed a new route by which to send supplies into South Vietnam. Chinese Premier Chou En-lai asked Sihanouk for permission to bring supplies through the Cambodian port of Sihanoukville (later renamed Kompong Som) and to truck the materials over Cambodian highways to the sanctuaries along the eastern border. Because Cambodia lacked the military strength to do otherwise, Sihanouk acquiesced.[11]

Cambodia was also pressed by the United States. In March 1969, Menu operations—extensive B-52 raids—against the Communist sanctuaries within Cambodia secretly began.[12] Just as Sihanouk had helped the North Vietnamese and Vietcong, he aided U.S. actions through his public silence about the attacks. According to investigative journalist William Shawcross, Cambodia could prevent neither Communist nor U.S. infringements of its neutrality; therefore, Sihanouk tolerated intervention from both parties to protect his nation from outright war.[13] Publicly, Sihanouk claimed that Cambodia remained neutral; privately, the prince aided both the Communists and the Americans. Such was the state of affairs within Cambodia in January 1970 when Sihanouk left the country for his annual obesity treatment on the French Riviera. Sihanouk left his government in the hands of two men: Prime Minister Lon Nol and Deputy Prime Minister Sisowath Sirik Matak.[14]

In Sihanouk's absence, Lon Nol and Sirik Matak decided to crack down on the Vietnamese Communists in Cambodia. Staged demonstrations were held at the North Vietnamese and Vietcong embassies in Phnom Penh. In March, Sirik Matak announced that the Communists could no longer make use of Sihanoukville or buy Cambodian goods. Lon Nol, meanwhile, ordered all Vietnamese Communists to leave Cambodia within seventy-two hours, even though the Cambodian army could not possibly enforce such a policy. When Lon Nol's deadline passed, his government asked South Vietnamese troops to provide artillery support against the Communist camps.[15] Throughout March and April, South Vietnamese units and their American advisers quietly crossed the Cambodian border for attacks against enemy positions.[16] Despite this action, North Vietnam and China attempted to negotiate with the Lon Nol government to keep Communist supply lines in Cambodia open.[17]

On March 18, the Cambodian National Assembly and Council of the Kingdom unanimously decided to remove Sihanouk from office. Although Cheng Heng was named interim head of state, Lon Nol and his cohort, Sirik Matak, held the actual reins of power. Five days after the coup, Sihanouk formed a coalition—the National United Front of Kampuchea (FUNK)—with the

Khmer Rouge, the Cambodian Communist movement. FUNK immediately declared war on the new Lon Nol regime and received the support of the North Vietnamese, the Vietcong, and the Pathet Lao.[18]

By April, Cambodia was in complete upheaval. To gain domestic support for his actions, Lon Nol had exploited Cambodians' historic distrust of the Vietnamese, which resulted in widespread atrocities against the more than 400,000 Vietnamese civilians who lived in Cambodia.[19] Meanwhile, South Vietnamese border attacks had pushed the North Vietnamese and Vietcong further west into the heart of Cambodia. For the first time, Communist troops began to attack Cambodian soldiers and to promote the Cambodian Communist movement as the way to restore a sympathetic government to Phnom Penh.[20]

Against this backdrop of internal conflict within Cambodia, President Nixon told Americans that an end to U.S. involvement in Vietnam was in sight. In his April 20 televised address, Nixon announced that 150,000 American soldiers would leave Vietnam within the next year. He declared, "We can now say with confidence that pacification is succeeding. We can now say with confidence that the South Vietnamese can develop the capability for their own defense. And we can say with confidence that all American combat forces can and will be withdrawn." The president noted that enemy escalations in Cambodia and Laos made his decision risky, but the overall tone of the speech was positive. According to Nixon, "the just peace we are seeking" would soon be at hand.[21]

Ten days later, on April 30, Nixon shocked many citizens when he appeared on television to announce that U.S. troops had invaded Cambodia. The president claimed that increased enemy activity in that country posed a threat to American soldiers in South Vietnam and, hence, to the U.S. withdrawal program. Nixon argued that "the possibility of winning a just peace in Vietnam . . . is at stake." For these reasons, the commander-in-chief said, he had launched a joint American–South Vietnamese operation to attack enemy sanctuaries.[22]

Reactions to the president's speech were swift but divided. On the one hand, a Gallup poll showed that most Americans supported Nixon's actions, just as citizens usually rally around the president during times of crisis. Nevertheless, Gallup also found that a substantial number of citizens—39 percent of those surveyed—disapproved of Nixon's decision.[23]

In notes about the disadvantages of the upcoming Cambodian operation, the president observed that the invasion was bound to create division in the United States.[24] Nixon's recognition of the potential political problems that awaited him led to extensive White House efforts to shape and control public information about Cambodia. Indeed, perhaps no contemporary administration left such a complete record, albeit unwillingly, of its attempts to promote and manage a foreign crisis. Assistant to the President H. R. Haldeman, for instance, wrote that the White House should engage in "preconditioning" for the invasion announcement by asking congressional hawks, partisan groups, and key newspapers to advocate stronger action.[25]

On April 30, in the minutes before he went on the air, Nixon articulated concern over the visual impact his message would make when he commented to a CBS camera crew that panning one camera sometimes was "just as effective as moving to another shot" and wondered aloud about whether there was enough color contrast for him and the set to show up well on black-and-white television. The president also joked about the use of the Oval Office phone as a prop and asked, "What if the hotline rang? Wouldn't that really be . . . That'd give you really a first."[26]

Once the Cambodian operation was made public, the White House communicated with organizations such as United We Stand, Tell It to Hanoi, and Young Americans for Freedom, groups with close ties to the administration, in order to generate letters and telegrams in favor of the president's decision.[27] Capitol Hill provided Nixon with support in the form of conservative stalwarts like Senators Bob Dole and Barry Goldwater, Congressman Gerald Ford, and others. The president attempted to gain additional endorsements when he sent three governors, four senators, and four congressmen to Vietnam and Cambodia on a fact-finding mission. Each received a "CKC rifle and . . . Chicom belt and holster" as souvenirs.[28] The administration even asked comedian Bob Hope to end his show with a public statement of support for Nixon, which he did, and Hope promised to continue to discuss the issue when he appeared on television in the immediate future.[29]

Nixon also looked to members of his own administration to send particular messages about Cambodia, such as the need to "protect American troops" or to "support our fighting men."[30] William Safire, Special Assistant to the President, wrote public relations pieces for the press about how Nixon made the invasion decision. Safire, too, followed prepared lines, such as "the decision was a tough one to make and the President showed a great deal of courage" and "he did it in a cool, calm, rational and very Nixon-like way."[31]

Because his guest spot on the *Dick Cavett Show* went especially well, Director of Communications Herb Klein was told to appear on television as much as possible.[32] National Security Adviser Henry Kissinger did his part by talking to members of the intellectual community and briefing the press. White House memos indicate, however, that some dissatisfaction existed over Kissinger's performance with both of these audiences. On May 14, the president asked Haldeman to fill up Kissinger's schedule so that he did not waste his time talking to academics since these individuals "even if they were for us could do no good for us."[33] Similarly, Haldeman recorded that he and Nixon had discussed how the mercurial National Security Adviser apparently basked in the attention of the press and then took far too long with his briefings. Haldeman's notes asked, "where can K. get ego satisfaction?" On another occasion, Haldeman and Nixon complained that Kissinger had to "make a harder *sell.* . . . [The] purpose of briefing is not to inform/it's to sell."[34]

If the White House put forth great effort to craft and to send its messages about Cambodia, then Nixon and his aides expended just as much energy to punish media outlets that interfered with the administration's campaign. In May, Nixon quietly initiated an administration boycott of *Time, Newsweek,* the *New York Times,* and the *Washington Post.* Nixon and Haldeman told Press Secretary Ron Ziegler not to return phone calls or to give interviews with these publications and to keep *Time,* in particular, out of the plane pool. The president also ordered sanctions against the Associated Press.[35]

In some cases, the administration orchestrated letter and phone campaigns against particular media. Nixon went so far as to suggest the types of arguments the letters and calls should use. In one set of meeting notes, Haldeman recorded how he and the president had discussed the need to "put someone on [the] *Post*—to needle Kay Graham/call everyday—I hate N—but you're hurting *our* cause."[36] On June 3, Nixon and Haldeman developed a letter theme in which the writer would claim that no president in the twentieth century had received as much media criticism as Nixon and that perhaps this fact should raise questions about the credibility of the press.[37]

Television networks, too, received their share of attention. Haldeman told one of his staff members, Jeb Magruder, to get his "boiler shop set up to hit both CBS & NBC"; about five weeks later, Magruder organized a letter-writing campaign against Walter Cronkite and CBS to protest a story by reporter John Lawrence.[38] Such efforts were part of what Nixon and Haldeman referred to as the "PR tide of battle" in the wake of Cambodia.[39] In a May 12 memo to Klein and Magruder, Haldeman underscored the importance that Nixon attached to an offensive, cohesive communication strategy when he wrote, "the orchestration of the Cambodian public information effort between now and June 20, and then the follow-up to the withdrawal of American troops are primary in the President's mind."[40]

For all of Nixon's efforts to control public perceptions, however, his announcement of the invasion and his subsequent communication in the months that followed seemed to bring great discord. A mere two weeks before the operation, the Vietnam Moratorium Committee had announced that it would close its Washington office due to a lack of public interest in the peace movement.[41] With the president's April 30 address, however, hundreds of college campuses exploded with protest once more. At Kent State University in Ohio, one demonstration ended in the deaths of four students. When that news broke, Nixon and Haldeman discussed the need to get out a story that a sniper had been involved.[42] In fact, national guardsmen had fired on the students. The victims included a devoted ROTC student and a young woman who was caught in the rifle fire as she walked to class. Several days later at Jackson State College in Mississippi, two more students were killed.[43]

Student protestors were angry, and substantial numbers in the House and the Senate felt the same way. Many representatives and senators were disturbed that Nixon had not consulted with them. Instead, the president had informed congressional leadership of the invasion just prior to his nationwide address. Even Lon Nol had heard about the operation only after it was underway.[44] Nixon justified his action on the basis of the commander-in-chief's authority to defend American soldiers abroad. According to Schlesinger, Nixon had so little concern about the legitimacy of his actions that he waited until four days after the invasion began before he directed the State Department to draft a legal justification.[45]

Another reason that Capitol Hill reacted so negatively to Nixon's news had to do with Secretary of State William Rogers. A week before the operation, Rogers had testified before a House appropriations subcommittee, where he stated that, "We [the administration] recognize that if we get involved in Cambodia with our ground forces, our whole program is defeated." Rogers had met with the Senate Foreign Relations Committee a few days later, where he said nothing about the possibility that the administration would soon launch an invasion. When the White House did just that, the senators felt deceived and immediately introduced legislation that would prevent a deep American commitment in Cambodia.[46]

Negative reactions to Nixon's announcement did not end with students and Congress. Even members of the president's own administration publicly expressed their disapproval. Assistant Secretary of Education James Allen openly objected and was forced to resign.[47] Interior Secretary Walter Hickel told the president of his views in a letter that one of Hickel's aides leaked to the press. Although the White House claimed there was no animosity between the president and Hickel, the administration immediately began plotting behind his back. Haldeman's notes from a May 8 meeting with Nixon read, "start a quiet job chopping Hickel/screwed everything up—behind scenes/encourage his enemies—build as incompetent/build pressure on him." Months later, Hickel was fired.

In addition to Allen and Hickel, more than two hundred State Department employees signed a public petition against Nixon's policy, and three of National Security Adviser Henry Kissinger's aides resigned in protest.[48] For his part, Daniel Patrick Moynihan, Counsellor to the President, encouraged Nixon to call off the administration's fierce public attacks against anyone who dissented from White House policy.[49] The president and his inner circle did not respond well to the dissent or the suggestions. Communication analyst Douglas Freeman observes that their tolerance for free speech typically extended only to that speech with which they agreed, regardless of the source.[50] In the case of Cambodia, Haldeman's notes recorded that the president would accept "no more crap" from Moynihan and the others. Haldeman wrote, "We're in a war now/when people don't shape up they've got to go." At another meeting, Nixon and his aides discussed the need for "a little housecleaning."[51]

Whether they came from outside the administration or from within, many who disagreed with the president found his sudden invasion announcement, at best, somewhat odd. At worst, they considered it bizarre. One obvious reason for this was that Nixon's announcement contradicted his positive message of April 20. Klein later commented, "Here we were facing a public sentiment to limit the war or get out of it, and our policy was to decrease American involvement—yet suddenly we were enlarging the theater of action."[52]

Furthermore, prior to the president's speech, the White House released news that South Vietnamese troops and their American advisers had crossed the Cambodian border. Officials described the operation as an incursion of "limited action" or a "surgical strike" of "relatively brief" duration.[53] The contrast between these relatively low-key depictions and Nixon's emotional announcement that U.S. ground troops had entered Cambodia contributed to the surreal nature of the crisis.

Beyond these inconsistencies, the Cambodian crisis seemed strange because of the incongruities of the discourse with which Nixon promoted it, both on April 30 and in the months that followed. The president's depiction of the situation, at first glance, seemed similar to the descriptions that Kennedy provided about the Cuban missile crisis and that Johnson provided about the Gulf of Tonkin. But his portrayal of the crisis situation contained nagging inconsistencies in regard to where the enemy was, how Nixon had decided upon a U.S. response, and whether Cambodia was even a crisis.

Likewise, the style of Nixon's rhetoric depicted a selfless "I" who would risk political repercussions in order to help a powerful U.S. actor prove its character, at the same time that his style revealed an obsession with personal concerns that belied his claims of self-sacrifice. Finally, the president employed identificational appeals that alternately scorned and entreated those who dissented from his policies. Despite his administration's efforts to rally support and control media coverage about the crisis, Nixon could not get around the incongruities of his public rhetoric about Cambodia and the way in which they contributed to an overall crisis of peculiar dimensions. The President's discourse exemplified "the grotesque."

THE GROTESQUE:
NIXON'S RHETORIC ABOUT THE CAMBODIAN CRISIS

Eight years before his Cambodian crisis, Richard Nixon published *Six Crises,* in which he discussed six of his most critical moments in politics, such as his Checkers speech and the "kitchen" debate with Nikita Khrushchev. He claimed in the book that the character traits an individual brings to a crisis determine how that person will respond to the situation at hand. Incongruously, a page later, Nixon instead maintained that most character traits are "acquired suddenly" during the stress of crises, rather than brought to those situations.

Nixon also gave voice to his ambivalent feelings about crisis. He wrote, "Crisis can indeed be agony. But it is the exquisite agony which a man might not want to experience again—yet would not for the world have missed."[54] Thus, Nixon depicted crisis as an intensely personal experience that was both wonderful and terrible at the same time.

In many ways, *Six Crises* foreshadowed Nixon's later talk on the 1970 invasion. An analysis of the key terms of Nixon's Cambodian discourse indicates that the president constructed a highly personal role for himself in his crisis talk. More so even than Lyndon Johnson, Nixon referred to himself in the first person as an important actor. Indeed, "I" was the dominant actor of Nixon's discourse. The coactor, though not nearly so prevalent, was "we," which usually seemed to refer to Americans or the United States. As in *Six Crises,* frequent incongruities existed, many of which seemed to arise out of the personal character of the president's discourse.

To say that Nixon's rhetoric was inconsistent does not, in and of itself, make his talk remarkable. Presidents are, after all, human, and human discourse contains disparities. The inconsistencies of Nixon's Cambodian rhetoric were noteworthy, however, for two reasons. First, Nixon constantly talked in incongruities, which made the disparities of his talk far more noticeable than the minor inconsistencies that typically appear in everyday presidential discourse. Second, Nixon rarely—if ever—*resolved* his inconsistencies, which gave his crisis rhetoric as a whole a rather chaotic quality. These characteristics of the president's discourse can be illumined by an ancient poetic structure called "the grotesque."

In *The Grotesque in Art and Literature,* Wolfgang Kayser writes that the term *grotesque* originally referred to a type of ancient Roman ornamental painting, which fused human elements with nonhuman elements such as plants and animals.[55] Since the discovery of these paintings in the fifteenth century, critics have used the term *grotesque* to describe everything from the gargoyles of Notre Dame to the artwork of such individuals as Goya, Bruegel, Hogarth, and Dali.[56] Kenneth Burke claims that the grotesque is a poetic structure that also includes the literature of authors like James Joyce and Thomas Mann.[57] Despite the apparent diversity of these so-called grotesques, all of these works have one thing in common: they are composed of constant incongruities.

According to Kayser, the grotesque is "the fusion of realms which we know to be separated" or "incompatible elements juxtaposed."[58] Not every aspect of the grotesque is bizarre; rather, elements that make sense in and of themselves are combined in strange ways.[59] Incongruities alone, however, do not constitute the grotesque. Irony, for instance, is also characterized by incongruent words or images, but its conflicts assume a higher meaning. According to Richard Brown, irony has "a transcendent perspective" in which these inconsistencies unite.[60] Conversely, the grotesque consists of irresolvable conflicts because no overarching perspective exists to give the conflicts meaning. Hence, humanities scholar Geoffrey Galt Harpham writes that the grotesque is "a medley of recognizable forms, in unrecognizable combinations, with no dominant principle."[61]

As a result of these odd juxtapositions, any grotesque portrayal fashions a world that appears both real and unreal. Thomson claims, for example, that the effect of the grotesque is alienation:

> Something which is familiar and trusted is suddenly made strange
> and disturbing. Much of this has to do with the fundamental
> conflict-character of the grotesque, with the mixture of incompat-
> ibles characteristic of it. The sudden placing of familiar elements of
> reality in a peculiar and disturbing light often takes the form of the
> flinging together of disparate and irreconcilable things, which by
> themselves would arose no curiosity.[62]

The grotesque takes familiar elements and combines them in unfamiliar ways with no larger frame to provide resolution or explanation. The consequent incongruities of this structure depict what is familiar and dependable about our world as strange and unreliable. According to Harpham, individuals simultaneously witness the grotesque, recognize its incongruities, and reject its depiction of the world.[63]

Nixon's Cambodian discourse typified the grotesque, for his talk consisted of terms and appeals that, individually, could stand on their own in meaningful ways. Nixon's rhetoric, however, juxtaposed these terms and appeals and involved them in relationships with one another that did not make sense. As a result, each aspect of Nixon's discourse—situation, style, and identificational appeals—contained unresolved incongruities. The immensely personal quality of his talk further underscored its resemblance to the grotesque, for Burke notes that subjective, personal symbols exemplify this poetic structure.[64]

Nixon's Cambodian rhetoric sounded as if he had taken selected elements from other presidential crisis discourse, personalized them, then thrown them together, regardless of the inconsistencies, in his own crisis promotion. The president also provided no larger frame in which these incongruities might be resolved. Consequently, the unexplained conflicts of Nixon's rhetoric made his crisis promotion appear both credible and incredible. Those who recognized the grotesque incongruities of the president's talk therefore reacted as one might expect: students, journalists, senators, representatives, and others understood Nixon's portrayal of events in Cambodia, but they did not believe him.

Situation

The representative anecdote, or typical way in which Nixon portrayed the crisis situation, can be described as follows:

> Because of increased enemy activity in Cambodia and anarchy both at home and abroad (scene), Nixon—"I"—and the United States—"we" (coactors)—cleaned out enemy sanctuaries (act) through a joint U.S.–South Vietnamese military operation (means), in order to protect U.S. soldiers in Vietnam, to ensure the U.S. withdrawal program, to demonstrate the character of the United States, and to attain a just peace (purposes).

Nixon described a scene of extensive "Communist occupied territories" in Cambodia that contained "major base camps, training sites, logistics facilities, weapons and ammunition factories, air strips, and prisoner-of-war compounds." These enemy sanctuaries were part of a larger scene of world crisis that involved attacks against "great institutions," both in the United States and in other "free" nations.[65]

The crisis scene of Nixon's rhetoric dictated that "I" and "we" realize particular purposes: to "reduce American casualties," to "guarantee the continued success of our withdrawal and Vietnamization programs," to demonstrate U.S. "will and character," and to "serve the cause of a just peace in Vietnam." In order to fulfill these goals, the president maintained, the key actors of his rhetoric must "clean out" major North Vietnamese and Vietcong sanctuaries in Cambodia. "We" and "I" were to carry out this act through a combined American and South Vietnamese military operation.[66]

Throughout Nixon's Cambodian discourse, two terminological relationships consistently appeared in his depictions of the situation: terms for scene-purpose and terms for purpose-act, the same ratios that characterized Kennedy's rhetoric about the Cuban missile crisis and Johnson's about the Gulf of Tonkin.

In his televised April 30 address, Nixon spent a great deal of time depicting a scene located in Cambodia, just across the South Vietnamese border. He explained, "Cambodia, a small country of 7 million people, has been a neutral nation since the Geneva Agreement of 1954—an agreement, incidentally, which was signed by the Government of North Vietnam." Despite the Geneva accord, Nixon noted, North Vietnam had "occupied military sanctuaries all along the Cambodian frontier with South Vietnam" for five years.[67] The president's words portrayed Cambodia as a tiny, harmless nation unable to prevent the hypocritical North Vietnamese from building bases within its borders.

Moreover, the phrase "military sanctuaries" implied that the Communist camps were unholy places of refuge where the enemy had immunity from punishment, especially since "American policy . . . has been to scrupulously respect the neutrality of the Cambodian people." Although the North Vietnamese and Vietcong remained safe from U.S. reprisals, Nixon claimed that they used their sanctuaries "for hit and run attacks on American and South Vietnamese forces in South Vietnam" and that they had "stepped up" their "guerrilla actions" considerably in the past two weeks.[68]

Like Kennedy and Johnson, Nixon discussed the crisis scene of his discourse in terms of a broader context. He argued that the crisis in Cambodia was related to a larger scene of crisis that the free world faced in 1970. He told his listeners on April 30 that "we live in an age of anarchy both abroad and at home. We see mindless attacks on all the great institutions which have been created by free civilizations in the last 500 years. Even here in the United States, great universities are being systematically destroyed. Small nations all over the world find themselves under attack from within and from without."

Nixon's discourse presented a truly nightmarish vision of world turmoil and domestic unrest. According to the president, our enemies, "the forces of totalitarianism and anarchy," were everywhere.[69] His delineation of the immediate crisis scene in Cambodia warned of North Vietnamese and Vietcong aggression, and his association of Cambodia with a more encompassing scene alerted Americans to domestic subversion, as well. Nixon's reference to universities, for example, implied that academics and student protestors were undermining the country. In a later passage, Nixon pointed the finger at "opinion leaders," which inferred that others—most notably journalists—were also involved.[70] The president heightened the apparent threat that Cambodia posed by casting the challenge there as part of a worldwide conspiracy against democracy.

On several occasions, Nixon also made parallels between the scene of crisis in Cambodia and previous scenes of aggression that the United States had faced. His April 30 address, for example, mentioned World War I, World War II, the Korean War, and the Cuban missile crisis.[71] Likewise, Nixon compared the Cambodian crisis to the Cuban missile crisis during a July 1 television interview with newsmen Howard K. Smith, Eric Sevareid, and John Chancellor; he even made allusions to the battle of Stalingrad and the D-Day invasion.[72]

In a meeting with student protestors on May 9, the president said that "in 1939 I thought Neville Chamberlain was the greatest man living and Winston Churchill was a madman. It was not until years later that I realized that Neville Chamberlain was a good man, but Winston Churchill was right."[73] The president's discussion of Cambodia in the context of World War II again revealed the imprint that experience seems to have left on so many American presidents. Like Kennedy during the Cuban missile crisis and Johnson during the Gulf of Tonkin crisis, Nixon discussed the scene in Cambodia in terms of a broader context where aggression, unless stopped by force, would only lead to further aggression.

Out of the president's key terms for scene, his terms for purpose arose. His June 3 speech to the nation, for example, asserted that enemy escalation in Cambodia "posed an unacceptable threat to our remaining forces in South Vietnam. It would have meant higher casualties. It would have jeopardized our program for troop withdrawals. It would have meant a longer war."[74] Given this scene, the purpose of American actions seemed clear. Nixon claimed in both his April 30 and June 3 addresses that "I" and "we" must act to "protect our men who are in Vietnam" and to ensure "the continuance and success of our troop withdrawal program."[75]

The president's discourse also exemplified another scene-purpose ordering of terms. According to Nixon, the United States faced aggression not only in Cambodia, but at home and in other places abroad. He argued, therefore, that the United States must prove that it had the character "to lead the forces of freedom in this critical period in world history." Unless this purpose were fulfilled, dire consequences would result. He warned, "If, when the chips are down, the world's most powerful nation, the United States of America, acts like a pitiful, helpless giant, the forces of totalitarianism and anarchy will threaten free nations and free institutions throughout the world."[76] Nixon's scenic terms of tumult implied what purposes must be met.

The president also subsumed his stated goals of protecting U.S. soldiers, ensuring the withdrawal program, and proving American character under the more transcendent purpose of attaining a "just peace." Nixon frequently talked about "the just peace we all desire" and his promise "to win a just peace."[77] During his final speech on the crisis, the president said: "Peace is the goal that unites us. Peace is the goal toward which we are working. And peace is the goal this Government will pursue until the day we reach it."[78] Reflective of the nation's World War II experience and the rhetoric of so many other presidents engaged in military conflict before and since, Nixon justified the necessity of force in an Orwellian fashion by arguing that only violence could bring peace.

The scene-purpose terminological ratio in Nixon's discourse was, in many ways, quite similar to that exemplified in the rhetoric of Kennedy and Johnson. In contrast to his immediate predecessors, Nixon's scene-purpose ordering of words also contained a number of unresolved incongruities.

Perhaps the most striking contradiction dealt with Nixon's entitlement of the scene. Throughout his discourse, the president portrayed the enemy buildup in Cambodia as threatening and part of an even more dangerous scene of aggression worldwide. At one point in his first televised address, Nixon labeled the scene as "critical" and referred to it as "this crisis." Incongruously, Nixon also declared, "If we fail to meet *this challenge,* all other nations will be on notice that despite its overwhelming power the United States, *when a real crisis comes,* will be found wanting."[79] He claimed that the United States faced a scene that was both a crisis and yet *not* a crisis. This contradiction cast Nixon's terms for scene in a very strange light.

Another inconsistency of the president's discourse pertained to the location of the enemy in Cambodia. In his April 30 speech, Nixon pointed out enemy camps on a map for viewers and mentioned—perhaps for the benefit of radio listeners and those who had black-and-white television sets—that the Communist sanctuaries were shaded the appropriate color of red. He claimed that Communist forces were "building up" along the eastern border of Cambodia "to launch massive attacks on our forces and those of South Vietnam." Nixon also argued that the enemy simultaneously had traveled west to attack the rest of Cambodia. As he put it, "Thousands of their soldiers are invading the country from the sanctuaries; they are encircling the capital of Phnom Penh. Coming from these sanctuaries, as you see here, they have moved into Cambodia and are encircling the capital."[80] Nixon said, in other words, that the Communists were headed in opposite directions at the same time.

According to Newman, the president's description posed a major contradiction, for how could enemy soldiers "be building up the sanctuaries when they are emptying them of soldiers to attack Phnom Penh"? Newman adds that this depiction was particularly puzzling to journalists since the presidents' advisers and Defense Department representatives had maintained that the enemy was not expanding the sanctuaries, but heading west to the Cambodian capital.[81]

A further incongruity of Nixon's discourse had to do with a particular element of the scene he described. According to the president, COSVN—the nucleus for Communist aggression against South Vietnam—was located within Cambodia's borders. He told listeners on April 30, "Tonight, American and South Vietnamese units will attack the headquarters for the entire Communist military operation in South Vietnam. This key control center has been occupied by the North Vietnamese and Vietcong for 5 years in blatant violation of Cambodia's neutrality."[82] In spite of the importance he attached to COSVN, Nixon never again mentioned the Communist headquarters in his subsequent crisis talk, including his televised June 3 address on the results of the Cambodian operation.

The president issued a report on June 30 that recounted "the background for the decision, the results of the operation, [and] their larger meaning in terms of the conflict in Indochina,"[83] but no references to COSVN appeared. Haldeman's May 3 notes of a meeting with the president explain why. According to Nixon's assistant, a major problem in the wake of the invasion was the fact that *"military reports—COSVN not there."* In light of this, the administration chose to focus on the supplies and materials captured in the operation instead.[84]

In addition to terms for scene-purpose and their attendant inconsistencies,

Nixon's crisis discourse was characterized by terms for purpose-act. This ratio dominated the president's crisis talk, just as it prevailed in Johnson's Gulf of Tonkin rhetoric, for Nixon constantly told citizens what purposes were behind his actions. During his first televised address, he stated that we were taking military action "not for the purpose of expanding the war into Cambodia but for the purpose of ending the war in Vietnam and winning the just peace we all desire."[85] Similarly, Nixon told reporters on May 8 that the invasion "will shorten this war. It will reduce American casualties. It will allow us to go forward with our withdrawal program. . . . It will in my opinion serve the cause of a just peace in Vietnam."[86] Nixon also maintained that the United States had attacked enemy sanctuaries in order to prove its character.

These key terms for purpose pointed to Nixon's key terms for act, for he argued that only the cleaning out of enemy sanctuaries could have fulfilled the purposes that he described. In his announcement of the crisis, Nixon claimed that the United States had three options. We could "do nothing," but this option really was "wishful thinking" and would not fulfill the goal of defending American soldiers. Or the United States could provide "massive military assistance" to Cambodia. Unfortunately, this option would make Cambodia an "active belligerent" and thereby expand the war. For Nixon, only one action could fulfill the purposes he had delineated: the United States must "go to the heart of the trouble" and begin "cleaning out" enemy camps through a joint U.S.–South Vietnamese operation.[87] Accordingly, the president's terms for purpose led to only one plausible act.

About a month later, Nixon's second major address on the crisis reinforced the relationship between the purposes he had professed and the action he had taken. The president's discourse intertwined key terms for purpose and act in such a way that the sanctuary operation appeared to have fulfilled all of his stated goals. For example, Nixon declared:

> First, we have eliminated an immediate danger to the security of the remaining Americans in Vietnam, and thereby reduced our future casualties. Seizing these weapons and ammunition will save American lives. Because of this operation, American soldiers who might not otherwise be ever coming home, will now be coming home.
>
> Second, we have won some precious time for the South Vietnamese to train and prepare themselves to carry the burden of their national defense, so that our American forces can be withdrawn. . . .
>
> Third, we have insured the continuance and success of our troop withdrawal program. As a result of the success of the Cambodian operations, Secretary Laird has resumed the withdrawal of American forces from Vietnam.[88]

In a memo to Haldeman, Nixon said that Gerald Ford had impressed upon him the need to "find a way to dramatize the capture of weapons, rice, etc."[89] The response to this counsel appeared in the form of a short Department of Defense film, which Nixon showed on nationwide television during his speech—a presidential first—to prove how the invasion had fulfilled its purposes. The president contended, "Had this war material made its way into South Vietnam and had it been used against American and allied troops, U.S. casualties would have been vastly increased." According to Nixon, his policy had fulfilled the goal of protecting American lives.

Nixon also indicated that U.S. military action had demonstrated the nation's character. If the leader of the United States had not met the Communist challenge, he asked, would our allies "in Latin America, Europe, the Mideast or other parts of Asia—retain any confidence in the United States?"[90] Since U.S. allies had provided no signs of panic or loss of confidence, Nixon suggested that his Cambodian policy had successfully preserved the nation's credibility.

Despite the president's extensive efforts to legitimize his actions, his terms for purpose-act also contained a number of puzzling incongruities. These contradictions dealt with Nixon's explanation of possible policy responses to the Cambodian crisis and why he had selected the course of action that he did. First, Nixon rejected the policy of no response because it would endanger the lives of American soldiers in Vietnam. He also argued against large-scale military assistance to Cambodia.[91] As Nixon explained at a May news conference, "the United States, as I indicated in what is called the Guam or Nixon Doctrine, cannot take the responsibility and should not take the responsibility in the future to send American men in to defend the neutrality of countries that are unable to defend them themselves."[92] Yet his April 30 speech had justified the U.S. invasion, in part, on just such grounds when he said, "Cambodia . . . has sent out a call to the United States, to a number of other nations, for assistance. Because if this enemy effort succeeds, Cambodia would become a vast enemy staging area and a springboard for attacks on South Vietnam along 600 miles of frontier."[93] Given these explanations, many of Nixon's constituents may have found his chosen policy troubling.

The president, by his own estimate, had sent 31,000 Americans into battle—thereby endangering their lives—and had sent troops to defend Cambodia's neutrality, an action that seemed to violate the Nixon Doctrine just as it ended Cambodia's attempts at impartiality in the Vietnam conflict. From this perspective, Nixon's policy seemed incommensurate with the criteria he claimed to have used in selecting it.

A second incongruity lay in the framework Nixon constructed for his discussion of possible responses to the crisis. He stated in his April 30 address that "we have three options," which implied that these were the *only* options available. Later in his speech, the president incongruously alluded to other possibilities—

such as diplomacy or immediate troop withdrawal—and then dismissed them.[94]

A third incongruity of Nixon's terms for purpose-act was the way in which he justified the invasion as an action that would help the United States attain peace. Nixon claimed, "It is tempting to take the easy political path: to blame this war on previous administrations and to bring all of our men home immediately, regardless of the consequences."[95] Nixon maintained that the decision to invade—the "right" decision—was "terribly difficult" or "hard."[96] According to communication professors Lynn Hinds and Carolyn Smith, the president often described policies in this way. They explain, "He contrasted the easy way with the right way, as though the right way could never be easy, or that his way was right because it wasn't easy."[97]

In his Cambodian discourse, Nixon argued that the purpose of peace would be best served by cleaning out the sanctuaries *because* of the difficulty such an action posed. At the same time, he indicated that perhaps the policy he had chosen *was* the easy one and that immediate withdrawal was the more difficult choice. The president claimed that to bring U.S. troops home immediately

> would mean defeat for the United States; to desert 18 million South Vietnamese people, who have put their trust in us and to expose them to the same slaughter and savagery which the leaders of North Vietnam inflicted on hundreds of thousands of North Vietnamese who chose freedom when the Communists took over North Vietnam in 1954; to get peace at any price now, even though I know that a peace of humiliation for the United States would lead to a bigger war or surrender later.[98]

This description portrayed immediate withdrawal, rather than Nixon's military action, as the more difficult policy to implement because of its horrendous consequences and thereby contradicted his odd equation of easiness with what was wrong and difficulty with what was right.

The interpretation of Nixon's terms for situation reveals two terminological relationships of note: words for scene-purpose and words for purpose-act. The president's rhetoric depicted a peculiar scene of crisis in Cambodia and worldwide, which dictated that Nixon and the United States act to protect American soldiers, to ensure the withdrawal program, to prove the nation's character, and, above all, to obtain a just peace. In turn, Nixon's discourse argued that these purposes could be fulfilled through only one act—the cleaning out of enemy sanctuaries—but again the inconsistencies of his rhetoric hinted that other actions might be possible and even preferable.

Moreover, the implied relationship between the president's terms for scene and his terms for act contributed to the disjointed nature of the situation he portrayed. Although Nixon typically described the scene as a crisis of massive proportions, recall that he undercut this depiction when he contrasted Cambodia with a future "real" crisis. The president's terms for act also cast doubts on the seriousness of the scene. In his April 30 speech, he said U.S. and South Vietnamese forces would "clean out" enemy sanctuaries,[99] a phrase that connoted action of short duration. Nixon likewise discussed in an interview "this limited, very precise action which was limited in terms of the time, limited in terms of 21 miles [inside Cambodia] as far as we were going to go."[100] The president may have chosen such terminology to reassure Americans that he was not expanding the war, particularly after the immediate outbursts his invasion announcement prompted. Nonetheless, the U.S. response that Nixon described seemed incompatible with the threatening nature of the scene he depicted, which lent further credence to the idea that perhaps Cambodia was not a "real" crisis after all.

Just as the situation of the president's discourse exemplified the grotesque, the style of his rhetoric also typified the chaos of this poetic structure. Nixon portrayed a selfless "I" that had assumed serious responsibilities in order to help the United States prove its character. Upon closer examination, Nixon's style appeared to contradict this representation, for his discourse revealed a leader more concerned with the nation's view of his character than with the well being of the nation.

Style

In Nixon's talk on Cambodia, the most common term for actor was "I"; the next most frequent actor was "we," or less often, "the United States." The dominance of "I" is consistent with Hart's computer-based analysis of Nixon's White House rhetoric. According to Hart, Nixon referred to himself more often than any contemporary president except Gerald Ford.[101] Rhetorical critics Ruth Gonchar and Dan Hahn observe that Nixon held "a highly personalized view of the Presidency."[102]

In Nixon's discourse on the Cambodian crisis, the actor "I" took center stage, in part because of the active role that Nixon played in his speechwriting. Drafts of the president's Cambodian messages reveal that he frequently personalized his talk by replacing "we" with "I"; adding the possessive to describe "my decision" and "my advisers"; and contributing numerous personal notations such as "I have concluded," "I have noted that," and "I have announced."[103] Nixon's habit of placing himself at the center of his discourse also served to portray him as an active leader who not only had the constitutional responsibility to make particular types of decisions, but who also willingly assumed accountability for the consequences of those decisions.

Nixon often referred to his titles, "Commander in Chief of our armed forces" and "President," when emphasizing the responsibility that came with these positions.[104] He told the American people on June 3 that he had "a solemn obligation to make the hard decisions which I find are necessary to protect the lives of 400,000 American men remaining in Vietnam."[105] In his interview with Smith, Sevareid, and Chancellor, Nixon emphasized the presidential duties of "I." He explained that "the President of the United States has the constitutional right, not only the right, but the responsibility to use his powers to protect American forces when they are engaged in military actions." Nixon claimed this obligation had forced him to "weigh the risk of dissent from those who would object if I did act, against the risks to 435,000 American lives who would be in jeopardy if I did not act, and as Commander in Chief, I had no choice but to act to defend those men."[106] The president's statement implied that "I" was a brave and selfless actor because he had been faced with a difficult decision and had made the proper choice, in spite of the political risks. In a May 8 news conference, he gave a similar account of how he had made the decision to send U.S. troops into Cambodia:

> Every one of my advisers . . . raised questions about the decision, and, believe me, I raised the most questions, because I knew the stakes that were involved, I knew the division that would be caused in this country. I knew also the problems internationally. I knew the military risks. And then after hearing all of their advice, I made the decision. Decisions, of course, are not made by vote in the National Security Council or in the Cabinet. They are made by the President with the advice of those, and I made this decision. I take the responsibility for it. I believe it was the right decision. I believe it will work out. If it doesn't, then I am to blame. They are not.[107]

The president portrayed "I" as a knowledgeable leader who had willingly chosen a policy that might prove politically detrimental to him and who would assume full culpability for it—regardless of the consequences—rather than blaming his subordinates.

In contrast to "I," Nixon depicted the secondary coactor of "we," or the United States, as both powerful and peaceful. His announcement of the Cambodian crisis described the United States as "the world's most powerful nation" and "the richest and strongest nation in the history of the world." At the same time, Nixon discussed how we had "patience" when it came to peace and how U.S. commanders had not taken action against Communist sanctuaries in Cambodia until enemy activity had escalated beyond the point of acceptability.

In spite of the U.S. invasion, the president also maintained that "the time came long ago to end this war through peaceful negotiations. We stand ready for those negotiations."[108] Nixon likewise discussed with reporters how we desired "a just peace" and reaffirmed in his June 3 address that as far as we were concerned the "door to a negotiated peace remains wide open."[109] Like Kennedy and Johnson, Nixon described "we" as a nation of power that could enforce its will and as an agent of peace that would act reasonably, rather than precipitously.

Both the key actor of "I" and the secondary coactor of "we," or the United States, were involved in the dominant terminological ratio of act-actor, the same ratio that played a major role in the style of Kennedy's and Johnson's crisis talk. Terms for act, in this scheme, revealed what kind of actors "I" and "we" were. Despite the central role of "I" in his discourse, Nixon seemed—at least on the surface—primarily concerned with the way in which actions reflected upon "we," a characteristic that Windt also observed in Nixon's rhetoric.

Nixon's April 30 speech asserted, for example, that if we reacted to Communist sanctuaries with diplomacy, "the credibility of the United States would be destroyed in every area of the world where only the power of the United States deters aggression." Any act other than military invasion would make our nation, in terms Nixon himself coined for the speech, look like "a pitiful, helpless giant" in the eyes of our allies and enemies. He explained, furthermore, "The action that I have announced tonight puts the leaders of North Vietnam on notice that we will be patient in working for peace, we will be conciliatory at the conference table, but we will not be humiliated."[110]

According to the president, our invasion of Cambodia served a necessary symbolic function: it proved our character to friend and foe alike. In his June 3 address, Nixon repeated this theme when he said that "failure to deal with the enemy action would have eroded the credibility of the United States before the entire world."[111] The president also indicated in a press conference that the United States could not afford to run from enemy aggression. He explained, "if we do what many of our very sincere critics think we should do, if we withdraw from Vietnam and allow the enemy to come into Vietnam and massacre the civilians there by the millions, as they would . . . let me say that America is finished insofar as the peacekeeper of the Asian world is concerned."[112] If the United States failed to combat the enemy, it would lose credibility and no longer serve as a deterrent to Communist aggression in Asia.

Although the president expressed concern with what actions we would perform and how these actions would reflect upon the national character, his April 30 address indicated, as Gregg and Hauser found, that Nixon also was concerned with the actions that "I" as commander-in-chief had to undertake. He stated several times that the act of invasion might make him a "one-term President." Nevertheless, the president contended, in words that he helped pen,

> I have rejected all political considerations in making this decision. . . . Whether I may be a one-term President is insignificant compared to whether by our failure to act in this crisis the United

States proves itself to be unworthy to lead the forces of freedom in this critical period in world history. I would rather be a one-term President and do what I believe is right than to be a two-term President at the cost of seeing America become a second-rate power.[113]

Nixon claimed that the invasion might "remake" him as an actor: he might become a one-term president. This threat notwithstanding, the president said he would selflessly accept the personal consequences of the sanctuary operation because the act would reflect positively on the United States as a whole.

The style or attitude of Nixon's rhetoric may not seem very different from that of the other presidents examined thus far. Kennedy and Johnson both described the actors of their discourse in glowing terms, just as Nixon did. Moreover, the act-actor ordering of terms typified the style of Johnson's crisis talk and was one of two predominant ratios in Kennedy's style. Regardless of these similarities, however, Nixon's style set his rhetoric apart from that of other presidential crisis promoters. His style contained distinctive incongruities that were rooted in the highly personal quality of his discourse.

One peculiar aspect of Nixon's style was the time and effort he spent denying that political considerations had affected his decision to invade Cambodia. According to Gonchar and Hahn, this depiction of selflessness was a consistent characteristic of all Nixon rhetoric.[114] In his Cambodian discourse, however, the commander-in-chief seemed to emphasize his selflessness in the extreme. As the *Washington Post* observed of Nixon's first speech, "The President devoted so much time to disavowing political motivations that one suspects politics."[115] There was a sense that the president "doth protest too much." The fact that Nixon would not face election again for more than two years made his assertion about the political risk he faced seem hollow. Even members of his own administration thought his claims went too far.[116] In *Six Crises,* Nixon had written that selflessness was the greatest asset a leader could have in the midst of crisis,[117] and his Cambodian crisis discourse seemed to mirror this belief.

Another incongruity of Nixon's style—and one related to the first—was that his discourse frequently contradicted his portrait of himself as a responsible and selfless leader. According to Nixon, the "easy political path" would be "to blame this war on previous administrations,"[118] but this was something that Nixon said he refused to do. In subsequent rhetoric, however, the president was quick to point out that he was not the one responsible for the Vietnam War. He told reporters, for example, "When I came to the Presidency—I did not send these men to Vietnam—there were 525,000 men there. And since I have been here, I have been working 18 or 20 hours a day, mostly on Vietnam, trying to bring these men home."[119] Nixon depicted himself as a victim of circumstances who was making a Herculean effort to clean up the mess that his predecessors had left him.

On another occasion, he said, "as you know, this war, while it was undeclared, was here when I became President of the United States. I do not say that critically. I am simply stating the fact that there were 549,000 Americans in Vietnam under attack when I became President." According to Nixon, it was "under these circumstances, starting at the time I became President" that he had ordered military offensives against the North Vietnamese and Vietcong in order to protect the lives of Americans who were already there. The Cambodian operation, then, was just one more instance of his fulfilling his presidential duties.[120] Although Nixon claimed that he did not intend to be critical, his statement nonetheless served to shift responsibility for the invasion of Cambodia and continuing American involvement in Vietnam to those who preceded him in office.

For one who portrayed himself as selfless, the president seemed inordinately self-centered. His discourse throughout the crisis was full of depictions about what "I" thought and felt, how "I" had made the decision to invade, and the obligations that "I" had. In addition, Nixon seemed just as anxious to prove *his* character as he did that of "we" or the United States.

In his June 3 speech to the nation, Nixon said: "Ask yourselves this question: If *an American President* had failed to meet this threat to 400,000 American men in Vietnam, would those nations and peoples who rely on America's power . . . retain any confidence in the United States?"[121] The president seemed to indicate that it was he who was integral to U.S. credibility, a perspective that heightened his own importance in the crisis over that of the nation he served. This same undercurrent can be seen in Nixon's speech notes to himself during the crisis. On one of the yellow legal pads that Nixon so liked to use, he asked, "Break President?"; on another, he wrote, "I will not be broken."[122]

Although Nixon portrayed himself as a selfless leader who assumed responsibility, the style of his talk indicated that he was frequently self-obsessed and sometimes anxious to make his predecessors accountable for decisions that he had made. As *Newsweek* observed of the president's April 30 announcement, Nixon sounded like "a beleaguered man who had suddenly come to regard foreign challenges as a test of Presidential manhood."[123]

In the situation of his Cambodian rhetoric, Nixon described a crisis scene that was full of inconsistencies and provided an account of his crisis decision-making that also contained a number of contradictions. Stylistically, the president's discourse disavowed political and personal considerations even as he lavished attention on such concerns. The grotesque incongruities of Nixon's rhetoric continued in his identificational appeals. He may have argued that he was impervious to politics, but the president attempted to gain the support of all citizens, including those he had named as domestic subversives. Hence, Nixon simultaneously castigated and appealed to the vocal minority.

Identificational Appeals

In his analysis of Nixon's April 30 speech, Windt argues that antithetical appeals dominated the president's talk.[124] An examination of Nixon's other discourse about the Cambodian crisis indicates that this same identificational strategy characterized his talk as a whole, just as it dominated Kennedy's discourse about the Cuban missile crisis. Unlike Kennedy, however, Nixon employed antithetical appeals in two distinct ways: he attempted to unite all American citizens against Communists in Southeast Asia, and he tried to unite a majority of American citizens against dissenters at home.

The president devoted a great deal of his discourse to the description of an evil Communist foe, as personified by the North Vietnamese and Vietcong. Nixon's initial announcement of the crisis claimed that the enemy "rejects every effort to win a just peace, ignores our warning, tramples on solemn agreements, violates the neutrality of an unarmed people, and uses our prisoners as hostages." Furthermore, both the president's April 30 and June 3 addresses contended that the North Vietnamese and Vietcong had tried to take advantage of the U.S. withdrawal program and that they had placed American soldiers in grave danger.[125]

Nixon's rhetoric made the enemy appear even more evil when he contrasted their behavior with that of the United States. The president claimed—in what he would later admit was a lie—that our country had not moved against the sanctuaries earlier because "we did not wish to violate the territory of a neutral nation." In contrast, North Vietnam "has stripped away all pretense of respecting the sovereignty or the neutrality of Cambodia."[126] Nixon's April 30 speech also contrasted our efforts to end the war with the enemy's reaction to those efforts.

> We have stopped the bombing of North Vietnam. We have cut air operations by over 20 percent. We have announced withdrawal of over 250,000 of our men. We have offered to withdraw all of our men if they will withdraw theirs. We have offered to negotiate all issues with only one condition—and that is that the future of South Vietnam be determined not by North Vietnam, not by the United States, but by the people of South Vietnam themselves.
>
> The answer of the enemy has been intransigence at the conference table, belligerence in Hanoi, massive military aggression in Laos and Cambodia, and stepped-up attacks in South Vietnam, designed to increase American casualties.[127]

Through such language, Nixon's discourse attempted to unite *all* American citizens against the evil North Vietnamese and Vietcong. Such a strategy was not surprising. For thousands of years, leaders have exhorted their fellow citizens to fight common enemies. The unusual aspect of Nixon's rhetorical strategy was that he coupled it with antithetical appeals aimed against American citizens.

In his early discourse about the crisis, the president strongly attacked domestic critics of his policies. For instance, Nixon had Pat Buchanan add to his initial speech a passage that compared his decision to invade Cambodia with the crisis decisions that previous U.S. presidents had made. Despite the similarities, Nixon bitterly observed, "In those decisions, the American people were not assailed by counsels of doubt and defeat from some of the most widely known opinion leaders of the Nation."[128] The president also launched barbs against student protestors; he warned of anarchy "at home" and the systematic destruction of "great universities."[129] One day after his invasion announcement, Nixon visited the Pentagon where he denounced student radicals as "these bums . . . blowing up the campuses."[130] The president's terse statement on Kent State was also less than sympathetic toward the victims and their families; it warned that "when dissent turns to violence, it invites tragedy."[131]

Throughout his discourse, Nixon employed antithetical appeals as a way to unite U.S. citizens behind him and his policies. The president simultaneously attempted to unite the majority of citizens against fellow citizens who dissented. Among this book's case studies of contemporary crisis promotion, Nixon's combination of these appeals was unique. Most presidents apparently preferred to unite their constituents against a foreign—and distant—foe, rather than stir up animosity among Americans at home.

Although Nixon's strategy of polarization may have been unusual for presidential crisis promoters, it was not unusual for him personally. He had, after all, begun his career on the House Un-American Activities Committee. In *Presidents and Protesters,* Windt points out that people supported Nixon "mainly because he *opposed specific things.* Realizing that people become politically active when they are agitated about something, Nixon rode the crest of those resentments to the presidency."[132] The analysis of Nixon's Cambodian rhetoric indicates that he exploited such resentments once he was in the White House as well.

By combining antithetical appeals aimed against Vietnamese Communists with those hurled against American dissenters, Nixon encouraged the silent majority to become as agitated and active as protestors were. Even if Middle America did not vocalize its support, Nixon could still claim that consensus was on his side since the "majority" was "silent." The impact of the president's discordant antithetical appeals may have been to unite members of the silent majority more closely, both in their support of him and in their opposition to dissenters at home, and to alienate even further those who disagreed with his policies.

In addition to antithetical appeals, Nixon employed extensive explicit appeals in a number of ways. First, he appealed to all American citizens through an emphasis on his constitutional authority and responsibilities. At a news conference, he told reporters, "As Commander in Chief, I have found for 525,000 Americans it has been my responsibility to do everything I could to protect their lives and to get them home as quickly as I can."[133] On two occasions, Nixon made links between his decision on Cambodia and the decisions that revered presidents of both parties had made during past foreign conflicts. His April 30 address, for example, discussed the policy decision he had made and then observed:

> In this room, Woodrow Wilson made the great decisions which led to victory in World War I. Franklin Roosevelt made the decisions which led to our victory in World War II. Dwight D. Eisenhower made decisions which ended the war in Korea and avoided war in the Middle East. John F. Kennedy, in his finest hour, made the great decision which removed Soviet nuclear missiles from Cuba and the Western Hemisphere.[134]

Seated in the Oval Office where other extraordinary decisions had been made, Nixon associated himself with the greatness of the Democratic and Republican presidential heroes he described and aligned his decision with their successes.

Nixon also made explicit appeals based on his presidential office and authority when he mentioned at various times the promises he had made to the American people during his campaign and first year in the White House. In his second major speech on the crisis, Nixon said:

> Let us look at the record.
>
> In June of 1969, I pledged a withdrawal of 25,000 troops. They came home. In September of the same year I said I would bring home an additional 35,000. They came home. In December I said an additional 50,000 Americans were coming out of Vietnam. They, too, have come home.
>
> There is one commitment yet to be fulfilled. I have pledged to end this war. I shall keep that promise.[135]

Nixon cited his presidential accomplishments as a means to reassure citizens that the Cambodian invasion did not mean a longer war. In the past, the president had made pledges and fulfilled them; he argued that he would do so again.

Beyond these broad, explicit appeals based on his office, Nixon also made a concerted effort to appeal directly to his silent majority supporters. In his June 3 speech, for instance, Nixon expressed his "deep appreciation to the millions of Americans" who had supported him and the Cambodian operation.[136] Similarly, in his initial announcement of the invasion, the president stated:

> Now let me give you the reasons for my decision.
> A majority of the American people, a majority of you listening to me, are for the withdrawal of our forces from Vietnam. The action I have taken tonight is indispensable for the continuing success of that withdrawal program.
> A majority of the American people want to end this war rather than to have it drag on interminably. The action I have taken tonight will serve that purpose.
> A majority of the American people want to keep the casualties of our brave men in Vietnam at an absolute minimum. The action I take tonight is essential if we are to accomplish that goal.[137]

Through such appeals, Nixon told the silent majority what their goals were, depicted these goals as ones with which no reasonable person would disagree—who, for example, would want the war to last longer than necessary?—and then told the silent majority that his acts would accomplish these goals. Because Nixon connected his policy to what the "majority of the American people" wanted, the president also talked as if the invasion already had widespread support. Nixon reinforced this idea in his July 1 interview with Smith, Sevareid, and Chancellor when he said, "a majority of the American people, even in this difficult period, have seemed to support me."[138]

Yet another example of the administration's explicit appeals to the silent majority came after blue-collar workers held rallies in support of the president. Over the objections of Assistant for Domestic Affairs John Ehrlichman and Secretary of Labor George Schultz, Nixon invited construction and longshoremen union members to the White House for a much-publicized visit. The president briefed the men on Cambodia and thanked them for their "very meaningful" public demonstration of support. The invited guests attached an American flag pin to Nixon's lapel and presented him with a hard hat of his own that had the words "Commander-in-Chief" emblazoned across the front.[139]

The fact that several hard hat workers had beaten up war protestors in previous weeks during pro-Nixon marches lent a subtle antithetical cast to the president's overt attempts to reach out to blue-collar Americans. After the demonstrations and counterdemonstrations of early May, Tom Huston, the coordinator for security affairs at the White House, had written a memo to the president and his men about how "we need to quit talking about the great Silent

Majority and start talking to it."[140] With the organizational help of Special Counsel Chuck Colson, Nixon followed Huston's advice. The president also referred to "a union leader from New York" in his June 3 address as a credible figure who had endorsed his Cambodian policy.[141]

At first blush, Nixon's explicit identificational strategy seemed quite ordinary. Based on his constitutional role and responsibilities, he petitioned all Americans. Furthermore, he made overt entreaties to citizens, such as blue-collar workers, who composed a special constituency for him. If the president's explicit appeals to the silent majority sometimes had an antithetical tinge to them, this, too, was consistent with Nixon's typical rhetorical posture. As with the situation and style of his discourse, though, the president's explicit identificational strategy resembled the grotesque.

The glaring contradiction of Nixon's explicit appeals lay in his attempts to reach out to student protestors. Despite his earlier descriptions of students as subversives, Nixon began, several days after Kent State, to make direct appeals to them. At a May 8 news conference, the president asserted, "Those who protest want peace. They want to reduce American casualties and they want our boys brought home. I made the decision, however, for the very reasons they are protesting."[142] Nixon portrayed student protestors—the anarchists of his initial announcement—as individuals who had the same goals that Nixon claimed he and the majority of Americans had. Nixon continued such explicit appeals when he met with university presidents, brought six Kent State University students to the White House, and publicly made a commitment to improve communication efforts with university students and administrators.[143]

These efforts were surpassed, however, by one of the most bizarre communication events in presidential history: a discussion between student protestors and the president, who had decided to pay a surprise sunrise visit to the Lincoln Memorial just prior to a major peace demonstration. By Nixon's own account, he had been on the phone until 2:15 on the morning of May 9; he then slept until shortly before 4:00 A.M., when he awoke and spoke with his valet Manolo Sanchez. Sanchez, it turned out, had never been to the Lincoln Memorial at night, and the president decided to rectify this situation. He and his valet left for the Lincoln Memorial at 4:35 A.M. with nervous Secret Service agents in tow.

According to Nixon, he told students gathered at the Memorial that he "came from a Quaker background" and as a young person he had been "as close to being a pacifist as anybody could be." The president also discussed such varied topics as his support for environmental issues and civil rights for ethnic minorities, how the hometown of one of the protestors was a favorite of his, and places he thought the students should visit. Nixon told the young people that he hoped their protest would not turn into hatred for their country. In what had to be one of the president's most overt and amusing attempts to appeal explicitly to the students, he said, "I know that probably most of you think I'm an S.O.B. but I want you to know that I understand just how you feel." The visit to Lincoln Memorial ended with Nixon posing for a photograph with one of the bearded protestors.[144]

Afterward, to complete his odd sojourn, the president took Sanchez, along with the Secret Service agents and the aides who had gathered, to the chamber of the House of Representatives where they had Sanchez sit in the Speaker's chair while they applauded. The group then went to the Mayflower restaurant for a breakfast of corned beef hash. Once they returned to the White House, the president, in true Nixonian fashion, wrote an account of it all, which Ron Ziegler released to the press.[145] Later, when media coverage of that evening's events were not as positive as Nixon desired, he wrote to Haldeman that it was "*our* P.R. failure."[146] For a time at least, Nixon's inconsistent use of explicit appeals cast student protestors as no different from "the majority of Americans."

These conflicting appeals may be explained, in part, by the president's own conflicting attitudes toward those who dissented from his policies, particularly young people. Immediately after Nixon announced the Cambodian invasion, he, Haldeman, and others discussed how "we *have* to go on [the] offensive against peaceniks" and how the administration could turn student protests to its advantage.[147] According to the president and his men, it also was "time for Goldwater, Reagan, inflammatory types to attack Senate doves—for knife in back disloyalty—lack of patriotism."[148]

The events at Kent State on May 4 seemed to shock Nixon, however, for Haldeman's notes of their daily meetings show a sudden shift in strategy. For instance, the president wanted Vice President Spiro Agnew, the resident offensive lineman, to say nothing about student protests and to be more conciliatory. Nixon and his aides even talked about whether there was a way to hook up universities by television so the president could answer questions. According to Haldeman's May 6 notes, "somebody around here has *got* to emote."[149]

Nixon's gentler approach was relatively short lived, and by May 12, the president and his aides were examining the possibility of withdrawing defense money from universities that had been sympathetic to the protestors' cause. Later, Colson would investigate how the administration could strip universities of their tax-exempt status.[150] Publicly, the White House focused its attentions on the silent majority and mounted "an all-out attack on critics."[151] Simultaneously, it went through the motions of attending to students.

The minutes from one meeting suggested that the administration "about once a week put out something re what P. has done re students—ie a new report— May, etc./so it looks like we're staying in touch."[152] Perhaps Haldeman signaled the shift in focus most clearly when he recorded on May 11, "re kids/ get them out of their self torturing self-pitying attitudes & see the world as it is/ no one [is] lining up for [a] passport to leave."[153]

From start to finish, the identificational appeals in Nixon's crisis rhetoric were idiosyncratic. The president appealed to *all* citizens through an antithetical strategy, which pitted Americans against Communists, and an explicit strategy, which relied on Nixon's office and authority. At the same time, the president encouraged polarization among Americans by employing an antithetical strategy that attempted to unite the majority of citizens against American dissenters and an explicit strategy that joined Nixon's interests with those of the majority. This stance, while peculiar for presidential crisis promoters, was typical of much of Nixon's rhetoric during his political career.

Just as *Six Crises* portrayed Nixon as one who enjoyed the agony that crises bring, the commander-in-chief's crisis discourse likewise seemed to reveal a rhetor who throve upon conflict. Nixon's assistant preserved a private instance of such sentiments when he recorded the president's position at a staff meeting: "don't worry about divisiveness/we've created division—drawn the sword/ don't take it out—grind it hard."[154] The polarizations that, Nixon claimed, plagued him politically were also frequently of his own making. More than anything else, however, the truly perplexing part of the president's discourse was his attempt to identify explicitly with student protestors, those individuals that he previously had referred to as bums and anarchists. Nixon alternately attacked dissenters and aligned himself with them.

Throughout his rhetoric on the Cambodian crisis, Nixon spoke in the constant incongruities of the grotesque. The situation, style, and identificational strategies of his discourse were composed of terms and appeals that did not seem strange in and of themselves, but that were combined in peculiar and distinctive ways. Just as Frankenstein's monster appeared to be human and inhuman at the same time, Nixon's crisis rhetoric seemed both credible and incredible. And just like Frankenstein's monster, Nixon's discourse was assembled from various parts that did not match.

REFLECTIONS OF THE GROTESQUE

The comparison of Nixon's Cambodian discourse with the grotesque, a poetic structure that deals with incongruous monstrosities, may shed light upon his other presidential rhetoric, for numerous observers claim that Nixon often spoke incongruently. Hinds and Smith, for instance, write that "Nixspeak" was a "rhetoric of opposites."[155] Garry Wills notes that Nixon's "last press conference," following his defeat in the 1962 California gubernatorial election, actually alternated between condemnation and praise for the media, such that one could not be separated from the other.[156] According to communication scholar Robert Scott, Nixon's first inaugural was full of unresolved tensions, and Karlyn Kohrs Campbell and William Benoit each contend that the president's talk about Vietnam and Watergate, respectively, was contradictory.[157]

Rhetorical critic Carol Jablonski asserts that Nixon managed to turn what should have been a somber occasion, the resignation of Spiro Agnew, into a celebration or Irish wake.[158] Edwin Black comments that the president's talk was frequently paradoxical, and Ted Windt claims that Nixon was "a complex mass of contradictions."[159] More than any of these authors, Hart perhaps best sums up Nixon's rhetoric when he says, "Like Iago, Richard Nixon was consistently inconsistent."[160] The evidence from these other studies indicates that Nixon's habitual attitude, or style, may have resembled the grotesque. The president may have been—to adapt a phrase from Burke—a "modern linguistic gargoyle."[161]

If such evidence is correct, the grotesque also may explain why people love to hate Richard Nixon. Hart observes that no modern president has seemed "so ripe for parody even by amateur parodists," and he asserts that the many parodies of Nixon center around his rhetorical personality.[162] According to Thomson, the grotesque is related to parody. Citizens who despised Nixon may have been frightened by the habitual unresolved incongruities of his talk, and these same characteristics provided tempting targets for ridicule. In the case of Nixon's Cambodian rhetoric, Thomson's observation may be the most insightful. The real meaning of the grotesque, he contends, is that "the vale of tears and the circus are one, that tragedy is in some ways comic and all comedy in some way tragic and pathetic."[163]

In the wake of the 1970 U.S. invasion, the vale of tears came to reign for many years in Cambodia. When U.S. troops withdrew on June 30, Cambodia was left with virtually no defense against Communist soldiers, and Khmer Rouge forces captured Phnom Penh on April 17, 1975. The Pol Pot regime proceeded to murder as many as two million Cambodians—one-quarter of the population—over the next three years.[164] In 1982, Kissinger fixed the blame for this turn of events squarely on North Vietnam, the "master architect of disaster"; he said America had failed not by doing too much but by doing "too little."[165]

Conversely, critics like Shawcross claimed that it was the American invasion that brought the war to Cambodia. Shawcross argued that Nixon and Kissinger had committed a "crime" when they "consciously sacrificed" Cambodia for their own interests.[166] Just like Nixon's discourse on the crisis, interpretations of the impact of U.S. policy on Cambodia were wrought with conflict.

The Cambodian crisis also prompted congressional attempts to curb presidential power, but these attempts corresponded—incongruously—with the expansion of presidential power over crisis promotion. On May 1, 1970, the Senate Foreign Relations Committee approved a concurrent resolution that would terminate the legislative legacy of the Gulf of Tonkin: the Southeast Asia Resolution. Ten days later, the Committee approved the Cooper-Church amendment to the Foreign Military Sales Act. The amendment prohibited the use of funds to support U.S. ground troops in Cambodia, American advisers in that country, or Cambodia's own military forces.[167] This flurry of legislative activity indicated that Congress would wrest back from the presidency at least some control over foreign policy. In the end, however, almost nothing changed.

Nixon had long maintained that the Southeast Asia Resolution was irrelevant because of the immense prerogative powers he held as commander-in-chief. Nevertheless, Nixon did not want a great deal of public attention given to a repeal, so he had Republican senator Robert Dole attach the rescission to a military sales bill *before* the repeal could be brought up separately for a vote. According to Austin, Nixon's move ensured that the rescission received little notice and also reinforced the president's assertion that the resolution had no bearing on his powers as commander-in-chief. Nixon continued to rely on his prerogative powers and conducted policy in Southeast Asia as he had in the past.[168]

The other attempt to curb the president's power met a similar fate. By the time the vote on Cooper-Church began, Nixon had already withdrawn troops from Cambodia; the amendment passed on June 30, 1970, but did not become law until 1971.[169] As with the repeal of the Southeast Asia Resolution, the Cooper-Church amendment changed events relatively little. The amendment did not prevent the United States from bombing Cambodia in order to halt Communist forces and supplies headed toward South Vietnam; this loophole allowed the Nixon administration to conduct overtly a policy begun covertly two years earlier.[170] In addition, the Defense Department regularly violated Cooper-Church.[171] Congressional critics may have won legislative victories over the presidential power to conduct war, but Nixon made sure that little of the legislation became enacted as policy.

Later, of course, Nixon's Cambodian policies would contribute to his downfall. In 1973, the White House officially acknowledged the secret bombing of Cambodia, which increased the demands for Nixon's impeachment. Moreover, the Watergate hearings revealed that Nixon had developed a surveillance program for domestic critics after senators had begun to oppose him on Cambodia. This revelation provoked further condemnation.[172]

Despite Nixon's personal misfortunes, the presidential power to promote and manage crises remained intact. In 1973, Congress passed the War Powers Resolution, which was intended to limit the president's right to commit troops abroad without the approval of Congress. Two years later, when Nixon's successor, Gerald Ford, promoted and managed a crisis of his own, he demonstrated that the resolution did little more than formalize the expansive prerogative powers contemporary presidents had already assumed.

Chapter Five

THE QUIET MAN
Ford's Portrayal of Leadership During the *Mayaguez* Crisis

In the spring of 1975, the Vietnam War was about to end and with it, a long and tragic chapter in the history of both Southeast Asia and the United States. American combat involvement in Vietnam had officially concluded in 1973, but the United States still attached strategic and emotional significance to the region. Nearly 58,000 Americans had died there, and billions of dollars had been spent for the war effort. Despite these sacrifices, a Communist victory was at hand. The United States' worst fears were realized when Phnom Penh fell to the Khmer Rouge on April 17, and Saigon collapsed to Communist forces thirteen days later.[1]

For many Americans, the United States' hasty evacuation from Southeast Asia—immortalized by photographs of U.S. helicopters on Saigon rooftops—was fraught with humiliation. The abandonment of American embassies in Cambodia and South Vietnam focused attention on Southeast Asia and underscored America's defeat. At home, the nation's unelected president, Gerald R. Ford, presided over the foreign policy debacle. He said that the war was "finished as far as America is concerned" and encouraged citizens "to avoid recrimination about the past."[2] As if the war's end were not tumultuous enough, however, the United States soon found itself embroiled in yet another foreign crisis.

On May 12, 1975, White House Press Secretary Ron Nessen announced that Khmer Rouge forces had seized an American merchant ship, the *Mayaguez,* while it traveled on "the high seas" in the Gulf of Thailand.[3] The Ford administration reportedly attempted diplomacy to free the ship, but finally resorted to a military rescue mission. On the evening of May 14, the *Mayaguez* crew was released unharmed. U.S. citizens and members of Congress reacted ecstatically. From the jaws of America's Vietnam defeat, the nation had snatched a minor victory.[4]

Commanders-in-chief typically talk about the foreign crises they and the nation face. According to rhetorical critics Jeff Bass and Gerard Hauser, one reason for this is that presidents have a great deal of control over foreign policy and over the interpretation of that policy's success. Foreign crises thereby allow presidents to portray themselves as wise, efficient leaders.[5] Certainly, other occupants of the Oval Office have seized upon crises as the opportunity to strike a presidential pose through stirring public talk. Kennedy, Johnson, and Nixon all appeared on television to announce crises in Cuba, the Gulf of Tonkin, and Cambodia, respectively. And each of these presidents engaged in public rhetoric once his foreign crisis had been resolved. Presidents Jimmy Carter and Ronald Reagan also spoke volumes about crisis events that were similar, in many ways, with the circumstances that Ford faced. From 1979 through 1981, Carter attempted to resolve a hostage situation in Iran through diplomacy and a military rescue mission, whereas Reagan dealt with a short-term crisis in Grenada in 1983 when he launched a military operation in order to forestall the taking of American hostages on the island.

In contrast with these five other presidents, Ford's initial promotion of the *Mayaguez* crisis violated the expected form. Rather than make a dramatic public announcement about the ship's seizure, Ford said absolutely nothing. This is not to imply that no discourse emanated from the White House. Ford's press secretary, Ron Nessen, acted as the president's surrogate, providing the public with brief updates throughout the crisis and subsequent rescue mission. More importantly for Ford, his press secretary's rhetoric focused upon the president as a competent and capable leader firmly in control of the situation. Ford's silence was not meaningless. To paraphrase Robert Scott, in remaining silent, the president still spoke.[6]

Once the crisis had been resolved, Ford broke his silence and made several short public statements. The president appeared on television for a few minutes to announce the rescue of the crew, and he commented briefly about the *Mayaguez* in the months that followed. Throughout his sparse public talk about this crisis, Ford concentrated almost exclusively on what the crisis said about him as president and thereby reinforced the meaning of his initial silence. The success of the *Mayaguez* crisis may have helped Americans feel better about their national character, but Ford's silence and subsequent talk about this crisis emphasized his own presidential character. Just as other presidents have used discourse to manage their image of leadership, Ford used a combination of silence, followed by economical public statements, to do the same.

Ford's resolution of the *Mayaguez* crisis also marked a major test of the War Powers Resolution, which Congress had passed in 1973 to end unilateral executive decisions on matters of war and peace. At the time of the *Mayaguez,* Frank Church and Jacob Javits, two Senate sponsors of the legislation, agreed that Ford had complied with the War Powers Resolution during the crisis. Senator Mike Mansfield took a different view. He insisted that Congress had no voice in the decision to rescue the crew and that "we were informed, not consulted."[7] Contrary to its authors' purpose, the War Powers Resolution legitimized prerogative powers and gave commanders-in-chief the authority to engage in acts of war. The *Mayaguez* crisis bears testament to this legal precedent.

Just as the War Powers Resolution increased presidential power, Ford's unique approach to communication about the *Mayaguez* crisis improved his personal presidential image by depicting him as a strong, forceful leader and viable candidate for 1976. In my analysis of the *Mayaguez* crisis, I answer the question of how Ford communicated such messages through his combination of silence and sparse public talk. During the crisis itself, the president's surrogates portrayed Ford as a competent leader who had events under control, and his own discourse after the crisis reinforced such depictions. The situation of Ford's discourse centered upon the president and his administration and the actions they took, rather than upon the crisis scene, the nation's purpose, or some other element. In the style of his rhetoric, Ford continued this theme, emphasizing how the successful management of the *Mayaguez* crisis reflected favorably upon the character of the Ford administration. The president also encouraged citizens to identify with him and his crisis resolution almost exclusively through explicit appeals that, again, focused upon him: his office, his duties, and his responsibility for the successful rescue of the *Mayaguez* crew.

In this chapter, I examine the rhetorical context of the *Mayaguez* crisis, Ford's employment of silence and subsequent public talk, and how this particular crisis expanded presidential power over matters of war and peace.

THE RHETORICAL CONTEXT OF THE *MAYAGUEZ* CRISIS

Gerald Ford entered the White House under trying political circumstances. Nixon picked Ford as his vice president in 1973 when then-Vice President Spiro Agnew entered a plea of nolo contendere to income tax evasion and stepped down. In August 1974, Nixon resigned rather than face impeachment over the Watergate scandal, and Ford became the nation's first chief executive not to be elected either to the presidency or to the vice presidency.[8] Because of this, Ford began his term without the advantage of an electoral mandate and the added legitimacy it bestows. The president's position was made even worse by the monumental problems the nation faced.

Domestically, the United States suffered from the final throes of Watergate and from increasingly high inflation. Ford's attempts to resolve these issues often seemed to exacerbate them instead. In September 1974, the president appeared on television to grant Nixon a complete pardon. Ford's approval rating plunged. A Phillips-Sindlinger survey noted, "Ford is the *first* President in memory to trigger a negative job rating by the end of his first month in office."[9] The president's attempts to conquer inflation met a similar fate. In what Ford himself would later call a "gimmicky" campaign, the president donned a WIN button and urged citizens to Whip Inflation Now. Reactions to the war on inflation included criticisms about its simplicity and, perhaps worse, jokes about its corniness. Even some of Ford's own aides referred to one presidential address on inflation as the "lick-your-plate-clean" speech.[10]

On the issue of Vietnam, the president fared no better. The military predicament in Cambodia and South Vietnam deteriorated daily, and by the spring of 1975, Communist victories seemed imminent. As enemy forces encircled Phnom Penh and Saigon, U.S. helicopters hurriedly evacuated Americans and many of those who had worked with them. The hasty and unceremonious retreat raised questions about the United States' reliability as an ally. Furthermore, many Americans felt humiliated and demoralized by their country's much-publicized defeat. Ford assured citizens, however, that "America can regain the sense of pride that existed before Vietnam. But it cannot be achieved by refighting a war that is finished."[11] In the spring of 1975, Americans lamented their country's plight, and the new president attempted, as best he could, to console his fellow citizens.

On May 12, less than two weeks after the fall of Saigon, the United States suddenly found itself faced with yet another foreign crisis: the Communist Khmer Rouge had captured an American merchant ship, the *Mayaguez,* about sixty miles from the coast of Cambodia near the Wai Islands. The ship was a commercial vehicle owned by Sea-Land Service, Inc., a subsidiary of R. J. Reynolds Industries, and was run by a forty-man crew. On its way from Hong Kong to Sattahip, Thailand, the *Mayaguez* carried general cargo for American soldiers and embassy officials in Thailand. The reason for the ship's seizure was not clear.[12]

In Washington, Ford reacted quickly to the news. He later recalled, "My feeling was that seizure of a U.S. vessel and crew, especially by a country which had so recently humiliated us, was a very serious matter."[13] Ford concerned himself with the same issue of credibility that Nixon had raised during the invasion of Cambodia five years earlier. The *Mayaguez* incident also conjured up images of the 1968 *Pueblo* disaster, in which North Korea had captured eighty-three Americans at sea and imprisoned them for eleven months. In a press briefing after the crisis, Press Secretary Nessen admitted that "the *Pueblo* episode was in people's minds here" during the crisis.[14]

To avoid a repetition of history, Ford instructed the State Department to demand the ship's immediate release. Diplomacy was problematic because the United States had no relations with the new Khmer Rouge regime, so State Department officials asked China to deliver the message. Meanwhile, Ford put American military forces in the Western Pacific on alert and sent 1,100 marines to Utapao Air Base in Thailand. Nessen announced the ship's seizure to the press.[15]

Over the course of the next few days, the Cambodians kept their captives constantly on the move. Initially, the *Mayaguez* anchored at Koh Tang Island, about thirty miles from the mainland port of Kompong Som, formerly called Sihanoukville. The Cambodians then put the crew on a fishing boat and headed for Kompong Som. United States planes strafed and gassed the boat, but could not turn it back. Unknown to Washington, the Cambodians later took the crew to Koh Rang Island, about fifteen miles west of Kompong Som.[16]

By the afternoon of May 14, some two days after the initial seizure, Ford believed a diplomatic end to the crisis was unlikely. China had refused to deliver U.S. messages to Cambodia. To make matters worse, the United States was uncertain of the crew's whereabouts. Given the dire situation, Ford decided to launch a military rescue mission. He ordered the destroyer escort *Holt* to wrest control of the *Mayaguez,* the marines to land on Koh Tang Island in search of the crew, and the carrier *Coral Sea* to carry out air strikes against military installations on the Cambodian mainland.[17]

After the orders were executed, Ford briefed congressional leaders on his decision. Three Democratic senators—Mike Mansfield, Robert Byrd, and John McClellan—voiced their disapproval of the planned air strikes; the president defended the attacks as essential to prevent Cambodian reinforcements from attacking the marines on Koh Tang. According to Nessen, the argument was superfluous since Ford had already issued the orders.[18]

Indeed, the operation was well underway. Marines from the *Holt* had recaptured the *Mayaguez,* only to find no crew on board. Other marines were pinned down in heavy combat on Koh Tang. In the meantime, the Cambodians had released their captives and put the men in a fishing boat to make their way back to the *Mayaguez.* The destroyer *Wilson* intercepted the fishing boat one hour and eleven minutes after marines had landed on Koh Tang. Because Washington was unaware of the *Mayaguez* crew's release, air strikes against an oil depot at Kompong Som and the airfield at Ream took place as scheduled. Around 11:00 P.M., the Pentagon informed Ford that the *Mayaguez* crew was safe. The president then ordered the withdrawal of the marines on Koh Tang.[19]

Although the marines suffered many casualties, news of the successful mission met with widespread public and congressional support. The White House received thousands of letters, calls, and telegrams in favor of Ford's crisis management, and opinion polls showed the president's stock on the rise. In Congress, liberal Democrats and conservative Republicans alike offered words of praise for the president.[20] Ford's supporters undoubtedly were pleased that the *Mayaguez* crew was safe, but underlying the enthusiastic reactions was a sense that America had somehow restored its national credibility. *U.S. News and World Report* claimed that the president's response "was meant as a signal to U.S. allies and adversaries. In essence: Don't take us lightly. The humiliating setbacks in Indo-China . . . have not paralyzed America's will to play its role as a global power."[21]

Other observers sounded almost gleeful. According to Senator Barry Goldwater, if Ford had "not done what he did, every little half-assed nation in the world would be taking shots at us, and I think now they're going to think twice before they try it." Journalist Hugh Sidey echoed this sentiment when he called the crisis "a lovely bit of rascality," and a senior State Department official referred to the operation as "our thirty seconds over Tokyo."[22] The Cambodian Communists may have humiliated America only a few weeks before, but the *Mayaguez* crisis had provided the United States with an opportunity to fight back and win at least a minor victory.

Public support for the rescue mission and the commander-in-chief who launched it was only natural given the rally effect that foreign crises induce in public opinion polls. What was different about the *Mayaguez* crisis was the way in which President Ford promoted it. Unlike other contemporary presidents, Ford did not make a dramatic public announcement of the crisis. On the contrary, until the *Mayaguez* crew was safe, the president said nothing. One reason may have been Ford's belief that action was preferable to rhetoric. In *A Time to Heal,* Ford recalled his concern about U.S. credibility after the fall of Phnom Penh and Saigon, then said, "Rhetoric alone, I knew, would not persuade anyone that America would stand firm. They would have to see proof of our resolve." According to the president, the opportunity to provide that proof came with the Cambodian seizure of the *Mayaguez* and its crew.[23]

Ford remained silent, allowing others to speak for him throughout the *Mayaguez* seizure. Once the crew was safe, he talked publicly about the crisis, but even then his comments were few in number and quite brief. To dismiss the president's silence would be a mistake, for both his silence and his words served to portray him as a competent leader. Indeed, the analysis of Ford's crisis communication shows that public talk should not be valued for its own sake. As Pindar once observed, "full oft is silence the wisest thing for a man to heed."[24]

SILENCE AND SPEECH:
FORD'S PROMOTION OF THE *MAYAGUEZ* CRISIS

Gerald Ford may have spoken disparagingly of rhetoric in his memoirs, but the president and his aides paid a great deal of attention to his public persuasion. According to Rod Hart, the record shows that Ford spoke publicly more frequently than any president from Harry Truman through Ronald Reagan, an especially noteworthy feat when one considers the brief time that Ford served. Hart argues that the president and his aides, fully aware that Ford lacked an electoral mandate, settled on speechmaking as a way for Ford to display his leadership.[25]

Along with the administration's recognition that speechmaking was important, however, came the realization that the president was not gifted in this area. Ford and his staff took steps to compensate for this. The president hired Bob Orben, a former comedy writer for Red Skelton, to give him advice. In memos marked "administratively confidential" and initialed "GRF," Orben suggested that the president grasp the podium when he spoke to emphasize a "sense of bigness and strength," that he smile without laughing or showing his teeth, and that he consider a voice coach akin to "Prof. Henry Higgins in *My Fair Lady*" to help him develop vocal variety.[26]

Ford was especially pleased when Orben told the administration to emphasize the president's great sex appeal and to stop defending Ford in response to jokes about his clumsiness. In a passage that today would make Ronald Reagan's admirers chuckle, Orben wrote that Reagan posed no political challenge to Ford because "*Bedtime for Bonzo* and selling borax for Death Valley Days will last longer as a joke subject than the current stumbling fad. Anyone can and has stumbled. Hardly any Presidents have been foster father to a chimpanzee."[27]

If Ford felt unsure of his communicative abilities, then much of Orben's advice, albeit well-intentioned, may have added to the president's lack of confidence. As early as April 1975, Ford's adviser remarked that his public comments needed to be briefer. This theme was repeated in the months ahead. Orben even went so far as to time Ford's answers at press conferences and praised the president when his average answer went from seventy-eight seconds to only thirty-six seconds.

For public speeches, Orben suggested a wrist alarm that would vibrate to signal Ford to stop.[28] Finally, he argued that perhaps other people should speak up for the president at public meetings and banquets and in endorsements. According to the former comedy writer, "The concentration should not be on the greats of yesteryear which would tend to be counterproductive, but the people who influence their peer groups today. . . . Robert Redford, Woody Allen, Mary Tyler Moore, Valerie Harper, Rich Little."[29] In all of these comments, one can discern apprehension over Ford's communicative abilities and, simultaneously, a recognition that communication was central to establishing his image as a leader.

Public appearances provided the opportunity for citizens to witness Ford—in person and through the media coverage his speeches drew—enacting the role of president through his talk. Despite his weaknesses as a rhetor, the president doggedly continued with his frequent public speeches and did his best to improve. Hart points out, nonetheless, that Ford's "quantity of speech hardly contributed to quality—of language or ideas."[30]

Ford's need for communication, coupled with his inability to communicate particularly well, raises an intriguing question: why would the president choose to remain silent during a foreign crisis? After all, crises cede a great deal of control to presidential rhetors. Commanders-in-chief have immediate access to nationwide television during emergencies, which means that their message will get wide dissemination. Moreover, television allows them to speak directly to the American people without the distractions and alternative interpretations of events that a live audience, such as reporters, might interject. Foreign crises prompt citizens to support the president and therefore to think of him as their president. Chief executives can further encourage this during crises by speaking authoritatively in their role as commander-in-chief.

Given all these benefits, the *Mayaguez* crisis would appear to have been an ideal opportunity for Ford to speak and to enhance his image as a leader, but he refrained from doing so. One explanation of the president's behavior that might be proffered is that he was hesitant to talk because the outcome of the crisis was uncertain. Rather than give a great deal of attention to a potential failure— particularly on the heels of Saigon—Ford may have chosen to downplay the *Mayaguez* crisis, thus reducing the risk of additional damage to America's ego and to the nation's credibility abroad.

Such a strategy would also allow him to decrease the negative repercussions a crisis failure would have on perceptions of his own leadership skills. But this hypothesis does not provide a complete answer to the president's unusual behavior. Even after the crisis ended successfully, Ford bypassed the opportunity to celebrate through extensive rhetoric, saying little, even when public discourse might have served to bolster the nation's spirits and credibility, and, concomitantly, his own public image.

Ron Nessen offers another explanation for the president's silence and sparse public talk. According to the press secretary, "Ford preferred to make his big decisions in an atmosphere of calm deliberation. Throughout the *Mayaguez* episode, Ford appeared cool, precise, and very low-key. Just as he rarely showed anger . . . he remained impassive during crises no matter how intense the pressures."[31] Nessen claimed the president's unique approach to crisis communication had its basis in the man himself.

A third explanation, and one compatible with the other two, is that silence afforded the president a number of advantages. According to rhetorical critics Keith Erickson and Wallace Schmidt, "silence during a national emergency can create a 'social reality' of a duty-bound president whose behavior and symbolic activities demonstrate leadership, a role reminder of what the presidency can be."[32] In the case of the *Mayaguez* crisis, Ford delegated rhetorical tasks to other members of his administration who, in turn, portrayed the president as busily involved in behind-the-scenes efforts at crisis resolution. The benefit of this strategy for Ford was that he avoided the discomfort of a public speech in which he might have sounded less than eloquent or made a verbal gaffe. At the same time, his surrogate speakers depicted him as an active, competent commander-in-chief who had the crisis under control.

Ron Nessen, for example, served as Ford's chief spokesperson throughout the crisis and announced the *Mayaguez* seizure with the following statement: "We have been informed that a Cambodian naval vessel has seized an American merchant ship on the high seas and forced it to the port of Kompong Som. The President has met with the NSC. He considers this seizure an act of piracy. He has instructed the State Department to demand the immediate release of the ship. Failure to do so would have the most serious consequences."[33]

In this discourse, terms that described the crisis scene were followed with references to the president and the actions he had taken. Nessen's rhetoric associated the need for crisis resolution with the crisis management of President Ford. In other statements the press secretary made, Ford was also the dominant figure. Nessen described the scene off the coast of Cambodia, for instance, and then noted, "the President was kept informed of developments during the night." Similarly, Nessen announced that Ford had directed the military to launch a rescue operation.[34]

At a news briefing, the press secretary provided reporters with a timetable of the president's activities, including the fact that he had been briefed on the crisis throughout the night and then had awakened for good at 5:20 A.M. which, according to Nessen, was his usual time.[35] The press secretary portrayed Ford as a capable, alert commander-in-chief who was clearly in command.

Other surrogates in the administration reinforced this depiction. According to Robert Hartmann, one of Ford's speechwriters and an old friend, Nessen tried to "muzzle" the State and Defense Departments to prevent them from giving statements to the press.[36] State Department spokesman Robert Funseth constantly told reporters, "This has been a presidential action, and I refer you to the White House for comment." After a National Security Council meeting, Secretary of State Henry Kissinger flew to Missouri. His conspicuous absence from Washington again underscored Ford's leadership. According to journalist Roy Rowan, "The president wanted it known that he personally had taken command of the crisis. State and Defense were to play supporting roles."[37] The president's silence, but obvious involvement as director behind-the-scenes, during the *Mayaguez* crisis did much to convey this impression to the public. Because the crisis lasted only four days and resulted in the release of the crew, Ford appeared to be an efficacious leader, as well.

Only *after* the *Mayaguez* sailors had been freed did Ford make his first public statement, and even this discourse had not been planned. According to Hartmann, the Defense Department announced the rescue before Nessen could, which violated Ford's order that the outcome of the operation come from the White House. Nessen quickly rectified the problem with his suggestion that the president interrupt Johnny Carson's *Tonight Show* and make his own statement. Ford's brief televised appearance before reporters apparently occurred only because his plans for strategic silence were thwarted. Once he finished his announcement, the president somberly folded up the statement he had read and strode silently from the room.[38]

In his announcement and subsequent rhetoric on the *Mayaguez*, Ford continued to emphasize his leadership capabilities, just as his silence had, and constructed the most personal role for himself in his discourse of any president examined in this study. More than even Richard Nixon, Gerald Ford talked about himself. Hart maintains that Ford's overall presidential discourse contained more self-references than any chief executive from Truman through Reagan.[39] According to political commentator Richard Reeves, Ford's aides may have encouraged him in this regard. His advisers wrote a memo in which they told Ford to portray himself as a man in charge—"You have to establish forcefully that *you* are the President!" Specifically, this meant he was to make greater use of the first-person singular and to stop referring to his advisers and other administration officials, particularly Henry Kissinger. As a result of this advice, Reeves contends that Ford's televised statement to announce the rescue of the *Mayaguez* crew made it clear that the president had issued all orders.[40]

My analysis of Ford's crisis discourse supports Reeve's assertion. In his portrayal of the crisis situation, the president concentrated on the actor of Gerald Ford or the Ford administration, and the actions this actor performed. The style of his discourse, consistent with the situation, emphasized how the management of the *Mayaguez* crisis reflected upon the character of the president. Likewise, Ford's identificational appeals tended to be explicit in nature and to encourage citizen support through references to his official role and obligations and to his responsibility for the crisis's successful resolution.

Situation

In his discourse about the *Mayaguez* crisis, Ford described the situation in the following way:

> When Cambodia captured the *Mayaguez* near the island of Koh Tang (scene), President Ford or the Ford administration (actor) took firm action (act) to rescue the ship and crew (purpose) through attempted diplomacy and a military rescue operation (means).

Like the other presidents examined in this study, Ford portrayed a scene of danger abroad. His May 15 announcement of the crew's release, for instance, explained that "the American merchant ship SS *Mayaguez*" had been "illegally seized by Cambodian forces" near "the Island of Koh Tang."[41] Through these terms, the president emphasized that the *Mayaguez* was an innocent commercial ship, as opposed to a U.S. military vessel. His reference to the illegality of Cambodian actions also served to delineate a scene in which Americans had been placed in danger, even though they had done nothing wrong.

In response to this scene, President Ford or the Ford administration took action "for the purpose of rescuing the crew and the ship." The president said he accomplished this goal through a military operation, which included landings on Koh Tang and "supporting strikes against nearby military installations" in

Cambodia.[42] Later, when a Government Accounting Office (GAO) report criticized Ford for a lack of diplomatic efforts during the crisis, he made it clear that he had sought a peaceful solution prior to ordering the rescue mission. Ford said in an October 1976 debate with Jimmy Carter, "Every possible diplomatic means was utilized."[43]

Although the president's situational portrayal of the *Mayaguez* crisis described a threatening scene, terms for scene did not dominate his talk as they did in the other cases of crisis promotion examined in this book. Words for the nation's purpose and actions also failed to play a major role. Moreover, the actor of the president's rhetoric was not the United States or an ambiguous "we," nor did these figures play supporting roles as coactors. Instead, Gerald Ford portrayed a crisis situation that revolved around him and his actions, for the key actor of Ford's crisis promotion was Gerald Ford. The president talked about "I" and "me" and discussed himself as the head of a corporate presidency when he identified the key actor as "the Ford administration" or as "we," which seemed to refer to him and the government he led.

Among Ford's terms for situation, the terminological ratio of actor-act prevailed and served to depict the president as a dynamic leader. During a May 1975 interview with *Time*'s Hugh Sidey, for instance, the president emphasized his role as the key actor who had overseen the entire *Mayaguez* rescue.

> I issued the order to prevent boats going in and out from the island. That was the first order. The second order I issued was to have the Marines, the ships and the Air Force ready to go. This was an order issued at that night meeting on Tuesday. In other words, everybody was to be put on one hour's notice. Then I issued the order Wednesday afternoon when we were in here with charts and every-thing. . . . I issued the orders in all three cases.[44]

In this passage, Ford clearly represented himself as the leader in charge during the crisis. His announcement of the *Mayaguez* crew's release was equally careful to point out who had given the orders. According to the president, "At my direction, United States forces tonight boarded the American merchant ship SS *Mayaguez* and landed at the Island of Koh Tang for the purpose of rescuing the crew and the ship. . . . I have now received information that the vessel has been recovered intact and the entire crew has been rescued."[45]

Ford's televised statement depicted him as a dynamic actor in two ways. First, the phrase "at my direction" accentuated the president's leadership role, as he was the one who had instigated the rescue. Second, Ford referred to the military's actions in passive voice—the ship "has been recovered intact" and the crew "has been rescued"—which diminished the role of the military in the accomplishment of these goals, but still allowed the president to associate himself with these positive results.

The actor-act terminological relationship took center stage in Ford's crisis rhetoric on other occasions as well. At a 1976 news conference, for example, he asserted, "I can assure you that this administration has taken a firm action wherever we have been confronted with any illegal international action. The best illustration of course is what we did in 1975 in the *Mayaguez* incident."[46] When a Wisconsin high school student asked Ford during a campaign stop what his most important presidential decision had been, Ford responded, "I would say that probably the one that took the most forceful action was the decision to make certain that the *Mayaguez,* the merchant ship, was recovered from the Cambodians. That was probably one of the most meaningful decisions because that ship was attacked, it was seized by the Cambodians, and we sent in our forces to get it back and we got it back."[47]

The president's recollection described his administration's actions as "forceful," or strong, and emphasized the efficacy of those actions by pointing out that they had resulted in the return of the *Mayaguez*. Likewise, Ford defended his administration's crisis management in a 1976 presidential debate when he said, "I can assure you that if we had not taken the strong and forceful action that we did, we would have been criticized very, very severely for sitting back and not moving."[48]

During the *Mayaguez* crisis, Ford remained silent while Press Secretary Nessen made statements that exemplified the terminological relationships of scene-actor, in which terms for the crisis scene were associated with terms for the president, and actor-act, in which terms for Ford were paired with terms for the actions he was taking to release the crew. In his own subsequent crisis talk, Ford exemplified the actor-act ratio of terms when he concentrated on himself as the key actor during the crisis, and then described the firm, successful action he had taken.

The *Mayaguez* crisis seemed somewhat less threatening and urgent than the other crises examined in this book due to the lack of emphasis on terms for scene in Ford's discourse and the way in which Nessen and Ford accentuated the president's leadership role. As one reporter put it, the ship's seizure was depicted as a "mini-crisis" with the administration emphasizing, "we are calm, we are cool."[49] Ford's crisis rhetoric, in other words, described a crisis situation that was less frightening *because* Ford was in command. In the style of his crisis discourse, the president continued to focus on his leadership capabilities.

Style

Although Ford spoke very little about the *Mayaguez* crisis, his public words frequently described what the key actor of Ford or the Ford administration was like. The president said at various times, for instance, that his administration took "forceful," "firm," and "strong" action.[50] In addition, Ford maintained in a

1976 campaign debate that he and his officials had handled the *Mayaguez* crisis "responsibly." The president insisted, "We did the right thing."[51] Hence, Ford portrayed the key actor as a strong and moral leader.

More often than he engaged in these descriptions, however, Ford depicted himself or his administration as an actor who was decisive and capable under even the most difficult of circumstances. The president commented at a June 1975 news conference, for example, that his rise in the polls "reflects some of the hard decisions we had to make in the area of foreign policy. Obviously, the *Mayaguez* incident and the way it was handled has had a good reaction." He continued to explain that his management of the *Mayaguez* crisis and other problems "have been good for the country. And when something is good for the Nation, people who have something to do with it do benefit to some extent."[52]

Through his explanation, Ford described the *Mayaguez* crisis as representative of the other difficult decisions his administration had faced. He also asserted that the outcome had been beneficial for the United States and implied that this must be the case because citizens had supported his actions. In a similar fashion, Ford told an audience at a Wisconsin campaign stop that the decision to order a military rescue operation had been "a tough decision," but it had proved successful because it resulted in the return of the *Mayaguez*.[53]

The president also remarked to reporters in the fall of 1976 that the GAO report critical of his actions was "another example of partisan politics." According to Ford, "I don't believe the American people will believe somebody who, with the luxury of 18 months afterwards, can sit back and write a report. I think they will believe a President who was there and had to make the tough decisions on an incident that was important to the American foreign policy."[54] Once more, Ford depicted himself as the man in the arena, the one who had made the difficult decisions needed during a critical period. All in all, the president represented himself as strong, moral, decisive, and competent.

The dominant terminological ratio of Ford's style further reinforced such depictions. Stylistically, the president emphasized the terminological relationship of act-actor, which indicated that Ford's actions were reflective of his character. At a 1976 public forum in Indiana, a questioner praised the president on his handling of the *Mayaguez* crisis. Ford responded, "Well, first let me thank you for your comments concerning the *Mayaguez*. That, I think, should be a good warning to any country that thinks they can challenge us. If any country does any act of that kind, I think the *Mayaguez* incident and the action we took ought to be a fair warning to them to the decisiveness of the Ford administration."[55] Ford's discourse was similar to that of Kennedy on the Cuban missile crisis, Johnson on the Gulf of Tonkin, and Nixon on Cambodia in that the style of all four of these presidents exemplified an act-actor ordering of terms.

Unlike these other rhetors, however, Ford did not concern himself with the nation's character, nor did he, as Richard Nixon had done, divide his attentions between U.S. character and his own. Instead, Ford's style focused almost exclusively on himself and the administration that bore his name. In a July 1976 news conference, he talked about "what we did" during the *Mayaguez* crisis and added, "I think that was a clear warning to any nation that violates international law that this administration will act swiftly and firmly and, I think, successfully."[56] Ford also told Hugh Sidey that his administration's management of the *Mayaguez* crisis "ought to be a very clear signal, Hugh, that we are going to act with responsible caution but firm action."[57] According to the president, the actions taken during the crisis reflected favorably upon him and his government. Ford's management of the *Mayaguez* crisis was, in other words, emblematic of his ability to lead.

Identificational Appeals

To encourage citizen identification with—and thus support for—him and his crisis management, the president could have chosen antithetical appeals that focused on the Cambodian enemy, or spoken implicitly about "America" or an ambiguous "we." Instead, Ford relied on an explicit identificational strategy that consisted of overt attempts to identify himself with the office of the presidency and with the success of the operation.

In his sparse public talk on the *Mayaguez* crisis, Ford twice referred to himself in the third person as "a President" or "President Ford,"[58] which underscored his authority and official role. Ford's interview with European journalists in May 1975 also linked him to his title when he reassured allies that the *Mayaguez* crisis was one of several indications that "the United States—the President, the Congress, and the American people—can and will work together in an extended commitment."[59] This statement not only associated Ford with the presidency, but also overtly connected him with the legislative branch and the citizens he served.

In a campaign debate with Carter the following year, Ford responded to the charges of the GAO report through explicit appeals that focused on the special burdens of his position: "Let me assure you that we made every possible overture to the People's Republic of China and, through them, to the Cambodian Government. . . . Every possible diplomatic means was utilized." Ford added, "But at the same time, I had a responsibility . . . to meet the problem at hand."[60] Ford implied that the policy he chose to resolve the *Mayaguez* crisis was based upon an official obligation he held, presumably to protect American citizens abroad.

In addition to identifying himself with the role of president, Ford made explicit attempts to identify with the positive outcome of the *Mayaguez* crisis. The situation of his discourse highlighted portrayals of the president involved in efficacious action. The style of his discourse, through the act-actor ordering of terms, also made clear connections between the success of the actions Ford took and Ford himself. Beyond this, the president's identificational appeals overtly associated him with *Mayaguez* crew members, particularly the ship's captain, who served as credible endorsement figures for him.

In July 1975, Ford invited Captain Charles Miller, as well as seamen from the U.S.N.S. *Greenville* who helped rescue the *Mayaguez,* to the White House. Miller presented the president with the wheel of the *Mayaguez* as reporters watched. The two men also engaged in a rather awkward exchange that the White House recorded and later circulated in a press release. According to the transcript, Captain Miller and the president briefly talked about the sequence of events during the crisis. Ford then encouraged the captain to give his sanction to the rescue operation.

> THE PRESIDENT: Those American planes looked pretty good to you?
> CAPTAIN MILLER: Those American planes looked like angels coming out of the sky.
> THE PRESIDENT: I bet it was good to see these fellows when you saw them on board.
> CAPTAIN MILLER: Yes, sir.

After this interchange, Ford went on to show how he and Miller shared common interests.

> THE PRESIDENT: What does the ship's log say? I used to be the assistant navigator on a carrier out there in the Pacific, and part of my job, along with the quartermaster, was to keep the ship's log. . . . It would be nice to have a copy of the ship's log the day that it all happened and a copy of the ship's log the day that you all boarded it and you got back home.
> CAPTAIN MILLER: We can give you a copy of the log, Mr. President. We can also give you a copy of our charts and all the navigation reports that we had on it.
> THE PRESIDENT: That would be very interesting.[61]

Through his explicit appeals in this public appearance, Ford was able to elicit an endorsement for his actions during the *Mayaguez* crisis from a person who would have great credibility in the matter with American citizens: the captain of the ship, a man who actually had been on the crisis scene and whose life had been endangered. Not only had the captain given the president a token of the crew's appreciation, he had also publicly articulated his approval. Ford's other comments, and the joint appearance itself, functioned to link the president and the person who had validated his leadership in much the same way that political aspirants benefit when they pose for photo opportunities with union leaders, prominent business executives, and movie stars.

When the GAO report was released in 1976, Ford again relied on Captain Miller for persuasive support in his answer to a question about the report during a debate with Carter. The president said, "This morning I got a call from the skipper of the *Mayaguez*. He was furious, because he told me that it was the action of me, President Ford, that saved the lives of the crew of the *Mayaguez*. . . . Captain Miller is thankful, the crew is thankful."[62] Through this response, Ford indicated that people in the best position to evaluate his crisis policy, Captain Miller and the other *Mayaguez* sailors, approved of his crisis management. Although possibly an attempt to correct a syntactical error, the president's assertion—"it was the action of me, President Ford, that saved the lives of the crew"—also made abundantly clear that Ford felt the operation had been a success and who he believed was responsible for it.

As a whole, Ford's crisis talk treated the *Mayaguez* crisis as representative of his leadership capabilities. Key terms for situation emphasized Ford in action, rather than distant crisis scenes or the nation's goals and actions. Meanwhile, key terms for style depicted the president as strong, moral, decisive, and competent and argued that the positive nature of his acts revealed his character. The explicit appeals of Ford's talk also centered on the president by overtly identifying Ford with his office and the success of the operation, including Captain Miller of the *Mayaguez* who endorsed his crisis management.

From the president's early refusal to talk and his reliance on surrogate speakers, to his brief public remarks that focused on his leadership, Ford represented himself as the strong, silent type: a man too busy leading to engage in unnecessary chatter; a president who understood what to do, then did it; an individual who was happy to receive public support for his efforts and took credit when he thought he had earned it, but who did not dwell excessively on his crisis victory. Gerald Ford showed that sometimes the best way for a president to demonstrate leadership in a foreign crisis is to whisper rather than shout.

THE *MAYAGUEZ* CRISIS AND THE WAR POWERS RESOLUTION: THE LEGAL AUTHORITY TO PROMOTE CRISES

In addition to its rhetorical interest, the *Mayaguez* crisis holds historical and political significance. The crisis posed a major test for the 1973 War Powers Resolution, which set new legal precedents for the presidential authority to promote crises. Before Ford's adherence to this law can be examined, the resolution's history and principles must be explained.

In the fall of 1973, the House and the Senate enacted, over Richard Nixon's veto, the War Powers Resolution, in order to reestablish congressional participation in decisions of war and peace.[63] Supporters of the resolution were confident that it clearly delineated the respective powers of the legislative and executive branches. Even so, Pat Holt, former chief of staff for the Senate Foreign Relations Committee, observes that the resolution's procedures posed problems that actually thwarted the intended purpose of the resolution.[64]

According to the statute, the president must consult with Congress only when hostilities have occurred or are imminent. Congress need not be consulted when the president merely has enlarged the number of troops in another country or has committed troops "into the territory, airspace or waters of a foreign nation, while equipped for combat"—if hostilities are not expected. This loophole allows the president to avoid consultation altogether if he plausibly can define a deployment as one that does not involve imminent hostilities. Furthermore, the War Powers Resolution does not indicate which senators and representatives the president must consult if hostilities are expected, nor does it require consultation in all threatening cases but rather "in every possible instance."[65] Since time is at a premium during crises, Holt points out that rarely will presidents deem consultation possible.[66]

The president must file a report with Congress within forty-eight hours whenever he sends armed forces abroad, regardless of whether imminent hostilities are expected. Because Congress need not receive the report until after the president has committed troops, this means that Congress probably will have little information about the deployment until it has already taken place. If the commander-in-chief wants troops to remain in actual or imminent hostilities longer than sixty days, he may commit them for an additional thirty days if he "determines and certifies to the Congress in writing that unavoidable military necessity respecting the safety of United States Armed Forces requires the continued use of such armed forces in the course of bringing about a prompt removal of such forces."[67]

The president, therefore, will find it easy to send troops abroad for as long as three months on his own authority. Once troops have been sent, Congress will probably approve of the decision, as citizens tend to rally around the commander-in-chief and his interpretation of crisis events. No doubt, legislators will be particularly reluctant to withdraw support from the president if American soldiers have lost their lives in hostilities. When young men or women die in battle, their fellow citizens frequently cling to the belief that the fallen were martyrs in a just cause; to think that their deaths had no meaning is simply too painful. Hence, bloody conflict frequently begets more conflict.

For all of these reasons, the War Powers Resolution actually strengthened the presidency and legitimized the prerogative powers that commanders-in-chief had previously assumed. Ford's application of the resolution revealed that it had even more problems in practice.

In the spring of 1975, Ford became the first president to file reports under the War Powers Resolution, and he did so four times between April 4 and May 15. The first two instances were the evacuation of Vietnamese refugees from Danang to safety further south and the evacuation of the American embassy in Phnom Penh. Because troop deployment took place in a nonhostile environment, Ford did not have to consult Congress, nor did he have to start the sixty-day clock and the possibility that Congress would end the evacuations through a concurrent resolution.[68]

Ford's third report to Congress concerned the evacuation of Americans and Vietnamese from Saigon. On April 10, the president asked Congress to revise a law that prohibited the use of appropriations for military operations in Southeast Asia. Ford claimed this law did not allow U.S. armed forces to evacuate Vietnamese from Saigon under what would most likely be hostile conditions.[69] On April 25, the Senate passed the Vietnam Humanitarian Assistance and Evacuation Act of 1975, which carefully justified the use of U.S. troops for evacuation purposes through reference to the War Powers Resolution. The House, however, delayed voting until May 1 and then rejected the bill. In the meantime, of course, Communist forces had surrounded Saigon, so Ford had ordered the evacuation without congressional approval.[70]

In this case, congressional mismanagement ceded even greater power to the White House. Ford had asked Congress for its permission, and, after nearly three weeks, the House had still not made a decision. Congress's failure to act would later prompt former-Congressman Gerald Ford to remark, "You cannot have 535 commanders in chief."[71] When the House decided not to ratify the president's actions, even after the fact, it left the impression that congressional permission was no longer needed.[72] Less than two weeks after the Saigon operation, the *Mayaguez* crisis provided the ultimate proof that the War Powers Resolution had merely legalized claims of presidential prerogatives.

During the *Mayaguez* crisis, the Ford administration "consulted" with congressional leaders three times. This consultation procedure exhibited several flaws, one of which was that White House aides did not contact members of Congress until thirty-six hours after Ford had learned about the *Mayaguez*. In addition, the president had already ordered the military operation by the time he met with congressional leaders on the evening of May 14. As Holt remarks, "The executive branch has a long history of using 'inform' synonymously with 'consult.'"[73]

The Ford White House's own preference for this usage became clear when an administration official, most likely Nessen, attempted to sketch out the administration's *Mayaguez* crisis consultation process: "After the information was given to the Congressmen and Senators, the comments of the members were written down by the Congressional liaison staff and transmitted to the president. The president couldn't talk to every one of them, but their feelings were transmitted to him. This is consultation, or discussion."[74] One suspects that most lexicologists would be hard-pressed to call this procedure a consultation. Despite the War Powers Resolution's stipulations, Ford's consultations were no better than the briefings that Kennedy, Johnson, and Nixon had provided congressional leaders during their respective crises.

This points to another flaw of the War Powers Resolution: it only restrains presidential action after the fact.[75] Three senators—Mansfield, Byrd, and McClellan—told Ford that they opposed his decision to launch air strikes against the Cambodian mainland. Even if Ford's orders had not already gone out, the senators had no legal authority under the War Powers Resolution to stop the immediate implementation of his plans. The War Powers Resolution stipulates that only a concurrent resolution can terminate U.S. involvement in armed conflict before sixty days have elapsed.[76] By the time such a resolution can be passed, hostilities may have ended.

The *Mayaguez* crisis also exemplifies the problems of the reporting procedure contained in the War Powers Resolution. In accordance with the statute, Ford sent a report to Congress within forty-eight hours of launching the *Mayaguez* operation, but by then the *Mayaguez* crew had been released. The War Powers Resolution gives presidents short-term control over military conflicts because the crisis may be over by the time the required report reaches Congress.[77]

Ford's report to Congress remains of interest for another reason. In his letter, the president claimed he was "taking note" of the War Powers Resolution. Ford then closed the report with the following statement: "This operation was ordered and conducted pursuant to the President's constitutional Executive power and his authority as Commander-in-Chief of the United States Armed Forces."[78] Like the contemporary presidents who came before him, Ford based his actions on his prerogative powers. The War Powers Resolution merely functioned as a touchstone to legitimize prerogative claims.

The *Mayaguez* crisis and Ford's implementation of the War Powers Resolution illustrate that the law merely legalized the prerogative powers contemporary commanders-in-chief have long assumed. Rather than encourage congressional participation, the resolution's flaws ensure that presidents will make important crisis decisions by themselves. In 1977, Senator Church, a supporter of both the War Powers Resolution and Ford's adherence to it during the *Mayaguez* crisis, had a change of heart as he reflected upon the events that had taken place. Church noted: "If the President . . . uses the Armed Forces in an action that is both swift and successful, then there is no reason to expect the Congress to do anything other than applaud. If the President employs forces in an action which is swift, but unsuccessful, then the Congress is faced with a *fait accompli,* and although it may rebuke the President, it can do little else."[79]

Rather than restraining the president, the War Powers Resolution transferred more power from Congress to the Oval Office. Inherent flaws in the resolution and Ford's interpretation of the law further strengthened the presidential power to promote and manage crises.

A PERSPECTIVE ON SILENCE: FORD AND THE *MAYAGUEZ* CRISIS

After the *Mayaguez* crisis had ended, critics raised questions about Ford's lack of congressional consultation, the use of force rather than diplomacy, the decision to launch the attack from Utapao Air Base after Thailand had explicitly asked the United States not to do so, and especially, the extensive casualties—more men died than were saved.[80] Nine members of the *Mayaguez* crew even tried, albeit unsuccessfully, to sue the U.S. government for negligence. Despite Ford's claims that the crew was "thankful," the legal brief of these particular *Mayaguez* sailors argued that "armed United States aircraft . . . negligently shrapneled, maced and wounded the crew during the Government's bungled rescue attempt." The crew members alleged that the Cambodian seizure of the ship had been legal because the *Mayaguez* was not in international waters, but only 1.75 miles from the Cambodian Wai islands. Consequently, the plaintiffs argued, the United States should have used diplomacy rather than military force.[81]

None of this criticism, however, seemed to dampen immediate public enthusiasm for U.S. actions or for the president who had directed those actions. On May 30, 1975, William Baroody told Hartmann that the campaign for Ford's election had already begun; he maintained that the public's perception of how the president handled domestic issues like the economy and international issues like the *Mayaguez* would be a major factor in the presidential race.[82] In June, Lou Harris wrote that Ford's chances of winning the White House in 1976 had appeared slim prior to the *Mayaguez* crisis. After the return of the ship and crew, however, Harris's opinion research showed the president running ahead of Ted Kennedy, thought to be a leading contender for the Democratic nomination.[83] More than a year later, the White House Office of Communications issued a report on the president's "first two years" in office, a phrase that implied that more would follow, and listed the rescue of the *Mayaguez* and its crew as one of his achievements.[84]

Certainly, Ford benefited from the fact that the *Mayaguez* operation coincided with the safe release of the sailors. Nevertheless, the president also strengthened his image as a leader through a unique variant of crisis promotion that combined silence with economical public remarks. By Ford's own account, he did not place much stock in rhetoric. The president explained in his memoirs that after Watergate, he needed to restore Americans' trust in the White House. According to Ford, "rhetoric alone would not suffice. . . . The country didn't need more promises. It yearned for performance instead."[85] His protests to the contrary, Ford did rely upon rhetoric. He may have remained silent during the crisis, but his spokespersons' discourse imbued that silence with meaning.

Similarly, the president's postcrisis statements were few, but they reinforced the message of his silence. Ford thus avoided extensive public speaking, an activity he engaged in frequently as president but with little finesse or enjoyment, while he and his administration nonetheless projected an image of Ford as a dynamic and efficacious leader. Through his promotion and management of the *Mayaguez* crisis, Ford demonstrated that a president may say very little and still communicate a great deal.

Four years after the *Mayaguez* seizure, Ford's successor, Jimmy Carter, would face a hostage situation of his own when Iranian students seized the American embassy in Teheran. In contrast to Ford's understated approach, Carter would go to great lengths to promote the crisis and his role as crisis manager. He would also discover that the political dividends of crisis promotion can be fleeting.

Chapter Six

IDEALISM HELD HOSTAGE
Jimmy Carter and the Crisis in Iran

In early 1979, Iran was in the midst of revolution. Shah Mohammed Reza Pahlevi, a long-time U.S. ally, had fled his country, seeking sanctuary elsewhere. Meanwhile, Ayatollah Ruhollah Khomeini, an Islamic fundamentalist who had guided the revolution from his exile in France, returned to Iran, where he publicly attacked the shah and his international sponsor, the United States. President Jimmy Carter increased tensions further when he admitted the shah to the United States for medical treatment eight months later. In response to this news, Iranian students overran the U.S. embassy in Teheran and took its American occupants hostage. The students demanded that the shah be returned to Iran to face trial, while Khomeini publicly applauded the embassy seizure.[1]

At first, the Carter administration played up this latest crisis with great political effect. The president froze Iranian assets and turned away shipments of Iranian oil. On Thanksgiving, Carter asked the nation to pray for the hostages. In December, he proclaimed National Unity Day to show support for the captured Americans and left the White House Christmas tree unlit.[2] According to the president, "anything that happens in this country to take the mind of the world off the American hostages is damaging to our nation, is harmful to me in my efforts and is also threatening to the lives and the safety of those hostages."[3] Carter also announced his candidacy for reelection, but told Americans that he would not actively campaign so that he could devote his full attentions to the hostage issue.[4]

During the *Mayaguez* seizure, Gerald Ford refrained from public statements about the crisis he faced. Jimmy Carter, during the initial months of his own crisis, spoke volumes about the hostages, but refused to engage in traditional campaign discourse and public debates. In both cases, the commanders-in-chief succeeded in portraying themselves as leaders. For Carter, however, public support was short lived. As months went by and no tangible progress had been made, citizens began to lose patience. Even First Lady Rosalynn Carter urged her husband to "do something—anything" to bring the crisis to an end.[5]

Jimmy Carter's discourse on Iran presents an interesting case for the study of crisis promotion and management. Carter illustrates the problems a president faces when he adopts a crisis terminology with little forethought as to its long-range implications or when he cannot resolve the crisis he has promoted. According to rhetorical critic Gerard Hauser, the attention the Carter White House focused upon the hostages necessarily increased their public importance and encouraged citizens to evaluate the president's leadership abilities by how well he managed the crisis.[6] The contrast between Carter's initial flurry of activity on behalf of the hostages and his later apparent passivity contributed to citizen perceptions of his ineffectuality.

Beyond the president's decision to call the events in Iran a crisis, Carter undermined his long-term public support through the type of argument that he typically employed. Unlike the crisis discourse of many other contemporary presidents, Carter's public talk rarely discussed progress that had been made toward the resolution of the crisis. Instead, the president focused almost exclusively on principles. Carter repeatedly claimed that he had two goals in mind: to "persist in our efforts, through every means available, until every single American has been freed" and to "preserve the honor and integrity of our Nation and to protect its interests."[7] That is, the president said he would seek the release of the hostages, but he would do so only through means that were in keeping with our country's character.

Carter grounded his discourse about the crisis in an idealist's terminology, distinctive because of its emphasis on genus—specifically, his definition of who Americans were and what they were like—and the application of that genus to public problem-solving. Through such arguments, Carter constrained his ability to take effective action. He insisted that policies must not only achieve pragmatic results, but also be consistent with his definition of the nation's moral character. Herein lay the strength of Jimmy Carter the man and the weakness of Jimmy Carter as presidential rhetor.

This does not mean, however, that Carter's talk was completely atypical. Other commanders-in-chief have argued that their policies were consistent with the character of the nation and/or the president. Nonetheless, these rhetors legitimized their policies by pointing to their efficacy and success, thereby intertwining strains of idealism and pragmatism in their public words. In Carter's case, his crisis rhetoric relied too heavily on idealism and displayed far too little pragmatism. The president repeatedly promised Americans that his policies would support the nation's interests, protect the country's integrity, defend the United States' honor, and bring the hostages safely home, but Carter was unable or unwilling to indicate how his crisis resolution efforts had accomplished any of these ends. Progress toward the hostages' release may have been slow, but the president also failed to provide citizens with encouragement as to how his policies were fulfilling his other stated goals. Carter's decision to promote the hostage seizure as a crisis, in tandem with his heavily idealistic talk, made a trying political circumstance even worse.

To explain the president's persuasive efforts further, I first examine the rhetorical context of the hostage seizure, including the Carter administration's strategic decision to engage in crisis promotion, then analyze the overwhelmingly idealistic emphasis on principles and character in Carter's rhetoric.

THE RHETORICAL CONTEXT OF THE IRANIAN HOSTAGE CRISIS

When Iranian students seized the U.S. embassy in Teheran, it appeared initially that they would hold their captives only a short while. Prime Minister Mehdi Bazargan and Foreign Minister Ibrahim Yazdi immediately tried to gain the Americans' release, but Khomeini was otherwise inclined. Rather than urge the freedom of the hostages, the Mullah praised the student captors for their actions and encouraged them to keep the hostages until the shah was returned. Other public officials in Iran were afraid to confront the students once Khomeini had thrown his support to them. Soon after, Bazargan and Yazdi resigned, which shifted political power to Khomeini and other fundamentalist leaders.

At Khomeini's request, the students freed thirteen hostages, all women and black men, an action that the Mullah justified on the grounds of women's special status in the Islamic religion and blacks' historic persecution in the United States. Khomeini also warned that if the shah were not returned, the remaining hostages might be tried as spies and executed.[8]

Surely no one in the Carter White House was happy about events in Iran. At the same time, the hostage seizure provided the president with a political opportunity. Only a few months before, Gerald Rafshoon, the Assistant to the President for Communications, had sent Carter a memo on the subject of "style." He said the public believed the president had failed to show leadership on foreign policy issues, inflation, and energy. Because of this, Rafshoon argued that the president's reelection hopes hinged not on what Carter did during the next year but on *how* he did it. According to Rafshoon,

> *You're going to have to start looking, talking and acting more like a leader if you're to be successful—even if it's artificial.* Look at it this way: changing your position on issues to get votes is wrong; changing your style (like the part in your hair) in order to be effective is just smart and, in the long run, morally good. I know you think it's phony and that you're fine the way you are but that pride is, by far, your greatest political danger.[9]

As if in answer to Rafshoon's wishes, Iranian students took over the U.S. embassy in November, which provided an opportunity for Carter to assume the role of leader.

In his first public statement about the seizure, the president thanked Americans for the restraint they had shown "during this crisis" and asserted that the United States would not "permit the use of terrorism and the seizure and the holding of hostages to impose political demands." Carter also took several measures to exert pressure on Iran. He announced that the United States would no longer purchase Iranian oil.[10] In addition, the president prevented the delivery of military equipment to Iran and directed the attorney general to deport any Iranian students who were in the United States illegally. When Iran threatened to withdraw billions of dollars from its accounts in American banks, Carter froze Iranian assets to prevent the transaction.[11] Whether these measures encouraged Iranian students to rethink their hostage-taking may be open to question, but the policies clearly served to highlight the conflict between the United States and Iran in a public way and to portray Carter as a man in charge who knew how to play hardball.

The administration also took other symbolic actions. At Thanksgiving, the president released a statement asking citizens to engage in "a special prayer" on behalf of the hostages. He himself met with hostage families for an interfaith prayer service.[12] A few days later, Press Secretary Jody Powell sent a letter to 10,000 editors and news directors across the nation for publication. The letter encouraged citizens to ring church bells every noon until the hostages were freed and to write the Iranian consulate in New York to demand the hostages' release.[13]

In addition, the White House actively recruited the help of a variety of individuals and organizations to send petitions, letters, and telegrams to the Iranian embassy. The administration contacted union bartenders, Lane Kirkland, assorted universities, the U.S. Student Association, the National Education Association, the National Council of Churches, the U.S. Catholic Conference, the Baptist Joint Commission on Public Affairs, the United Church of Christ, the American Jewish Committee, the Christian Broadcast Network, Jim and Tammy Bakker's *Praise the Lord* television program, and Robert Schuller, among others.[14]

The following month, Carter continued to focus public attention on the hostages at the White House Christmas tree lighting ceremony where only the star at the top of the tree was lit. Traditionally, the fifty small trees around the national Christmas tree had represented the fifty states. The president departed from this custom when he said, "there are 50 small Christmas trees, one for each American hostage, and on the top of the great Christmas tree is a star of hope. We will turn on the other lights on the tree when the American hostages come home."[15] Three days later Carter declared December 18 to be National Unity Day. He called on citizens and groups to observe the day and to demonstrate their concern for the hostages by displaying the American flag. In a public proclamation, the president reflected on how the American flag "stands for freedom. It stands for justice. It stands for human dignity. It stands too for our united determination to uphold these great ideals."[16] Through all these actions, the administration transformed the hostage seizure into an issue of paramount importance. The White House also used the crisis to show Carter "looking, talking and acting" like a leader.

Perhaps no better example exists of how the president magnified the urgency of the hostage issue and his role in its management than his announcement that he planned to run for reelection. Carter said that his campaign trips would be postponed so that he could stay in Washington, D.C., "to define and to lead our response to an ever-changing situation of the greatest sensitivity and importance." The president claimed that as a result of the hostage seizure, Americans were more unified than they had been at any time since Pearl Harbor. Carter then went on to make even loftier comparisons: "At the height of the Civil War, President Abraham Lincoln said, 'I have but one task, and that is to save the Union.' Now I must devote my concerted efforts to resolving the Iranian crisis."[17]

By cloaking himself in the national interest, the president helped ensure, at least initially, that the public would support him. Carter also held off-the-record meetings with members of Congress and the press in which he detailed the actions he was taking to resolve the crisis situation and asked the legislators to support him, at least publicly, on the issue.[18] By giving these opinion leaders an inside view, the president helped curtail possible criticism of his crisis management and encourage positive portrayals of his actions. Hauser sums up the situation well when he writes that Carter and his aides "were quick to employ the Iranian crisis as a shield with which they could protect the president's administration from scrutiny while simultaneously displaying him in a leadership role."[19]

For a while, the strategy worked. A Gallup poll taken in December showed that Carter's job approval rating had doubled to 61 percent, the sharpest one-month increase Gallup ever had recorded for a president. This rise in public support notwithstanding, a White House summary of Gallup, Harris, and Roper polls warned that "data suggests that the proportion of the public wanting the U.S. to 'do something' retaliatory and with a visible effect will increase significantly if the situation is perceived as worsening."[20]

In early 1980, Americans saw a sign of tangible progress in the crisis when six embassy officials made their way safely to the United States. The Americans had lived underground since the seizure first occurred, and Canada's ambassador to Iran, with the help of the CIA, had managed to spirit the diplomats out of the country.[21] The United States also began a flurry of diplomatic initiatives with Iran. Those who appealed on the United States' behalf included former attorney general Ramsey Clark, former foreign service officer William Miller, Argentine businessman Hector Villalon, French lawyer Christian Bourguet, and U.N. Secretary-General Kurt Waldheim.[22] For all their efforts, though, these envoys and intermediaries met with no success.

Every time the hostages' release seemed imminent, quick disappointment followed. The shah had left the United States for Panama in December and then had gone to Egypt in the spring, where President Anwar Sadat had offered him asylum from the start. His departure from the United States made no impact on the hostage negotiations, however, for the marines and embassy personnel had become pawns in Iran's internal power struggle between Khomeini's militants and President Abolhassan Bani-Sadr's moderates. In the face of continued stalemate, Carter's approval rating plunged.[23]

On April 1 at 7:20, the morning of the Wisconsin primary, some sun seemed to break through the clouds momentarily when the president invited reporters to the Oval Office to give them good news: the Iranian students had agreed to transfer control of the hostages to the Iranian government, a step that Carter had sought for quite some while. News of what the president called "a positive development" quickly spread, and he won most decisively in Wisconsin. Shortly thereafter, Americans learned that the Iranian government had refused to take custody of the captives. The president's own aides commented that the early morning statement made Carter appear manipulative and soured his relationship with the press.[24]

In an attempt to punish the Iranians for their recalcitrance, the president announced new sanctions on April 7. Carter broke diplomatic relations, expelled Iranian diplomats and military personnel in the United States, invalidated visas issued to Iranians for future travel to the United States, and imposed a trade embargo of all goods headed to Iran, with the exception of food and medicine. In addition, the president directed Treasury Secretary G. William Miller to make an inventory of Iran's frozen assets and to catalog American financial claims against Iran, which might be repaid through those assets.[25]

Several weeks later, on April 24, Carter found it necessary—as had other presidents before him—to take military action. The commander-in-chief sent eight helicopters and six C-130 transport planes to Iran in a rescue attempt, which ended in an on-ground collision that killed eight of the servicemen. Although the president sent the requisite report to Congress on April 26, he did not meet with legislative leaders until after the mission had been aborted, a fact that distressed many members of Congress. Carter justified the operation through reference to his "powers under the Constitution as Chief Executive and as Commander-in-Chief of the United States Armed Forces."[26]

President Carter's claim reinforced Ford's assertion that a president could take military action on the basis of his power as commander-in-chief, regardless of the dictates of the War Powers Resolution. Furthermore, Counsel to the President Lloyd Cutler made the case that:

> Section 3 of the War Powers Resolution does require consulting with Congress "in every possible instance" before introducing the United States Armed Forces into "hostilities or into situations where imminent involvement in hostilities is clearly indicated by the circumstances." In this case, the first stage of the operation— introducing the rescue team into Iran during the night of April 24—

did not involve any hostilities. The rescue effort itself was not to be initiated before the following night, and could have been aborted before involvement in hostilities was "clearly indicated," and this is in fact what occurred.[27]

Despite the criticism Gerald Ford received, he insisted that he had consulted with Congress during the *Mayaguez* crisis. The Carter White House, conversely, made no pretense in this matter. Instead, the administration creatively argued that it was not required to discuss the matter with legislators unless hostilities seemed imminent. Given CIA estimates that as many as 60 percent of the hostages could be killed in the operation, it seems unlikely that Carter expected no hostilities.[28] The administration's arguments reinforced and also extended, albeit slightly, the precedent for presidential military initiatives.

In his televised announcement of the failed operation, Carter did not concern himself with legalities but instead emphasized the "humanitarian" character of the operation. The haggard President claimed the mission "was not directed against Iran; it was not directed against the people of Iran. It was not undertaken with any feeling of hostility toward Iran or its people. It has caused no Iranian casualties."[29] In a Gallup poll, 71 percent of surveyed Americans supported the rescue attempt, but only 46 percent approved of the way Carter was handling the crisis in general.[30] The president had other problems as well. Secretary of State Cyrus Vance resigned because he disagreed with Carter's decision to use force. Worst of all, the Iranian student militants declared that they had moved the American hostages to a number of secret locations, which would make future rescue impossible.[31]

The president's dwindling political fortunes convinced his aides that he needed to leave the Rose Garden for the campaign trail. Carter had retreated to the White House to resolve the crisis, but the hostages were not yet free. The question he faced was how to justify this change in plan. As early as April 8, Hamilton Jordan had told the president, "I believe that one of our problems now after months of protracted crisis is that you are seen increasingly in a passive state after the first couple of months of great activity." Jordan suggested that Carter call an emergency session of Western allies in Belgium to get their pledge of support for U.S. initiatives to end the hostage crisis and for the boycott of the Moscow Olympics. According to Jordan, the president then "could return to the States and say that you had decided that the need for you to explain your programs and actions to the American people in this time of international crisis and great domestic difficulty outweighed the benefits of your staying in the White House." Carter seemed to realize that his aide was grasping at straws and responded that the proposal was not a good idea, especially since Prime Minister Thatcher of Great Britain and Chancellor Schmidt of West Germany wanted to avoid U.S. pressure and had already rejected the idea of a NATO meeting.[32]

The strategy that Carter eventually adopted to justify his campaign activities was not much better. On April 30, the administration planted a question with Charles Manatt of the Democratic National Committee so that the president could give his prepared response. As reporters listened, Manatt asked if there were any chance that Carter would leave the White House so that citizens could talk with him. The president replied that "a lot of the responsibilities that have been on my shoulders in the past few months have now been alleviated to some degree" and that many of the issues he had dealt with lately were "manageable enough now for me to leave the White House for a limited travel schedule, including some campaigning if I choose to do so."[33] With the hostages still in Iran and the failed rescue mission fresh in everyone's mind, Carter's statement seemed both ill-conceived and opportunistic.

The summer and fall of 1980 brought no further progress toward a resolution to the crisis, and, at least until the autumn campaign was underway, the Carter administration kept a low rhetorical profile on the subject.[34] In July, the Iranians freed one hostage who was very ill and rejoiced over news that the shah had died of cancer.[35] Iranian officials renewed negotiations with the United States through German intermediaries, but the eruption of the Iran-Iraq War distracted attention from the hostage issue. Although discussion continued, no final settlement was reached. Finally, the November elections delivered Carter a landslide defeat. Election Day had fallen, ironically, on the one-year anniversary of the hostages' captivity. Iran was not the only issue of the campaign, but the lingering crisis and Carter's apparent inability to resolve it certainly contributed to Ronald Reagan's victory.[36]

After the election, Carter continued his efforts to release the hostages with the help of Algeria, who mediated between Iran and the United States and at last struck an agreement that satisfied both countries. The settlement was remarkably complex, but essentially amounted to a trade: Iranian assets for American hostages. Under the terms of the agreement, the United States would transfer the Iranian assets in its possession to an Algerian bank account. Iran, in exchange, would turn the hostages over to Algerian officials.[37]

On January 20, after fourteen months of crisis and just minutes after Ronald Reagan became president, the American hostages were released.[38] Jimmy Carter had lost the presidency, but the hostages had returned safely home. According to National Security Adviser Zbigniew Brzezinski, Carter deserved the credit for this accomplishment because he had refused to take military action that would have gained him popular support but placed the hostages in danger.[39] Although Brzezinski clearly overlooked the failed rescue mission, many agreed that the president's dogged diplomatic efforts had eventually met with success.

According to then-Iranian President Bani-Sadr, however, a different mechanism was at work: the ayatollahs had made a deal with the Reagan campaign to delay the release of the hostages in exchange for arms that Iran needed in the war with Iraq. Journalist Christopher Hitchens supports Bani-Sadr's account with the fact that the first weapons shipment of the infamous Iran-Contra arms scandal arrived in Iran in February 1981, when there were no American captives in Teheran or Beirut.[40]

Regardless of the reason for the hostages' release, the Iranian crisis clearly had a devastating impact on Carter's reelection efforts. Press Secretary Powell explained in December 1980 that "certainly for the first three or four months, really even longer than that, I suppose—it was very hard to get either the press or the public to focus their attention on much else." Because of this, Powell argued that the crisis dominated the campaign and also made it difficult for the administration to communicate with citizens about other pressing matters.[41] If Americans' preoccupation with the seizure caused problems for the White House, however, Carter officials had no one to blame but themselves.

Carter's decision to call the events in Iran a crisis was, without a doubt, his most important action in the resolution of the hostage question. The crisis terminology defined the issue and thereby affected the way the president chose to discuss the issue and to manage it. In retrospect, Carter's language choice also was a crucial political misstep, for it focused attention upon the hostages and raised public expectations for their release. Of course, some observers might respond that Carter referred to the hostage-taking as a crisis because it most assuredly was one. But this need not have been the case.

Hauser points out that in February 1980, U.S. Ambassador Diego C. Asencio and several other Americans were taken hostage at the Dominican embassy in Colombia. Despite the similarities between this situation and the one in Iran, the *Department of State Bulletin* and the *Weekly Compilation of Presidential Documents* show that the administration made no public statements on the matter.[42] Reagan, too, publicly downplayed the existence of American hostages in the Middle East during his tenure in office and suffered few adverse consequences as a result of this decision.

Carter certainly could not have avoided all news coverage of Iran, but his urgent language and the public attention his administration lavished on events there firmly established the hostage situation as a crisis that demanded an immediate solution. Cyrus Vance lent support to this idea when he later noted that the administration's constant public declarations about the Iranian hostages contributed "unwittingly to Iran's exploitation of the nation's heartfelt anxiety by letting it appear that the hostages were the only concern of the U.S. government."[43] Early on, before the crisis became a liability, Carter himself seemed to be aware of the political dividends a crisis terminology could bring. Ray Jenkins took notes of a staff meeting with the president on January 16, 1980, and recorded Carter's desire to "escalate [the] rhetoric." Jenkins quoted the president as saying that we have "got a patriotism wave & we ought to pursue it."[44]

During the early days of the hostage crisis, officials in the Carter administration were absorbed in their efforts to manage public perceptions. Al McDonald, the staff director in charge of presidential speechwriters, summed up White House strategy when he told Powell on November 26, 1979, "As one part of dealing with the leadership issue, we need to move out more aggressively to 'merchandise' the President's record and views and to provide more complete Administration perspectives on what we are doing, why we are doing these things and how they fit together."[45] McDonald may have been referring to Carter's overall presidential leadership, a likely campaign issue in 1980, rather than his leadership in the specific case of the embassy seizure. Nevertheless, McDonald and the rest of the White House staff seemed to recognize that the two were intertwined, that the president could demonstrate leadership in the hostage crisis and simultaneously resolve questions about his leadership on other matters.

As early as November 7, 1979, the president's Assistant for Public Liaison, Anne Wexler, asked Powell and Jordan whether the administration was "developing a strategy to show the public that the President is in control of the situation?" She suggested that a group of "wise men" should meet with Carter about the crisis and then "make public statements to the effect that the President is in control."[46] Similarly, McDonald recommended that Carter appear before television cameras to make his first public comment on the seizure, but only *after* the departure of the Irish Prime Minister so that he would "clearly be seen alone as the American leader in charge of the handling of this problem." Furthermore, McDonald argued that "each statement by the Secretary of State should indicate that he has been 'authorized by the President to make the following statement'" and that Powell's briefings with reporters should depict Carter as a leader who had the crisis under control.

McDonald also concerned himself with the timing of the president's announcement that he would freeze Iranian assets. According to the staff director, the announcement should occur before Carter's meeting with state governors and should be portrayed "as another positive Presidential action."[47] Jody Powell tried to convince the president to let White House photographers stay in the Oval Office for longer periods of time. He explained that a White House–released shot gave the Press Office greater control over public depictions of Carter. In addition, Powell argued that "in the current situation it is an especially valuable tool since there is a steady demand for pictures of you working and managing these crises."[48]

The Press Secretary also did what he could to portray Carter's Rose Garden strategy as a selfless political act. In the early weeks of the crisis, Powell wrote a memo in which he recommended that the president agree to debate Jerry Brown and Ted Kennedy, his chief Democratic opponents in the Iowa caucuses, in order to protect his own political self-interests in the 1980 campaign. At the bottom of the memo, Carter responded in language that was much more formal than that which he used in other internal documents at the time: "Jody—I can't disagree with any of this, but I cannot break away from my duties here, which are extraordinary now and ones which only I can fulfill. We will just have to take the adverse political consequences & make the best of it. Right now both Iran & Afghanistan look bad, & will need my constant attention. J."[49]

According to journalists such as David Broder, Powell leaked the memo to the press to encourage support for Carter's withdrawal from election activities. One of the president's top campaign advisers, Robert Strauss, later would comment on the strategic memorandum and Carter's response to it with, "Well, it was somewhat overwritten."[50]

If Carter and his aides accentuated the urgency of the hostage seizure initially and used it to highlight the president's leadership, then they also began to realize fairly quickly the dangers of the road on which they had embarked. On January 12, 1980, Powell said at a presidential staff meeting that there was a need to lower public expectations about Iran. Two weeks later, families of the hostages invited the president and First Lady to a rededication of the national Christmas tree to tie fifty yellow ribbons to its branches. Powell wrote on an internal memorandum about the request, "I hate to see us involved in another one of these but I don't see how we can refuse."[51]

Adviser Hedley Donovan also seemed to sense that the administration was losing control of the crisis. He warned Carter that "if there is no progress with the hostages by February 11—the 100th day—I suggest that will be a very sensitive day for 'the media' and public opinion. Congressmen and others would begin talking about the date before it arrives. There would be TV specials. If there is no progress to be reported on the hostages, it would be well to have something else to report."[52] There is no evidence that the administration attempted to divert attention from the hostages on February 11, but the president made no public statement about Iran and concerned himself instead with routine reports and nominations on that day. Nevertheless, Donovan's warning articulated concerns expressed in other quarters.

In April, a draft of Carter's announcement of further sanctions had begun with the sentence, "Today is the 156th day of imprisonment for 50 Americans in our Embassy in Tehran." The text was changed to read "Ever since Iranian terrorists imprisoned American Embassy personnel in Tehran early in November," a phrase that did not emphasize the length of the hostages' captivity quite so much.[53] Throughout the summer of 1980, Carter made relatively few public statements about Iran, and his speechwriters recommended that he "maintain his present low public profile of this issue."[54] As the fall election loomed ahead, Pat Caddell's Cambridge Survey Research Report told the president what he did not want to hear: citizens saw him as passive, overpowered by events, and lacking in leadership. These public perceptions, the report concluded, would prove formidable challenges in Carter's reelection bid.[55]

Without thinking of the long-term ramifications, the president had supported a crisis definition of the hostage seizure, depicting himself as the leader who would gain the hostages' release. When the captives' freedom was not forthcoming, Carter was impaled on the terminological structure he had erected. After all, Hauser explains, the crisis was "an issue Carter himself defined as an important index of his presidential qualities."[56] The president's decision to promote a hostage "crisis" and his inability to gain the captives' quick release were not his only problems. Carter's communication efforts floundered because of the kind of argument he customarily used. Although Americans expect to hear strains of both idealism and pragmatism in their leaders' rhetoric, Carter's crisis discourse focused almost exclusively on idealism, which served to reinforce his public image as a passive leader.

THE FAILURE OF IDEALISM:
CARTER'S LACK OF PRAGMATISM IN HIS IRANIAN CRISIS DISCOURSE

According to Richard Weaver, idealistic rhetoric employs arguments based on definition, genus, or fundamental principles; it argues from "the nature or essence of things."[57] Idealistic discourse may define a certain class of things in terms of the principles they hold in common, or idealistic rhetoric may apply an already established classification or genus. In either event, rhetors employ definitions of ideational "essence" in order to convince auditors to follow one course of action rather than another. For example, Weaver notes: "If a speaker should define man as a creature with an indefeasible right to freedom and should upon this base an argument that a certain man or group of men are entitled to freedom, he would be arguing from definition."[58]

In *A Grammar of Motives,* Kenneth Burke supports Weaver's conception of idealistic argument when he points out that idealistic discourse emphasizes terms for agent (genus) and the principles and qualities that characterize that agent.[59] Implicitly or explicitly, idealistic rhetoric focuses on a "philosophy of being," or principles of definition, and requires that auditors comply with those principles. For Weaver, idealistic discourse constitutes the most ethical form of argument because it deals with the realm of enduring ideas, rather than sensory experience, and consequently concerns itself with a Platonic sense of Truth.[60] Burke, too, observes that idealistic rhetoric has a special concern with ethics because it argues that action must be taken in accordance with an absolute moral reality that transcends experiential phenomena.[61] In idealistic discourse, the means, or policy, adopted must allow one to stay true to held ideals.

In contrast to idealistic talk, pragmatic rhetoric consists of arguments from cause and effect or consequence. Weaver states that pragmatic rhetoric portrays a particular subject as "the cause of some effect or as the effect of some cause."[62] For instance, a president might argue that the massive production of cocaine in South American countries is the cause of drug abuse in the United States; in this scheme, the rhetor would then make the case for policies that attempt to curb drug abuse by decreasing the drug supply. A social worker, conversely, might claim that the South American drug trade is merely an effect of the demand for cocaine in this country and, accordingly, plead for policies that focus on American drug users. Were their policies instituted, these rhetors might point to the positive consequences of their actions for evidence of success.

Burke notes that pragmatic discourse "evaluates a doctrine by its 'consequences,' by what it is 'good for,' by 'the difference it will make to you and me,' or by its 'function,' or by asking whether it 'works satisfactorily.' "[63] According to Weaver, pragmatic argument is not as ethical as idealistic argument because it fails to concern itself with enduring principles or defined ideas. He also worries that rhetors who habitually engage in pragmatic discourse may play "too much upon the fears of their audience by stressing the awful nature of some consequence or by exaggerating the power of some cause." Yet, Weaver recognizes that everyone relies on pragmatic argument from time to time because their sense of history leads them to discern and to speak about particular relationships of cause and effect.[64]

The rhetorical themes of both idealism and pragmatism play an important role in political discourse. Rhetoricians as venerable as Aristotle and Cicero have argued that deliberative speeches concern expedience consistent with values or, in Cicero's terms, "what is honourable and what is advantageous."[65] This intertwining of idealistic and pragmatic themes in political rhetoric has been especially true of American society. According to communication scholar Ernest Bormann, the Puritans were the ones who institutionalized this persuasive tradition, which he calls "romantic pragmatism." The Puritans idealistically defined themselves as "God's chosen people." They also exhorted one another to choose policies with transcendent principles in mind or, in other words, to consider how their course of action reflected the values by which they defined their lives. At the same time, the Puritans pragmatically looked to "the usefulness, workability, and practicality of ideas and proposals for criteria of judgment" in deciding whether policies should be instituted and whether they had proved successful.[66]

Rod Hart claims that the twin rhetorical traditions of idealism and pragmatism are still with us. Because Americans are equally fond of both, Hart asserts that "American politicians . . . have normally balanced ideals and practicality for their constituents."[67] Rhetorical critic Carroll Arnold goes one step further when he argues that "successful public debates have been marked by an almost

anti-philosophical mixture" of idealism, pragmatism, and—he adds—
doctrinality. Arnold states that when public problem-solving has failed, it
usually has been because rhetors stressed one of these themes too heavily.[68]

The case of Jimmy Carter and Iran provides an example of the phenomenon
that Arnold discussed. During the hostage crisis, Carter relied almost entirely
on idealistic discourse and rarely embraced pragmatic appeals. The unabashed
idealism of the president's talk encouraged public perceptions of his passivity
and ineffectiveness. Although ideals are important to Americans, pragmatic
concerns are also of great significance. Jeff Bass, in his analysis of Lyndon
Johnson's rhetoric on the Dominican crisis, points out that claims of efficiency
are particularly appealing in contemporary times when foreign policy rarely
achieves quick, satisfactory solutions.[69] Moreover, citizens' desire for pragmatism may become especially great in times of crisis.

The word *crisis* focuses public attention on the circumstances to which it is
attached, arouses fears, and raises public expectations for practical policy
solutions. Once a president decides to call an event a "crisis," he heightens
citizens' need for swift results and for pragmatic presidential rhetoric about
those results.

This is *not* to say that presidents should ignore idealism in their crisis
discourse, for Americans still want to hear that U.S. policies are in accordance
with the principles they ascribe to their country. A scholar of international
affairs, Cecil V. Crabb, Jr., explains that American foreign policy is opera-
tionally pragmatic, but that leaders still must refer to principles of character as a
way to legitimize their policy decisions. He says that "the exercise of power by
the United States abroad must be related to some ostensible, worthwhile *human
purpose* that is understood (or at least intuitively sensed) by the American
people." If it is not, "applications of American power overseas . . . are not likely
to succeed or prove enduring." Crabb adds, however, that citizens tend to use
pragmatic standards of efficacy to evaluate the degree to which ideals have been
upheld.[70]

From the rhetorical perspective taken in this book, presidents must legitimize
policies with references to the sacred values through which our nation defines
itself because cause-effect arguments of expediency alone will not prove
sufficiently persuasive. At the same time, commanders-in-chief must point to
results not only to prove the practical success of policies, but also to convince
citizens that U.S. policies have upheld the nation's principles. Presidents
therefore must balance their idealistic and pragmatic talk with the greatest of
care. During the Cuban missile crisis, for example, Kennedy idealistically
claimed the United States was both peaceful and honorable, and that our policy
in regard to the missiles was consistent with our national character.

Likewise, Johnson declared that the limited nature of the Gulf of Tonkin
reprisals reflected our great responsibility, and Nixon asserted that only the

policy of a Cambodian invasion would be in accordance with U.S. will and character. During the *Mayaguez* crisis, Ford primarily discussed how his actions demonstrated his own innate leadership qualities, but even he emphasized on one occasion that "the handling of the *Mayaguez* incident should be a firm assurance that the United States is capable and has the will to act in emergencies, in challenges."[71] Reagan, too, as discussed in chapter 7, insisted that America was the personification of freedom and that U.S. policy in Grenada was consistent with that ideal.

These presidents also attended to pragmatic concerns in their crisis rhetoric. Kennedy, for instance, talked about the terrible, tangible consequences that Soviet policy had wrought and emphasized how the missile installation posed a threat to the Western Hemisphere. Kennedy later proved the worth of his quarantine policy when he announced its effects: the Soviets had agreed to withdraw their missiles. The other commanders-in-chief examined in this book also reported on the positive, tangible effects of their policies: we had destroyed the boats that fired on U.S. forces in the Gulf of Tonkin; we had captured North Vietnamese and Vietcong military supplies; we had gained the release of the *Mayaguez* crew; we had rescued Americans in Grenada. Presidential discourse about these positive consequences served as proof that the United States had succeeded in standing by its principles.

Although Jimmy Carter could not have prevented media coverage of Iran, he contributed to his own political difficulties through the urgent language and public attention his administration lavished on the issue and, hence, clearly established the hostage situation as a crisis that demanded an immediate solution. In addition, the extreme idealism of Carter's talk constrained his ability to resolve the crisis that he had done so much to promote. Unlike Kennedy and other presidents, Carter did not merely pay homage to ideals by describing U.S. character and asserting that U.S. policies were consistent with American principles. The president discussed ethics as a most important factor in determining what policies should be implemented.

According to Carter, he would only institute policies that upheld what he defined as the nation's honor and ideals. He announced at the start of the hostage seizure that the crisis "is a serious matter, as you know. . . . It's not a reason to abandon the principles or law or proprieties in our own country."[72] This meant, first, that Carter sought the safe release of the hostages, rather than simply an end to the crisis. According to the president, the United States had to be concerned with the hostages' lives because policies that were not would violate the nation's principles about the value of "human life" and "compassion."[73] Even Carter's most pragmatic goal therefore was constrained by other purposes consonant with his definition of American character.

Faced with the same political circumstances, other presidents might have made a quick end to the crisis their goal and ordered the captors to release the hostages by an impending deadline or to face the consequences of a military attack. This type of policy is often the most advantageous option a president can pursue when large numbers of Americans are held and their captivity is highly visible. If the hostages are released, the commander-in-chief can point to pragmatic results, and the country's honor and integrity will still appear intact. If, on the other hand, the president must resort to a military operation that results in harm to the hostages, U.S. citizens may mourn the loss but, nevertheless, praise the president for bringing the crisis to an expedient close. The devastating effects of an attack on the enemy serve as proof that the captors have been punished and the United States' national honor maintained.

Although such a scenario may seem callous, the overwhelmingly positive public reaction to the *Mayaguez* crisis—in which members of the *Mayaguez* crew were injured, dozens of American military personnel killed, and countless other Cambodian casualties incurred—points to its plausibility. In contrast, Jimmy Carter articulated a pragmatic goal, the safe release of the hostages, that was based on his definition of who Americans were and what they were like. His idealism hindered his ability to end the crisis because this goal was extremely difficult to attain given the lack of government in Iran.

The idealism of Carter's rhetoric also constrained his crisis management by narrowing the range of policy options he could pursue to those that he deemed consistent with the moral principles he set forth. As a result, Carter was left with few means that he was willing to pursue to free the hostages. He refused to order bombing raids, for example, which might harm the hostages and threaten other human life. He excluded the possibilities of a public apology for the U.S. role in propping up the shah's regime or the paying of ransom in the form of money or military equipment because these policies would violate U.S. honor and integrity.

Nonetheless, Carter was able initially to balance his appeals to ideals with pragmatic words about how he had frozen Iranian assets and stopped the import of Iranian oil and the adverse consequences these steps would have on the Iranians. But Carter quickly ran out of policies by which he could demonstrate practical effectiveness. Instead, he increasingly emphasized the nation's ideals and how its crisis policies ought to be consistent with those ideals. The president appeared increasingly passive. Burke writes that "ideals are never practicable; indeed, they are *by definition* something that you don't attain; they are merely *directions* in which you aim. (You can't hit 'North,' for instance, though you may hit a target placed to the North of you.)"[74]

The president's rhetoric on the Iranian crisis displayed little practicality, emphasizing instead directions in which the United States should aim. In the situation of his discourse, Carter portrayed events in Iran as a crisis and heightened a sense of public urgency and citizen expectations for quick results. The president's situational description also made idealistic concerns paramount, for he discussed his attempts to seek an ethical and pragmatic goal—the safe release of the hostages—which was largely beyond his control, and emphasized ideals for which he wanted the nation to strive in its crisis policies.

The style of Carter's rhetoric similarly emphasized that the United States ought to pursue policies compatible with its moral character. But he rarely pointed to tangible results or provided evidence that demonstrated how the United States had remained faithful to its ideals and why it was important to do so. This lack of pragmatism hurt the president's ability to maintain public support. Although his identificational appeals consistently sought to unite citizens behind his leadership through declarations of "our" shared principles, these statements rang hollow when Carter provided little evidence of progress, either in the attempt to gain the hostages' release or in the efforts to uphold the nation's honor and integrity.

Situation

Carter depicted the situation of the Iranian hostage crisis as:

> Because the Iranians seized American embassy personnel in Teheran (scene), the United States—or "we"—and Jimmy Carter—or "I"—(coactors) are pursuing (act) every possible channel (means) in order to secure the safe release of the hostages and to protect the integrity and interests of the United States (purposes).

Like most of the presidents in this study, Carter described a frightening scene. He claimed, for instance, that "American citizens continue to be held as hostages" in a climate of "terrorism and anarchy."[75] On another occasion, the president somberly noted that the captives were in particularly grave danger because Iran had no government that could enforce order and protect them. These circumstances dictated Carter's goal: "to get the hostages home and get them safe. That's my total commitment."[76] This statement to the contrary, the president's rhetoric revealed other obligations, as well. He maintained that the coactors of "we" and "I" also must "protect the integrity and the honor and the interest of our Nation."[77]

To accomplish all these goals, Carter did not, as one might expect, invoke dynamic terms for action. He claimed that we would "persist in our efforts" and "continue to pursue" our ends.[78] Even when the president announced sanctions against Iran, his terms for these acts frequently lacked the forcefulness of Kennedy, Johnson, Nixon, or Ford in their crisis talk. In an April 1980 speech, for instance, Carter edited out phrases such as "I have ordered that" or "I have directed that," which his speechwriters had included. The president instead made comments like "the Secretary of Treasury [State] and the Attorney

General will invalidate all visas issued to Iranian citizens for future entry into the United States effective today."[79]

Such complexity sapped Carter's statements about administration actions of their dynamism and made them sound like excerpts from a legal document. According to Hart's computer-assisted analysis, Carter produced the most passive presidential rhetoric of any chief executive from Truman through Reagan. Rather than discuss change, motion, or the implementation of ideas, the president spoke in patient, quiet terms and relied upon words that referred to mental functions, such as "consider" or "believe."[80] The passivity of Carter's crisis rhetoric distinguishes him from the other commanders-in-chief examined thus far, all of whom conveyed a sense of action in their public talk.

In the discourse of Kennedy, Johnson, Nixon, and Ford, at least one of the dominant ratios of terms for situation included words for act, as did each of the terminological relationships that characterized their style. Rather than accentuate action, Jimmy Carter emphasized means and, most importantly, how those means must be consistent with our nation's principles. Carter stated at a news conference, for instance, "I am pursuing every possible avenue to have the hostages released."[81] But he made it clear that the policy alternatives he considered "possible" were ones that would both free the hostages safely and preserve our country's interests, honor, and integrity.

Two predominant relationships existed among Carter's key terms for situation: scene-purpose and purpose-means. At first glance, these ratios appear to violate the expectations of an idealist terminology and its corresponding emphasis on actors and their properties. One even might argue that a purpose-means ratio looks suspiciously pragmatic, as if the rhetor were concerned with the most efficient policy to reach a desired goal. Nonetheless, a closer examination indicates that Carter's terms for purpose dealt with moral principles, the concern of the perennial rhetorical idealist.

The first ratio of situational terms in Carter's talk, terms for scene-purpose, corresponded to that found in the crisis discourse of Kennedy, Johnson, and Nixon. Like these presidents, Carter described a menacing scene and then argued that the scene dictated what purposes must be fulfilled. Like Johnson, President Carter, particularly with the passage of time, devoted less of his discourse to a depiction of the scene in Iran and more of his talk to a description of the purposes emanating from that scene. The ordering of these terms, however, always remained clear. The president told State Department employees, for example, that "there is one issue and that is the early and safe release of the American hostages from their captors in Tehran. And it's important for us to realize that from the very first hour of the captivity of our hostages by a mob, who is indistinguishable from the Government itself, that has been our purpose."[82]

Rather than argue for an immediate end to Iranian blackmail—whether through the Iranians' release of the hostages or a U.S. military attack on Teheran—Carter proffered a tangible goal that was shaped by abstract moral ideals: the United States must seek the safe return of American marines and embassy personnel, rather than a purely expedient resolution to the crisis regardless of the risk to the hostages. Beyond this aim, Carter professed other purposes, as well. He told state governors in November 1979 that "I've just gotten a report that there are maybe 80,000 Iranians demonstrating outside our Embassy in a highly emotional state." Therefore, Carter said, he would do whatever he could to protect the hostages' lives and to defend the country's honor.[83] Likewise, the president told reporters on *Meet the Press* in January 1980 that the hostage crisis was "an abhorrent violation of every moral and ethical standard and international law." Because of this, Carter said, our nation would seek

> to protect, first of all, the short-term and long-range interests of our country; secondly, to protect the safety and the lives of the hostages themselves; third, to pursue every possible avenue of the early and safe release of our hostages; fourth, to avoid bloodshed if possible, because I have felt from the very beginning that the initiation of a military action or the causing of bloodshed would undoubtedly result in the death of the hostages; and fifth, and perhaps most difficult of all, is to arouse and sustain the strong support by the vast majority of nations on Earth for our position.[84]

As if these purposes were not exhaustive enough, Carter provided even more. He told voters during a campaign stop in California that we had to uphold "the principles of our Nation" and mentioned to citizens at a town hall meeting in Texas the importance of protecting "the honor of our country and the integrity of our Nation."[85] For Carter, the embassy seizure dictated that we seek the safe return of the hostages and also that we fulfill more abstract goals related to U.S. character. These two sets of goals were potentially incompatible. After all, one could defend the nation's honor and at the same time, bring harm to the hostages. That possibility notwithstanding, the president told citizens that the United States could protect its honor, integrity, and national interests, and still gain the hostages' safe release.

The espousal of multiple and potentially incompatible purposes alone did not make Carter's crisis discourse any different from that of Kennedy, Nixon, and Johnson. During the Cuban missile crisis, Kennedy claimed that Americans could achieve the tangible goal of the withdrawal of Soviet missiles and simultaneously accomplish the more abstract aim of protecting freedom and peace. Similarly, Nixon asserted that the United States wanted to protect U.S.

soldiers in Vietnam, to ensure the U.S. withdrawal program, to attain a just peace, and to demonstrate U.S. character. Kennedy and Nixon took action and pointed to the observable consequences of that action—the removal of the Cuban missiles and the caches of captured Vietcong weapons and supplies. The presidents appeared to have achieved their concrete goals expediently, and the achievement of these goals, in turn, served as evidence that the presidents' less tangible purposes had also been fulfilled. For his part, Johnson argued for the unitary goal of peace and the defense of freedom during the Gulf of Tonkin crisis, and he, too, emphasized the success of U.S. retaliation as evidence that this purpose had been realized. Only later, after Johnson had repetitively engaged in indirect dissociation and the implications of his moderate Vietnam policy had made themselves known, did peace and the defense of freedom appear to be inconsistent with one another.

Carter's rhetoric was distinguished by its extreme idealism. Although Kennedy and Nixon implied that their goals were compatible and Johnson outwardly treated peace and defense of freedom as one and the same, Carter emphasized his terms for purpose and overtly, repeatedly argued that his goals were completely harmonious with one another. His talk also was distinct because his focus on ideals as goals constrained the policy avenues open to him. According to Carter, U.S. policies had to be in keeping with the way he defined U.S. character. Carter accentuated the consistency of his goals when he told reporters in April 1980 that aims he articulated could be reached "on an equal basis."[86] As late as October 1980, when the hostages had been imprisoned for nearly a year and no sign of their imminent release was in sight, Carter persisted in claiming at a New Jersey campaign stop that his many purposes could be reached "compatibly" and said to voters in Flint, Michigan, "I've never seen any incompatibility between doing these things at the same time."[87]

Burke writes that such assertions are typical of idealists, for the idealist's world is one in which incompatibilities among one's principles do not exist. For instance, the idealist would claim that individuals can live up to the various principles by which they define themselves—spouse, parent, teacher, and friend—in a perfect way, or that our nation simultaneously can actualize the ideals of individual rights and collective national interest upon which it is founded. Burke explains that "an unwritten clause" of idealism is that "in this realm all contradictions are to be reconciled; hence it would simply be irrelevant to concern oneself with contradictions at all."[88] Throughout his public statements, Carter pointed to one tangible goal—the release of the hostages—and to numerous constitutive ideals for which the United States should strive. The president's insistence on the compatibility of these goals, especially when he could present little evidence that any of them had been reached, raised questions about his leadership abilities.

Furthermore, the idealism of Carter's situational portrayal limited, in a unique way, the policy avenues open to him. Carter chose to pursue a tangible aim, the safe release of the hostages, that was exceedingly difficult to attain given the political circumstances in Iran. The second terminological ratio prevalent in his talk, purpose-means, placed further constraints on Carter's crisis management. He stipulated that crisis policies were feasible only if they could safely free the hostages *and* allow the United States to remain true to its other moral purposes. Like Kennedy, Nixon, and Johnson, Carter employed talk of principles as a way to legitimize his policies. Unlike those presidents, Carter also idealistically applied principles of character as a way to determine the appropriateness of any given policy.

Carter consistently emphasized that the means he pursued must meet not only pragmatic demands, but also idealistic demands. In response to the embassy seizure, the president initially took the route of economic sanctions. He announced, for example, that the United States would no longer buy oil from Iran. Carter maintained that the ban would help bring the release of the hostages (pragmatism) and also would "eliminate any suggestion that economic pressures can weaken our stand on basic issues of principle" (idealism). The president pursued "every peaceful means, through every diplomatic means, to bring about a resolution of this crisis, to protect the honor and integrity of our country, and to secure the safe release of our people back to freedom."

In April 1980, Carter broke diplomatic relations with Iran, expelled Iranian diplomats and military personnel from the United States, and took additional economic sanctions. The president again portrayed these policies as consistent with his pragmatic and idealistic goals when he said that he was "committed to the safe return of the American hostages and to the preservation of our national honor"; his new steps were "necessary" to attain these goals.[89]

That same month, Carter also had to deal with a possible conflict between the moral purposes he had advocated since November and the military rescue mission he had ordered. The operation appeared, on its face, to be an expedient attempt to bring the crisis to a close. Had hostages or innocent Iranian citizens been killed, the president would probably have faced charges of hypocrisy from a number of quarters given the great emphasis he had placed on the desire to avoid bloodshed and keep the hostages safe. The consistent and blatant idealism of Carter's rhetoric encouraged citizens to scrutinize his behavior and to apply higher ethical standards when evaluating him than they usually applied to politicians.

When the mission ended before the U.S. military reached Teheran, Carter appeared on television and addressed this potential problem by arguing that the rescue attempt was consistent with the purposes he had upheld in previous months. According to the president, increased anarchy in Iran had posed new dangers to the hostages. Thus the military operation had been both practical and moral, for it was designed to "safeguard American lives." Carter also called the operation a "humanitarian mission" and claimed it was ethical because it upheld our nation's moral principles:

> Our goal in Iran is not to conquer; neither was theirs [the men of the rescue team]. Their goal was not to destroy nor to injure anyone. As they left Iran, following an unpredictable accident during their withdrawal stage, with eight of their fellow warriors dead, they carefully released, without harm, 44 Iranians who had passed by the site and who were detained to protect the integrity of the mission.[90]

According to Carter, the military operation was consonant with his goals of safe release for the hostages and the preservation of U.S. ideals. Americans also supported the rescue attempt,[91] perhaps because it spoke to their desire for expediency, at the same time that Carter's discourse and the fact that hostages and innocent Iranians were not harmed prevented the operation from appearing inconsistent with the bold idealism the president had espoused.

In other public statements, Carter also made it clear that not all peaceful means to end the crisis were feasible. He told voters at a town meeting in California, "There are some things that I could not do in order to secure the release of the hostages if it meant embarrassing our country or apologizing for something which we have not done or bringing our Nation to its knees to beg those terrorists to do what they should do under international law and in the realm of human compassion." The president also declared that the United States would not pay a ransom to get the hostages back.[92] He maintained that we could acquiesce to Iranian demands and bring the hostages home, but at the cost of the nation's honor. Only a special means could meet all the purposes Carter articulated.

According to Burke, a terminological relationship like that between purpose and means in Carter's discourse is ethically of great significance. He explains that "a man may deliberately choose a less 'efficient' means for doing something because it is 'his way' (if he is concerned not merely for the successful outcome of the given operation, but also for its performance in keeping with his 'character,' or norms of his being)."[93] Carter idealistically claimed that we could resolve the hostage crisis only through those policies that befitted our character as a nation. As a result, the president inadvertently robbed his discourse of activity, because only rather vague terms for means, such as "diplomatic avenues" or "peaceful means," could attain all of the goals he had espoused. Carter, unable to tell citizens what specific policy he was pursuing to end the crisis, tended to talk in generalities instead.

He told reporters in November 1979, "We are proceeding, I guarantee you, in every possible way, every possible moment, to get the hostages freed and, at the same time, protect the honor and the integrity and the basic principles of our country." In a similar fashion, Carter asserted at a February 1980 press conference, "We have pursued every possibility to achieve those goals. No stone has been left unturned in the search for a solution."[94] Although it is not unusual for presidents to be brief or to speak of policy in broad terms, statements like these prevailed in Carter's crisis rhetoric about Iran and portrayed him as a man who spoke in generalities because he had few specifics to offer.

Carter portrayed the situation in Iran as a frightening crisis scene that dictated U.S. purposes: to seek the safe release of the hostages and to uphold the nation's moral principles. The president's terms for purpose were highly idealistic. Even the tangible goal he advocated incorporated concern for the value of human life, and Carter repeatedly emphasized that his many purposes were completely compatible with one another. According to the president, "we" and "I" simply needed to pursue means that were consistent with the nation's moral principles and that could also attain tangible ends. Carter's focus on means and abstract ideals made his discourse sound exceedingly passive.

Moreover, political circumstances in Iran and the narrow range of policies Carter considered "appropriate" hindered his efforts to free the hostages and pointed to potential incompatibilities among the various purposes he espoused. Because the idealistic constraints upon the president's choice of policy left him with increasingly fewer options, Carter was reduced to speaking in generalities. His continual references to "any possible channel" depicted him as an ineffectual leader frantically in search of some solution. The characteristics of idealism present in the situation of the president's discourse, as well as the persuasive obstacles that they posed, were deeply rooted in Carter's style.

Style

The president described the key actors of his discourse as "I" and "we." Frequently, "we" seemed to refer to the United States as a whole, whereas at other times it seemed to represent the U.S. government. Like Kennedy's crisis talk, the term "we" played the more important role in Carter's style. The president described what "we" were like and how "we" acted, but provided almost no descriptive terms in conjunction with "I." Because Carter was a part of the larger "we," however, his glowing descriptive terms for this actor reflected upon himself as well.

The president depicted "we" as an actor who had courage, persistence, patience, maturity, moral decency, and common sense.[95] On the surface, Carter did not appear to portray the actor of his discourse in a way that differed markedly from the descriptions ascribed to actors by Kennedy, Johnson, Nixon, and Ford. Like Carter, these other presidents often described their actors as courageous, persistent, patient, or moral, and Lyndon Johnson claimed that the actor of his talk had common sense. Yet, none of these other presidents depicted the actor of their crisis resolution as mature, a quality our society claims to value. Because of this, the actor of Carter's rhetoric appeared to be much more rational and ethical than the actors these other presidents portrayed.

The "we" of Carter's talk acted in a correspondingly rational and ethical manner. The president said to journalists in April 1980, "We believe in treating others with respect and with good will and with decency." Carter maintained that our country continued to exemplify these characteristics throughout the hostage crisis. He held that "what we have tried to do is to act with moral decency, with restraint, with sensitivity." The president told Michigan voters in October 1980, "we've acted in a very mature way." In addition, he remarked before the American Society of Newspaper Editors that our nation would act "with courage and also with wisdom."[96]

Carter's terms for actor were involved in one dominant ratio: terms for actor-means. For the president, the means we employed to free the hostages had to be consistent with our character as actors. Carter told reporters on Election Day, for instance, that any proposal to end the crisis would have "to uphold our Nation's honor and integrity."[97] This statement echoed Carter's purpose-means ordering of terms for situation, for almost all of Carter's terms for purpose dealt with genus, or principles, that constituted actors. Carter exploited terminological ambiguity, equating the nation's purposes with who "we" were.

In fact, the president explained how even the goal of safety for the hostages was based upon the United States' moral principles and that the peaceful and humanitarian channels we pursued therefore emanated from our national character. Carter commented to journalists,

> the relationship between our national interests, the national honor on the one hand, and the hostages' lives on the other has never been separated in my mind. The two are directly interrelated. If I should do anything to lessen the importance paid by us to the hostages' lives and safety and freedom, it would obviously be a reflection on our own Nation's principles, that we value a human life, we value human freedom, that we are a country with compassion, and that we are not callous about the value of the lives of those 53 hostages.[98]

Because of the relationship between the nation's principles and the hostages' lives, Carter maintained in November 1980 that "we'll continue to deal with it [the crisis] using the principles that I've outlined to you before, which we will certainly honor, to protect the hostages, their lives and safety, to work for their earliest possible release, but not to do anything that would violate the honor and integrity of our country."[99] We would, in other words, continue to pursue means consistent with our character.

To examine the style of the president's discourse is to come face-to-face with incurable, irrepressible idealism. Carter's style gave terms for actor preeminence and focused intently on how U.S. policy could reflect the actor's principles. In addition, the president's style constrained his portrayal of the situation. The situation of Carter's rhetoric argued that purposes arose from the scene and that these purposes dictated the type of means that could be employed. Meanwhile, the style of the president's discourse insisted that the principles of the key actor must guide the choice of means. Terms for purpose and terms for actor thereby overlapped in Carter's talk. Even in dealing with the pragmatics of a political problem, the president only advocated policies to end the crisis that also met the ethical principles he ascribed to the country. Carter's penchant for rhetorical idealism further revealed itself in his efforts to encourage citizens to identify with his crisis management.

Identificational Appeals

Like many of the presidents in this book, Carter sometimes engaged in antithetical appeals that urged citizens to support him and his policies in opposition to the Iranians, but this identificational strategy was not characteristic of his talk. Carter's discourse on Iran relied most often on implicit appeals that encouraged citizens to unite under the rubric of "we." Johnson's rhetoric about the Gulf of Tonkin featured this same identificational strategy, but where Johnson used "we" to identify Americans with specific actions—such as the successful sinking of enemy boats—Carter's discourse attempted to unite citizens behind repeated declarations of national principle and statements of the pragmatic goal he could not seem to reach. Shortly after the hostages were taken, for instance, Carter asserted that "we are trying as best we can to protect the honor of the country and to protect the lives of the hostages who are courageous, dedicated, and who deserve every protection that we can give them."[100] The president's use of implicit appeals here portrayed his goals as "our" goals.

More than a year later, Carter continued to invoke this identificational strategy in almost the same way. He told journalists, "We'll continue to protect our Nation's honor, to work for the hostages' release and make sure that we do everything we can to protect them from any abuse, and to make sure they stay alive and well."[101] According to Burke, rhetorical idealism displays a "futuristic stress upon kinds of social *unification*" by emphasizing a future utopia in which rhetor and listeners will become one through the realization of shared ideals.[102] Carter's use of "we" in his Iranian crisis discourse encouraged listeners to unite with him in the accomplishment of future goals, rather than allowing citizens to bask in the glory of goals "we" already had achieved.

Because of this, Carter found the allure of this identificational strategy difficult to sustain. As a president expected to engage in practical problem-solving, Carter instead invoked implicit appeals that conjured up the image of a social movement leader or a Baptist minister urging his followers to stay true to communally held, abstract ideals. The use of "we" in presidential crisis rhetoric can implicitly link citizens with the nation's achievements—and its leader— and consequently provide a sense of personal efficacy over "our" success. In the case of Carter and Iran, the president was unable to free the hostages quickly and provided little indication of what "we" were doing to achieve that or any of the other more idealistic goals he discussed. Carter's consistent and insistent claims about what "we" would do may have grown increasingly frustrating to Americans who could discern no sense of progress. In this context, the president appeared to lack competence. Citizens also may have wondered whether he had interpreted the nation's principles correctly—whether morality and integrity really meant the wimpishness and weakness of which Carter was often accused.

In addition to implicit appeals, Carter supported his crisis talk with extensive explicit appeals through his references to what "I"—Jimmy Carter—had done. Johnson, Nixon, and Ford also employed a number of explicit appeals in their crisis discourse when they emphasized their constitutional authority and pointed to the action they had taken. Carter, conversely, contributed to percep- tions that he was passive because he rarely referred to his authority as president and typically refrained from dramatic descriptions of his actions or accomplish- ments. During the early months of the hostage seizure, the president used dramatic symbolic actions such as the Unity Day Proclamation, the White House Christmas tree ceremony, and his withdrawal from campaign activities to focus attention on the crisis. Carter did not, however, balance his promotion of the crisis with an equally dramatic portrayal of his management of the crisis. Instead, the president's explicit appeals depicted him as involved in only the most passive of activities.

In an interview with the *Detroit Free Press,* for instance, Carter said, "I have never failed, any morning when I woke up, to pray that God would let those hostages come home safe at the earliest possible moment."[103] The president's other explicit appeals were equally passive. Over the course of the crisis, Carter claimed: "I must emphasize," "I am proud," "I appreciate," "I've tried to make the best judgment," "I am concerned," "I am committed," "I wanted," and "I've had two goals in mind."[104] These explicit appeals reflected his concern with ideas, rather than pragmatic policy implementation.

When other avenues failed in early 1980, the president took no bold action. Instead, he sought additional knowledge from Islamic scholars whom he invited to the White House to discuss how the crises in Iran and Afghanistan had affected the United States' relationship with Islamic countries.[105] Carter articu- lated his great idealism in this remark to reporters in the spring of 1980: "I have spent hundreds of hours, literally, studying Iran and the composition of its people and the religious and political attitudes, the character of the specific people who are involved, so I could make the proper judgments according-ly."[106] Faced with crises of their own, other presidents claimed they had retaliated or taken action. Carter, instead, studied the character of his opponent so that he could make better judgments, assuming (and reflecting simultaneous-ly) that one's character guides one's actions.

The president's discourse about the Iranian hostages consisted primarily of implicit appeals, supported by a fair number of explicit appeals, but neither of these identificational strategies maintained their long-term attractiveness. When the hostages remained imprisoned for more than a year, the president continued to claim that "we" could gain the hostages' safe release, protect our country's honor, defend the United States' interests, and preserve our national integrity. Citizens' experience with the prolonged crisis told them otherwise. In the end, Carter no longer could speak for "us" and no longer could represent "our" principles.

Beyond this, Carter's crisis rhetoric depicted the president as no different from many other Americans. He studied the crisis; he prayed about it; he thought about it. Carter may have been elected as one of "the people," but in the midst of crisis, citizens expected him to be more than this: they wanted him to be a leader. Finally, the president's steady employment of explicit appeals clearly linked him with the stalemated crisis. Just as his association with the crisis had politically benefitted Carter early on, his long-term identification with the seizure harmed him irreparably. In many ways, Carter's idealism held him hostage, unable to project the image of presidential leadership that Americans expected.

If Carter made a major mistake when he promoted the embassy seizure as a crisis, then the idealistic character of his crisis talk only added to the political difficulties he later faced. Presidents who embrace a crisis terminology must produce rhetoric that employs not only idealistic arguments, but also pragmatic arguments. Although citizens want to hear that their government's policies are consistent with the nation's moral principles, they desire relatively quick, concrete results and discourse about those results. Carter instead espoused an array of moral principles and a pragmatic goal constrained by those principles. The safe release of the hostages could not be accomplished quickly because of political conditions in Teheran. Moreover, Carter severely limited the policy options he considered "possible" by requiring that they be consistent with his definition of American ethics.

As months passed, the president found it increasingly difficult to find a resolution to the crisis. He also failed to reassure citizens through pragmatic discourse that could have shown him attending to practical concerns and provided Americans with encouragement as to *why* they should continue to pursue the principles he set forth or evidence as to *how* we were fulfilling these abstract goals. Instead, Carter restated the same point again and again: our nation must act in accordance with its principles. End of story.

According to rhetorical scholar Dan Hahn, Carter's discourse about the crisis and about foreign policy in general frequently demonstrated that "any leader who oversells problems without overselling his solutions is bound to be perceived as incapable of coping with the problems."[107] Political scientist Mark Rozell cites Carter's own speechwriters, who claimed that the president's "tendency to identify bad news without offering any immediate cure" was a political liability.[108] Had Carter balanced his idealistic and pragmatic appeals equitably in his Iranian discourse, he might have articulated the more expedient aim of bringing the crisis to a speedy end. Even if the president had maintained his ethical stand on this goal, however, a greater concern with pragmatics might have led him to explore a wider range of policy options or to present citizens with more compelling reasons for continuing to support his management efforts, despite his inability to end the crisis quickly.

A second lesson to be gleaned from Carter's experience is that once a president adopts high-minded principles to manage an issue, he had best remain above reproach in his management of other issues as well. The contrast between Carter's political machinations for the 1980 campaign and the idealism of his crisis talk added to public cynicism about the president. Carter's idealistic rhetoric and his inability to free the hostages already placed him in a precarious political position. Although he portrayed the rescue mission as consistent with his principles, the president's strategic announcement the day of the Wisconsin primary and, especially, his return to the campaign trail days after the failed military operation seemed like instances of blatant political pragmatism. Citizens may have wondered whether Carter's idealistic statements were sincere or just a public con job to obscure his incompetence.

Angered by the president's opportunism, journalists wrote about his mean streak and began to speculate on whether he planned to resolve the crisis in time for the November elections. The Reagan campaign also warned of what it called an impending "October surprise."[109] If Carter's crisis talk was too intensely idealistic, then his surprise announcement and decision to leave the Rose Garden seemed too expedient, or pragmatic. The contrast between the two cast doubts on the veracity of the president's crisis management efforts and upon his character. Hauser might add that the Carter administration probably overlooked such possibilities because of its technological image of the public; that is, the president and his aides perceived Americans as passive and highly impressionable.

According to Hauser, the administration relied heavily on public opinion polls to construct messages that it thought would be popular in the short term. What the White House did not consider was what would prove persuasive in the long run or how citizens would analyze and judge all of the president's messages rather than just the most recent one.[110] Once Carter committed himself so completely to ideals in the hostage crisis, he needed to stay faithful to that commitment in regard to the 1980 campaign.

IDEALISM HELD HOSTAGE:
JIMMY CARTER AS PRESIDENTIAL RHETOR

In 1979, just months before the attack on the U.S. embassy in Iran, Gerald Rafshoon told the president that

> your natural style—low-key, soft spoken, gentleness—was perfect for 1976. People were looking for the antithesis of Richard Nixon—a non-politician. In 1980 they're looking for a leader. . . .
>
> You've got to improve your speaking style. It should be more forceful, less gentle, harder and more interesting. Your ability (or lack of it) to move an audience and a nation by your words is no longer a minor matter of personal concern to you. It is the single greatest reason (under our control) why your Presidency has not been more successful than it has.[111]

Rafshoon's observations about the style of Carter's presidential communication could as easily have been written during the hostage crisis as before. Possibly the idealism of his Iranian crisis discourse was present in his other talk as well. During the 1976 campaign, Carter had displayed a propensity for intensely idealistic rhetoric. He defined the American people as good, honest, and decent. In the aftermath of Watergate, the candidate also reassured citizens that "our government can express the highest common ideals of human beings—*if* we demand of government true standards of excellence."[112] Carter's talk idealistically focused on the characteristics of a genus. According to communication analyst Martha Martin, the governor's campaign rhetoric constantly emphasized personality traits like morality, intelligence, and competence.[113] Carter not only concentrated on the qualities and principles that defined American citizens, but also argued that these ideals should guide our actions.

In his analysis of Carter's campaign talk, rhetorical critic John Patton writes that "in upholding an idealized conception of what the people should become in conformity with their essential character, Carter provides an ultimate, directive goal." Carter's discourse provided, in Patton's terms, "an ethical grounding for politics."[114] Carter the rhetorical idealist did not talk about specific programs or policy implementation and the positive effects they would have. Instead, his discourse advocated abstract moral action. The added appeal of his talk, of course, was that nearly everyone could agree with the broad principles of humanity that he espoused.[115]

After Carter entered office, he continued to give voice to principles, rather than specific policies, and soon found himself under attack for his passivity. Senator Henry ("Scoop") Jackson, for instance, quipped that the president had "abulia," the abnormal inability to act. According to Tad Szulc, Carter did nothing to stop the devaluation of the dollar except to lecture citizens about economic principles.[116] The president seemed to feel more at home in the realm of principles and ideas rather than pragmatics. Communication scholars Les Altenberg and Robert Cathcart provide further support for this idea when they argue that the president constantly advocated the principle of human rights, but never defined it in a precise way so that it could be implemented credibly in his administration's foreign policy.[117]

The president's reliance on abstractions was just one consistent flaw of his rhetoric. To make matters worse, Carter also exemplified the idealist's inability to set priorities for commitments or to see any incompatibility among the various principles he espoused. James Fallows, one of the president's speech-writers, said Carter would not discuss one particular issue in a speech, but instead inserted lists of topics into his addresses and then mentioned them all.[118] The president eschewed talk of policies for talk of principles, and he was unable to focus on any single principle as the preeminent goal for the nation to attain. In a typically idealistic fashion, Carter asserted that Americans could achieve them all.

The president's rhetoric not only emphasized principles but, more importantly, the actors who embodied those principles. Carter's 1976 campaign talk had appealed to voters because it offered optimistic promises of a future in which the American people would realize their full potential. Once Carter became president, he continued to emphasize national character—and *his* character—over policy action. Fallows explains that the president spoke with "gusto" when

> he was speaking about the subject that most inspired him: not what he proposed to *do,* but who he *was.* Where Lyndon Johnson boasted of schools built and children fed, where Edward Kennedy holds out the promise of the energies he might mobilize and the ideas he might enact, Jimmy Carter tells us that he is a good man. His positions are correct, his values sound. Like Marshal Petain after the fall of France, he has offered his person to the nation. This is not an inconsiderable gift; his performance in office shows us why it's not enough.[119]

When Carter the candidate became Carter the president, citizens expected him to do more than state his high principles. They demanded him to act and to lead.

Perhaps because of this, many Americans remember Jimmy Carter as "a nice man who meant well but who lacked the capacity to be an effective president."[120] His public persona seemed to reflect that of a born-again Baptist who asked Americans to save themselves through faith in the nation's ideals.

Carter's discourse on the Iranian hostage crisis exemplifies the idealism that permeated much of his presidential rhetoric. In addition, his crisis talk demonstrates that appeals to ideals and principles alone cannot inspire citizens for long. Nevertheless, the failure of the president's discourse is no reason to scoff at principles, for Americans demand both idealism and pragmatism of their leaders. In his 1983 talk about the crisis in Grenada, Ronald Reagan demonstrated just how perfectly these two rhetorical threads could intertwine.

Chapter Seven

MISSION AND MANIFEST DESTINY IN GRENADA
Ronald Reagan Rallies the American Faithful

In October 1983, Americans found themselves in the midst of two crises. The first crisis erupted in Beirut, where the United States suffered both humiliation and great loss of life with a suicide terrorist attack on U.S. marines. A second crisis, one that quickly eclipsed events in Beirut, was Operation Urgent Fury, the U.S. invasion of Grenada. Indeed, Americans seemed only too happy to put the Middle East tragedy out of their minds and to concentrate, in President Reagan's words, on how "the United States came to the rescue of democracy and of hundreds of American students in Grenada."[1] Through such discourse, the president turned attention away from the failure of Beirut and focused it instead on the victory of American forces over a Communist coup in Grenada. Anchorwoman Beverly Williams noted, "Coming on the heels of Beirut and the frustration over the deaths there, it [Grenada] was something to cheer about."[2] For many citizens, Grenada was not only a moment of exhilaration in the aftermath of Lebanon, but a symbol of the glory that epitomized America.

Viewed from a more detached perspective, the U.S. victory in Grenada hardly seemed worthy of the celebratory mood it evoked. President Reagan himself had described Grenada as "only twice the size of the District of Columbia, with a total population of about 110,000 people," and Reagan's Deputy Press Secretary Larry Speakes observed that the invasion "was the equivalent of the Washington Redskins scheduling my old high school team, the Merigold Wildcats."[3] This disparity in size notwithstanding, Ronald Reagan claimed that U.S. military forces had achieved two significant accomplishments. They had captured an airfield that Grenada said it was building to encourage tourism, but which the president maintained was intended to export Communism, and they had rescued American medical students on the island. Questions about the value of these accomplishments arose a few months later with the Reagan administration's announcement that the United States would help Grenada complete its airport in order to "boost tourism," which was "vital to the revival of Grenada's economy."[4] Moreover, numerous critics pointed out that the students had been free to leave Grenada and had not considered themselves in danger until after the invasion began.[5]

The public outpouring of support for the invasion of Grenada and the president who launched it seemed even more puzzling in light of Reagan's

175

responsibility for U.S. policy in Beirut and the foreign policy fiasco that took place there only days earlier. In order to explain U.S. public reaction to the Grenadian crisis, one has to turn not to a policy analysis of Grenada and Beirut, but to American culture and to the implicit understanding of that culture reflected in Ronald Reagan's rhetoric.

According to communication scholar D. Ray Heisey, the foreign policy discourse of world leaders is grounded in their cultures' "acceptable images of political reality." Heisey claims that Reagan's October 27 address on Grenada and Beirut emphasized a Communist enemy that the United States faced and the United States' power to resist that enemy, portrayals consonant with American history and culture, which depict Communism as a perennial foe and the United States as defending its national self-interests.[6] Rhetorical critic David Procter similarly argues that Reagan's invasion announcement and subsequent televised speech exemplified the cultural tradition of American "rescue mission" rhetoric in which presidents justify military action based upon the need to combat chaos abroad.[7] Bonnie Dow supports this finding through her own observation of how Reagan's nationwide address emphasized the precarious situation in Grenada.[8]

In his study of Reagan's October 27 speech, rhetorical analyst David Klope also firmly roots Reagan's rhetoric in American culture, for he contends that it tapped into the myths of progress, freedom, national self-interest, and mission, or selfless patronage. Klope argues that the president's speech allowed him to shift guilt for both the bombing in Beirut and the invasion of Grenada to the Soviet Union and thereby to escape personal culpability for these events.[9] Likewise, David Birdsell indicates that Reagan intertwined Grenada and Beirut in his televised address.[10]

In this chapter, I examine Reagan's October 27 speech and his other discourse about the Grenadian crisis. Although my analysis corroborates previous findings, it amplifies them by examining how the president's discourse invoked two sacred American myths—mission and manifest destiny—and by exploring the role of these myths in the presidential promotion and management of foreign crises. I argue that the incorporation of mission and manifest destiny in Reagan's rhetoric served to legitimize U.S. intervention in Grenada and to portray the victory in Grenada as a victory over U.S. foes in Lebanon. Hence, the president absolved himself of blame for events in Beirut, diverted public attention from Beirut to Grenada, and further reinforced the importance of mission and manifest destiny in American culture.

Although people often think of myths as fairy tales intended only to entertain, religious historian Mircea Eliade argues that myths constitute sacred truths for the communities in which they develop.[11] Rene Wellek and Austin Warren elaborate on this idea in *Theory of Literature* when they define myths as "the explanations a society offers its young of why the world is and why we do as we do, its pedagogic images of the nature and destiny of man."[12] In this sense, myths constitute the foundation of a community, for they describe how the society first came to be, and they provide principles for behavioral guidance through sanctions and taboos.[13]

Myths may be religious in nature, or they may emanate from the political/ cultural context of a society. In either case, myths are sacred to the people who hold them; they also shape the way people interpret the world. According to political scientist W. Lance Bennett, political myths "are like the lenses in a pair of glasses in the sense that they are not the things people see when they look at the world, but they are the things they see with. Myths are the truths about society that are taken for granted."[14]

In American culture, two myths have been of special importance: the myth of mission and the myth of manifest destiny. The myth of mission has its origins with our Puritan forebears, who considered themselves to be God's chosen people. According to this myth, the United States has a moral duty to serve as a model for other countries in the world and thus to encourage freedom around the globe.[15] The myth of manifest destiny, on the other hand, was first articulated explicitly in the mid-1800s by U.S. imperialists who wanted to create, in historian Frederick Merk's words, a "free, confederated, self-governed republic on a continental scale." Imperialists argued that the United States was divinely destined to expand its boundaries to the Pacific Ocean and, eventually, to the rest of North America. Many even claimed that the United States would eventually encompass the entire Western Hemisphere.[16]

Although distinct, the myths of mission and manifest destiny have much in common. Both consider the United States to be divinely blessed. Both emphasize the principle of freedom. And both postulate that the world would be better if more of its peoples emulated the United States. The essential difference between mission and manifest destiny lies in the methods through which they carry out their goals; mission argues that the United States should serve as a model of virtue, whereas manifest destiny takes a more interventionist approach.[17]

In contemporary America, these two myths are intertwined. Although the United States no longer serves as a passive model of virtue in foreign affairs, its presidents and its citizens often beam with pride over U.S. actions abroad and claim that we are the envy of the world. Likewise, Americans and their leaders may not actively encourage the acquisition of new territories; nonetheless, the United States intervenes in other countries in the name of freedom and tries, on a regular basis, to expand its reign of influence around the globe.

In his discourse on the crisis in Grenada, Ronald Reagan embraced both manifest destiny and mission. He romantically portrayed the United States as a noble nation that had engaged in selfless heroics in order to "save" freedom and democracy in this hemisphere, and he emphasized the safe rescue of medical students as proof that we had succeeded in fulfilling our national destiny. According to the president, U.S. actions in Grenada also served as an exemplary model of the United States' devotion to freedom. Ronald Reagan's rhetoric about Grenada invoked two of America's most sacred myths, thus encouraging citizens to view the invasion through lenses that increased the significance of the military triumph and made Grenada a symbol of U.S. virtue and accomplishment. Even more importantly, Grenada symbolically served to absolve him of blame for the debacle in Beirut.

Reagan linked events in the Caribbean with events in the Middle East and argued that Grenada had served as a victory over U.S. foes in both places. If the deaths of marines in Beirut raised questions about America's role in the world and the competence of its commander-in-chief, Grenada served as proof that America's myths remained true and that its president was a strong and credible leader. Through his invocation of myth, the president made his crisis discourse appealing and difficult to criticize. Those who opposed Reagan's foreign policy also seemed to attack the national myths that his rhetoric embodied.

To shed further light on Reagan's crisis talk, I discuss the rhetorical context of the Grenadian crisis and then examine the mythic character of the situation, style, and identificational appeals in his discourse, and how the president's use of myth enhanced his crisis promotion.

THE RHETORICAL CONTEXT OF THE GRENADIAN CRISIS

From September 1982 through October 1983, Ronald Reagan found himself embroiled in a conflict with Congress over the power to make foreign policy. The president had committed U.S. marines to Lebanon in August 1982 as part of a multinational contingent to oversee the evacuation of Palestinian guerrillas. According to Reagan, the marines would play a "carefully limited, noncombatant role" and would stay no longer than thirty days.[18] The marines left within the allotted time, but events in Lebanon quickly took a turn for the worse. Lebanese President Bashir Gemayel was assassinated, Israeli forces moved into West Beirut, and hundreds of Palestinian refugees were massacred just outside the city.[19] To help restore order, President Reagan announced on September 20 that he would redeploy marines to Lebanon as part of a multinational peacekeeping force composed of U.S., Italian, and French soldiers.[20]

Reagan waited until the day the troops arrived, September 29, to file a report about the deployment with Congress. According to the president, he wrote the report in "accordance with my desire that the Congress be fully informed on this matter, and consistent with the War Powers Resolution." Like Ford and Carter before him, Reagan claimed he had a constitutional right to send the marines since he was commander-in-chief of the United States armed forces.[21] What was unusual about the president's report was that he had sent American soldiers into imminent hostilities, but had not referred to the hostilities clause of the War Powers Resolution in his report to the House and the Senate.

According to Section 4(a) of the resolution, the president must send a report to Congress within 48 hours whenever he introduces troops

(1) into hostilities or into situations where imminent involvement in hostilities is clearly indicated by the circumstances;

(2) into the territory, airspace or waters of a foreign nation, while equipped for combat, except for deployments which relate solely to supply, replacement, repair, or training of such forces; or

(3) in numbers which substantially enlarge United States Armed Forces equipped for combat already located in a foreign nation.[22]

If the commander-in-chief files a report under Section 4(a)(1), the hostilities clause, the sixty-day clock begins to run. The president must then withdraw the troops he has dispatched after sixty days unless Congress approves the deployment before that deadline. In his report about the *Mayaguez* crisis Gerald Ford took note of "Section 4(a)(1) of the War Powers Resolution," but the military rescue was over well before the forty-eight-hour deadline for the report was reached.[23] In contrast, Jimmy Carter did not refer to the hostilities clause in his report on the failed Iranian rescue mission because he said the U.S. military team was withdrawn before hostilities could occur.[24] Since American servicemen died as a result of an accident, rather than armed conflict with the Iranians, Carter's report was technically correct. The rescue mission, like the *Mayaguez* operation, had ended before the president's required report reached Congress. In both the *Mayaguez* and the Iranian crises, the brief duration of the military operations made the matter of the sixty-day deadline moot.

Reagan's report on the U.S. deployment to Beirut was quite different from Ford's and Carter's. Although the president insisted that "there is no intention or expectation that U.S. Armed Forces will become involved in hostilities,"[25] hostilities did, in fact, seem likely, and the troops would be deployed for an extended period of time. Nonetheless, Reagan refused to cite Section 4(a)(1) of the War Powers Resolution; constitutional law scholars Francis Wormuth and Edwin Firmage claim that he wished to avoid the sixty-day clock and to keep the length of the marine deployment under presidential control.[26] Congress appeared to be losing authority over foreign policy in the fall of 1982, and a court decision the following summer weakened the legislature's position even more.

In June 1983, the Supreme Court decided the case of *Immigration and Naturalization Service v. Chadha*. According to the Court, the House of Repre-

sentatives acted illegally when it overturned the Immigration and Naturalization Service's decision to let Chadha remain in the United States. The Court
ruled, seven to two, that the House's legislative veto had been unconstitutional.
The majority opinion argued that both houses of Congress must pass legislation
and the president must approve that legislation for it to become a law, unless
Congress could override a presidential veto of legislation by a two-thirds
majority.

Although some uncertainty remained, many observers agreed that the
Court's decision invalidated the concurrent resolution provision of the War
Powers Resolution. According to this interpretation, Congress could no longer
force the president to withdraw troops immediately through a concurrent
motion, which does not require the president's signature.[27] The Court's decision seemed to make the War Powers Resolution—which was, at best, a feeble
attempt to constrain presidential power in foreign affairs—even weaker.

In August 1983, U.S. marines were still in Beirut when intense fighting broke
out. Two marines were killed and fourteen were injured. Given these casualties,
Reagan could not deny that the marines were involved in hostilities. He made a
report to Congress "consistent with Section 4 of the War Powers Resolution,"
but again failed to mention Section 4(a)(1) or to acknowledge a sixty-day
deadline for the troops' withdrawal.[28] Perhaps bolstered by the *Chadha* decision, the president went even further when he ordered navy gunboats to the
coast of Lebanon to launch strikes against Syrian positions, the apparent source
of attacks against the marines.[29]

When news of the navy attacks broke, Reagan's congressional opponents
gained support and insisted that the president withdraw the marines or, at the
very least, report to Congress under Section 4(a)(1). Reagan refused to follow
either course of action. Eventually, a compromise was struck with the Multinational Force in Lebanon Resolution, which the president signed into law on
October 12, 1983. The resolution approved the marines' involvement in
Lebanon for eighteen months, but stipulated that the sixty-day clock had been
started on August 29, the day two marines were killed.[30] Once again, however,
Reagan took issue with the War Powers Resolution.

In his statement at the bill-signing, the commander-in-chief said he did not
agree that Section 4(a)(1) became operative on August 29. Reagan claimed that
"the initiation of isolated or infrequent acts of violence against the United States
Armed Forces does not necessarily constitute actual or imminent involvement
in hostilities." Furthermore, the president argued that the War Powers Resolution's sixty-day deadline was "arbitrary and inflexible" and created "unwise
limitations on Presidential authority." Although Reagan agreed to act in accordance with the Multinational Force in Lebanon Resolution, he was quick to say
that he did not believe legislation could infringe "impermissibly" on his
constitutional authority, or that congressional authorization was needed to

allow troops to remain in hostilities or imminent hostilities for more than sixty days.[31]

The president's decision to sign the compromise legislation into law appeared, at first, to be an indication that Congress had reasserted its authority, albeit tentatively. Actually, Reagan had obtained everything he wanted: Congress had agreed that the marines could remain in Lebanon, and the president, while publicly praising Congress for its support, had made clear that its attempts to constrain presidential power were irrelevant. In many ways, the legislative branch's efforts *were* irrelevant, for the only thing Congress gained was Reagan's written acknowledgment that the sixty-day clock began on August 29, a meaningless agreement since the president denied it in his public statement, and legislative approval of the marines' mission made the automatic sixty-day withdrawal immaterial. Through such maneuvers over the deployment of marines in Beirut, Reagan established a precedent that would serve him during the invasion of Grenada. Later, the president would link events in these two locales symbolically as well.

On October 23, 1983, less than two weeks after Reagan signed the Multinational Force in Lebanon Resolution into law, Beirut again became a focal point. More than two hundred marines, sent to Lebanon on the president's orders, were killed in a terrorist attack as they slept in their barracks. Americans suffered the loss of their soldiers and loved ones and, reminiscent of the Iranian hostage crisis, found their national security and power threatened by events in the Middle East. According to journalist Lou Cannon, the White House worried over a poll conducted by Richard Wirthlin that showed "a precipitous overnight decline in Reagan's approval rating."[32]

In Washington, D.C., legislators from both parties insisted that Reagan clarify the role of the marines in Beirut.[33] The same expressions of frustration and fear over the president and his policies were expressed in the media. The *New York Times* commented that "once again America is held hostage by a Middle East circumstance beyond its control. And this time there's no escape through daring rescue missions or ransom negotiations. Honor and prestige are again on the line, but the marines who claim them are dead, victims of a murky diplomatic cause that the President feels bound to reaffirm but still cannot fully define."[34] Events in Beirut placed great demands on the president's credibility, demands that were too large for even the popular Reagan to meet. Somehow, he had to restore his good will with the American public.

One alternative that Reagan could pursue was to reassure the country about its losses through patriotic, transcendent rhetoric that might unify the nation behind him. At his first press conference following the bombing, for example, he comforted his fellow Americans with "We cannot pick and choose where we will support freedom; we can only determine how. If it's lost in one place, all of us lose."[35] Unfortunately, such symbolic reassurance quickly loses its persuasive appeal. As the analysis of Jimmy Carter and Iran proves, citizens may comply with presidential requests to rally around the president, but a limit exists as to how long they will do so. In Reagan's case, the magnitude of the death and destruction in Beirut probably overwhelmed the symbolic reassurance he had to offer. Citizen and congressional reactions showed that the nation's unity was still far from complete.

Another avenue open to the president was to obtain the return of resources lost in Lebanon, such as power and security, by taking action against the terrorists and then dramatically informing the American public of the retaliation. This, too, was problematic, for Reagan had no feasible way to carry out such a goal: the terrorist truck driver was dead; his organizational headquarters were unknown; and the marines, as peacekeepers, could take no overt offensive action. Furthermore, the most important tangible resource lost in Beirut, American lives, could never be reclaimed. As a result, Reagan could unite the nation neither through the allocation of symbolic reassurance nor through the return of lost resources.

Faced with the quandaries that Beirut posed, the president found an opportunity to reverse his political fortunes through events taking place in another corner of the globe. A coup had occurred on the Caribbean island of Grenada, and the United States was about to launch a military invasion of the tiny nation. Through the promotion and management of a crisis in Grenada, Reagan was able to mask his Mideast foreign policy failure and to bask, instead, in the glory of an obvious success. This is *not* to say that Reagan launched the invasion of Grenada purely to counteract the problems of Beirut, for the administration was apparently in the midst of its plans for the Grenadian operation when the Beirut bombing occurred.[36] But Reagan exploited the rhetorical possibilities of Grenada in a way that drew attention from Beirut and helped to resolve the anxieties citizens felt about his foreign policy as a result of events there.

Grenada, a tiny nutmeg-exporting island in the Caribbean, hardly seemed a likely location for an international crisis. From the time Reagan first took office, however, he made clear that he disapproved of the country's Marxist ruler, Prime Minister Maurice Bishop, and his strong ties to Fidel Castro. The president's discourse provided a persuasive context for the later invasion of Grenada. In March 1983, for example, Reagan deemed the island a potential trouble spot. He addressed the annual meeting of the National Association of Manufacturers and warned his audience about "the extraordinary buildup of Soviet and Cuban military power" on Grenada. Two weeks later, the president delivered a televised speech on national security, one section of which was devoted to Grenada. He claimed a Communist militarization of Grenada was underway, complete with military training grounds, barracks, and storage bases for munitions. Even more troubling to the president, reconnaissance photos indicated that the island nation was building an airfield with a ten-thousand-foot runway. Reagan declared, "Grenada doesn't even have an air force. Who is it intended for?" According to the president, the answer was obvious. "The Soviet-Cuban militarization of Grenada, in short, can only be seen as power projection into the region. And it is in this important economic and strategic area that we're trying to help the Governments of El Salvador, Costa Rica, Honduras, and others in their struggle for democracy against guerrillas supported through Cuba and Nicaragua."[37]

In October 1983, just prior to the attack on marines in Beirut, events in Grenada provided an additional rationale for the president's actions. A military coup, under the direction of General Hudson Austin, overthrew and killed Bishop, along with several of his cabinet ministers. Reagan then ordered a naval task force on its way to Lebanon to go instead to Grenada in order to protect the safety of about one thousand Americans on the island, most of them medical students. According to the president, the Organization of Eastern Caribbean States (OECS) sent a cable to him the morning of October 23 asking that the United States intercede in Grenada.[38]

Forty-eight hours later and just two days after the Beirut bombing, Reagan obliged with a military operation whose name itself—Operation Urgent Fury—capitalized on the rich imagery that "crisis" has to offer. Like so many of his predecessors, the president briefed congressional leaders only after he had ordered the invasion. House Speaker Thomas ("Tip") O'Neill commented, "We weren't asked for advice. We were informed what was taking place."[39] In his report to Congress, Reagan again relied upon his power as commander-in-chief to justify the invasion and, despite the fact that U.S. troops were clearly involved in hostilities, refused to cite the hostilities clause of the War Powers Resolution.[40]

The House and the Senate responded when each attached riders to legislation in order to invoke the resolution and its sixty-day time limit, but a procedural impasse prevented the passage of any joint legislation. Led by Representative Ted Weiss of New York, some members of Congress demanded that Reagan immediately withdraw U.S. troops from Grenada. Weiss and his allies even introduced a resolution to impeach the president for his unconstitutional actions, but found few colleagues willing to support their efforts.[41] Although it had not done so vigorously, Congress had challenged Reagan's legal justification for the deployment of marines to Beirut and had convinced the president to go through the motions of a compromise. When Reagan used the same legal strategy with Grenada, few members of Congress questioned his usurpation of congressional authority.

As a successful military operation that came on the heels of Beirut, U.S. intervention in Grenada quickly won popular support among Americans, aided in no small measure by the Reagan administration's expert news management. The Defense Department pushed the commander-in-chief for a press ban, in part because it was convinced that media coverage had hurt efforts in Vietnam and because the British news blackout during the Falklands war had been so successful. As a result of this lobbying, Reagan banned all reporters from Grenada during the first two days of the invasion and placed restrictions on newsgathering in the week that followed. Journalists who attempted to violate rules were incarcerated, and Rear Adm. Joseph Metcalf threatened to sink press boats that approached Grenada illegally. When reporters were, at last, allowed on the island, armed guards guided them to stockpiles of military arms and ammunition the United States had captured, but denied the journalists access to other areas of the island.[42]

Reporter Charles Kaiser explained that Reagan's news management kept pictures of the bloody conflict on Grenada off television screens where it might have alarmed Americans. According to Kaiser, "The first Grenada-related pictures with people in them were just what the administration wanted: grateful students evacuated from St. George's University School of Medicine, kissing the ground when they reached America." When visuals from Grenada itself finally appeared on television, they consisted of film that the U.S. military had shot and carefully edited.[43]

By restricting access and allowing the release of only approved photos and film, Reagan maintained tight control over the public presentation of events in Grenada. For many days, Americans who consumed news of the invasion saw and heard only what the president wanted them to see and hear. The death and destruction in Grenada were almost wholly omitted; the dramatization of heroism and bravery was left intact. Because the administration alone had access to desired information, those with different perspectives on Grenada found it difficult to attack the president's arguments or to establish the credibility of their own arguments. Like a number of presidents before him, Reagan had discovered that news management was a valuable tool in the successful promotion and resolution of crisis.

In tandem with his news management, Ronald Reagan's crisis rhetoric further encouraged support for him and his policies. The president urged citizens to unite in a fight against the common enemy of Communism, which he claimed was responsible for both the deaths of marines in Beirut and the coup in Grenada. Unlike Jimmy Carter in his rhetoric about Iran, Reagan appealed to idealism when he told Americans that they personified the principle of freedom and gave a nod to pragmatism when he pointed to the safe return of the students as evidence that we had lived up to our principles. Overnight, Grenada became a symbol of victory and pride; the crisis reminded citizens of both tangible (the return of the students) and symbolic (security, action) gains. Lebanon's failures seemed blunted, almost forgotten, in the wake of Grenada's triumph. Most importantly for Reagan, he replenished his symbolic reserves and accrued a surplus of public goodwill he could draw on during future policy decisions. In the president's rhetoric, Grenada exemplified America's sacred myths of mission and manifest destiny.

THE MYTHS OF MISSION AND MANIFEST DESTINY IN REAGAN'S RHETORIC ON THE CRISIS IN GRENADA

If myths are the sacred truths about a society that its citizens take for granted, then the two most prominent myths in American culture have been mission and manifest destiny. Intellectual historian Loren Baritz argues that the myth of mission has its origins with the Puritans and their leader, John Winthrop, who claimed that the Puritans' settlement in the new world "shall be as a City upon a Hill" for "the eyes of all people are upon us."

According to Baritz, Winthrop's discourse implied that Americans were God's chosen people and that the rest of the world looked to America as a model of morality. Baritz writes, "It could not have occurred to him [Winthrop] that his small and weak band of saints should charge about the world to impose the One Right Way on others who were either too wicked, too stupid, or even too oppressed to follow his example."[44] Similarly, Merk contends that in the latter half of the nineteenth century, many American politicians continued to argue that the United States' mission was to improve the state of the world by serving as a model of democracy, rather than by intervening in other countries.[45] The myth of mission held that America had a special obligation to lead by example.

In contrast to the myth of mission, the myth of manifest destiny was born much later. Magazine and newspaper editor John L. O'Sullivan coined the expression in 1845 as part of his arguments for the annexation of Cuba, although the basic concept behind manifest destiny had existed since the time of the American Revolution.[46] According to Merk, manifest destiny referred to "expansion, prearranged by Heaven, over an area not clearly defined. In some minds it meant expansion over the region to the Pacific; in others, over the North American continent; in others, over the hemisphere." The goal of this expansion was to spread the practice of democracy in the world.[47]

Although American imperialists gained materially from the acquisition of new territories, rhetorical critics Jeff Bass and Richard Cherwitz argue that during its prime in the late 1800s, the rhetoric of manifest destiny emphasized "the pre-ordained destiny of the American people, acting as agents of the Divine, to somehow go out into the world spreading American institutions and precepts."[48] Where the myth of mission maintained that America had a moral duty to serve as a model of democracy, the myth of manifest destiny claimed that America was destined to succeed in spreading the practice of democracy through the expansion of its domain.

Despite these differences, the myths of mission and manifest destiny shared a number of similarities. Each espoused the principle of freedom, for example, and considered Americans to be divinely blessed. Foreign affairs scholar Cecil Crabb, Jr., observes that both schools of thought were also ethnocentric in character; they had the mutual goal of creating democracies in the outside world not only to improve conditions for the United States, but also to improve the condition of humanity in general. According to Crabb, "It was but a logical step from believing that the expansion of democracy was vital for the creation of a peaceful global system [mission and isolationist policies] to acting on that belief in U.S. relations with other countries [manifest destiny and interventionist policies]."[49]

According to rhetorical scholars Kurt Ritter and James Andrews, this transition began with the imperialism debates of 1898–1900 that pitted ardent anti-imperialists such as William Jennings Bryan and Adlai Stevenson against fervent expansionists like President William McKinley and Sen. Albert Beveridge of Indiana. Through this "cultural dialectic," Ritter and Andrews explain, a rhetorical reconciliation took place with the result that "both sides seemed to endorse the same ideal: America as the promoter of liberty in the world." According to Ritter and Andrews, this premise profoundly changed American ideology and, in regard to foreign policy, made it imperative that America "assume the active role of ensuring the survival of liberty around the globe."[50]

Baritz echoes this theme when he writes that mission underwent a transformation once the United States had accrued enough power to impose its will on others. Rather than fulfill its sense of mission by passively serving as an example, America actively sought to expand democracy by intervening in other countries.[51] For all these reasons, the myths of mission and manifest destiny are intricately intertwined in contemporary society. Americans today think of themselves as unique, blessed by God, possessed of high ideals, and destined to succeed. In addition, they consider it their special responsibility to spread freedom around the globe through active means and, in this way, to serve as a model of morality for the rest of the world.

Not surprisingly, strains of mission and manifest destiny have frequently found their way into the crisis talk of our nation's presidents, for presidents, too, feel compelled to pay homage to the sacred truths they learned as children and internalized as adults. Even if a chief executive did not believe in these American myths, he would be foolish to ignore them or, worse yet, to discount them publicly. In *Political Myth and Epic,* Gilbert Morris Cuthbertson writes that myths are "the means by which the political shaman maintains power." Myths imbue governmental policies with legitimacy, are relatively immune to factual attacks, and, hence, condition behavior in a way beneficial to political leaders.[52]

Whether the invocation of a deeply held belief or simply a shrewd political maneuver, the presidents examined in this study often paid tribute to mission and manifest destiny and the principle of freedom around which these myths revolve. John Kennedy asserted during the Cuban missile crisis that "the cost of freedom is always high—but Americans have always paid it."[53] Likewise, Johnson referred to the United States in his crisis rhetoric as "the guardian at the gate of freedom," and Nixon, in his announcement of the Cambodian invasion, urged Americans to prove we had the character "to lead the forces of freedom" in the world.[54] In all three of these cases, the presidents pointed to tangible results as an indication that our nation had, in fact, protected freedom.

Although Gerald Ford did not explicitly discuss freedom in his crisis discourse about the *Mayaguez,* even he implied the importance of this principle and America's leadership role in the world. Ford told European journalists that the United States' rescue of the *Mayaguez* symbolized how America would continue to respond to Communist challenges.[55] More often, Ford claimed that the crisis proved how his government, the ultimate representative of the American people, would act in similar emergencies.

In Carter's proclamation of Unity Day during the hostage crisis, he, too, discussed the United States' great reverence for freedom.[56] However, Carter typically was unable to balance his talk of this ideal—or many of the other ideals he invoked—with indications of how the United States was actualizing the principle. The myths of mission and manifest destiny are sacred to Americans, but Carter discovered that citizens will not settle for the mere invocation of freedom in presidential crisis rhetoric. Americans also expect their presidents to demonstrate, at some point, how this ideal has been upheld.

Perhaps no contemporary president's discourse exemplified the myths of mission and manifest destiny more than that of Ronald Reagan. Rhetorical critics Richard Crable and Steven Vibbert, Walter Fisher, G. Thomas Goodnight, David Klope, William Lewis, Kurt Ritter and David Henry, Janice Hocker Rushing, Craig Allen Smith, and American studies scholar Paul Erickson all have noted that Reagan's presidential communication had a mythic or religious quality.[57] I argue that Reagan's crisis discourse about Grenada called upon the myths of mission and manifest destiny and also provided his listeners with "proof" that these myths worked. Reagan romantically described the Grenadian crisis and the successful invasion of the island as an exemplar of the United States' pursuit of the ideal of freedom. At the same time, the president paid obeisance to pragmatism when he justified the military operation through arguments of expediency. Reagan's rhetoric, with its appeals to principles and practicalities, constituted a nearly pristine example of the myths of mission and manifest destiny in action.

Situation

In the case of Reagan and Grenada, the situation of the president's talk can be summarized as because of a Communist power grab on Grenada and the urgent request of the OECS (scene), America or "we" (actor) and our military (lesser coactor) took decisive action (act) through a rescue mission (means) in order to restore democracy and freedom and to save American lives (purpose).

In his initial announcement of the invasion, Reagan painted a bleak scene for his listeners. He claimed that "a brutal group of leftist thugs" in Grenada had "violently seized power, killing the Prime Minister, three Cabinet members, two labor leaders, and other civilians, including children." In addition, hundreds of American medical students and senior citizens remained on the island in possible danger. Because of this, "the United States," "America," or "we" had intervened, and our "armed forces" had interceded.[58]

Although Reagan's public image was that of a man of action,[59] the key terms for act in his discourse were not particularly strong, nor did they dominate his talk. Reagan claimed, both during the crisis and in the months that followed, that the United States "had no choice but to act," had "taken this decisive action," "acceded to the request" of the OECS, "joined in an effort," "displayed" resolve, and was "willing to take decisive action."[60] These words hardly described the forceful acts of a nation involved in military intervention. Rather than emphasize action, Reagan's discourse pointed toward goals. He told reporters on October 25, for instance, that the purpose of American actions was "to protect our own citizens, to facilitate the evacuation of those who want to leave, and to help in the restoration of democratic institutions in Grenada." To accomplish these important tasks, the president remarked at a White House ceremony and elsewhere that the United States had employed the means of a "rescue mission."[61] Within Reagan's rhetoric about Grenada, two terminological relationships also played especially important roles: terms for scene-purpose and terms for purpose-actor.

As with Kennedy, Johnson, Nixon, and Carter, Reagan's talk exemplified a scene-purpose ordering of terms in which a frightening crisis scene dictated what goals the United States should pursue. In his public discussion of the invasion, for instance, Reagan portrayed Grenada as a place of grave danger. He said that Bishop, a protégé of Fidel Castro, had overthrown the Grenadian government in 1979 and had begun a military buildup there. By October 1983, Reagan argued, conditions on the island had become even worse. He explained in his televised address:

On October 12, a small group in his [Bishop's] militia seized him and put him under arrest. They were, if anything, more radical and more devoted to Castro's Cuba than he had been.

Several days later, a crowd of citizens appeared before Bishop's home, freed him, and escorted him toward the headquarters of the military council. They were fired upon. A number, including some children, were killed, and Bishop was seized. He and several members of his cabinet were subsequently executed, and a 24-hour shoot-to-kill curfew was put into effect. Grenada was without a government, its only authority exercised by a self-proclaimed band of military men.[62]

According to Reagan, radical Communists had overthrown the Grenadian government, murdered children, and instituted a deadly curfew. He claimed that authority on the island was tenuous, that democracy in the Caribbean was in danger, and, most importantly, that American lives were at stake. Finally, the president added to his portrayal of an overpowering scene when he asserted, repeatedly, that the OECS had sent an "urgent request" for the United States to intervene in the "Communist power grab."[63]

From these key terms for scene, arose Reagan's terms for purpose. When the president first announced the invasion, for instance, he stated that the United States had three major objectives: "First, and of overriding importance, to protect innocent lives, including up to a thousand Americans, whose personal safety is, of course, my paramount concern. Second, to forestall further chaos. And third, to assist in the restoration of conditions of law and order and of governmental institutions to the island of Grenada."[64]

In the weeks that followed, Reagan would reaffirm these goals when he spoke of U.S. attempts "to protect American lives" and "to restore order and democracy" to Grenada, "that strife-torn island."[65] Overall, the president's discourse described a dangerous and urgent crisis scene, which dictated that the United States fulfill particular goals: to free Grenada and to save the American students there.

The second dominant ratio in Reagan's crisis talk was that of purpose-actor; that is, key terms for purpose led to corresponding terms for actor. In a 1985 radio address on the anniversary of the invasion, for instance, Reagan claimed that Grenada's Gov. Gen. Paul Scoon "appealed for our help to restore order" and that "all of us can be proud of the swift response of our country."[66] On the simplest of levels, the president asserted that the specific purposes of freedom and democracy—or the restoration of order—in Grenada had necessitated that the United States respond.

More often, though, the terminological relationship of purpose-actor appeared in Reagan's rhetoric in a different, more mythic form. For the president, the purpose of freedom was personified by the United States. He said at a political rally in November 1983, for example, that America was "the force for freedom and peace" and "the brightest star of hope in the world today."[67] In the president's discourse about Grenada, this pattern was the overwhelming characteristic of his portrayal of the situation. Reagan told military personnel at Cherry

Point, North Carolina, "America seeks no new territory, nor do we wish to dominate others. We commit our resources and risk the lives of those in our Armed Forces to rescue others from bloodshed and turmoil and to prevent humankind from drowning in a sea of tyranny."[68]

At other public ceremonies in 1983 and 1984, the president similarly declared that "peace with freedom is the highest aspiration of the American people" and that Grenada was one more instance of "America standing up for human freedom."[69] The purpose-actor ratio in Reagan's talk portrayed America as a nation that embodied the noblest of values and that intervened militarily in other countries out of a sense of moral responsibility, rather than greedy self-interest. The Grenadian crisis was merely one episode in our country's fulfillment of its mission and manifest destiny. During Reagan's tenure in the White House, Erickson, Goodnight, Klope, Lewis, and Smith observed this same romantic image of the United States in his presidential rhetoric.[70]

In Reagan's talk about Grenada, he personified the principle of freedom not only in the actor of America, but also in the less visible coactor of the American military. During his 1986 remarks to the Grenadian people, he said, "Nineteen of our sons died here; many were wounded. Our brave lads risked all because they believed in those ideals that we've spoken about today: justice, freedom, and opportunity."[71] The president portrayed the United States as a nation with a mission. Consistent with this image, he exclaimed on another occasion, "I don't know that we've ever had any better missionaries for our country abroad than GIs in uniform."[72] If America's calling were freedom, then America's soldiers were tied integrally to their country as propagators of the faith.

Reagan remarked in November 1983 that servicemen who died in Grenada and Beirut were "now part of the soul of this great country and will live as long as our liberty shines as a beacon of hope to all those who long for freedom and a better world."[73] At still other times, Reagan referred to the heroism of particular soldiers like Sgt. Steven Trujillo, who saved the lives of fellow soldiers while under enemy fire in Grenada. During his 1984 State of the Union address, the president told Sergeant Trujillo admiringly, "You inspire us as a force for freedom."[74] In Reagan's crisis rhetoric, the principle of freedom took concrete form both in America and in America's military. Furthermore, each actor derived strength from the other and renewed belief in their common cause.

The transformation of terms for purpose into terms for actor reveals the mythic thread woven throughout the president's rhetoric, for in myth, principles typically take their form in particular personalities or characters.[75] This statement may seem to contradict assertions made about the extreme idealism of Carter's rhetoric on Iran, in which almost all of the president's terms for purpose dealt with genus, or principles, that constituted actors. Stated more simply, Carter equated America's purposes with who "we" were. This in itself, however, did not make Carter's discourse idealistic. Rather, the interaction between his situational ratio of terms for purpose-means and his stylistic ratio of terms for actor-means led Carter to concern himself with the way in which actors could stay true to their many principles—principles he failed to establish priorities for—through the policies the nation pursued.

In contrast, Reagan's discourse about Grenada, with its situational purpose-actor ordering of terms, paid obeisance to American ideals, but did not reflect the purity of Carter's idealistic talk. Reagan's rhetoric focused on freedom as *the* overarching principle that personified our nation. And as stylistic analysis will show, he talked about the progress America had made in defending freedom, rather than pondering how America might do so. In this way, the president appealed to pragmatism, as well as idealism. His talk invoked the myths of mission and manifest destiny, indicated how the mythic ideal of freedom had been upheld, and provided Americans with reassurance as to why this ideal was so important.

Reagan's situational ratios of words for scene-purpose and words for purpose-actor also worked together in that his descriptions of the scene led to particular purposes and those purposes found their exemplification in America. During a Reagan-Bush campaign reunion right after Grenada, for instance, the president declared, "In foreign policy, we've let the world know once again that America stands for the political, religious, and economic freedom of mankind."[76] Here the larger scene of foreign policy pointed toward the principle of freedom that, in turn, was personified by America. In Reagan's crisis rhetoric, the purpose-actor ordering of terms played a much more important role than the scene-purpose ratio. The depicted scene of crisis in Grenada simply provided a rationale for why America had to fulfill its purposive mission or destiny.

Rhetorical critic Janice Hocker Rushing discovered a similar pattern in the president's "Star Wars" address. She argues that Reagan "revises temporal and spatial scene to be consistent with the nature of the purposive acts he calls upon his agents to perform."[77] In the discourse analyzed here, the president described Grenada as a place where freedom was threatened; this scene therefore justified America's decision to protect freedom with a military operation there. Reagan's tendency to imbue the nation with moral purpose in his portrayals of situation was also indicative of how the style of his crisis rhetoric treated the key actor of his talk.

Style

The central actor of America in Reagan's discourse was a strong and noble hero on a sacred mission. For example, he claimed that the nation had "courage and determination" and a "moral and spiritual character."[78] According to Reagan, the United States was a force for freedom and would fight for that sacred principle in order to help those in need.[79] Nonetheless, Reagan insisted, as he did in his 1984 nomination acceptance speech, "America is the most peaceful, least warlike nation in modern history. We are not the cause of all the ills of the world. We're a patient and generous people."[80] These depictions painted a flattering portrait of the United States as a selfless nation that made supreme sacrifices on behalf of others in the world.

In addition to this central actor, the president also described the coactor of the U.S. military in glowing terms. Reagan claimed that America's soldiers were "faithful to their ideals," "courageous," "truly gallant," "unselfish," and "inspiring." Furthermore, he said that our military forces were devoted and dedicated in their duty to country.[81]

In his discourse on the Grenada crisis, Reagan provided elaborate depictions of what both America and its military were like. Despite this, however, the president did little to indicate "how" the central actor of America acted. Instead, he used the lesser coactor of his talk, the U.S. military, to illustrate the way America behaved. Over the course of three years of talk about the crisis—from 1983 to 1986—the president's descriptions of how our armed forces acted served to represent the characteristic behavior of our nation as a whole. For instance, Reagan stated that our soldiers moved "quickly," "professionally," and "successfully" to save American students on Grenada and to restore freedom to the island. Because of such courageous actions, he explained, "our servicemen were hailed as saviors by the local population in Grenada" and "thousands of people lined the streets to cheer and shower them with gratitude." The bold and brave behavior of our military also reflected on the United States as a whole, for Reagan noted that the Grenadians were "hailing us as liberators," too.[82]

Once the battle of Grenada had been won, the president continued to indicate how America typically acted through his idyllic depictions of the military's activities on the island. He told those in attendance at a 1983 political rally: "And today, the engineers of the 82d Airborne are repairing roads and bridges and damaged buildings and homes down there. And the Medical Corps, now that our wounded have been evacuated, are taking care of the people on Grenada, vaccinating children, doing those things that are associated with public health chores. In other words, we're doing what America has always done."[83] Again, the actions of U.S. military men and women represented the way in which the United States typically acted or, in the words of Reagan's 1984 State of the Union speech, "what it means to be Americans."[84] The president told recipients of the Congressional Medal of Honor in December 1983, "Your efforts to serve remind us of America's heritage and its purpose."[85]

In Reagan's portrayal of the crisis situation, the purpose-actor ratio of terms played a major role. Stylistically, the president's words for actor were involved in two other important ratios, as well: scene-actor and actor-scene. The first of these relationships was exemplified when Reagan discussed scenes that called both for America and for America's military. After the invasion of Grenada, he told soldiers at Cherry Point, North Carolina, "The world looks to America for leadership. And America looks to the men in its Armed Forces—to the Corps of Marines, to the Navy, the Army."[86] Similarly, Reagan commented during a 1984 campaign stop that medical students on Grenada "told me, one group, of how they were lying under the beds in their dormitory with the bullets coming through the building and the gunfight. And then they heard an American voice."[87] In the president's discourse, this threatening scene called for a heroic U.S. actor.

In another sense, Reagan also described scenes from which actors arose. After giving tribute in a November 1983 radio broadcast to soldiers who were killed in Beirut and Grenada, the president asked from where such brave Americans came. The answer, he said, was that such "men and women can only come from a nation that remains true to the ideals of our Founding Fathers."[88] In the situational analysis of Reagan's discourse, terms for scene led to terms for purpose, and terms for purpose led to terms for actor. Not surprisingly, then, terms for scene in the president's style also pointed necessarily to particular actors—America and American soldiers.

Beyond this scene-actor ordering of terms, another important ratio of terms, actor-scene, prevailed in Reagan's crisis rhetoric. In recounting the Grenadian crisis before the 1984 convention of the Veterans of Foreign Wars, he asserted, "Because we were willing to take decisive action, our students today are safe, Grenada is free, and that region of the Caribbean is more peaceful and secure than before."[89] Correspondingly, Reagan told the Republican National Convention that thanks to America, our "students are safe, and freedom is what we left behind in Grenada."[90] The United States had changed the threatening scene into one of calm.

The president also associated the lesser coactor of the U.S. military with the outcome of the crisis. In his 1984 public tribute to Sergeant Trujillo, Reagan addressed the soldier personally and said, "you and your fellow service men and women not only saved innocent lives; you set a nation free. . . . God bless you."[91] Thus the scene-actor ratio in the president's discourse depicted a threatening scene that demanded noble and heroic actors. And Reagan indicated that these actors had succeeded in altering the scene. America and its soldiers had resolved the Caribbean crisis. On a more abstract level, the actor-scene ratio of Reagan's rhetoric implied that the United States would continue to ensure the existence of freedom, both within our own borders and in other areas of the world. According to the president, freedom "is never more than one generation away from extinction. Each generation must do whatever is necessary to preserve it and pass it on to the next, or it will be lost forever."[92]

The style of Reagan's crisis talk portrayed America as a moral, majestic nation whose good deeds and intentions were most evident in the way its military personnel behaved. When freedom was endangered, the commander-in-chief assured citizens that the United States and its armed forces would be there. Furthermore, these valorous actors would remedy threatening scenes and restore them to tranquility. Like Carter, Reagan's terms for act dominated neither in the situation nor in the style of his discourse. Unlike Carter, however, Reagan's crisis rhetoric seemed active. This finding corroborates Rod Hart's computer-based study, for Hart discovered that Reagan's presidential discourse had a higher activity rating than that of any of his seven predecessors.[93]

If the president's style in his crisis talk was at all like his typical style, it may explain why Reagan's rhetoric always sounded so active. The scene-actor ratio depicted the United States in motion, a special nation that had been called to a particular scene. Meanwhile, the actor-scene ratio demonstrated that our country had made a difference by altering that scene. Through this attitude, or style, Reagan invested his talk with a sense of progress and momentum. The president's style also helped him balance his idealistic appeals to freedom with pragmatic, cause-and-effect arguments of how we had actualized this principle in Grenada. Where Carter expounded upon ideals but failed to demonstrate how his policies upheld them, Reagan focused on one ideal and provided citizens with a sense of accomplishment in the present and a sense of promise for the future. He told citizens in his October 27 speech about Grenada that he was "more sure than I've ever been that we Americans of today will keep freedom and maintain peace."[94]

The president's focus on progress was also indicative of myth. According to Eliade, myth consists of a contest between the sacred and the profane, or cosmos and chaos. Those who believe in a particular myth champion their cosmogony by attempting to reduce or eliminate chaos. Eliade explains that this ritual frequently takes the form of a society's settlement of land: "To settle a territory is, in the last analysis, equivalent to consecrating it."[95] In our own nation's history, citizens have looked at migration westward and the colonial acquisition of territory as a way to progress and to actualize the American myth of manifest destiny. Now that the West is settled and the old form of imperialism dead, Americans have lost that means by which to satisfy their mythic appetites. To compensate, Rushing argues, Americans have looked skyward to our space program and the "Star Wars" project for a new frontier to conquer.[96]

The present stylistic analysis of Reagan's crisis discourse suggests another ritualistic outlet: progress through victory in a foreign crisis. Just as American politicians once justified war with Spain as a means to realize the United States' manifest destiny, Reagan found in Grenada the perfect opportunity for public proclamations about our country's fulfillment of its sacred destiny and successful accomplishment of its moral mission. His discourse, in turn, reinforced these American myths. After the demoralizing effects of Vietnam, Watergate, recessions, and Iran, citizens may have been especially eager to embrace the president's hopeful message that America was not in decline and to overlook the bloodshed his foreign policy provoked. For his part, Reagan offered the myths of manifest destiny and mission and their accompanying ritual of crisis as a cure for the country's ills, as well as his own. He may not have been the first president to discover that foreign crises could serve a valuable political function as rituals of progress, but Reagan's crisis discourse embraced this concept far more thoroughly than any of the other cases of crisis promotion examined in this study.

No doubt the sense of linear progress in Reagan's style was appealing to citizens. It also obscured the circularity of his rhetoric. According to communication critic Craig Allen Smith, Reagan as presidential rhetor frequently interwove themes of moral purpose into tautologies in his public talk.[97] My own analysis of the president's crisis discourse demonstrates how, stylistically, he did so. Purpose was everywhere in Reagan's style, for even the stylistic ratios of scene-actor and actor-scene were imbued with the purpose of freedom. The president's rhetoric described Grenada as a scene where freedom was threatened, which called for America, an actor that embodied freedom. Moreover, he insisted that our nation would restore Grenada and similar places to scenes of calm where freedom again existed.

The impact of Reagan's stylistic purposiveness can be observed in his terms for situation, as well. In addition to scene, actor, and purpose, the principle of freedom also appeared covertly in his terms for act and means. Reagan did not use forceful words for action, but instead he pointed toward goals; for him, to act was to fulfill a purpose. The president's overwhelming emphasis on the principle of freedom may also explain why his rhetoric emphasized that the military operation in Grenada was a "rescue mission."

In his initial discourse on U.S. intervention in the Caribbean, Reagan said that our country had employed a "landing or landings," a "military operation," or an "invasion" to fulfill its goals.[98] Shortly after the operation was completed, however, he adopted the term "rescue mission" and took time on a number of occasions to clarify the means the United States employed in Grenada. In a December 1983 interview with wire service correspondents, the president explained,

> Now, to invoke Grenada, here again I think the words of the Grenadian people themselves, the Governor General, the people of Grenada, our own people who were there and were rescued have revealed that this was not an invasion. This was something in the nature of a commando operation, and it was a rescue mission. And the people of Grenada have made it very plain that they feel they, too, were rescued.[99]

This shift from "invasion" to "rescue mission" made Reagan's terms for means more consistent with the rest of his talk. Just as his other terms for situation were imbued with purposiveness, the means of a rescue mission also contained the purpose of freedom, for to rescue means to free. In addition, a rescue mission, rather than a more aggressive-sounding military invasion, was more compatible with the noble actor of America who embodied freedom in Reagan's rhetoric.

The president's style infused his discourse with purposiveness. As a result, Reagan's talk provided citizens with a sense of linear progress that was based on rhetorical tautologies: in Grenada (the scene where freedom was threatened), America and its military (the personification of freedom) acted (upon the purpose of freedom) through a rescue mission (a means to freedom) in order to restore freedom to medical students and to the island of Grenada (the driving purpose of freedom). According to Burke, myths always express circular relationships in a deceptively linear, narrative form.[100] Reagan's crisis rhetoric did the same.

The circular quality of Reagan's style also exemplified the mythic idea that history is reversible and repeatable. In *Language and Myth,* Ernst Cassirer observes that myth concentrates on the here and now because mythic thinking makes all time the present time.[101] Eliade explains that this phenomenon is a result of involvement in the rituals that actualize myth. "Religious participation in a festival implies emerging from ordinary temporal duration and reintegration of the mythical time reactualized by the festival itself. Hence sacred time is indefinitely recoverable, indefinitely repeatable."[102] Rituals, more simply put, reinvigorate a myth and allow participants to recapture times gone by and to relive them.

Reagan emphasized history's reversibility. In a 1986 answer to a question from Radio Marti, for example, he claimed that Grenada was "the first time in history that a Communist regime, having consolidated totalitarian control, was replaced by a democracy. The world has now seen the proof—the old idea that communism is irreversible is itself being reversed."[103] Furthermore, Reagan warned that the only way Americans could continue to preserve and to expand upon freedom in the world was to repeat the ritual enacted in Grenada. As the stylistic analysis of the scene-actor and actor-scene ratios detailed, the president claimed that the United States not only had rescued freedom in Grenada, but also would continue to rescue freedom wherever it was endangered.

In his televised address about Beirut and Grenada, Reagan related to citizens why this ritual was so necessary: "Sam Rayburn once said that freedom is not something a nation can work for once and win forever. He said it's like an insurance policy; its premiums must be kept up to date. In order to keep it, we have to keep working for it and sacrificing for it just as long as we live. If we do not, our children may not know the pleasure of working to keep it, for it may not be theirs to keep."[104]

Unlike Carter in his discourse on Iran, Reagan explained to Americans the importance of fulfilling the nation's ideals. The American myths of mission and manifest destiny, as described in the president's talk, could be actualized only if Americans vigilantly worked to protect freedom and to expand its presence around the globe. He argued that, through rituals of consecration such as the one played out in Grenada, America could maintain its unique position in the world. Crisis rituals might entail sacrifice, but they were important if America were to actualize its mission and destiny. The commander-in-chief told U.S. military personnel immediately after Beirut and Grenada, "If this country is to remain a force for good in the world, we'll face times like these, times of sadness and loss."[105] America's victories on behalf of freedom were repeatable, but so, too, was the ritualistic loss of lives the nation had endured.

Identificational Appeals

Throughout his discourse about Grenada, Reagan most often employed antithetical identificational appeals, a strategy characteristic of myth, and one that assumed a prominent role in the crisis rhetoric of Kennedy and Nixon. Because myth personifies principles and consists of a battle between cosmos and chaos, myth naturally involves personified polar oppositions. Good cannot exist unless evil also lives.[106] In the case of Reagan and Grenada, evil took the form of a long-standing foe of the United States—Communism, as exemplified by the Soviet Union and Cuba. The president claimed in his October 27 televised address that it was "no coincidence" that Soviet advisers and Cuban military and paramilitary forces were in Grenada when the coup took place. Worse yet, these evil enemies had threatened democracy and American citizens. As proof of their intended crimes, Reagan discussed evidence discovered on the island:

> Two hours ago we released the first photos from Grenada. They included pictures of a warehouse of military equipment—one of three we've uncovered so far. This warehouse contained weapons and ammunition stacked almost to the ceiling, enough to supply thousands of terrorists. Grenada, we were told, was a friendly island paradise for tourism. Well, it wasn't. It was a Soviet-Cuban colony, being readied as a major military bastion to export terror and undermine democracy. We got there just in time.[107]

By dramatizing America's defeat of the enemy in Grenada, Reagan encouraged citizens to unite with him in the rejection of a shared object of hatred.

On another level, Reagan's antithetical appeals allowed him to use Grenada to demonstrate victory over other foes in Lebanon and Iran. He made clear links between the common enemy the United States faced in Beirut and in the Caribbean: "The events in Lebanon and Grenada, though oceans apart, are closely related. Not only has Moscow assisted and encouraged the violence in both countries, but it provides direct support through a network of surrogates and terrorists."[108] Because of this link, the victory in Grenada over Communism became a victory over our tormentors in Lebanon, as well. Reagan declared to the Congressional Medal of Honor Society in 1983, "now the world knows that when it comes to our national security, the United States will do whatever it takes to protect the safety and freedom of the American people."[109] He noted on another occasion that America "must not and will not be intimidated by anyone, anywhere."[110]

In a similar fashion, Grenada served as a victory over Iran and the haunting specter of the hostage crisis. By renaming the Grenadian invasion a "rescue mission," Reagan allowed Americans the chance to relive a hostage situation and win. He said in his 1983 speech to North Carolina soldiers, "With a thousand Americans, including some 800 students, on that island, we weren't about to wait for the Iran crisis to repeat itself, only this time in our own neighborhood—the Caribbean."[111] Reagan's statements served to bolster his perceived leadership capabilities by comparing his recent success with Carter's failure in Iran. In addition, the reference seemed to lessen Reagan's responsibility for Beirut through the association of Mideast problems with his predecessor.

The president's antithetical appeals allowed him to reassure the nation about two failures in its past, Lebanon and Iran, and to give the country hope for the future. Reagan told supporters at a 1983 campaign reunion that Grenada proved "our Nation is through wringing its hands and apologizing."[112] Eliade explains that in myth, any victory by one side over the other in a particular situation is equivalent to the victory of one principle over another.[113] For Reagan, Grenada was, as he said in a 1986 radio speech, "part of a Communist pattern of deception that has been repeated so many times in so many places."[114] Because the United States defeated enemy troops in Grenada, the president could claim that freedom had emerged victorious over Communism. Americans had won a battle over all of their foes, both past and present.

Although Reagan's appeals were primarily antithetical, his rhetoric shaded into implicit identificational appeals as well. He made great use of the word "we," for example, even when it was not juxtaposed with an enemy. Shortly after the invasion, Reagan said to Gannett newspaper editors, "In Grenada, we set a nation free."[115] Likewise, the president proclaimed in his 1984 convention acceptance address, "for the sake of our freedom and that of others, we cannot permit our reserve to be confused with a lack of resolve. Ten months ago, we displayed this resolve in a mission to rescue American students on the imprisoned island of Grenada."[116] The word "we" in these statements portrayed U.S. actions in Grenada as something of which all citizens could be proud.

Reagan also identified implicitly with his audience through more specific references to the nation. In a 1985 radio broadcast, for instance, he remarked, "the United States came to the rescue of democracy and of hundreds of American students in Grenada."[117] Just as the word "we" implicitly identified rhetor and audience, the term "United States" in this sentence quietly linked Reagan with his constituents. The commander-in-chief also made references in his crisis discourse to "America," "our Nation," and "our country."[118]

In *Myth and Mythmaking,* historian John Marcus argues that the Western mystique of American society provides a "sense of unity in purpose" and encourages citizens to believe that their "respective contributions to history give moral purpose to the life of the individual and to the existence of the group."[119] In the president's talk about the crisis in Grenada, his implicit appeals prompted individual Americans to unite as a nation, or "we." Furthermore, these appeals identified citizens personally with America's achievement in Grenada. Reagan subtly told Americans that the victory in Grenada was their victory and that the protection of freedom in the Caribbean was meaningful not only for the United States as a country, but also for them as individuals.

Ronald Reagan called upon the American myths of mission and manifest destiny to imbue the Grenadian invasion with legitimacy, to escape personal responsibility for Beirut, and to encourage citizen support for his management of foreign policy. Situationally, the president argued that the scene in Grenada called for the accomplishment of particular goals (scene-purpose) and that the United States and its military were the personification of one of these goals, the ideal of freedom (purpose-actor). Stylistically, Reagan's terminological ratios of scene-actor and actor-scene appealed to Americans' desire for progress by first depicting a crisis scene in Grenada that called for the United States and then describing how the United States had restored democracy to the Caribbean island. The president's identificational appeals simultaneously spoke to Americans' sense of idealism and their sense of pragmatism. His implicit appeals worked to unite citizens under the banner of freedom, whereas his antithetical appeals encouraged Americans to rally against Communism, the perceived enemy of the nation's most cherished ideal. Moreover, both forms of appeal served to identify citizens with the apparent success of the United States' Caribbean intervention.

The president's heavy reliance on mission and manifest destiny in his rhetoric may also explain why opponents found it difficult to criticize him and his policy in Grenada with any degree of success. The fact that the U.S. military emerged victorious from the crisis clearly did much to stifle dissent, but the circular quality of Reagan's arguments also served to protect him. Although obvious tautologies would have been a weakness, the president's seemingly linear, progressive tale of success in Grenada camouflaged the underlying circularity of his talk. As a result, his rhetoric did not appear to be unsound, and critics who attacked any one part of Reagan's argument were forced to attack the entire view of the world he described. That is, to criticize Reagan's policy in

Grenada, opponents also had to criticize, albeit implicitly, the principle of freedom that his policy intended to fulfill, and the brave soldiers and noble nation that embodied that principle and carried out the commander-in-chief's policy.

Rhetorical critics Kathleen Hall Jamieson, Kurt Ritter, and David Henry point out, for instance, that Reagan's epideictic tribute to Sergeant Trujillo during his televised 1984 State of the Union address prompted members of Congress—including opponents of the Grenada invasion—to applaud the Sergeant and thereby to appear supportive of the mission itself.[120] William Lewis and Craig Allen Smith note that Reagan's presidential talk typically transformed opposition to policy into opposition to principle and the people who personified that principle.[121] In the case of Grenada, the principle was freedom, the central belief of America's civil religion. The myths of mission and manifest destiny, like any myths, are sacred and true to their believers. Opponents of Reagan's intervention in Grenada had to make the unenviable choice either to remain silent about their qualms or to voice their concerns and thereby commit blasphemy. Little wonder, then, that relatively few raised their voices against the president's policy and that those who did were unable to convince a majority of citizens that the policy was flawed. Most Americans probably preferred Reagan's version of events because it reaffirmed revered myths and, in turn, the moral structure of our society. Hence, the president's talk discouraged criticism about Grenada and, instead, encouraged uncritical acceptance of U.S. intervention there as a fulfillment of the country's mission and manifest destiny.

Yet another reason that the president encountered so little criticism about the Caribbean crisis may have had to do with his own role in his rhetoric, for Reagan did not appear as a central actor very often. Jamieson and Lewis have even referred to him as "the narrator" of his presidential talk.[122] Given the mythic character of Reagan's rhetoric, a better way to conceive of him may be as a religious shaman or faith healer. In an analysis of the president's 1981 economic policy address before Congress, Richard Crable and Steven Vibbert argue that Reagan assumed the role of political faith healer, one who tells the sick, "By your faith, you shall be healed." They explain that if the sick become healthy again, the faith healer can take the credit. If, on the other hand, the sick remain ill, the faith healer may be able to blame them for their plight by claiming that they did not have enough faith. The key to where final responsibility will rest has to do with whether others interpret the faith healer's words as a prediction or as a command. If the sick interpret the faith healer's rhetoric as a prediction, the faith healer will have failed if the sick do not become well. If, however, the sick interpret the faith healer's words as a command, they will blame themselves if they are not healed; obviously, they did not have enough faith and therefore failed to obey. Clever faith healers, who also have popular support, will discover that the sick easily interpret their words as commands.

Crable and Vibbert observe that "in faith healing, the faith healer who enjoys the faith of others is seldom held personally accountable for failures in the healing process." These same principles, they argue, explain how the popular Reagan avoided responsibility for the nation's economic woes in 1981. Reagan as political faith healer told Americans that the economy would improve only if they believed in it. In his economic policy speech before Congress that April, the president intoned what he claimed to be a piece of Carl Sandburg poetry: "All we need to have is faith, And the dream will come true. All we need to do is act, And the time for action is now." Reagan placed responsibility for the nation's recovery on those who desired the cure.[123]

In a parallel fashion, the president's small role in his crisis rhetoric diminished his accountability for any negative results of the intervention in Grenada. Reagan certainly basked in the reflected glory of the military success on the island, but his mythic portrayals of how America once was and how it would be again also placed primary responsibility on citizens to decide the historical importance of events there. That is, the president insisted that Americans could preserve America's heritage and improve upon its future if only they would support his foreign policy.

In his 1983 televised address on Lebanon and Grenada, Reagan told Americans that the armed forces "were not afraid to stand up for their country or, no matter how difficult and slow the journey might be, to give to others that last, best hope of a better future. We cannot and will not dishonor them now and the sacrifices they've made by failing to remain as faithful to the cause of freedom and the pursuit of peace as they have been."[124] Grenada could contribute to America's special legacy if citizens believed in their country's cause there and remained faithful to their nation's ideal. Through such assertions, Reagan's rhetoric helped him to escape responsibility by placing the burden on citizens. At best, the president was just one small part of the "we" in his crisis talk. If citizens were faithful to freedom, then Grenada would be considered a success and Reagan as the commander-in-chief could take some of the credit. If citizens were not faithful to freedom, then Grenada would not be remembered as a success and Americans' lack of faith would be at fault. The president reinforced this idea in a 1986 radio address about Grenada when he implored citizens, "Let's make certain we all live up to our responsibility."[125]

Nowhere, perhaps, was Reagan's assumption of the faith healer role more evident than in his 1984 State of the Union address. He discussed Grenada and other noteworthy events of the previous year and asked, "How can we not believe in the greatness of America?" The president then asserted,

> I've never felt more strongly that America's best days and democracy's best days lie ahead. We're a powerful force for good. With faith and courage, we can perform great deeds and take freedom's next step. And we will. We will carry on the tradition of a

good and worthy people who have brought light where there was
darkness, warmth where there was cold, medicine where there was
disease, food where there was hunger, and peace where there was
only bloodshed.[126]

With the help of a literary license and the gospel, Reagan once again called
upon Americans to improve their country by remaining faithful to its principles.
If better days came, the president as the nation's leader would benefit; if better
days did not come, then Americans needed to try harder. Reagan's reliance on
myth in his talk about Grenada was what allowed him to invoke political faith
healing and to deflect personal criticism so easily. If the style of the president's
crisis rhetoric was much like his typical style, it may also elucidate his so-called
Teflon presidency. Opponents hurled attacks at Reagan and his policies
throughout his eight years in office, but until the Iran-Contra affair and its
violation of American myths, none of the criticisms seemed to stick.

Lastly, mythic rhetoric's proclivity for religious allusions explains, at least in
part, why Reagan always seemed so pious despite his infrequent church attendance. In his own way, the president was faithful, for his words constantly paid
homage to the sacred American myths of mission and manifest destiny. Reagan's faith was one that Americans of almost all denominations could share and,
especially in regard to Grenada, they joined in communion with him.

REAGAN, MYTH, AND THE POLITICAL DIVIDENDS OF THE CRISIS IN GRENADA

Through the successful promotion and management of a crisis in Grenada,
Reagan unified a nation divided by events in Beirut, and his approval rating
soared to its highest level in two years. An ABC–*Washington Post* survey found
that 71 percent of American citizens supported the U.S. intervention in Grenada. Furthermore, the invasion attracted few public critics in the United States,
while its supporters included prominent political figures from both parties.[127]
Grenada appeared to be an unmitigated political and rhetorical success.

In addition to uniting the nation after Beirut, Reagan's investment in promoted crisis earned him a surplus of public goodwill to be drawn upon in the
future. The president discovered just how valuable such a surplus can be when
terrorists bombed the U.S. embassy in Beirut, killing thirteen people, in September 1984. This was the third attack of a major U.S. installation in Lebanon in
less than eighteen months. Once again, Reagan was, in effect, powerless to act
against an ephemeral enemy. The difference, however, was that the president
had a reservoir of support still full from his successful management of the crisis
in Grenada. Sixty-five percent of Americans polled considered Reagan "good
in times of crisis" and 63 percent felt he was an "effective leader."[128]

Reagan also reaped a third dividend from Grenada: the replenishment of his symbolic resources. When the president visited the Caribbean island in February 1986, he talked about Grenada and the victory it represented to provide some timely symbolic reassurance about American intervention in Central America. Reagan told Grenadian crowds, "I will never be sorry that I made the decision to help you." He added that the United States also "must help those struggling for freedom in Nicaragua." Extensive media coverage of the president's visit carried his message home to citizens and members of Congress. Even House Speaker O'Neill recognized the valuable symbolic resource Grenada had provided the president. The Speaker claimed Reagan's visit to Grenada could be "a Hollywood kickoff to a greater military involvement in Nicaragua."[129]

As public disclosure of the Iran-Contra arms scandal proved, O'Neill's fears had merit. The mythic combat between good and evil that appeared in the president's crisis rhetoric about Grenada seemed to reflect a world view that necessitated that the United States defeat Communism anywhere and everywhere it appeared. As noted earlier, those who truly believe in a myth reaffirm it through rituals of consecration. In *The Sacred and the Profane,* Eliade writes that some myths are "tragic, blood-drenched" and that "as imitator of the divine gestures, man must reiterate them."[130] American presidents' fascination with foreign crises may lend credence to Eliade's claim, for strains of this mythic foundation frequently appear in presidential crisis discourse.

When our nation becomes involved in a foreign crisis, commanders-in-chief assume the moral high ground and portray the United States as a force for good that has only the most honorable of reasons behind its use of military force: we wish to protect freedom, to rescue hostages, to protect democracy, or to accomplish some other worthy goal. All too often, these same rhetors point to victories in military conflicts as the standard by which Americans should measure their success in upholding revered principles, particularly the principle of freedom. Reagan may have exploited the myths of mission and manifest destiny to their fullest in his crisis rhetoric, but traces of these myths permeate the crisis talk of other commanders-in-chief, as well.

Reagan's promotion and management of a crisis in Grenada clearly provided him with significant benefits, but this is not to say that he was invincible. Toward the end of his White House tenure, the president lost some of his luster when he violated the mythic principles of his earlier talk by allowing the secret sale of weapons to Iran, a nation he had described as our enemy. This episode demonstrated once more that successful crisis victories may not protect a commander-in-chief if unpopular policy decisions or failures elsewhere make large demands on his public good will and symbolic resources. When such demands are made, presidents may choose to replenish these important reserves through crisis promotion and management yet again. The danger, however, is that this gambit will fail and subject both the commander-in-chief and the nation to even greater losses.

Despite these potential drawbacks, the sheer frequency of crisis promotion demonstrates that it remains an appealing issue management option for presidents. Reagan's public talk about the Grenadian crisis and, later, the Libyan crisis, provides ample evidence of the temptation involved. In *The American Jeremiad,* Sacvan Bercovitch offers evidence that crisis has long been a part of American culture. Bercovitch claims that Puritan political sermons made use of crisis talk and the anxiety it provoked to provide the community with a sense of purpose and direction. According to Bercovitch, Puritan leaders exploited crisis for their own ends; they "fastened upon it, gloried in it, even invented it if necessary."[131] Years later, American presidents followed in their Puritan predecessors' footsteps when they, too, realized the persuasive potential of crisis and the political advantages it could provide.

Chapter Eight

"AN ENDLESS SERIES OF HOBGOBLINS"
The Rhetoric and Politics of Crisis
from John Kennedy to George Bush and Beyond

At the outset of this book, I argued that foreign crises are not objective, independent entities, but are instead linguistic constructions. Political events occur, but the meaning given to those events lies with the language that people use to interpret them. The shipment of weapons from one country to another, for instance, may be ignored as insignificant, depicted as a valid defensive measure, or portrayed as a threatening escalation in arms that constitutes a crisis. In the United States, the major source of such interpretations today is the nation's president, for average Americans have little direct experience with foreign affairs, and they defer to presidential words of expertise for guidance in such matters. The interpretations of the president—rather than those of individual legislators, State Department officials, special interest groups, and others— have particular strength because of advantages that the presidential office brings. Presidents can, for example, easily draw on the institutional credibility of the presidency, traditional American values, and historical examples to lend legitimacy to their claims. Presidents can also obtain quick and ample access to the media in order to circulate their views and can expect most citizens to be predisposed to believe them when they speak. Hence, presidential rhetoric plays a crucial role in the forging of political reality about foreign affairs.

Throughout the preceding chapters, I have concentrated on one particular aspect of the presidential construction of political reality: the promotion and management of foreign crises. Contemporary commanders-in-chief promote foreign crises by explicitly advancing a claim of crisis or implicitly treating a circumstance as a crisis in their public discourse. To manage foreign crises, presidents utilize military or other means and, most importantly, attempt to persuade American citizens that their resolution was the most appropriate one available. In keeping with the significance I have attributed to political language, I have focused my attention not on historical and political analyses, but on presidential words themselves in order to understand foreign crises as most citizens experience them and to shed light on the characteristic arguments and themes of presidential crisis promotion.

The presidents examined here exhibited a great deal of overall consistency in their portrayal of the crisis situation, the style, or attitude, that their discourse regularly exhibited, and the characteristic strategies they used to encourage citizens to identify with and to support them and their policies. Situationally, commanders-in-chief typically emphasized a menacing crisis scene that threatened American lives and American principles, thus dictating that the United States act to achieve both pragmatic (the protection of lives) and idealistic (the protection of principles) purposes that would serve to rectify, or correct, the crisis scene. Through such situational portrayals, presidents imbued political events—events that might otherwise attract little attention—with great significance and urgency.

These rhetors' appeals to American ideals also deflected troubling questions about the ethicality of U.S. policy by infusing military intervention with moral purpose. In this way, presidents' situational portrayals served to reinforce the American myths of mission and manifest destiny, for commanders-in-chief contended that the nation must act to defend its moral ideals and then pointed to the accomplishment of pragmatic goals as evidence that the United States had fulfilled its moral destiny.

Stylistically, the presidents discussed in this book most often spoke through the national voice of "we" and frequently described foreign crises as tests of character. Presidents depicted "we" as a patient, peaceful actor who was reluctant to intervene in other countries, but who felt compelled to do so because of our sacred moral responsibilities in the world. The style of crisis rhetoric thereby appealed to the American self-concept of morality, treated U.S. intervention as an appropriate response to tests of national character, and implied that blame for the crisis must lie with some other, less scrupulous party. At the same time, presidents stylistically depicted "we" as strong, which again served to reinforce the nation's self-concept and also to signal American resolve to enemies and allies alike.

The identificational appeals that commanders-in-chief used showed a bit more variety than the situational portrayals and style of their rhetoric. In three cases, presidents relied primarily upon antithetical appeals that encouraged Americans to unite against a foreign enemy, but in three other case studies, this type of identificational appeal did not play a central or even secondary role. Therefore, my analysis irrevocably refutes earlier research findings, which indicated that antithetical appeals were an identifying characteristic of presidential crisis rhetoric.

Half of the presidents examined here showed a special fondness for implicit appeals, which united citizens with the president through a language of shared values and achievements, or for explicit appeals, which made overt links between the president and some other positive element such as his office, the values and desires of the American people, or the success of the crisis resolution. Moreover, explicit appeals appeared much more frequently in the discourse of all presidential crisis promoters, albeit most often as a secondary identificational strategy, than earlier research indicated.

In addition to the characteristics of presidential crisis rhetoric, I have examined the structural/legal bases for crisis promotion and the news management techniques that presidents use to enhance their persuasive efforts. The characteristics of crisis discourse may have stayed fairly constant since Kennedy's time, but presidents have employed crisis promotion to accrue more power and then used accumulated power to promote more crises. Furthermore, news management techniques have grown increasingly more sophisticated and, because of the legitimacy that each apparently successful crisis resolution bestows upon these techniques, increasingly more extensive and widely accepted.

The term *crisis,* which derives from the Greek word κρίσις, refers to the critical moment of decision in the life of an issue or dispute.[1] Although people usually perceive crises as threatening events, this study shows that presidential rhetors have frequently found their discourse about foreign crises to be personally beneficial because it allows them to expand their powers and to enhance their political standing. This aspect of crisis can be illumined further by turning to another Greek term related to crisis: καιρός. According to Liddell and Scott, καιρός means *"the right time for action, the critical moment . . .* generally, *convenience, advantage, profit."*[2] What is dangerous for some may prove advantageous for others. These etymological origins reveal the multiple connotations of crisis. In addition, they provide a context for discussing this study's conclusions.

In this chapter, I detail the characteristic situation, style, and identificational appeals of presidential crisis rhetoric and note significant differences among the particular cases examined. I then turn to the structural/legal state of affairs that now encourages crisis promotion, to the current status of news management techniques that further perpetuate this phenomenon, and to the dangers crisis promotion poses to our political system.

THE RHETORIC OF PROMOTED CRISIS

Although the cases examined in this book involved six different presidents over the course of two decades, the situation, style, and identificational appeals of presidential crisis promotion were remarkably constant. At the same time, each president's discourse exhibited unique traits that differentiated his persuasive efforts from those of his peers. In the following pages, I attempt to make sense of the commonalities and the differences that inhere in the crisis promotion of presidents Kennedy through Reagan; I also demonstrate how George Bush followed the rhetorical traditions of his predecessors when he promoted a crisis in Panama.

Situation

Just as scholars from other fields firmly root their conception of situation in the subject matter they study—be it psychology, history, political science, or some other discipline—in this communication analysis of presidents and foreign crises, I have accounted for situations through the examination of how presidential rhetors portrayed situations in their discourse. Accordingly, I have employed Burke's pentadic method to scrutinize each president's crisis rhetoric in order to answer five questions: (1) what took place? (terms for act); (2) who performed the deed? (terms for actor); (3) what was the background of the act or where did it take place? (terms for scene); (4) by what avenue was the act performed? (terms for means); and (5) what was the goal of the act? (terms for purpose).

After constructing the situational portrayal of each president's talk, I then examined the central ratios, or relationships, that existed among these words. The key terms and terminological relationships of a president's situational portrayal are of great significance because they illumine how that president depicted a crisis situation and the linguistic form that his motives or strategies for managing the situation took. Given the central role that presidential words play in the construction of political reality, pentadic analysis reveals the characteristic ways that presidents portray foreign crises to Americans and, thus, the characteristic ways in which average Americans experience these crises.

If *crisis* refers to a turning point, then the crisis discourse examined in this study remained true to its etymological roots, for presidents typically depicted crises as menacing scenes that could rapidly change for better or worse. Whether dealing with missiles in Cuba or a Communist coup in Grenada, presidents gave special prominence to terms that described the international setting of the crisis, its causes, and, especially, its potential dangers. Commanders-in-chief claimed that crisis scenes posed a threat to American lives and were of transcendent significance because of the test they posed for American principles. According to presidential rhetors, these scenes were so urgent that they demanded immediate action to fulfill both pragmatic (protection of American lives) and idealistic (protection of American principles) goals. Presidents consistently emphasized the urgency of a scene and the compelling necessity of goals arising from that scene to rally support for the policies they had enacted and to discourage dissent and open debate.

This line of reasoning was exemplified in the terminological relationship that arose on a regular basis in the situation of presidential crisis rhetoric: terms for scene-purpose, which appeared in the talk of Kennedy, Johnson, Nixon, Carter, and Reagan. These presidents' terms for situation explained what the nation's purposes must be, in view of a particular crisis scene. In Kennedy's rhetoric, for example, he argued that because the Soviets had placed offensive nuclear weapons on Cuba, "we" and "I" must act to prevent the use of the missiles, to secure their withdrawal, and to protect freedom and peace (scene-purpose). Similarly, Carter described a scene in which Iranian students had taken U.S.

embassy officials hostage and contended that this scene dictated that the United States work for particular purposes: to gain the hostages' safe release and to protect the integrity, interests, honor, and principles of the United States.

Terms for purpose in presidential crisis rhetoric usually assumed the form of goals that would serve to correct the crisis scene by achieving practical ends and upholding American principles. Nixon, for instance, talked about a crisis scene in which U.S. soldiers and the withdrawal program were endangered and in which a just peace and U.S. credibility had been threatened. According to the president, the United States' purposes must be to modify this scene by acting to safeguard American soldiers, the U.S. withdrawal program, the chances of a just peace, and the nation's credibility.

Reagan likewise described his purposes in terms of the need for a corrected scene; he discussed both practical ends (the protection of American lives) and more transcendent ones (the restoration of democracy and freedom), as did Kennedy and Carter. More recently, the crisis discourse of another president, George Bush, exemplified the same scene-purpose ordering of principles and articulated purpose. In his televised speech about Panama, the president explained how Manuel Noriega, a convicted drug trafficker, posed a threat to the United States.

> Last Friday, Noriega declared his military dictatorship to be in a state of war with the United States and publicly threatened the lives of Americans in Panama. The very next day, forces under his command shot and killed an unarmed American serviceman; wounded another; arrested and brutally beat a third American serviceman; and then brutally interrogated his wife, threatening her with sexual abuse. That was enough.[3]

Because of this dangerous scene, Bush said he had ordered military action "to protect the lives of American citizens in Panama and to bring General Noriega to justice in the United States." The invasion also had other goals: "to defend democracy in Panama, to combat drug trafficking, and to protect the integrity of the Panama Canal Treaty."[4] According to the president, the invasion sought to remedy the crisis scene by achieving both pragmatic (the protection of lives, the apprehension of Noriega, the alleviation of drug trafficking) and idealistic (the preservation of democracy and the integrity of the Panama Canal Treaty) goals. For a summary of Bush's discourse about the crisis in Panama, as well as a summary of the crisis rhetoric of the other presidents in this study, see the table on page 211.

In contrast to these presidents, Johnson's terms for purpose consisted almost exclusively of the abstract principles of peace and the defense of freedom, rather than practical or concrete goals. Nonetheless, his words for purpose still represented a corrected crisis scene because the president claimed that attacks against American ships in the Gulf of Tonkin constituted a threat to peace and freedom and that the United States' purposes must be to uphold these ideals.

The one exception to the recurrent situational emphasis on terms for scene-purpose occurred in the discourse of Gerald Ford; his words for situation highlighted neither of these principles. In his case, however, Press Secretary Ron Nessen, who spoke for Ford during the crisis, used language that ex-emplified a scene-actor ordering of words; he associated the scenic need for crisis resolution with the crisis leadership of President Ford. That terms for scene were not important in Ford's rhetoric may be explained—at least in part—by the post hoc nature of his talk: the president did not need to establish the existence of the crisis for citizens because Nessen had already done so. Moreover, the fact that Nessen *did* focus on the crisis scene serves to underscore the important role that words for scene play in the situational portrayals of presidential crisis discourse.

In addition to his lack of concern for the terminological scene, Ford also chose not to accentuate terms for purpose, perhaps because he had less need to legitimize his actions in this way. Since the *Mayaguez* crisis came on the heels of the United States' unceremonious withdrawal from Cambodia and Vietnam, the emotional context of the crisis and Nessen's description of the scene may have infused the military rescue mission with all the legitimacy that Ford needed.

The scene-purpose ordering of terms prevalent in presidential crisis rhetoric focused attention on a threatening crisis scene in which American citizens and American principles faced grave danger and on the unavoidable necessity of fulfilling goals that constituted a correction of the crisis scene. Hence, this study confirms and extends Procter's finding that presidents justify foreign interven-tion on the basis of the need to combat chaos abroad and to uphold American ideals.[5] Situational portrayals in crisis promotion encouraged citizens to view foreign crises as urgent matters in which debate over policy options—let alone debate over the presidents' interpretation of the crisis scene—was simply not feasible. Instead, presidents exhorted the public to support the policies they had enacted so that the threat could be swiftly eliminated.

Commanders-in-chief also heightened the significance of each crisis scene when they depicted it as one that challenged American principles and pro-claimed that the protection of these principles was a necessary goal of presiden-tial crisis management. In the cases examined here, the appeal to revered ideals rationalized the loss of human life, the depletion of the nation's economic reserves, and other sacrifices by endowing them with a transcendent meaning. Bloody military interventions apparently become more palatable to citizens, even heroic, when presidents can successfully imbue them with moral purpose.

In addition to terms for scene and purpose, terms for act played an important

Summary of the Situation, Style, and Identificational Appeals of Presidential Crisis Rhetoric

	Kennedy	Johnson	Nixon	Ford	Carter	Reagan	Bush
Situation	terms for scene-purpose and terms for purpose-act	terms for scene-purpose and terms for purpose-act	terms for scene-purpose and terms for purpose-act	terms for actor-act	terms for scene-purpose and terms for purpose-means	terms for scene-purpose and terms for purpose-actor	terms for scene-purpose and terms for means-scene
Style	actor = peaceful, determined "we"; terms for act-actor and terms for actor-act	actor = strong, yet restrained "we" and "I"; terms for act-actor	actor = responsible "I" and powerful "we"; terms for act-actor	actor = capable President Ford or the Ford administration; terms for act-actor	actor = patient, principled "we"; terms for actor-means	actor = noble America or "we"; terms for scene-actor and terms for actor-scene	actor = responsible "I" and patient, determined "we"; terms for scene-actor and terms for actor-purpose
Identificational Appeals	strongly antithetical	implicit supported by explicit	mostly antithetical; also extensive explicit	strongly explicit	implicit; also extensive explicit	antithetical; some implicit	strongly explicit; also antithetical

situational role in the crisis discourse included in this book. Presidents seemed to recognize that citizens look to them to resolve crises as soon as possible. In political scientist James Barber's words, Americans expect their president "to be a take-charge man, a doer, a turner of the wheels, a producer of progress even if that means some sacrifice of serenity."[6]

Murray Edelman adds that citizens' desire for "resolute action" becomes even greater in times of crisis.[7] The rhetoric of the presidents examined in this study reflected an awareness of such expectations. Not only did presidents describe dangerous scenes and the purposes emanating from those scenes, they frequently detailed the action they had taken to restore those scenes to normalcy. Kennedy, Johnson, Nixon, and Ford all emphasized how they had personally taken action to resolve their crises.

In the discourse of these four presidents, situational terms for act were also important because of their relationships with other terms. Kennedy, Johnson, and Nixon explained that the crisis scene dictated particular goals (scene-purpose) and that those goals, in turn, mandated particular acts (purpose-act). In his crisis rhetoric, for instance, Johnson argued that a scene of renewed enemy aggression in the Gulf of Tonkin indicated that the United States should attempt to maintain and to demonstrate its commitment to peace and the defense of freedom. Johnson claimed that to fulfill this purpose, retaliatory action and legislative action were needed. In contrast, Ford's crisis talk portrayed him as an active leader through the terminological ratio of actor-act. In all four of these cases, terms for act provided a sense of momentum. The nation—and the president—appeared to be doing something or had done something about the threat from abroad.

Terms for act did not, however, play a major role in the situation of Reagan's or Carter's crisis discourse. Reagan discussed his situation through a scene-purpose and purpose-actor ordering of terms, whereas Carter's rhetoric reflected the dominant terminological relationships of scene-purpose and purpose-means. Nonetheless, Reagan's words for situation conveyed a strong sense of momentum; Carter's crisis talk did not. One explanation for this is that Reagan's terms for purpose were active terms. The president said the United States acted to restore democracy and to save American lives. The situational ratio of purpose-actor also conveyed a sense of motion by portraying an actor called to fulfill these goals.

In contrast to Reagan, Carter portrayed our nation's purposes through comparatively passive terms: to secure the safe release of the hostages and to protect the integrity and interests of the United States. Carter also decreased his talk's activity, through the purpose-means terminological relationship. The reliance on terms for ends and means abetted the reduction of action to motion and gave the president the appearance of one who reacted to events instead of acting upon them. Rather than state that we had acted to achieve particular goals, Carter pondered what means we could follow to attain our ends.

Like Reagan and Carter, Bush paid little attention to terms for act in his crisis discourse about Panama, but like his mentor, Bush managed to convey a sense of action in his talk. For Bush, ratios of words for scene-purpose and words for means-scene played key situational roles. The president claimed that the scene of crisis in Panama demanded the fulfillment of a number of goals, all of which were articulated in active terms: to save American lives, to defend democracy, to fight drug trafficking, and to bring Noriega to justice in the United States.

Bush also mentioned that we aimed "to protect the integrity of the Panama Canal treaty."[8] This goal was more passive and abstract in character. One could, conceivably, point to tangible evidence to prove that Americans were safe, democratic government in Panama protected, drug trafficking thwarted, and Noriega forced to face charges; to point to similar results that proved the "integrity" of a treaty had been upheld would be more difficult. In Bush's crisis talk, this latter goal played a rather small role, whereas the more dynamic terms for purpose dominated; thus the president's talk sounded quite active.

Related to this, the terminological ratio of means-scene emphasized how Bush's policies had led to crisis resolution. In his December 1989 televised speech, for example, the president cautioned that not all goals had yet been achieved. At the same time, he quietly linked the U.S. invasion policy with the results of an improved scene in Panama. Bush said that "the operation is not over yet. General Noriega is in hiding. And nevertheless, yesterday a dictator ruled Panama, and today constitutionally elected leaders govern." Ten days later, Bush reported that the military operation had "restored peace and tranquility" to Panama and argued that this, in turn, would help clear the way "for the orderly implementation of the Panama Canal treaty."

On January 3, 1990, the president announced that Operation Just Cause had now fulfilled all of its objectives because Noriega had "turned himself in to U.S. authorities" that evening and was currently on a "U.S. Air Force C-130" that was taking him to the United States to face charges of drug trafficking. Shortly thereafter, Bush told a joint session of Congress that "one year ago, the people of Panama lived in fear, under the thumb of a dictator. Today democracy is restored; Panama is free. Operation Just Cause has achieved its objective."[9] Just as Bush's terms for scene had indicated what purposes must be fulfilled, the president demonstrated how his policy had realized its goals by pointing to changes the operation had brought to the crisis scene.

The examination of situation indicates the centrality of words for scene, purpose, and act in presidential crisis rhetoric. Presidents talk about the urgency of crisis scenes and the compelling need to fulfill goals that will correct crisis scenes as a way to justify their policies. Moreover, presidential rhetors' discussion of resolute action functions to convey momentum and to demonstrate their leadership. In Ford's case, where terms for scene and purpose did not predominate, the context of the crisis and Nessen's explanation of the threatening scene apparently served to legitimize presidential policy. Similarly, Reagan and Bush, who did not accentuate words for act, gave their discourse a sense of activity in other ways.

The presidents discussed in this book also demonstrated an Orwellian tendency to justify acts of war in terms of seemingly contrary purposes. Kennedy, for example, closed his televised address with the statement, "Our goal is not the victory of might, but the vindication of right—not peace at the expense of freedom, but both peace *and* freedom, here in this hemisphere, and, we hope, around the world."[10] The president who brought our nation to the brink of nuclear war claimed that one of his goals was peace. Likewise, Ford's purpose and actions seemed at odds. The president said his aim was to free the *Mayaguez* crew, but his actions, in fact, placed those men in great peril. Taken as a group, all seven presidents examined here showed a disturbing propensity to justify violence as a way of attaining peace (Kennedy, Johnson, Nixon), American intervention in another nation's affairs on behalf of freedom or democracy (Kennedy, Johnson, Reagan, Bush), and dangerous military missions, ostensibly to protect American lives (Kennedy, Nixon, Ford, Carter, Reagan, Bush). Even more troubling, perhaps, U.S. citizens have shown a predisposition to accept such arguments.

The situational portrayals of presidential crisis talk also tended to balance appeals to idealism with appeals to pragmatism. On the one hand, commanders-in-chief infused their actions with a sense of moral purpose by appealing to national ideals such as peace and freedom and by insisting that their policies were consistent with these ideals. At the same time, presidents appealed to pragmatism by emphasizing the concrete success of their crisis management as proof that their policies had also upheld national ideals. Johnson, Kennedy, Nixon, Reagan, and Bush all pointed to the apparently successful military action they had taken and, in the latter four cases, to their attainment of the tangible goals they had set forth, as evidence that more abstract purposes, such as the protection of peace and freedom, had been obtained or were within reach.

Bush told reporters after Noriega was in U.S. custody, "The return of General Noriega marks a significant milestone in Operation Just Cause. The U.S. used its resources in a manner consistent with political, diplomatic, and moral principles."[11] With Noriega safely in U.S. custody, the president had proof that he had managed the crisis successfully. The general's capture symbolized how Bush had fulfilled both pragmatic and idealistic ends by correcting the crisis scene. My research therefore reaffirms the case study findings of both Bass and Klope, who argue that presidents make appeals to progress in their crisis rhetoric in order to win public support.[12]

Unlike the other presidents, Ford did not emphasize purposive principles in his crisis talk. His terms for purpose were also more pragmatic, for he aimed merely to rescue the *Mayaguez* and its crew. Despite this practical focus, though, Ford paid homage to idealistic expectations when he talked about how the mission's success symbolized a higher principle: that the United States still had the will and capability to respond to foreign challenges.[13] The symbolic context of the *Mayaguez* crisis appealed to American ideals, but Ford also tipped his hat to idealism when he indicated that his crisis management had fulfilled more transcendent goals. All in all, the presidents examined here recognized the need to appeal both to Americans' sense of idealism and to their desire for pragmatism and results.

One president in this study, Jimmy Carter, did not fulfill these expectations, for his discourse was extremely idealistic in its appeals. Although Carter featured terms for scene-purpose in his situation, just as other presidents did, the situation of his talk was constrained by a second terminological ratio of purpose-means. Other presidents insisted that their stated purposes were consistent with their acts (Kennedy, Johnson, Nixon), that the key actor exemplified the purposive principles they had articulated (Reagan), or that their policy had successfully remedied the crisis scene in accordance with the purposes they had set forth (Bush). But Carter idealistically agonized over what policies or means might allow the nation to stay true to its principles. He argued, as did the other presidents in this study, that the crisis scene dictated particular purposes. Nevertheless, the idealistic bent of Carter's rhetoric was obvious even in his decision to make the hostages' safe release his practical goal—rather than to articulate the purpose of an expedient close to the crisis in which the embassy siege would end, albeit at the risk of harm to the hostages. He maintained that his stated purpose was in keeping with the United States' compassion and respect for human life. Carter also contended that the hostages' freedom was only one goal and emphasized how the United States must implement policies consistent with various abstract purposes: the protection of our nation's integrity, interests, honor, and principles.

Although the president initially had strong public support, citizens gradually grew disenchanted with his crisis management. As explained in chapter 6, one reason for this reaction was that Carter had promoted the crisis extensively, but then found its resolution was largely outside his control. In addition, the president's idealistic insistence that all policies be in accordance with our nation's character constrained his policy options. Carter's discourse did not feature terms for act, nor did it indicate whether or how progress toward his stated goals was being made. Instead, the president passively contemplated through a situational purpose-means ratio of terms what policy might safely free the hostages *and* allow the United States to remain true to its principles.

The lesson of Carter's rhetoric appears to be this: a president cannot promise the attainment of a tangible goal and then not obtain it. Furthermore, one must take quick military action that *appears* successful, or attain concrete goals, in order for citizens to sustain their belief that more abstract ends have been realized. Carter was unable to gain the hostages' release. When he finally ordered a rescue mission, a *Newsweek* poll found that Americans approved of the attempt, but most citizens surveyed said they would not vote for Carter in the upcoming November election.[14] His public support continued to decrease rapidly in the months that followed. The president idealistically described the operation as compatible with the nation's character, but the mission's failure to rescue the hostages implied that "we" also had failed to fulfill the more symbolic ends of protecting the United States' integrity, interests, honor, and principles.

Carter's problems notwithstanding, his promotion and management of the Iranian hostage crisis should not imply that idealism in crisis discourse is unimportant, for one can imagine that presidential rhetors who focused exclusively on pragmatism would also meet their share of political problems, in the form of attacks on their apparent lack of principles. In the fall of 1990, for example, Secretary of State James Baker argued pragmatically that if Iraqi leader Saddam Hussein's conquest of Middle East oil were not stopped, severe economic consequences in the United States would result. During an interview with CNN, President George Bush defended Baker's statement and claimed that U.S. involvement in the Persian Gulf crisis was about "jobs." In the controversy that followed, political commentator William Safire described Baker as "ever the pragmatist" and lambasted both men for their "cynical" explanations.[15] The Bush administration, shortly thereafter, abandoned its emphasis on purely pragmatic concerns.

To win enduring public support, presidents who engage in crisis promotion reject extreme idealism and extreme pragmatism and rely instead on rhetorical appeals that embrace both. The balance between these appeals helps presidents avoid the perception of passivity and ineptitude that purely idealistic talk may encourage and the perception of unprincipled expediency that purely pragmatic discourse may conjure. The combination of these appeals exemplifies the American myths of mission and manifest destiny. These myths emphasize the principle of freedom, argue that our nation is divinely blessed, claim that the United States is a model of morality for the rest of the world, and contend that the United States is destined to spread freedom around the globe.

In presidential crisis talk, mission and manifest destiny function to romanticize U.S. military intervention and to give it moral significance (idealism). At the same time, these mythic themes point to practical success as evidence that we have upheld our ideals and present military action as the primary way to do so (pragmatism). Presidents argue that we *must* take military action or we will suffer defeat, and yet later point to the resolution of foreign crises through military intervention as proof of how our principles were *destined* to win. Crisis promotion serves as a contemporary ritual that reinforces the myths of mission and manifest destiny by upholding American ideals and by providing citizens with a sense of progress.

Style

Style, as treated in this study, is the "character-istic" attitude exhibited in a rhetor's language, or the way a rhetor adheres to personal values in his or her discourse. To shed light on individual presidents' unique styles of crisis promotion, I ascertained in previous chapters each commander-in-chief's key terms for actor, descriptions of that actor, and the dominant ratios in which terms for actor were involved. The comparison of these presidents reveals that a characteristic style of contemporary crisis discourse also exists. Although style may be "the man himself,"[16] the role of president also apparently impacts on the stylistic choices that commanders-in-chief make.

In times of crisis, occupants of the Oval Office cannot speak merely for themselves, but must assume the voice of the nation in their role as leader. Accordingly, presidents tended to portray the key stylistic actor of their discourse as "we." Reagan's style, for example, revealed a rhetor who almost always hid behind the collective "we" or "America" and rarely referred to himself. In their own crisis promotion, Kennedy, Johnson, and Carter featured "we" as their most prominent stylistic actor, whereas Nixon and Bush both referred to "we" as a lesser coactor. The prevalence of this stylistic characteristic points to the important role that presidents perform when they articulate the country's crisis policies and justifications.

Next to "we," the key stylistic actors that presidents depicted most often were themselves. Ford's style, for instance, revolved exclusively around himself as "President Ford" and the head of "the Ford administration." Although no other commander-in-chief was quite as self-absorbed as Ford, three others—Johnson, Nixon, and Bush—referred to "I" as a stylistic coactor with "we." If foreign crises provide presidents with an opportunity to act especially presidential, then presidents frequently exploit that opportunity by casting themselves as key actors in their crisis rhetoric so that no one will overlook their leadership capabilities.

Beyond naming who the key actors were, presidents also described, with a good measure of consistency, what those key actors were like and how they acted. Most often, commanders-in-chief attributed patience to the actors in their discourse; Kennedy, Johnson, Nixon, Carter, and Reagan all claimed that "we" possessed this character trait or acted in accordance with it. In addition, presidents portrayed actors as determined, resolute, or firm (Kennedy, Johnson, Ford, Reagan), peaceful (Kennedy, Nixon, Johnson, Reagan), courageous

(Kennedy, Carter, Reagan), selfless (Nixon, Reagan), powerful or strong (Johnson, Nixon, Ford), and restrained (Kennedy, Johnson, Carter). The style of presidential crisis promotion, in other words, was akin to that of Lyndon Johnson in his rhetoric on the Gulf of Tonkin: presidents balanced depictions of strength with portrayals of restraint.

President George Bush, for example, at a December 1989 question-and-answer session with reporters, after Noriega had found refuge in the Vatican embassy, claimed that "we" had a great deal of "determination" to see Noriega turned over to the United States. In fact, he explained, "we're going to pursue every avenue to bring him to justice, and I'm satisfied that it will happen." Bush then added cautiously, however, that "we're not going to go in there and run roughshod over the Panamanians" and "we don't want to act too precipitously."[17]

Although strength and restraint are not necessarily opposed to one another, crisis discourse in the nuclear age reflects the tension between these concepts. The advent of the atomic bomb has meant that commanders-in-chief can no longer wage all-out war without facing the possibility of nuclear destruction. Because of this, a president must reassure both domestic and international publics that he will not rashly start a nuclear war in response to a crisis and, simultaneously, that he will act forcefully enough to defend freedom and keep the peace. Presidents therefore are at pains to convince their listeners that military responses are properly judicious and that diplomatic endeavors are appropriately forceful.

In President Johnson's discourse about the Gulf of Tonkin, he further encouraged the dichotomization of restraint and strength when he dissociated peace from the defense of freedom and publicly articulated the possibility that these goals might be at odds. With the public furor that later developed over American involvement in Vietnam, peace came to be associated with restrained diplomatic efforts, whereas defense came to connote military intervention—at least for a significant number of Americans. These new meanings, in conjunction with the constraints of the nuclear age, seem to have led contemporary presidents to offset depictions of restraint with descriptions of strength. In this book, presidents represented the key actor of "we" in a way that fulfilled Americans' dualistic expectations of themselves and portrayed "I" as a strong yet compassionate president who was worthy to lead American citizens.

Presidential characterizations of our nation as patient and peaceful assumed added importance, especially when considered in conjunction with terms for situation, because of the way in which they helped presidents justify harsh policy responses. In their linguistic construction of the crisis situation, commanders-in-chief described crisis scenes that consisted of a threat brought about by some foreign country or group's aggressive action: the Soviets had smuggled nuclear missiles to Cuba; North Vietnamese vessels had attacked

U.S. ships on the high seas without provocation; Communists had set up sanctuaries in Cambodia and posed a threat to U.S. soldiers; Cambodian Communists had captured the *Mayaguez;* Iranian students had seized American embassy personnel in Teheran; Communists had taken over Grenada and placed Americans there in danger; and the Noriega government in Panama had declared itself at war with the United States, killed a U.S. serviceman, and threatened other Americans. In all of these cases, the presidents argued that someone else had precipitated the crisis and that the United States had been forced to respond.

Stylistic attributions of patience, peacefulness, and restraint to "we" and "I" provided further support for these accounts of crisis origins. In previous case studies, Cherwitz and Zagacki, Brockriede and Scott, Klope, and Heisey observed this same tendency.[18] The image presidents created of an essentially passive United States and president who were forced to act also served to underscore the righteous fury with which the key actors undertook military retaliation.

According to President Bush, for example, the United States peacefully tried to resolve its differences with General Noriega of Panama. He said, "Many attempts have been made to resolve this crisis through diplomacy and negotiations. All were rejected by the dictator of Panama, General Manuel Noriega." Because of Noriega's "reckless threats and attacks upon Americans in Panama," Bush claimed that a military response could not be avoided because "as President, I have no higher obligation than to safeguard the lives of American citizens." Bush also assured citizens that no commander-in-chief "takes such [military] action lightly" and that he considered "every human life" to be "precious." In fact, the president contended the invasion had taken place at night in order to minimize civilian casualties in Panama. Bush asserted that "the Panamanian people want democracy, peace, and the chance for a better life in dignity and freedom. The people of the United States seek only to support them in the pursuit of these noble goals."[19] Bush depicted patient, peaceful, and principled coactors who had invaded Panama only when they had no other choice.

Along with their stylistic portrayals of an actor reluctant to take military action, commanders-in-chief also justified why the United States and its president had acted by emphasizing America's sacred responsibilities in the world. Kennedy, Johnson, Nixon, Reagan, and Bush especially incorporated the myths of mission and manifest destiny in their stylistic depictions of "we" or the United States. According to Kennedy, for example, Americans willingly sacrificed whenever freedom was at stake. Likewise, Johnson portrayed the nation as the protector of global freedom, and Nixon described the United States as the country that must act to prevent "the forces of totalitarianism and anarchy" from threatening "free nations and free institutions throughout the world."[20] In his discourse about Panama, Bush spoke of "the mission of our nation" and how the "sacrifice" of servicemen who had been wounded or killed had been for "a noble cause and will never be forgotten. A free and prosperous Panama will be an enduring tribute."[21]

None of these presidents, however, described the nation more romantically than Ronald Reagan, who claimed the United States was the world's "force for freedom" and its most brilliant "star of hope." He said that America had no other goal than to rescue others from oppression and pointed to Grenada as evidence that "the quest for freedom continues to build."[22] In general, the style of presidential crisis rhetoric characterized "we" as a nation that had to act, when challenged, in order to fulfill its moral responsibilities and destiny as the world's foremost protector and propagator of freedom.

Ford and Carter typically described the key actors of their discourse somewhat differently. Ford, for example, used relatively few descriptive terms to encapsulate the key actor of his rhetoric, Ford or the Ford administration. One explanation for this aberration may lie with the generally understated quality of the president's crisis promotion. Since Ford talked about the crisis so little, it stands to reason that he would invoke fewer stylistic descriptions of himself. Another answer, compatible with the first, may be that presidents typically find it undignified to focus too much upon themselves. When Ford chose to describe the key actor in his crisis discourse, for example, he centered attention, more often than not, on his administration, rather than himself alone. This allowed the president to depict his own worthy characteristics in a slightly less direct way by pointing to the positive qualities of the government he led.

Further evidence of the need for presidential decorum can be gleaned from Richard Nixon, whose crisis discourse lavished a great deal of attention upon himself and his selfless attributes and prompted large amounts of negative commentary in turn. *Newsweek,* for example, complained that Nixon's announcement of the Cambodian invasion was that of a "beleaguered man" who was personally obsessed with foreign challenges, and even National Security Advisor Henry Kissinger later pronounced that the president had "personalized the issue excessively."[23] Although presidents may talk about themselves and their motivations, as Bush did directly in regard to Panama and as Ford did more indirectly through references to his administration's performance during the *Mayaguez* crisis, Nixon proves that limits also exist as to how much they can do so. Americans apparently feel that presidential depictions of personal leadership should err on the side of earnest understatement.

A second distinctive depiction of a key actor occurred in Carter's crisis style. Carter emphasized that the chief actor of his discourse, "we," had maturity and integrity, and he repeatedly emphasized how the United States treated others with respect and sensitivity. Presidential crisis promotion typically did not attribute such characteristics to key actors. Carter also failed to balance his portrait of the United States' gentle moral traits with depictions of its strength and forcefulness of action. As a result, the president contributed to perceptions that the country—and its leader—were responding to the hostage crisis with weakness and incompetence.

According to Windt, Gregg and Hauser, and Birdsell, presidents have a predilection to elevate foreign crises into tests of national will in their public speeches.[24] My own analysis of presidential discourse corroborates these scholars' findings. In four of the cases examined, an act-actor ordering of terms characterized the style of presidential crisis promotion. These presidents talked about foreign crises as tests of credibility for the nation and, in some cases, for themselves. In his discourse on the Cuban missile crisis, for example, Kennedy argued that the United States could not accept the presence of nuclear missiles in Cuba if "our courage and our commitments are ever to be trusted again by either friend or foe."[25]

In a similar vein, Johnson claimed that retaliatory air strikes and the passage of the Southeast Asia Resolution revealed that the two coactors of his style, "we" and "I," were resolute and restrained when it came to the defense of freedom in Vietnam. Nixon's rhetoric on Cambodia constructed a similar, if somewhat more complex, scenario. On the one hand, Nixon insisted that the United States must invade Cambodia or become "a pitiful, helpless giant."[26] To ensure that the country lived up to this test, Nixon—or "I"—launched the invasion, even though this action might make him a one-term president. Nixon's style indicated that the act of invasion would remake the coactors of his discourse, one for the better and one for the worse. In Ford's crisis talk, he pointed to his management of the *Mayaguez* crisis as an indication of his leadership capability. Ford said that his administration's quick and effective actions were a clear demonstration of how it would respond to future violations of international law.

In contrast to these act-actor orderings of terms, the stylistic ratios of Carter's and Reagan's discourse initially seemed to mark a change from the tendency to represent foreign crises as tests of character. Although Carter's talk did, in fact, diverge from this trend, Reagan's crisis promotion followed the theme of earlier crisis rhetoric. But he conveyed this meaning through a different linguistic means. In Reagan's discourse about Grenada, terms for situation portrayed the United States as an actor that personified the principle of freedom (purpose-actor). In turn, the president's style featured a scene that called for the United States (scene-actor) and that demonstrated how "we" had managed the crisis in Grenada successfully (actor-scene). Reagan's rhetoric argued that the crisis called upon America to impose its character and that the crisis resolution wrought in Grenada was proof that we had done so. Although his talk accomplished the effect in slightly different ways, Reagan's crisis promotion followed the pattern of many of his predecessors when he depicted Grenada as a test of national character.

In his rhetoric about Panama, Bush, too, emphasized crisis as a test of character through the stylistic ordering of terms for actor-purpose and terms for scene-actor. The president made clear, for instance, that the actors of his discourse, "I" and the United States, had a special devotion to the protection of American citizens and to the defense of freedom. According to Bush's nation-wide address, he had a moral duty to safeguard the lives of Americans abroad. He was also "determined not to neglect the democracies in this hemisphere." Likewise, he told listeners at a January 1990 executive forum that "Americans" considered democracy to be "a noble cause."[27]

In conjunction with this actor-purpose terminological relationship, Bush established a scene-actor ratio of terms, as well. Given the actors' dedication to their principles, the president argued that they were compelled to act in response to the challenge that the Panamanian crisis posed. Bush said that the "threat to the lives of Americans" and "the abortion of democracy" in Panama had "caused American action." During a December 1989 press conference, the president responded to news of criticism from Soviet leader Mikhail Gorbachev by asserting that the crisis had demanded that Bush act on his personal commitments: "Look, if they kill an American marine, that's real bad. And if they threaten and brutalize the wife of an American citizen, sexually threatening the lieutenant's wife while kicking him in the groin over and over again, then, Mr. Gorbachev, please understand this President is going to do something about it."

Bush also took time to explicate how the Panamanian crisis had dictated that the United States act upon its principles. The president claimed at a March 1990 ceremony that "the people of . . . Panama, needed us to stand with them to defend that struggle for democracy and for the opportunity that Americans have enjoyed for over 200 years."[28] For Bush, like most of the contemporary presidents who preceded him, foreign crises constituted a challenge to princi-ples of character and demanded that the nation and its president assert themselves.

The one exception to this general rule was, once again, Jimmy Carter, whose style exemplified an actor-means terminological relationship. Carter's style alone emphasized the actor's principles—integrity, honor, and interests—over all other key terms and insisted that "we" only implement policies that were in accordance with those principles. Like other presidents, Carter justified his resort to a military rescue mission by claiming that this means was consistent with our character. More often, though, the president told of his difficult search for policies that would lead to the hostages' safe release and that also would be consonant with what he construed to be national beliefs. That Carter's style accentuated such concerns reveals his unique interest in ethics and the true test of character that the Iranian hostage crisis may have posed for him. That the president, like other commanders-in-chief, justified military action as a policy consistent with the country's character bespeaks of a larger presidential need to dispel the difficult moral questions that bloodshed may bring by cloaking military intervention in the sacredness of national morals and commitments.

Overall, the style of presidential crisis promotion presented crises as tests of credibility where the actors of "we" and "I" must prove their courage and capability through daring, and all too often reckless, acts of military intervention. The emphasis on violence as a way to prove credibility is also a telling commentary on the cultural character of our nation. Indeed, Richard Slotkin argues that American culture has historically treated violence as a means of regeneration.[29] Political scientist Myron Hale elaborates on this idea when he writes that "the American social order is based on the values of profit, conflict, competition, 'stand and fight,' etc.," and that as individuals who have succeeded politically within the American system, presidents have internalized these values. As a result, Hale claims, "Whether born to the purple or self-made men, modern presidents, when faced with a perceived 'crisis,' have resorted to some type of violence, thinking it to be a demonstration of courage."[30]

United States presidents have also placed that reliance on violence in the best possible light through their insistence that "we" and "I" were peaceful, principled actors who were forced to act as a result of circumstances that foreign agents instigated and out of a corresponding need to fulfill the American dedication to freedom. Through this prototypical style of crisis promotion, commanders-in-chief elevate military interventions into unavoidable, imperative responses to tests of national commitment.

Identificational Appeals

Although presidential crisis rhetoric evidenced significant similarities in situation and style, the identificational appeals—or ways in which presidents encouraged citizens to identify with them and to support their policies—exhibited much more variety. Previous rhetorical criticisms of presidential crisis discourse have consistently mentioned how commanders-in-chief rely heavily on scapegoating, victimage, the portrayal of a wicked enemy, and other forms of antithetical identificational appeals in order to rally citizens behind them and their policies.[31] The claim that presidential crisis rhetoric necessarily stresses antithetical appeals, however, is one that this study definitively refutes. Although presidents claimed that foreign parties had instigated crises, only three presidents—Kennedy, Nixon, and Reagan—actively and consistently encouraged citizens to unite with them against a common foe. George Bush relied upon antithetical identification as a secondary strategy, and Presidents Ford, Carter, and Johnson rarely indulged in such entreaties.

The lack of such appeals in Carter's communication can be explained by his need to negotiate with the Iranians for the hostages' release. If a president hopes to resolve a foreign crisis through diplomacy, then he had best keep his rhetoric under control. Lack of restraint in the public description of one's adversaries may convince those adversaries not to negotiate or, equally harmful, may raise questions among one's own citizenry about why their country seeks a diplomatic solution with the devil incarnate. Although this constraint elucidates the scarcity of antithetical appeals in Carter's crisis discourse, it does not explain the dearth of these appeals in Ford's and Johnson's rhetoric. Perhaps the best answer is that the strategy of antithetical identification appears to be a common, but by no means essential, characteristic of presidential crisis promotion.

Among those presidents who featured antithetical appeals as a primary or secondary strategy, the central focus was on the construction of a diabolical villain who posed a grave threat to the United States. For Kennedy, the enemy was the Soviet Union; for Nixon, the antagonists were North Vietnam and its Vietcong allies; and for Reagan, the foes were the Soviet Union and Cuba. These presidents also tended to discuss their adversaries as representative of a more general enemy—Communism. As Kennedy said, the individual players were merely the "puppets and agents" of a larger Communist threat.[32]

Unlike these presidents, Bush claimed that the United States' chief rival was an individual, General Manuel Noriega, rather than a country. And the president made no attempt to label Noriega a Communist, no doubt because it was widely publicized that the general had been on the CIA payroll for years[33] and because changes in the Eastern bloc had dissipated public fear about Communism per se. But Bush stayed consistent with the antithetical appeals his predecessors employed when he repeatedly described Noriega as a "dictator" who had fought against democracy and prevented a freely-elected government from ruling in Panama. Just as Kennedy, Nixon, and Reagan had established a villain that represented the antithesis of freedom, Bush did the same.

To encourage Americans to unite against foreign foes, these commanders-in-chief emphasized the threat the enemy posed to American citizens and depicted the enemy as a ghastly agent who must be fought. Kennedy, for instance, detailed the proximity of Cuba's nuclear missiles to the United States. He also contrasted the benign actions of the nation he led with the evil actions of the enemy. In his announcement of the Cuban missile crisis, Kennedy asserted that the United States had never transferred missiles secretly to another country and had never tried to dominate the world as the Soviet Union had. Similarly, Nixon pointed to enemy sanctuaries that endangered American soldiers in South Vietnam as one reason for ordering an invasion of Cambodia. He also said that the United States had been conciliatory toward North Vietnam and the Vietcong, but that these adversaries had responded to the offer of negotiation with inflexibility, bellicosity, and increased attacks against American soldiers.

In Reagan's rhetoric about Grenada, he, too, magnified the danger of what he called a "Communist power grab" on the island and the menace it posed to American medical students there. Furthermore, Reagan claimed that the Soviet Union and Cuba had planned to use Grenada as a base to "export terror and undermine democracy" in the Western Hemisphere.[34] In a kindred fashion, Bush argued that Manuel Noriega had directly imperiled American citizens through "the brutalizing, really obscene torture" of a navy lieutenant and through his activities as "a fugitive drug dealer." Of greater importance, the president claimed that Noriega was an active opponent of freedom: he had "aborted" democracy in Panama, ordered the beatings of freely elected officials, and commanded "forces of repression" in order "to brutalize the Panamanian people." Bush maintained that the General was a thug who had so much personal arrogance and so little respect for freedom that he had "usurped power and declared war against the United States."[35]

In presidential crisis promotion, antithetical appeals provided a villain and highlighted the danger that the villain posed to Americans—through nuclear missiles, enemy sanctuaries, potential hostage-taking, actual torture—or to America's most revered principle of freedom. For many presidents engaged in crisis promotion, chaos continued to threaten the American cosmos.

One variation on this antithetical strategy occurred in Nixon's discourse on Cambodia where the president simultaneously attempted to unite all American citizens against Communism in Southeast Asia *and* to unite a majority of American citizens against dissenters at home. According to Nixon, the "enemies" included not only the North Vietnamese and Vietcong, but also those Americans who disagreed with his policies. The president complained, for instance, about opinion leaders, such as journalists who did not back his Vietnam policies enthusiastically enough, and about student protestors who did not support him at all. In this way, Nixon combined antithetical appeals aimed against Vietnamese Communists with those used against American citizens. The net result may have been to unite members of the silent majority more closely, both in their support of him and in their opposition to domestic critics, and to estrange further those who disagreed with the president's policies.

Through antithetical identificational strategies, presidents painted the portrait of an enemy too dangerous and too wicked to ignore. The fact that charges of villainy typically were made against countries, rather than individual leaders, also encouraged violence by depicting people of a particular nationality as one monolithic bloc. According to rhetorical critic Philip Wander, American foreign policy rhetoric personifies nations. Official government statements "agree that nations are the irreducible units in foreign affairs, that nations are to be understood as people, that they are, literally, actors in international affairs, and that nations live in a world where, if the freedom of one nation is threatened, other nations are obliged to help." The problem with this is that the abstract language used to describe enemy nations, such as that found in crisis promotion, "automatically dehumanizes the people most immediately and profoundly affected."[36]

The use of antithetical appeals may also increase the chances that innocent civilians will suffer. If presidents describe an enemy as extremely threatening and vile, their language creates a world in which the use of diplomacy seems fruitless at best, and, at worst, smacks of appeasement. Communication scholar Robert Ivie, who discovered that presidential war rhetoric relies on images of savagery, offers an explanation for why antithetical identifications, in spite of their dangers, remain so appealing. According to Ivie, "a people strongly committed to the ideal of peace, but simultaneously faced with the reality of war, must believe that the fault for any such disruption of their ideal lies with others. Hierarchic guilt would otherwise threaten to drive the nation toward some form of self-mortification."[37]

Antithetical appeals allow citizens to place the blame for bloodshed on others, rather than to assume responsibility and guilt themselves. Political scientists David Finlay, Ole Holsti, and Richard Fagen concur when they argue that portrayals of an evil enemy allow the nation to assume "a posture of self-righteousness" and to justify "any means" deemed necessary to win.[38] In the realm of presidential crisis rhetoric, antithetical identificational appeals frequently serve this same function and act as a comfortable rationalization for the use of military might.

In addition to antithetical identificational appeals, explicit appeals also appeared regularly in presidential crisis promotion. This form of appeal dominated the crisis rhetoric of both Ford and Bush and served a support role in the discourse of three other presidents. In his public talk about the *Mayaguez,* Ford made overt links between himself and the office of the presidency. He also used explicit appeals to highlight his administration's actions and accomplishments during the crisis and to solicit a public endorsement from the captain of the *Mayaguez.* Through this strategy, Ford portrayed himself not only as the president, but also as the capable president.

In his rhetoric about Panama, Bush likewise made use of explicit appeals in order to identify with the public. First, the president referred to his obligations and duties as "President" and as "Commander in Chief."[39] Furthermore, Bush overtly aligned himself with values that were sacred to the American populace, such as democracy and economic freedom. He told a nationwide television audience, for instance, that "I am committed to strengthening our relationship with the democratic nations in this hemisphere."[40]

Bush also repeatedly used explicit appeals to link himself with the soldiers who had served in Panama. The president visited the wounded in San Antonio in a December 1989 visit dutifully publicized by the mass media and appeared in a home video for one of the soldiers. In a January 1990 speech to American Farm Bureau Federation members, Bush said, "I know I don't have to tell you this, but let me just tell you from the bottom of a grateful heart that I am mighty proud of our courageous fighting men who have helped Panama."[41] The president's expression of such sentiments on this and other occasions was no doubt genuine, but it also served to bolster his own stature and help him duck criticism. Because he clearly identified himself with troops he described as courageous, selfless, heroic, and effective,[42] Bush subtly basked in the glory of such adjectives.

Furthermore, the president's explicit identification with members of the armed services who had been wounded or killed helped him to accomplish what Ronald Reagan's crisis rhetoric performed on a much larger scale: the transformation of opposition to policy into opposition to the people who exemplified that policy. More simply put, Bush's overt attempts to link himself with U.S. soldiers quietly reminded citizens that to attack the invasion of Panama was to attack the dedicated troops who had sacrificed much to carry out the invasion. The president's identificational strategy thereby took advantage of public sympathies to insulate him from potential criticism.

In addition to their primary role in Ford's and Bush's crisis promotion, explicit identificational appeals also served as a secondary strategy in the crisis rhetoric of Johnson, Nixon, and Carter. Johnson and Nixon, much like Ford and Bush, talked about the duties and responsibilities they had as "President" and "Commander-in-Chief," and neither president was shy about identifying himself with successful policies. Nixon, however, invoked this strategy in an unusual way by appealing to three different audiences, two of whom were at odds with one another. Through references to his title and authority, Nixon attempted to identify with all American citizens. He also overtly aligned his interests with those of the silent majority and made explicit appeals to the "vocal minority," or student protestors whose views were in conflict with those of the silent majority and his own. Because Nixon utilized explicit appeals in such an incongruous fashion, his attempts at persuasion proved divisive and grotesque.

In Carter's rhetoric about the Iranian hostage crisis, he, too, employed explicit appeals in a peculiar way. The discourse of Johnson, Nixon, Ford, and Bush made reference to their responsibility, authority, and actions. Carter mentioned his role and power as president relatively rarely, especially given the voluminous talk that he uttered about the crisis. More importantly, he refrained from dramatic accounts of his actions or explanations of how his actions were impacting the crisis. Instead, Carter's explicit appeals depicted him as passively engaged in mental activities such as prayer, study, and thought. Whereas other presidents used explicit appeals to emphasize their leadership, Carter's self-references portrayed him as no more active or powerful than other citizens, an image that proved unappealing to Americans because of their desire for dynamic presidential leadership in the midst of crisis.

Explicit identificational appeals played a surprisingly important role in the presidential crisis rhetoric examined in this study. In previous research, scholars noted a heavy emphasis upon antithetical appeals, but did not observe any marked reliance on explicit identificational strategies. But explicit appeals characterized the crisis promotion efforts of Ford and Bush and appeared as a secondary strategy in three other presidents' rhetoric. During a foreign crisis, a president's references to his office, title, and responsibilities serve to legitimize his policy decisions. Such references also function as authoritative appeals to forestall questions and criticism. In effect, the president argues that he alone has the necessary expertise and power to make the proper decisions, a viewpoint that encourages citizens who revere democracy to defer to the president as though he were king.

The fact that Ford and Bush relied on explicit appeals as a dominant identificational strategy may also tell us something about their perceived need to demonstrate leadership through depictions of their apparently successful resolution of foreign crises. For Ford, the issue of leadership credentials was especially significant in light of his pardon of Richard Nixon, his silly WIN campaign, and his public image as a not-so-bright bumbler. Unlike Ford, George Bush enjoyed widespread popularity, but his management of the Panamanian crisis nevertheless helped him to overcome "the wimp factor," charges that he was too weak and timid.[43] The degree to which Ford and Bush recognized that they could bolster their perceived leadership through these crises may be reflected in their constant attempts to identify overtly with citizens through explicit appeals that referenced their title, their capabilities, and, in Bush's case, his belief in values that most Americans held and his solidarity with troops who had suffered injury or lost their lives in Panama. My analysis of these presidents' linguistic choices reveals rhetors who made repeated, obvious attempts to identify themselves with the authority of their office and with the citizens they led.

In contrast to the strategies of antithetical and explicit identification, implicit appeals characterized the crisis rhetoric of only two presidents in this study. Both Johnson and Carter invoked "we" as the primary means to unite citizens behind them and their crisis management, and Reagan used implicit appeals such as "we," "our nation," and "America" as a secondary identificational strategy. Because presidents represent the United States, and citizens thereby are linked implicitly with them, perhaps presidential rhetors typically felt less need to draw upon this type of appeal. Even though the implicit identificational strategy appeared less often than antithetical and explicit strategies, it still played a substantial role. In Johnson's discourse about the Gulf of Tonkin, for instance, he claimed that "we" must exercise our power in accordance with the principle of calm restraint. The president also employed implicit appeals to portray air strikes that he had ordered as successful retaliatory action "we" had taken. In a similar way, Ronald Reagan talked about how "we" believed in freedom and how "the United States" had restored democracy to Grenada and saved American lives.

Unlike Johnson and Reagan, Carter rarely invoked "we" in conjunction with statements of action, but instead used this identificational strategy to rally citizens behind declarations of principle. Throughout his discourse, Carter maintained that "we" must strive to secure the hostages' safe release and that "we" must attempt to protect U.S. interests, to defend our country's honor, and to preserve the nation's integrity, principles he deemed important. The president's implicit appeals gradually lost their attractiveness when, after more than a year, he was unable to free the hostages and could not demonstrate that any of his principles had been fulfilled. Conversely, Johnson's and Reagan's actions appeared to be successful, which meant that most citizens were all too happy to be subsumed as part of the "we" of their crisis talk. The unattractiveness of Carter's appeals, compared with those of Johnson and Reagan, again indicates how citizens expect their leaders to demonstrate progress.

Implicit appeals provide individuals with a way to feel part of a communal effort and may give citizens a sense of personal efficacy when presidents discuss the successful actions that "we" have taken. At the same time, implicit appeals may have the effect of encouraging group conformity, especially when they invoke national myths. If the president claims that "we" all hold particular ideals and that "we" all approve of his crisis policies, his rhetoric and the public support it typically begets may convince individuals who feel otherwise to remain silent.[44] Implicit appeals may also encourage citizens to view those who articulate opposition to the president's policies as cranks or, more alarmingly, as traitors. Nonetheless, implicit appeals in and of themselves do not provide an invincible shield for presidents anxious to deflect criticism.

The case of Jimmy Carter and Iran shows that when policies go awry, citizens tend not to question the communal ship of state, but rather the captain of that ship. If Carter were unable to release the hostages and to live up to American principles, many citizens had reason to think that he lacked practical competence. Implicit appeals may foster identification between individual citizens and national policies, but those same linkages may prove frustrating to citizens when the president's policies seem inept.

In this study of crisis promotion, no two presidents talked about foreign crises in exactly the same way. Nevertheless, a great deal of consistency existed among the rhetoric that each commander-in-chief produced. The situation of presidential crisis discourse typically portrayed a threatening scene of crisis somewhere abroad that impelled Americans to fulfill both pragmatic and idealistic purposes that would serve to correct the crisis scene. Because crisis scenes were urgent and constituted threats to American ideals, crisis rhetoric endowed presidential policies with moral purpose and discouraged public debate over their propriety. Presidents' situational portrayals also reinvigorated the American myths of mission and manifest destiny by emphasizing how the United States must act to defend its ideals and then pointing to the accomplishment of pragmatic goals as evidence that it had done so.

Given the urgency and mission of the crisis situation, the style of crisis promotion, in turn, tended to treat foreign crises as tests of national character. Presidents were careful to portray the United States or "we" as a moral actor who embodied both power and patience, but also maintained that simply to have this character was not enough. Rather, they insisted that the United States must prove itself in some way, usually by engaging in an act of violence. Although the situation and style of presidential crisis discourse were rather rigid, commanders-in-chief tended to be more creative at using identificational appeals to forge a public consensus behind them and their policies.

Only two presidents, Johnson and Carter, combined the same types of identificational appeals in their persuasive efforts. This notwithstanding, particular trends also existed, and presidents showed an inclination to use specific strategies in similar ways. Presidents frequently employed antithetical identificational appeals to portray the challenge that Americans faced as one posed by an evil, inhuman foe. To one degree or another, most presidents also relied on explicit attempts to underscore the appropriateness of their actions and their capability as president through references to their authority and effective action. Lastly, some commanders-in-chief drew upon implicit appeals to provide a sense of solidarity that united citizens in a discourse of shared values and achievements.

The crisis rhetoric examined in this book exemplified what Paul Hernadi might call a generic "spirit."[45] That is, significant similarities existed among the situation, style, and identificational appeals of these presidents' discourse. This does not mean, however, that the conclusions presented here should be treated as a taxonomy of the essential characteristics of crisis promotion. Although I have attempted to examine exhaustively the particular cases selected, I have, nonetheless, limited myself to the crisis rhetoric of six presidents (plus Bush) and analyzed only how each commander-in-chief talked about one particular crisis. My findings indicate that the recurring characteristics detailed here will appear in other presidential crisis promotion, as well, but the proof will lie with future studies that challenge, corroborate, and/or expand upon this research.

Another, and more important, reason not to treat these principles taxonomically is that in this study I have also shown that the rhetoric of individual presidents exhibited a number of important differences. The conclusion reached here about the typical situation, style, and identificational appeals of presidential crisis promotion is that these principles serve as richly inviting parameters for creative talk about foreign crises. A focus solely upon similarities may lead to tidier explanations about the characteristics of crisis rhetoric, but ignore the unique rhetorical traits of each president's crisis promotion: the strategic deflection and pessimism of Kennedy's Cold War discourse; the indirect dissociation of peace and the defense of freedom in Johnson's talk; the constant, unresolved incongruities of Nixon's grotesque rhetoric; the use of silence to bolster leadership in Ford's crisis promotion; the perpetual idealism of Carter's crisis talk; the centrality of myths of mission and manifest destiny in Reagan's discourse; and the simplicity and overtness of Bush's persuasive efforts. To overlook these unique traits is to overlook the distinction between the institution of the presidency and the individual who occupies that office, for each president brings with him a distinctive rhetorical style, based upon his own personality and background. An emphasis upon similarities to the detriment of understanding differences also overlooks the vagaries of political and historical circumstances which lead particular presidents to promote and manage foreign crises in particular ways.

At the same time, one is struck by the consistencies in the presidential rhetoric examined in this book. Jack Kennedy and George Bush, though separated by nearly thirty years, have much in common when it comes to the characteristics of their crisis discourse. Since those tension-filled days of October 1962, each of Kennedy's successors, at least once during his tenure, has promoted and managed a foreign crisis. Each has done so in a unique way, yet the situation, style, and identificational appeals of these men's rhetoric have remained remarkably constant given the different personalities involved and the time that has elapsed.

THE ONGOING CONTEXT AND TOOLS FOR PROMOTED CRISIS: STRUCTURAL/LEGAL FOUNDATIONS AND NEWS MANAGEMENT TECHNIQUES

John F. Kennedy brought together the structural changes, legal justifications, and news management techniques that not only allowed him to promote and manage the Cuban missile crisis, but also established the context and tools by which later presidents could follow suit. The acclaim that Kennedy received for his efforts further served to encourage the same type of behavior in his successors. If the rhetoric of crisis promotion has remained fairly constant since Kennedy's time, however, the same is not true for the structural/legal framework that permits crisis promotion and the news management techniques that perpetuate the president's point of view. On the contrary, presidents have accumulated ever-greater degrees of power over foreign affairs and have developed increasingly sophisticated news management techniques to portray their resolution of foreign crises in the most positive way possible.

Today, the president and the White House staff are still actively involved in unilateral foreign policy making. Three years after the invasion of Grenada, Ronald Reagan claimed that his power as commander-in-chief allowed him to direct an air attack against Libya in which many innocent civilians were injured and killed.[46] The president, Vice President George Bush, Oliver North, and others also intentionally circumvented congressional policy by providing support for the Contras' efforts to overthrow the Nicaraguan government and secretly sold arms to Iran in the hope that American hostages in Beirut would be released. Bush still denies that he was involved in the scandal despite overwhelming evidence to the contrary.[47]

During the 1989 Panamanian crisis, President Bush continued the presidential trend of sending troops into combat without the advice or approval of Congress. Press Secretary Marlin Fitzwater, in a prepared statement, said Bush made the decision to invade Panama in consultation with his national security advisors, rather than Congress. Not until two days later, after plans were finalized, did the president call members of the congressional leadership. The invasion was scheduled to begin in seven hours. In his written report to Congress, dated one day after the president's public announcement of the crisis, Bush followed the lead of his predecessors by claiming that "the military operations were ordered pursuant to my constitutional authority with respect to the conduct of foreign relations and as Commander in Chief."

Like Ronald Reagan, Bush refused to cite section 4(a)(1) of the War Powers Resolution and to begin the sixty-day clock that should govern troop deployments. Instead, he claimed that he had provided the report in "accordance with my desire that Congress be fully informed on this matter, and consistent with the War Powers Resolution," virtually the same wording that Ronald Reagan used in his reports on Grenada and Libya.[48] Despite Bush's lack of genuine consultation with Congress and his obvious disdain for the War Powers Resolution, most members of the legislative branch rallied, in traditional fashion, to support the president's policy in Panama.[49]

In order to dispatch troops as they see fit, commanders-in-chief have exploited the weaknesses of the War Powers Resolution and have continued to treat Congress as irrelevant. Calls to representatives and senators about impending military adventures have taken on the aura of proper etiquette rather than the thorough consultation that the War Powers Resolution intended. In 1985, former Senator Jacob Javits, one of the original sponsors of the statute, expressed concern over a major obstacle to enforcement of the War Powers Resolution—the failure of Congress to assert itself—and urged members of Congress to unite and to fight for their constitutional authority.[50] This seems unlikely to happen, for the cases of crisis promotion examined in this study demonstrate that it is hard to attack a president or his policies during times of crisis or, at least, that it is politically inadvisable.

According to rhetorical analysts Robert Denton and Dan Hahn, the office of the presidency has attained a "symbolic supremacy" over Congress, which makes it difficult for Congress to win policy battles with the president.[51] Communication researchers Lynda Lee Kaid and Joe Foote point out that media coverage also favors the president over Congress because the chief executive has regular access to the television networks and at least one story about the president appears on all three networks every night.[52] Even if Congress could get adequate media attention for criticism of a president's crisis policies, the chances of uniting every single member of Congress against the president seem small, especially given the tempting political benefits that support for an apparently successful military operation can bring.

In 1990 and 1991, further evidence of presidential encroachment on constitutional war powers and the congressional inability to stop it became apparent. President George Bush ordered 400,000 U.S. troops to Saudi Arabia when the Persian Gulf crisis began in August 1990, and he did so without seeking congressional permission or invoking the War Powers Resolution. Despite this unprecedented action, the legislative branch meekly provided the money to implement Operation Desert Shield and waited months to debate the issue in any comprehensive way. One group of lawmakers, fifty-four Democrats, filed suit to ban the president from sending U.S. troops to war, but a federal judge threw the case out since "a majority" of Congress had not voiced such concerns.[53] The United Nations Security Council, largely at the urging of the United States, ratified Resolution 678, which authorized member nations to employ "all necessary means" against Iraq if it had not withdrawn from Kuwait by January 15, 1991. According to Bush, he was ready to use force "sooner rather than later" if Iraqi leader Saddam Hussein had not complied by the deadline.[54]

On January 12, as the crisis threatened to turn into war, Congress voted on the Authorization for Use of Military Force Against Iraq Resolution, which gave the president the authority "to use United States Armed Forces pursuant to United Nations Security Council Resolution 678." The measure passed in the Senate by a 52 to 47 margin and in the House by 250 to 183. The only constraint on the president's authority to launch offensive attacks was the resolution's stipulation that, prior to the use of force, he "make available to the Speaker of the House of Representatives and the president pro tempore of the Senate his determination" that all possible diplomatic and peaceful means had been used to seek Iraq's withdrawal from Kuwait, but that they had not and would not be successful.[55]

In essence, the resolution required only that Bush inform congressional leaders of his decision to go to war. Had the president sought congressional approval before he ordered troops to Saudi Arabia, American men and women might not have been sent there. Had Congress taken action earlier, before the brink of war, some representatives and senators might not have felt pressure to support the commander-in-chief and might have voted differently. Tragically, the presidential usurpation of war powers appears likely to continue.

Although the crisis discourse of contemporary presidents has sounded very much alike, each commander-in-chief has made ever-broader claims of legal authority and assumed ever-larger amounts of power. The rhetoric of crisis promotion has not evolved, but the structural/legal foundations that permit crisis promotion have. In many ways, the relationship between power and discourse here appears to be symbiotic. The president's control over foreign affairs allows him to indulge in crisis promotion; at the same time, crisis promotion frequently helps the commander-in-chief to expand and consolidate his power. This is a dangerous combination, indeed.

Just as the structural/legal context of crisis promotion has grown more expansive since the Kennedy administration, so the news management techniques that presidents use have grown more sophisticated. White House officials and journalists are also much more matter-of-fact about these efforts. In the first few days of the Panamanian crisis, for instance, a Bush administration official commented to the *New York Times* that "we have not done a good job of selling" the invasion to the American people. To correct this problem, journalist Michael Oreskes reported that the White House began its "public-relations day" with calls to ABC, CBS, NBC, and CNN to offer Defense Secretary Dick Cheney for morning interviews; all of the networks accepted with the exception of ABC, which had already arranged for Lt. Gen. Colin Powell, Chairman of the Joint Chiefs of Staff, to appear. According to Oreskes, Cheney and Powell stressed "the return of democracy to Panama," and Bush elaborated on this theme in his news conference later that day.[56]

The Bush administration also made other efforts to manage news coverage of the crisis. After Noriega found asylum in the Vatican embassy, the U.S. military command in Panama released a report to the press stating that Noriega had been unfaithful to his wife, practiced voodoo, wore red underwear, employed prostitutes, and had in his possession large amounts of what the military claimed was cocaine, but what actually turned out to be tamale powder.[57] These efforts at vilification got news coverage and helped reinforce the president's own antithetical appeals aimed against Noriega.

In addition, the Bush administration took steps to emphasize the president's leadership capabilities. Press Secretary Fitzwater read a statement to the press that described in almost excruciating detail how Bush had made the decision to invade, whom he talked to or met with, and how he prepared his speech. Fitzwater went so far as to specify what the president was wearing as he monitored the crisis situation throughout the evening ("a dark blue sweater over his shirt and tie") and what the mood of the Oval Office was ("businesslike").[58] Through these and similar efforts, the administration depicted Bush as a competent and dedicated leader involved in the complexities of crisis decision making. Fitzwater's fetish for facts also gave the White House the appearance of openness, even though such details obscured larger questions such as how many people might be killed, how much the invasion would cost, what the CIA's relationship with Noriega had been, and whether the CIA, like the much-defamed general, had been involved in drug trafficking.

During the invasion of Panama, the United States government did not institute a press blackout as it had during the crisis in Grenada. Instead, the Pentagon activated a National Media Pool, composed of rotating news organizations, which it had created after journalists' complaints about Grenada. Reporter Steven Komarow, who was part of the pool in Panama, said the military provided the journalists with good accommodations, but still did not allow them to cover the invasion freely. According to Komarow, the pool did not reach Panama until four hours after the invasion began. Once there, journalists were not allowed to accompany soldiers who were part of the invasion or to visit scenes of the fighting until it was over.[59]

According to former Sen. Donald Stewart, the United States government also hid the number of civilian deaths from journalists and other American citizens by offering Panamanians six dollars a body and then burying the dead in unmarked mass graves, a charge the Director of Public Affairs for the Southern Command in Panama denied.[60]

After the invasion was completed, non-pool journalists arrived. Many of them stayed at a hotel that overlooked the Vatican embassy where Noriega had fled, and the day after they arrived, the U.S. military set up loudspeakers and began to play rock music at the threshold of pain. Journalists initially reported that the music was designed to deprive Noriega of sleep. According to CNN correspondent C. D. Jaco, however, they then noticed that the speakers were actually pointed at the hotel, rather than the embassy. According to Jaco, "G.I.s said they had been told the roar of guitars and screech of post-punk vocals was to keep reporters from eavesdropping on conversations among troops or inside the embassy," an account that Press Secretary Fitzwater later confirmed. Media representatives informed the military command that they did not have the technology it would take to eavesdrop, but offered to set up white-noise generators if it would put the military at ease. The army refused, and the music continued, until at last a frustrated Vatican embassy declared that it would not proceed with further negotiations until the music stopped. That threat finally brought the ear-piercing noise to an end.[61]

Despite this treatment, most members of the media jumped on the crisis bandwagon and served as President Bush's publicity arm. Gilbert Cranberg, a former editor of the *Des Moines Register* and now a professor at the University of Iowa, summed up the situation when he observed that "major elements of the press simply parroted the government's rendition as fact." According to Cranberg, most major newspapers endorsed the invasion with language that echoed the government's own justifications. The television networks did no better. Their efforts were, perhaps, worse as they were unable to cover the actual fighting and then saturated the airwaves with official government statements and pictures of happy Panamanians, many of whom were wearing the Operation Just Cause T-shirts that the army had distributed.[62]

The only glitch in this positive coverage occurred when the networks simultaneously broadcast both a presidential news conference and the U.S. arrival of a transport plane that unloaded the first American coffins from Panama.[63] In spite of this setback, the administration was largely successful in using the media to convey its preferred interpretation of events. Although journalists frequently mentioned Bush's efforts to manage the news, their comments were lost amid headlines and leads that reflected the White House's message of the day and footage that depicted the government's point of view. The journalists may have been aware of their co-optation, but they were co-opted nonetheless.

Since 1962, U.S. presidents have made increasingly broader claims of power to promote foreign crises and have used crisis rhetoric to accrue more power. Commanders-in-chief have also recognized the important role the mass media play in successful crisis promotion and management. Indeed, Reagan aide and public relations wizard Michael Deaver argues that television has encouraged presidents to promote quick foreign crises rather than to engage in longer-term wars. According to Deaver, "I firmly believe that television has absolutely changed our military strategy, that we will never again fight a major ground war. Americans simply do not want to see mass killings on the TV screen in their living rooms."[64]

In comments about the Persian Gulf crisis in January 1991, President Bush seemed to reflect this same attitude when he stated that if the United States decided to attack Iraqi troops, the conflict would be over relatively quickly and not dragged out, as it was in Vietnam. Perhaps in the event that fighting would be prolonged, the president also instituted rules for media coverage that included military censorship of pool reports and that effectively prohibited broadcasters from "conveying the sights and sounds of casualties," among other things.[65]

The history of crisis promotion shows that even when presidents engage in short-term military conflicts, they rely on news management techniques to keep the brutality of death off American television screens and the untidiness of much of the politics involved out of American newspapers. In turn, media coverage helps convince ordinary citizens that a president's crisis resolution efforts were both proper and successful. Frequently the net result is, in words the late Republican National Chairman Lee Atwater used to describe the invasion of Panama, a "political jackpot."[66]

THE THREAT AND OPPORTUNITY OF PROMOTED CRISIS: "AN ENDLESS SERIES OF HOBGOBLINS"

H. L. Mencken once observed that "the whole aim of practical politics is to keep the populace alarmed (and hence clamorous to be led to safety) by an endless series of hobgoblins, most of them imaginary."[67] As I have shown in this book, more than one president has conjured up foreign hobgoblins and then dispelled them through the rhetoric of promoted crisis. This is not to say that every president has invoked crisis merely for political gain; no doubt many— perhaps all—of the commanders-in-chief involved truly believed that the nation faced a genuine, rather than imaginary, threat from abroad. But one wonders how many times presidents have viewed a military operation as the only response to threat or have perceived what otherwise might be ignoble actions as sudden demands for massive retaliation or a show of character.

Representative Charles B. Rangel of New York made exactly this point about the invasion of Panama: "I am of course distressed that prior to our action, an American was killed, an American arrested, an American brutally beaten, and an American military wife was threatened with rape. President Bush said, 'That was enough.' If that is so, far more than that happens on the streets of New York every day and night, and I say, that too is enough."[68] Through the rhetoric of crisis promotion, presidents imbue base events—but events that otherwise would arouse little national outrage—with great significance in order to justify military action. The reward, all too often, is an outpouring of public support. Although presidents may engage in crisis rhetoric for any of a number of reasons, crisis promotion always offers the possibility that presidents will succumb to political hobgoblins of their own.

The presidential penchant for crisis promotion also has some dangerous implications for our political system. First, foreign crises serve to divert national attention and resources from other problems. Reagan's rhetoric on Grenada, for instance, dissipated concern over the president's flawed policies in Beirut, just as Kennedy's crisis talk overshadowed his foreign policy failures elsewhere. More recently, Bush's crisis promotion efforts have focused citizen attention on Panama and Noriega's alleged drug trafficking, rather than on the demand for drugs in the United States, and on Saddam Hussein in the Persian Gulf, instead of pressing domestic issues such as education, the budget deficit, poverty, health care, energy, or the environment.

Because military operations involve huge financial costs, foreign crises may also drain national resources that could be better spent in other ways. According to army finance officials, for example, the Panamanian invasion cost U.S. taxpayers $27 million.[69] The Bush administration might have spent this money on education, an issue the president had targeted as a top priority. Of course, money is only one type of national resource, and crisis promotion tends to squander other resources as well, such as the time, attention, and energies of the president and his staff, not to mention the lives of the military personnel involved. In all of these ways, crisis promotion distracts both the populace and the government from issues that deserve their attention.

Crisis promotion also impacts negatively on the resolution of other issues because it encourages citizens to expect immediate and complete success. Through their crisis rhetoric, commanders-in-chief paint a romantic portrait of the United States as a righteous moral crusader, military action as an admirable and necessary sacrifice, and the effect of U.S. policies as an unambiguous success. Unfortunately, news management techniques prevent citizens from witnessing the terrible toll that military intervention inflicts, both upon the combatants and upon innocent civilians. Since crises typically involve the United States in Goliath versus David matches, armed conflict usually does not last very long, which means the president can declare U.S. actions to be both successful and efficient.

Shortly thereafter, the attention of the president and the media will shift to other issues, which leaves citizens with the impression that all is now well in the region where the crisis took place. Little public attention was paid, for example, to Panama after Operation Just Cause, even though the country's economy was in a shambles and many Panamanians still remained homeless a year after the invasion as a result of its destruction.[70] Because of the perceptions and expectations that crisis promotion encourages, citizens become frustrated when policy implementation in regard to other issues does not achieve the same sort of rapid results. Americans have little patience with long-term planning or policies that move incrementally rather than quickly, which means that presidents, in turn, have little interest in such approaches. Chief executives advocate policies that can give the appearance of immediate success, rather than policies that might take longer to implement but be more effective.

In the realm of foreign affairs, the apparent success of past military interventions serves to perpetuate violence, in particular, as a legitimate way to resolve problems. Diplomacy can take a long time to conclude and involves compromise to be successful, whereas military intervention tends to be quick, allows the United States to claim a total victory, and, because it takes place in another country, seems to involve relatively little cost to Americans. The discourse that presidents use to glorify such episodes also cultivates national megalomania and an intolerance for the complexities and the other cultures involved in foreign relations. Presidents foster the attitudes that might makes right, that the United States always stands on the moral high ground, and that the self-interests of Americans should come before the interests of everyone else.

More than anyone, of course, crisis promotion may serve the interests of the commander-in-chief by permitting him to assume the role of leader and to take the credit for a policy success. The legacy of previous crisis promotion is to perpetuate future crisis promotion. In *The Sound of Leadership,* Roderick Hart charts how contemporary presidents have chosen to speak in public more and more often and how rhetoric has become "the primary means of *performing the act* of presidential leadership." Hart argues that presidents use public speech to enact the role of leader and that citizens have come to believe that governance occurs only when their presidents talk to them.[71] If Hart is correct, and I believe he is, it may explain why presidents find crisis promotion so appealing. Foreign crises allow the president to arouse citizen anxieties, to dress himself in the authoritative trappings of commander-in-chief, to lead distressed citizens through a threatening moment, and then, if all goes well, to relieve anxieties and savor the sweetness of a foreign policy triumph.

According to Alexander L. George, "the character for 'crisis' in the Chinese language has a dual connotation: 'threat' and 'opportunity.'"[72] Through the alchemy of promoted crisis, presidents transform the rhetorical possibilities of threat into the promise of political opportunity, but they do so at the cost of the national interest. Crisis promotion diverts attention, money, and energies from important problems; it creates unrealistic expectations for the speed and success with which other issues can be resolved; it encourages violence and intolerance; and crisis promotion perpetuates itself as president after president attempts to emulate the foreign policy victories of his predecessors. According to Edelman, "the frequent and unremitting succession of crisis and detente" also produces "political docility."[73] This is the worst news of all, for the outrage of American citizens may be the only thing that will deter future presidents from engaging in crisis promotion.

During the last seven White House administrations, presidents have promoted foreign crises with the aid of a largely compliant media and a legislative branch that has proved unable, despite the efforts of individual members, to stop them. Only if citizens themselves begin to examine their president's words more carefully and to question those words more frequently will journalists, representatives, senators, and presidents start to take notice. The optimist would argue that this could, in fact, happen. The realist, however, would recognize that this goal is far away, while the pessimist might point to evidence that this goal will never be reached.

In 1990 and 1991, the United States became embroiled in yet another foreign crisis. Once again a president told Americans that events, this time in Kuwait, called upon them "to define who we are and what we believe." Once again a commander-in-chief, this time George Bush, asked citizens to support his deployment of troops, not to ensure cheap oil or to bolster his leadership, but "in the cause of peace" and "to protect the lives of American citizens abroad." He said, "America does not seek conflict, nor do we seek to chart the destiny of other nations"; nevertheless, the president claimed, "we must resist aggression or it will destroy our freedoms."[74] An end to crisis promotion does not appear to be in sight.

NOTES

Administration documents and recordings referred to here are from the Kennedy Library in Boston, the Johnson Library in Austin, the Nixon Presidential Materials in Alexandria, Virginia, the Ford Library in Ann Arbor, and the Carter Library in Atlanta.

Two abbreviations are used throughout these notes: *WCPD* (*Weekly Compilation of Presidential Documents*) and *PPP* (*Public Papers of the Presidents*). For full publication information for these sources, refer to the bibliography.

CHAPTER ONE—PRESIDENTS AND THE PROMOTION OF FOREIGN CRISES: AN INTRODUCTION

1. Nationwide Address, Dec. 20, 1989, *WCPD,* 1974.

2. Ibid., 1974–1975.

3. R. J. Barnet, "Bush's Splendid Little War," *Nation,* Jan. 22, 1990, 76.

4. R. L. Berke, "Noriega Arraigned in Miami in a Drug-Trafficking Case; He Refuses to Enter a Plea," *New York Times,* Jan. 5, 1990, A1.

5. M. Oreskes, "President Wins Bipartisan Praise For Solution of Crisis Over Noriega," *New York Times,* Jan. 5, 1990, A1.

6. R. W. Apple, Jr., "War: Bush's Presidential Rite of Passage," *New York Times,* Dec. 21, 1989, A1.

7. See A. M. Schlesinger, Jr., *The Imperial Presidency* (1973; rpt., New York: Popular Library, 1974).

8. News Conference, Jan. 5, 1990, *WCPD,* 13–14, 15.

9. Ibid., 14.

10. D. A. Graber, *Verbal Behavior and Politics* (Urbana: U of Illinois P, 1976), 20–21.

11. J. K. Tulis, *The Rhetorical Presidency* (Princeton: Princeton UP, 1987), 133–135, 186.

12. M. E. Stuckey, *The President as Interpreter-in-Chief* (Chatham, N.J.: Chatham House Publishers, 1991), 1.

13. R. P. Hart, *The Sound of Leadership: Presidential Communication in the Modern Age* (Chicago: U of Chicago P, 1987), 4.

14. M. Edelman, *Constructing the Political Spectacle* (Chicago: U of Chicago P, 1988), 104.

15. R. E. Crable and S. L. Vibbert, "Managing Issues and Influencing Public Policy," *Public Relations Review* 11 (1985), 5. For more on the strategies of definition, legitimation, polarization, and identification discussed here, see Crable and Vibbert, "Managing Issues," 3–16; S. L. Vibbert and D. M. Bostdorff, "Issue Management in the 'Lawsuit Crisis,' " *The Ethical Nexus,* ed. C. Conrad, (Norwood, N.J.: Ablex, 1993), 103–120.

16. Edelman, *Constructing the Political Spectacle,* 12–13.

17. R. E. Neustadt, *Presidential Power: The Politics of Leadership From FDR to Carter,* 2d ed. (New York: Macmillan, 1986), 25.

18. Cicero, *De Inventione,* trans. H. M. Hubbell (1949; rpt., Cambridge: Harvard UP, 1960), 1.10–14.

19. D. Zarefsky, *President Johnson's War on Poverty: Rhetoric and History* (Tuscaloosa: U of Alabama P, 1986), 8.

20. See H. G. Stelzner, "Ford's War on Inflation: A Metaphor That Did Not Cross," *Communication Monographs* 44 (1977), 284–297.

21. Zarefsky, 20.

22. "Crisis," *The Compact Edition of the Oxford English Dictionary* (New York: Oxford UP, 1971); "κρίσις", *Liddell and Scott's Greek-English Lexicon,* 1977 abridged ed.

23. M. Edelman, *Political Language: Words That Succeed and Policies That Fail* (New York: Academic, 1977), 44; Edelman, *Constructing the Political Spectacle,* 31.

24. For example: C. J. Lamb, *Belief Systems and Decision Making in the Mayaguez Crisis* (Gainesville: U of Florida P, 1989), 5.

25. Edelman, *Constructing the Political Spectacle,* 21.

26. R. E. Denton, Jr., *The Symbolic Dimensions of the American Presidency: Description and Analysis* (Prospect Heights, Ill.: Waveland, 1982), 5; T. O. Windt, Jr., "The Presidency and Speeches on International Crises: Repeating the Rhetorical Past," *Speaker and Gavel* 11 (1973), 8–9.

27. F. I. Greenstein, "Popular Images of the President," *The Presidency,* ed. A. Wildavsky (Boston: Little, Brown, 1969), 291; P. C. Light, *The President's Agenda* (Baltimore: Johns Hopkins UP, 1982), 31–32; J. E. Mueller, *Wars, Presidents and Public Opinion* (New York: John Wiley and Sons, 1973), 208–213.

28. Windt, "The Presidency," 13.

29. "A *Newsweek* Poll: Mr. Nixon Holds Up," *Newsweek,* May 25, 1970, 30.

30. Windt, "The Presidency," 7–8; R. A. Cherwitz and K. S. Zagacki, "Consummatory Versus Justificatory Crisis Rhetoric," *Western Journal of Speech Communication* 50 (1986), 317.

31. "The 'In' Party's Dramatic Triumph," *Newsweek,* Nov. 19, 1962, 31.

32. M. Edelman, *The Symbolic Uses of Politics* (1964; rpt., Urbana: U of Illinois P, 1967), 6; Graber, 289–321.

33. Remarks in Des Moines, Oct. 7, 1964, *PPP,* 2: 1230.

34. Windt, "The Presidency," 11–13; R. A. Cherwitz, "Masking Inconsistency: The Tonkin Gulf Crisis," *Communication Quarterly* 28 (1980), 30–37; Cherwitz and Zagacki, 311, 313; J. D. Bass, "The Appeal to Efficiency as Narrative Closure: Lyndon Johnson and the Dominican Crisis, 1965," *Southern Speech Communication Journal* 50 (1985), 119; B. J. Dow, "The Function of Epideictic and Deliberative Strategies in Presidential Crisis Rhetoric," *Western Journal of Speech Communication* 53 (1989), 296.

35. Radio Address, May 17, 1986, *WCPD,* 651–652.

36. For more on masking issues, see H. D. Lasswell, *Propaganda Technique in World War I* (1927; rpt., Cambridge: MIT, 1971), 205; W. L. Bennett, P. Dempsey Harris, J. K. Laskey, A. H. Levitch, and S. E. Monrad, "Deep and Surface Images in the Construction of Political Issues: The Case of Amnesty," *Quarterly Journal of Speech,* 62 (1976), 109–126.

37. Bass, 104, 118–119; G. A. Hauser, "Administrative Rhetoric and Public Opinion: Discussing the Iranian Hostages in the Public Sphere," *American Rhetoric: Context and Criticism,* ed. T. W. Benson (Carbondale: Southern Illinois UP, 1989), 354–356.

38. Windt, "The Presidency," 7. See also T. O. Windt, Jr., *Presidents and Protesters: Political Rhetoric in the 1960s* (Tuscaloosa: U of Alabama P, 1990), 5.

39. Hauser, 330.

40. W. Brockriede and R. L. Scott, *Moments in the Rhetoric of the Cold War* (New York: Random House, 1970), 79.

41. For example, see G. T. Allison, *Essence of Decision* (Boston: Little, Brown, 1971); B. J. Bernstein, "The Cuban Missile Crisis," *Reflections on the Cold War,* ed. L. H. Miller and R. W. Pruessen (Philadelphia: Temple UP, 1974), 108–142; S. G. Walker, "Bargaining Over Berlin: A Re-Analysis of the First and Second Berlin Crises," *Journal of Politics* 44 (1982), 152–164; C. F. Hermann, ed., *International Crises: Insights From Behavioral Research* (New York: The Free Press, 1972); R. N. Lebow, "The Cuban Missile Crisis: Reading the Lessons Correctly," *Political Science Quarterly* 98 (1983), 431–458; R. J. Leng, "Reagan and the Russians: Crisis Bargaining Beliefs and the Historical Record," *The American Political Science Review* 78 (1984), 338–355; G. M. Herek, I. L. Janis, and P. Huth, "Decision Making During International Crises," *Journal of Conflict Resolution* 31 (1987), 203–226; D. A. Welch, "Cuban Decision Making Reconsidered," *Journal of Conflict Resolution* 33 (1989), 430–445.

42. E. Black, *Rhetorical Criticism: A Study in Method* (1965; rpt., Madison: U of Wisconsin P, 1978), 7.

43. "Criticism," *The Compact Edition of the Oxford English Dictionary.*

44. These include: Brockriede and Scott, 80–93; J. W. Pratt, "An Analysis of Three Crisis Speeches," *Western Journal of Speech Communication* 34 (1970), 194–203; Windt, "The Presidency," 6–14; R. B. Gregg and G. A. Hauser, "Richard Nixon's April 30, 1970 Address on Cambodia: The 'Ceremony' of Confrontation," *Speech Monographs* 40 (1973), 167–181; R. A. Cherwitz, "Lyndon Johnson and the 'Crisis' of Tonkin Gulf: A President's Justification of War," *Western Journal of Speech Communication* 42 (1978), 93–104; Cherwitz, "Masking," 27–37; D. F. Hahn, "Corrupt Rhetoric: President Ford and the *Mayaguez* Affair," *Communication Quarterly* 28 (1980), 38–43; R. P. Newman, "Pity the Helpless Giant: Nixon on Cambodia," *Essays in Presidential Rhetoric,* rev. ed., ed. T. Windt with B. Ingold (1983; Dubuque, Iowa: Kendall/Hunt, 1984), 204–223; Bass, 103–120; Cherwitz and Zagacki, 307–324; D. R. Heisey, "Reagan and Mitterand Respond to International Crisis: Creating Versus Transcending Appearances," *Western Journal of Speech Communication* 50 (1986), 325–335; D. C. Klope, "Defusing a Foreign Policy Crisis: Myth and Victimage in Reagan's 1983 Lebanon/Grenada Address," *Western Journal of Speech Communication* 50 (1986), 336–349; R. E. Dowling and G. Marraro, "Grenada and the Great Communicator: A Study in Democratic Ethics," *Western Journal of Speech Communication* 50 (1986), 350–367; D. S. Birdsell, "Ronald Reagan on Lebanon and Grenada: Flexibility and Interpretation in the Application of Kenneth Burke's Pentad," *Quarterly Journal of Speech* 73 (1987), 267–279; D. E. Procter, "The Rescue Mission: Assigning Guilt to a Chaotic Scene," *Western Journal of Speech Communication* 51 (1987), 245–255; Hauser, 323–383; Dow, 294–310; Windt, *Presidents and Protesters,* 24–44, 52–60.

244 Notes to Pages 11–19

45. Cherwitz and Zagacki, 318–319. See also Brockriede and Scott, 82–84; Klope, 343; Heisey, 328.

46. Windt, "The Presidency," 11. See also Gregg and Hauser, 171–172; Birdsell, 272; Windt, *Presidents and Protesters,* 55.

47. Bass, 119; Klope, 338, 343.

48. Cherwitz and Zagacki, 313–314; Newman, 209; Heisey, 327; Klope, 346–347; Brockriede and Scott, 82–84; Windt, "The Presidency," 10–11; Gregg and Hauser, 173, 178; Cherwitz, "Lyndon Johnson," 99; Bass, 115; Birdsell, 272; Windt, *Presidents and Protesters,* 27, 39–40, 55.

49. Remarks at Annual White House Correspondents Dinner, April 17, 1986, *WCPD,* 505–506.

50. Remarks to National Legislative Conference, AFL-CIO, May 3, 1965, *PPP,* 480, 479.

51. R. P. Hart, "A Commentary on Popular Assumptions About Political Communication," *Human Communication Research* 8 (1982), 370.

52. K. Burke, *Language as Symbolic Action* (Berkeley: U of California P, 1966), 16.

53. K. Burke, *Permanence and Change,* 3d ed. (Berkeley: U of California P, 1984), 35.

54. B. Brummett, "The Representative Anecdote as a Burkean Method, Applied to Evangelical Rhetoric," *Southern Speech Communication Journal* 50 (1984), 1.

55. Burke, *Permanence and Change,* 35, 31.

56. K. Burke, *A Grammar of Motives,* (1945; rpt., Berkeley: U of California P, 1969), xxii, 317.

57. K. Burke, "Dramatism," *International Encyclopedia of the Social Sciences,* ed. D. L. Sills (New York: Macmillan/Free Press, 1968), 7: 445, 448. Burke also describes dramatism in: *A Grammar of Motives,* xxii; K. Burke, "Rhetoric, Poetics, and Philosophy," *Rhetoric, Philosophy, and Literature: An Exploration,* ed. D. M. Burks (West Lafayette, Ind.: Purdue UP, 1978), 29.

58. Burke, *A Grammar of Motives,* xv, 59. Burke refers to actor as "agent" and to means as "agency." I have adapted his terminology somewhat for the sake of clarity.

59. Address to American Society of Newspaper Editors, April 20, 1961, *PPP,* 304–306.

60. Burke, *A Grammar of Motives,* 15.

61. Address to American Society of Newspaper Editors, April 20, 1961, *PPP,* 304–306.

62. Ibid., 305–306.

63. Ibid., 306.

64. "Campaign," *The Compact Edition of the Oxford English Dictionary.*

65. Aristotle, *The "Art" of Rhetoric,* trans. J. H. Freese (1926; rpt., Cambridge: Harvard UP, 1959), 3.1–12; Cicero, *De Oratore,* trans. E. W. Sutton, rev. ed. (London: William Heinemann, 1959), 3; Longinus, *On the Sublime,* trans. G. M. A. Grube (New York: Library of Liberal Arts, 1957); H. Peacham, *The Garden of Eloquence,* ed. R. C. Alston (1577; rpt., Menston, Eng.: Scolar, 1971); R. Sherry, *A Treatise of Schemes and Tropes* (1550; rpt., Gainesville, Fla.: Scholars' Facsimiles and Reprints, 1961).

66. R. P. Hart, *Verbal Style and the Presidency: A Computer-Based Analysis* (Orlando, Fla.: Academic, 1984), 31, 244.

67. Burke, *Permanence and Change*, 268–269.

68. K. Burke, *The Philosophy of Literary Form*, 3d ed. (Berkeley: U of California P, 1973), 1; Burke, *A Grammar of Motives*, 236, 20; K. Burke, afterword to second edition, *Attitudes Toward History*, 3d ed. (Berkeley: U of California P, 1984), 348; K. Burke, "Attitudes Toward History: In Retrospective Prospect," afterword to third edition, *Attitudes Toward History*, 3d ed. (Berkeley: U of California P, 1984), 394.

69. See Burke, *A Grammar of Motives*, 443.

70. Nationwide Address, April 14, 1986, *WCPD*, 492, 491.

71. Ibid., 491.

72. Ibid.

73. Ibid., 492.

74. Ibid.

75. Ibid.

76. H. Blair, *Lectures on Rhetoric and Belles Lettres*, ed. H. F. Harding (Carbondale: Southern Illinois UP, 1965), 1: 183 (the spelling in this quotation has been modernized for ease in reading); J. D. Barber, *The Presidential Character*, 3d ed. (Englewood Cliffs, N.J.: Prentice-Hall, 1985), 5; G. Buffon, "Discours sur le Style," *The Art of the Writer*, ed. L. Cooper (Ithaca: Cornell UP, 1952), 153–154.

77. K. Burke, *A Rhetoric of Motives* (1950; rpt., Berkeley: U of California P, 1969), 43–45, 55, 20, 22.

78. K. Burke, *Dramatism and Development* (Barre, Mass.: Clark UP, 1972), 28; K. Burke, "The Rhetorical Situation," *Communication: Ethical and Moral Issues*, ed. L. Thayer (New York: Gordon and Breach Science Publishers, 1973), 268.

79. Nationwide Address, July 25, 1961, *PPP*, 539.

80. Ibid., 540.

81. Burke, *Dramatism and Development*, 28; Burke, "The Rhetorical Situation," 268–269.

82. Nationwide Address, Mar. 16, 1986, *WCPD*, 371, 372.

83. Ibid., 371.

84. Burke, *Dramatism and Development*, 28; Burke, "The Rhetorical Situation," 269–270.

85. Remarks to National Legislative Conference, AFL-CIO, May 3, 1965, *PPP*, 480.

86. Address Before Congress, April 27, 1983, *WCPD*, 609.

87. Burke, *Dramatism and Development*, 28.

88. D. F. Hahn, "The Media and the Presidency: Ten Propositions," *Communication Quarterly* 35 (1987), 261.

CHAPTER TWO—THE RHETORIC OF DEFLECTION: JOHN F. KENNEDY AND THE CUBAN MISSILE CRISIS OF 1962

1. Nationwide Address, Oct. 22, 1962, *PPP*, 806–808.

2. When Russian ships stopped short of the U.S. blockade, Secretary of State Dean Rusk reportedly quipped, "We're eyeball to eyeball, and I think the other fellow just blinked." See K. P. O'Donnell and D. F. Powers with J. McCarthy, *"Johnny, We Hardly Knew Ye"* (1972; rpt., New York: Pocket Books, 1973), 385.

3. R. F. Kennedy, *Thirteen Days* (1968; rpt., New York: New American Library, 1969), 173–175.

4. T. C. Sorensen, *Kennedy* (New York: Harper and Row, 1965), 717.

5. T. O. Windt, Jr., "The Presidency and Speeches on International Crises: Repeating the Rhetorical Past," *Speaker and Gavel* 11 (1973): 10–11; T. O. Windt, Jr., *Presidents and Protesters: Political Rhetoric in the 1960s* (Tuscaloosa: U of Alabama P, 1990), 54–55; J. W. Pratt, "An Analysis of Three Crisis Speeches," *Western Journal of Speech Communication* 34 (1970), 201; W. Brockriede and R. L. Scott, *Moments in the Rhetoric of the Cold War* (New York: Random House, 1970), 84, 107.

6. A. Hamilton, J. Madison, and J. Jay, *The Federalist Papers* (New York: New American Library, 1961), 447.

7. Constitution of the United States, Article I: Sec. 8; Article II: Sec. 2, Sec. 3; A. M. Schlesinger, Jr., *The Imperial Presidency* (1973; rpt., New York: Popular Library, 1974), 18–19, 47.

8. K. C. Clark and L. J. Legere, *The President and the Management of National Security* (New York: Frederick A. Praeger, 1969), 3. The National Security Act also created the Central Intelligence Agency.

9. 61 Stat. (1947), 496.

10. I. M. Destler, "National Security Management: What Presidents Have Wrought," *Political Science Quarterly* 95 (1980–1981), 575.

11. Clark and Legere, 58; Destler, 578.

12. Clark and Legere, 60–61.

13. Destler, 578; P. G. Henderson, "Organizing the Presidency for Effective Leadership: Lessons from the Eisenhower Years," *Presidential Studies Quarterly* 17 (1987), 54–55.

14. Clark and Legere, 68, 64.

15. Henderson, 55–56.

16. A. M. Schlesinger, Jr., *A Thousand Days* (1965; rpt., Greenwich, Conn.: Fawcett, 1967), 197–198; also see Destler, 578.

17. Clark and Legere, 71.

18. Schlesinger, *Thousand Days,* 276–277.

19. Destler, 578; Henderson, 58–61.

20. Clark and Legere, 80; Sorensen, 674–675.

21. Destler, 583.

22. R. M. Pious, *The American Presidency* (New York: Basic Books, 1979), 47.

23. Schlesinger, *Imperial Presidency,* 47–76, 107–134.

24. W. W. Stueck, Jr., *The Road to Confrontation: American Policy Toward China and Korea, 1947–1950* (Chapel Hill: U of North Carolina P, 1981), 177–180; Schlesinger, *Imperial Presidency,* 135.

25. Stueck, 180–181, 184–185; Schlesinger, *Imperial Presidency,* 135–137.

26. F. D. Wormuth and E. B. Firmage with F. P. Butler, *To Chain the Dog of War: The War Power of Congress in History and Law* (Dallas: Southern Methodist UP, 1986), 28.

27. S. E. Ambrose, *Eisenhower* (New York: Simon and Schuster, 1984), 2: 231–232; D. D. Eisenhower, *Mandate for Change, 1953–1956* (Garden City, N.Y.: Doubleday, 1963), 461, 472.

28. Eisenhower, 467, 472; Ambrose, 2: 232–236. Eisenhower and Ambrose also explain the role of the offshore islands, Quemoy and Matsu, in Eisenhower's decision.

29. 69 Stat. (1955), 7.

30. Ambrose, 2: 234–235.

31. Special Message to Congress, Jan. 24, 1955, *PPP*, 209–210; Eisenhower, 467–468.

32. 71 Stat. (1957), 5; see also Wormuth and Firmage, 205.

33. "Is Castro's Cuba a Soviet Base?" *U.S. News and World Report,* Sept. 10, 1962, 43; O'Donnell and Powers, 355–356.

34. News Conference, Sept. 13, 1962, *PPP,* 674, 675.

35. Ibid.

36. Position Paper, Anonymous, Sept. 7, 1962, Box 36, National Security Files: Countries.

37. Schlesinger, *Imperial Presidency,* 173–174; 76 Stat. (1962), 697.

38. O'Donnell and Powers, 378–380.

39. Nationwide Address, Oct. 22, 1962, *PPP,* 807.

40. Schlesinger, *Imperial Presidency,* 175.

41. J. Tebbel and S. M. Watts, *The Press and the Presidency: From George Washington to Ronald Reagan* (New York: Oxford UP, 1985).

42. A. Krock, "Mr. Kennedy's Management of the News," *Fortune,* Mar. 1963, 202; Tebbel and Watts, 441; B. H. Winfield, "The New Deal Publicity Operation: Foundation for the Modern Presidency," *Journalism Quarterly* 61 (1984), 45.

43. Krock, 82.

44. K. W. Thompson, *Ten Presidents and the Press* (Lanham, Md.: UP of America, 1983), 70; Krock, 82, 199. See also B. C. Bradlee, *Conversations with Kennedy* (1975; rpt., New York: Pocket Books, 1976), 49–51, 67–70, 108.

45. W. J. Small, "Crisis News Management in the Kennedy Years," *Media Power in Politics,* ed. D. A. Graber (Washington, D.C.: CQ Press, 1984), 326–327.

46. Ibid., 327.

47. Address to American Newspaper Publishers Association, April 27, 1961, *PPP,* 336, 337; P. Salinger, *With Kennedy* (Garden City, N.Y.: Doubleday, 1966), 155, 158.

48. Salinger, 158; "Kennedy Pledges Free News Access," *New York Times,* May 10, 1961, A3.

49. Salinger, 250–253, 261.

50. Ibid., 288–289.

51. J. E. Pollard, "The Kennedy Administration and the Press," *Journalism Quarterly* 41 (1964), 9–10.

52. Press Briefing #808, Oct. 29, 1962, Box 50, White House Staff Files: Pierre E. G. Salinger Papers.

53. History of Cuban Crisis, Frank Sieverts, Aug. 22, 1963, Box 49A, National Security Files: Countries.

54. M. Kern, P. W. Levering, and R. B. Levering, *The Kennedy Crises: The Press, the Presidency, and Foreign Policy* (Chapel Hill: U of North Carolina P, 1983), 127–129; Brockriede and Scott, 106–112.

248 Notes to Pages 35–42

55. Memorandum, Thomas C. Sorensen to U.S. Information Agency and Other Government Media Outlets, Oct. 22, 1962, Box 48, Theodore Sorensen Papers.

56. Cable, American Embassy in London to the White House, Oct. 24, 1962, Box 36, National Security Files: Countries; Salinger, 293–294.

57. Krock, 199, 201.

58. Memo, Pierre Salinger to Editors and Radio and Television News Directors, Oct. 24, 1962, Box 114A, President's Office Files: Countries.

59. Pollard, 12; R. J. Walton, *Cold War and Counterrevolution* (New York: Viking, 1972), 119.

60. Press Briefing #799, Oct. 25, 1962, Box 50, White House Staff Files: Pierre E. G. Salinger Papers.

61. Memo, Chester Clifton, Oct. 22, 1962, Box 115, President's Office Files: Countries.

62. Tebbel and Watts, 481.

63. Kern, Levering, and Levering, 140.

64. B. J. Bernstein, "Courage and Commitment: The Missiles of October," *Foreign Service Journal,* Dec. 1975, 9.

65. Schlesinger, *Imperial Presidency,* 205.

66. Schlesinger, *Thousand Days,* 730–734; Sorensen, 668, 673–674.

67. "Congressmen and Editors Choose Cuba as the Main Campaign Issue," *Washington Post,* Oct. 18, 1962, A2.

68. I. F. Stone, *In a Time of Torment* (New York: Random House, 1967), 19.

69. O'Donnell and Powers, 359.

70. Items 28.2 and 28A.1, Oct. 16, 1962, Meeting Recordings.

71. R. Kennedy, 30–50.

72. Items 28.2 and 28A.1, Oct. 16, 1962, Meeting Recordings.

73. Item 28.1, Oct. 16, 1962, Meeting Recordings.

74. See B. J. Bernstein, "The Cuban Missile Crisis," *Reflections on the Cold War,* ed. L. H. Miller and R. W. Pruessen (Philadelphia: Temple UP, 1974), 108–142.

75. O'Donnell and Powers, 374–375; J. G. Blight and D. A. Welch, *On the Brink: Americans and Soviets Reexamine the Cuban Missile Crisis* (New York: Hill and Wang, 1989), 246.

76. Items 28.2 and 28A.1, Oct. 16, 1962, Meeting Recordings.

77. Blight and Welch, 246. In recent years, McGeorge Bundy has expressed regret for what he calls "a certain excess in rhetoric." See M. Bundy, *Danger and Survival: Choices About the Bomb in the First Fifty Years* (New York: Random House, 1988), 457.

78. 1st Draft of Cuban Missile Crisis Speech, Oct. 20, 1962; Notes to Speech Draft, Oct. 20, 1962; and 4th Draft of Cuban Missile Crisis Speech, Oct. 21, 1962. All found in Box 48, Theodore Sorensen Papers. 3rd Draft, Oct. 21, 1962, Box 41, President's Office Files: Speech Files.

79. Items 28.2 and 28A.1, Oct. 16, 1962, Meeting Recordings.

80. Walton, 124.

81. J. F. Kennedy, *Profiles in Courage* (1955; rpt., New York: Harper and Row, 1964), 1, 16.

82. Nationwide Address, Oct. 22, 1962, *PPP,* 806.

83. White House Statement, Oct. 26, 1962, *PPP,* 812; Ibid., 806.

84. Nationwide Address, Oct. 22, 1962, *PPP,* 807–809.

85. Ibid., 807.

86. Ibid., 806–808.

87. Ibid., 807, 809.

88. Ibid., 807.

89. According to Walton, Nixon publicly called for a "quarantine" of Cuba on Sept. 18. See Walton, 113, 124.

90. Memo, Abram Chayes to McGeorge Bundy, Sept. 10, 1962, Box 49, Theodore Sorensen Papers.

91. Nationwide Address, Oct. 22, 1962, *PPP,* 808.

92. Ibid.

93. White House Statement, Oct. 27, 1962, *PPP,* 813.

94. News Conference, Nov. 20, 1962, *PPP,* 830.

95. Message in Reply to Khrushchev's Broadcast, Oct. 28, 1962, *PPP,* 815.

96. K. Burke, *A Grammar of Motives* (1945; rpt., Berkeley: U of California P, 1969), 17.

97. Nationwide Address, Oct. 22, 1962, *PPP,* 808, 807.

98. News Conference, Feb. 7, 1963, *PPP,* 150.

99. See ibid., 149; Nationwide Address, Oct. 22, 1962, *PPP,* 807, 808.

100. Nationwide Address, Oct. 22, 1962, *PPP,* 807.

101. Ibid., 809, 807, 808.

102. Ibid., 807.

103. Address to Economic Club of New York, Dec. 14, 1962, *PPP,* 876.

104. News Conference, Feb. 7, 1963, *PPP,* 149.

105. Windt, *Presidents and Protesters,* 10–11.

106. Nationwide Address, Oct. 22, 1962, *PPP,* 807–808. Pratt (197) also observed that Kennedy's televised address had an unusually high number of international appeals.

107. Windt, "The Presidency," 11.

108. Nationwide Address, Oct. 22, 1962, *PPP,* 809.

109. White House Statement, Oct. 27, 1962, *PPP,* 813.

110. Nationwide Address, Oct. 22, 1962, *PPP,* 807.

111. White House Statement, Oct. 26, 1962, *PPP,* 812.

112. State of the Union, Jan. 14, 1963, *PPP,* 16.

113. Nationwide Address, Oct. 22, 1962, *PPP,* 806, 807, 808.

114. Ibid., 807, 806.

115. Ibid., 807.

116. Ibid., 807, 808.

117. News Conference, Feb. 7, 1963, *PPP,* 149.

118. Sorensen, 678, 676–677.

119. Walton, 121. Walton also discusses Sorensen's account of Ex Comm's theories.

120. For more on Cold War rhetoric, see Brockriede and Scott; M. J. Medhurst, R. L. Ivie, P. Wander, and R. L. Scott, *Cold War Rhetoric: Strategy, Metaphor, and Ideology* (New York: Greenwood, 1990); L. B. Hinds and T. O. Windt, Jr., *The Cold War as Rhetoric: The Beginnings, 1945–1950* (New York: Praeger, 1991).

121. R. P. Hart, *Verbal Style and the Presidency: A Computer-Based Analysis* (Orlando, Fla.: Academic, 1984), 99.

122. Ibid., 107; C. A. Berthold, "Kenneth Burke's Cluster-Agon Method: Its Development and an Application," *Central States Speech Journal* 27 (1976), 308; Windt, *Presidents and Protesters,* 27, 39, 55.

123. Commencement Address at American University in Washington, June 10, 1963, *PPP,* 463.

124. Nationwide Address, July 26, 1963, *PPP,* 605.

125. Hart, 107.

126. Statement Following the Soviet Decision to Withdraw Missiles From Cuba, Oct. 28, 1962, *PPP,* 815.

127. R. C. Albright, "Key Legislators of Both Parties Back Blockade," *Washington Post,* Oct. 23, 1962, A14; "The 'In' Party's Dramatic Triumph," *Newsweek,* Nov. 19, 1962, 31.

128. Bernstein, "Courage and Commitment," 27.

129. G. Wills, *The Kennedy Imprisonment* (1981; rpt., New York: Pocket Books, 1983), 274–284; Walton, 103–142.

130. B. Keller, "Soviets Say Nuclear Warheads Were Deployed in Cuba in '62," *New York Times,* Jan. 29, 1989, A1.

131. Letter (Embassy Translation), Nikita Khrushchev to John Kennedy, Oct. 26, 1962, Box 115, President's Office Files: Countries Files; Current Intelligence Memorandum, CIA, Oct. 19, 1962, Box 51, National Security Files: Countries.

CHAPTER THREE—LBJ BALANCES STRENGTH AND RESTRAINT: THE 1964 GULF OF TONKIN CRISIS AND THE DANGER OF THE MIDDLE GROUND

1. Nationwide Announcement, Aug. 4, 1964, *PPP,* 2: 927.

2. M. Marder, "American Planes Hit North Viet-Nam After 2d Attack on Our Destroyers; Move Taken to Halt New Aggression," *Washington Post,* Aug. 5, 1964, A1.

3. J. C. Goulden, *Truth Is the First Casualty* (New York: James B. Adler, 1969), 13.

4. R. A. Cherwitz, "Masking Inconsistency: The Tonkin Gulf Crisis," *Communication Quarterly* 28 (1980), 36.

5. R. Evans and R. Novak, *Lyndon B. Johnson: The Exercise of Power* (New York: New American Library, 1966), 533; B. E. Altschuler, *LBJ and the Polls* (Gainesville: U of Florida P, 1990), 38.

6. K. J. Turner, *Lyndon Johnson's Dual War: Vietnam and the Press* (Chicago: U of Chicago P, 1985), 6.

7. D. Kearns, *Lyndon Johnson and the American Dream* (1976; rpt., New York: New American Library, 1977), 206.

8. "Dirksen and Halleck Say G.O.P. Must Make Vietnam an Issue," *New York Times,* July 3, 1964, A7.

9. "Transcript of Goldwater's Speech Accepting Republican Presidential Nomination," *New York Times,* July 17, 1964, A10; C. Mohr, "Goldwater and Scranton Clash on Military's Role," *New York Times,* July 10, 1964, A1.

10. K. H. Jamieson, *Packaging the Presidency: A History and Criticism of Presidential Campaign Advertising* (New York: Oxford UP, 1984), 171.

11. Altschuler, xi, 40.

12. T. W. Benham, "Polling for a Presidential Candidate: Some Observations on the 1964 Campaign," *Public Opinion Quarterly* 24 (1965), 189, 191.

13. M. Marder, "U.S. Destroyer Fights Off 3 PT Boats in Attack Off Coast of North Viet-Nam," *Washington Post,* Aug. 3, 1964, A1; J. G. Norris, "USS *Maddox* on Patrol as Attack Came," *Washington Post,* Aug. 3, 1964, A1; Statement by the President, Aug. 3, 1964, *PPP,* 2: 927.

14. L. B. Johnson, *The Vantage Point* (New York: Holt, Rinehart and Winston, 1971), 115–117; Marder, "American Planes," A1.

15. "Goldwater, Congressional Leaders Support President in SE Asia Action," *Washington Post,* Aug. 5, 1964, A1.

16. Notes Taken at Leadership Meeting, author presumed to be Walter Jenkins, Aug. 4, 1964, Box 38, National Security Files: NSC History; Revised Draft Statement by the President, Aug. 4, 1964, Box 2, National Security Files: Speech File.

17. Nationwide Announcement, Aug. 4, 1964, *PPP,* 2: 927–928.

18. A. Austin, *The President's War* (New York: New York Times, 1971), 51–52; Goulden, 38.

19. Interview Transcript, Robert McNamara with Peter Hackes of NBC, Aug. 5, 1964, Box 138, National Security Files: NSC History.

20. Remarks at Syracuse University, Aug. 5, 1964, *PPP,* 2: 928–930; Special Message to Congress, Aug. 5, 1964, *PPP,* 2: 930–932.

21. Goulden, 53–79.

22. E. F. Goldman, *The Tragedy of Lyndon Johnson* (New York: Alfred A. Knopf, 1969), 183, 180.

23. 78 Stat. (1964), 384.

24. M. Miller, *Lyndon: An Oral Biography* (New York: G. P. Putnam's Sons, 1980), 384.

25. Interview Transcript, Robert McNamara with Neil Strawser of CBS-TV and Robert McNamara with Peter Hackes of NBC News, Aug. 5, 1964, Box 38, National Security Files: NSC History.

26. "Vietnam: 'We Seek No Wider War,'" *Newsweek,* Aug. 17, 1964, 18.

27. R. N. Goodwin, *Remembering America: A Voice from the Sixties* (Boston: Little, Brown, 1988), 358.

28. Austin, 113.

29. Johnson, 46.

30. Remarks to the New Hampshire Weekly Newspaper Editors Association, Sept. 28, 1964, *PPP,* 2: 1161.

31. Remarks Upon Signing Joint Resolution, Aug. 10, 1964, *PPP,* 2: 946; Remarks at Syracuse University, Aug. 5, 1964, *PPP,* 2: 928, 929.

32. Remarks to the American Bar Association, Aug. 12, 1964, *PPP,* 2: 953.

33. C. Perelman and L. Olbrechts-Tyteca, *The New Rhetoric: A Treatise on Argumentation,* trans. J. Wilkinson and P. Weaver (1969; rpt., Notre Dame: U of Notre Dame P, 1971), 411–419, 445.

34. Memo, James L. Greenfield to Under Secretary at Dept. of State, June 3, 1964, Box 71, Confidential Files.

35. Memo, McGeorge Bundy to the President, Oct. 1, 1964, Box 2, National Security Files: Memos to President.

36. Second Draft of Memo, William Bundy, Sept. 5, 1964, Box 8, National Security Files/Country File: Vietnam.

37. Second Draft Memo, William Bundy, June 11, 1964, Box 39, National Security Files: NSC History.

38. "The 'Phantom Battle' That Led to War," *U.S. News and World Report,* July 23, 1984, 56–67; Austin, 276–287; E. G. Windchy, *Tonkin Gulf* (Garden City, N.Y.: Doubleday, 1971), 211–218, 259–293. See also Dept. of Defense, *United States-Vietnam Relations, 1945–67* (Washington, D.C.: U.S. Government Printing Office, 1971), 4: c.2(b)8, c.3.7.

39. Memo, Bill Moyers to Horace Busby, Dick Goodwin, Fred Dutton, Douglass Cater, and McGeorge Bundy, Sept. 21, 1964, Box 121; and Memo, Bill Moyers to the President, Sept. 23, 1964, Box 122. Both in Statements of Lyndon Baines Johnson.

40. Memo, McGeorge Bundy to the President, Oct. 1, 1964, Box 2, National Security Files: Memos to the President.

41. Memo, McGeorge Bundy to the President, Aug. 5, 1964, and Draft of Remarks for Resolution Signing Ceremony, McGeorge Bundy to the President, Aug. 9, 1964. Both found in Box 2, National Security Files: Memos to the President.

42. Kearns, 264, 265.

43. Turner, 1–4.

44. Kearns, 263.

45. Suggested Remarks for Signing of Joint Resolution on Monday, Aug. 10, 1964, Box 115; First Draft of American Bar Association Speech, Dick Goodwin, Box 116. Both in Statements of Lyndon Baines Johnson.

46. W. Brockriede and R. L. Scott, *Moments in the Rhetoric of the Cold War* (New York: Random House, 1970), 82–84; R. A. Cherwitz and K. S. Zagacki, "Consummatory Versus Justificatory Crisis Rhetoric," *Western Journal of Speech Communication* 50 (1986), 318–319; D. R. Heisey, "Reagan and Mitterand Respond to International Crisis: Creating Versus Transcending Appearances," *Western Journal of Speech Communication* 50 (1986), 328; D. C. Klope, "Defusing a Foreign Policy Crisis: Myth and Victimage in Reagan's 1983 Lebanon/Grenada Address," *Western Journal of Speech Communication* 50 (1986), 343.

47. Turner, 4.

48. Nationwide Address, Oct. 22, 1962, *PPP,* 807.

49. Turner, 4.

50. CBS President Frank Stanton had installed one of Johnson's famous three-way receiver television sets in the White House as early as May of 1964. Letter, Walter Jenkins to Frank Stanton, May 16, 1964, Box 518, White House Central Files: Name File.

51. Nationwide Announcement, Aug. 4, 1964, *PPP,* 2: 927.

52. Special Message to Congress, Aug. 5, 1964, *PPP,* 2: 931; ibid.

53. Remarks at Syracuse University, Aug. 5, 1964, *PPP,* 2: 928.

54. Special Message to Congress, Aug. 5, 1964, *PPP,* 2: 930.

55. News Conference, Aug. 8, 1964, *PPP,* 2: 938.

56. Nationwide Announcement, Aug. 4, 1964, *PPP,* 2: 927.

57. Remarks at Syracuse University, Aug. 5, 1964, *PPP,* 2: 928.

58. Nationwide Address, Oct. 7, 1964, *PPP,* 2: 1242; Remarks to the American Bar Association, Aug. 12, 1964, *PPP,* 2: 954; Remarks to the New Hampshire Weekly Newspaper Editors Association, Sept. 28, 1964, *PPP,* 2: 1161–1162; Remarks at Lindbergh Field, San Diego, Oct. 28, 1964, *PPP,* 2: 1510–1511; Remarks in El Paso at a Ceremony Marking the Chamizal Settlement, Sept. 25, 1964, *PPP,* 2: 1119.

59. Remarks to the National Association of Counties, Aug. 11, 1964, *PPP,* 2: 949.

60. Nationwide Announcement, Aug. 4, 1964, *PPP,* 2: 927.

61. Ibid.

62. News Conference, Aug. 8, 1964, *PPP,* 2: 938.

63. Remarks at Barbecue in Stonewall, Texas, Aug. 29, 1964, *PPP,* 2: 1021.

64. Special Message to Congress, Aug. 5, 1964, *PPP,* 2: 930–931.

65. Remarks at Syracuse University, Aug. 5, 1964, *PPP,* 2: 929.

66. Turner, 43.

67. Miller, 343.

68. Remarks Upon Signing Joint Resolution, Aug. 10, 1964, *PPP,* 2: 947.

69. Remarks at Syracuse University, Aug. 5, 1964, *PPP,* 2: 928; Nationwide Address, Oct. 7, 1964, *PPP,* 2: 1242.

70. Special Message to Congress, Aug. 5, 1964, *PPP,* 2: 931.

71. Remarks to the National Association of Counties, Aug. 11, 1964, *PPP,* 2: 949.

72. Remarks at Johns Hopkins University, Oct. 1, 1964, *PPP,* 2: 1177.

73. News Conference, Aug. 8, 1964, *PPP,* 2: 937.

74. Remarks in El Paso at a Ceremony Marking the Chamizal Settlement, Sept. 25, 1964, *PPP,* 2: 1119.

75. Remarks to the American Bar Association, Aug. 12, 1964, *PPP,* 2: 952.

76. Nationwide Announcement, Aug. 4, 1964, *PPP,* 2: 927, 928.

77. Remarks Upon Signing Joint Resolution, Aug. 10, 1964, *PPP,* 2: 946.

78. Nationwide Announcement, Aug. 4, 1964, *PPP,* 2: 928.

79. News Conference, Aug. 15, 1964, *PPP,* 2: 965–967.

80. Remarks in South Gate, California, Oct. 11, 1964, *PPP,* 2: 1294.

81. Remarks at Lindbergh Field, San Diego, Oct. 28, 1964, *PPP,* 2: 1511.

82. Statement by the President, Aug. 7, 1964, *PPP,* 2: 936.

83. News Conference, Aug. 8, 1964, *PPP,* 2: 937.

84. Remarks Upon Signing Joint Resolution, Aug. 10, 1964, *PPP,* 2: 947.

85. Remarks to the American Bar Association, Aug. 12, 1964, *PPP,* 2: 953–954.

86. Perelman and Olbrechts-Tyteca, 443.

87. Remarks to the American Bar Association, Aug. 12, 1964, *PPP,* 2: 952 (emphasis added).

88. Remarks to the New Hampshire Weekly Newspaper Editors Association, Sept. 28, 1964, *PPP,* 2: 1162 (emphasis added).

89. Remarks Upon Signing Joint Resolution, Aug. 10, 1964, *PPP,* 2: 947 (emphasis added).

90. Remarks at Johns Hopkins University, Oct. 1, 1964, *PPP,* 2: 1177.

91. Remarks to the American Bar Association, Aug. 12, 1964, *PPP,* 2: 953.

92. Nationwide Address, Oct. 22, 1962, *PPP,* 809.

93. J. W. Pratt, "An Analysis of Three Crisis Speeches," *Western Journal of Speech Communication* 34 (1970), 202.

94. Special Message to Congress, Aug. 5, 1964, *PPP,* 2: 931.

95. Remarks at Syracuse University, Aug. 5, 1964, *PPP,* 2: 930.

96. News Conference, Aug. 8, 1964, *PPP,* 2: 938.

97. Remarks in Des Moines, Oct. 7, 1964, *PPP,* 2: 1230.

98. Remarks at Barbecue in Stonewall, Texas, Aug. 29, 1964, *PPP,* 2: 1021.

99. R. P. Hart, *Verbal Style and the Presidency: A Computer-Based Analysis* (Orlando, Fla.: Academic, 1984), 110; F. Cormier, *LBJ the Way He Was* (New York: Doubleday, 1977), 137.

100. R. A. Cherwitz, "Lyndon Johnson and the 'Crisis' of Tonkin Gulf: A President's Justification of War," *Western Journal of Speech Communication* 42 (1978), 99.

101. Nationwide Announcement, Aug. 4, 1964, *PPP,* 2: 927.

102. Remarks Upon Signing Joint Resolution, Aug. 10, 1964, *PPP,* 2: 946, 947.

103. Nationwide Announcement, Aug. 4, 1964, *PPP,* 2: 927–928.

104. Remarks at Syracuse University, Aug. 5, 1964, *PPP,* 2: 929.

105. Remarks to the American Bar Association, Aug. 12, 1964, *PPP,* 2: 954.

106. For example, see Remarks to the New Hampshire Weekly Newspaper Editors Association, Sept. 28, 1964, *PPP,* 2: 1161.

107. Ibid., 1164.

108. T. W. Benson, "Rhetoric as a Way of Being," *American Rhetoric: Context and Criticism,* ed. T. W. Benson (Carbondale: Southern Illinois UP, 1989), 320.

109. Remarks at Lindbergh Field, San Diego, Oct. 28, 1964, *PPP,* 2: 1510.

110. Perelman and Olbrechts-Tyteca, 445.

111. Remarks to the New Hampshire Weekly Newspaper Editors Association, Sept. 28, 1964, *PPP,* 2: 1161–1165.

112. Ibid., 1165, 1166.

113. Ibid., 1165.

114. Remarks to the American Bar Association, Aug. 12, 1964, *PPP,* 2: 953.

115. Remarks at Barbecue in Stonewall, Texas, Aug. 29, 1964, *PPP,* 2: 1021, 1022.

116. Remarks at the Dedication of Oklahoma's Eufaula Dam, Sept. 25, 1964, *PPP,* 2: 1126.

117. Remarks to the New Hampshire Weekly Newspaper Editors Association, Sept. 28, 1964, *PPP,* 2: 1164.

118. T. H. White, *The Making of the President 1964* (New York: Atheneum Publishers, 1965), 300.

119. Benham, 190.

120. Turner, 4.

121. Memo, Horace Busby to W. Willard Wirtz, Clark Clifford, McGeorge Bundy, Douglass Cater, Dick Goodwin, and Eric Goldman, Oct. 14, 1964, Box 10, White House Central Files: EX FG 1 10/10/64–12/20/64. Comparisons of Johnson's prepared texts

with transcripts of the texts as they were delivered revealed the importance that ad-libs played in the President's indirect dissociation.

122. Douglass Cater Oral History Interview with David McComb, May 8, 1969, Tape II, 23.

123. Perelman and Olbrechts-Tyteca, 82.

124. Turner, 6.

125. Zarefsky, 204.

126. George Reedy Oral History Interview with Michael L. Gillette, Dec. 20, 1983, Interview XI, 20.

CHAPTER FOUR—RICHARD M. NIXON AND THE GROTESQUE: THE 1970 INVASION OF CAMBODIA

1. Nationwide Address, April 20, 1970, *WCPD,* 554, 556.

2. Nationwide Address, April 30, 1970, *WCPD,* 598–599.

3. "A *Newsweek* Poll: Mr. Nixon Holds Up," *Newsweek,* May 25, 1970, 30.

4. J. Kifner, "4 Kent State Students Killed by Troops," *New York Times,* May 5, 1970, A1, A17; "Jackson Police Fire on Students," *New York Times,* May 15, 1970, A1, A21; S. Rich, "Senators Denounce Nixon Move," *Washington Post,* April 30, 1970, A1, A15; S. Rich, "Congress Reacts," *Washington Post,* May 2, 1970, A1, A10; "Nixon's Gamble: Operation Total Victory?" *Newsweek,* May 11, 1970, 23.

5. J. Schell, *The Time of Illusion* (1975; rpt., New York: Vintage Books, 1976), 92; "Vietnam: Mr. Nixon's Quick Fix . . . ," editorial, *Washington Post,* May 2, 1970, A12; R. P. Hart, *The Sound of Leadership: Presidential Communication in the Modern Age* (Chicago: U of Chicago P, 1987), 79.

6. S. Karnow, *Vietnam: A History* (1983; rpt., New York: Penguin Books, 1984), 609; R. P. Newman, "Pity the Helpless Giant: Nixon on Cambodia," *Essays in Presidential Rhetoric,* rev. ed., ed. T. Windt with B. Ingold (1983; Dubuque, Iowa: Kendall/Hunt, 1984), 217–218.

7. R. B. Gregg and G. A. Hauser, "Richard Nixon's April 30, 1970 Address on Cambodia: The 'Ceremony' of Confrontation," *Speech Monographs* 40 (1973), 179, 177–178.

8. T. O. Windt, Jr., "The Presidency and Speeches on International Crises: Repeating the Rhetorical Past," *Speaker and Gavel* 11 (1973), 11.

9. P. Thomson, *The Grotesque* (London: Methuen, 1972), 24, 59.

10. N. Chomsky, "Cambodia in Conflict," *Cambodia: The Widening War in Indochina,* ed. J. S. Grant, L. A. G. Moss, and J. Unger (New York: Washington Square, 1971), 39.

11. A. R. Isaacs, *Without Honor: Defeat in Vietnam and Cambodia* (Baltimore: Johns Hopkins UP, 1983), 193–194; W. Shawcross, *Sideshow: Kissinger, Nixon, and the Destruction of Cambodia* (New York: Pocket Books, 1979), 64, 68.

12. Isaacs, 195.

13. Shawcross, 94.

14. Karnow, 604.

15. Shawcross, 117–118, 120.

16. Chomsky, 43.

17. Isaacs, 200–201.

18. P. C. Pradhan, *Foreign Policy of Kampuchea* (New Delhi: Radiant, 1985), 145–150; Shawcross, 125–126.

19. Shawcross, 132–133.

20. Chomsky, 43.

21. Nationwide Address, April 20, 1970, *WCPD*, 554, 556.

22. Nationwide Address, April 30, 1970, *WCPD*, 597–598, 601.

23. "A *Newsweek* Poll," 30.

24. Notes, Richard Nixon, April 26, 1970, Box 58, President's Personal Files: Speech File.

25. Notes of Meeting with the President, H. R. Haldeman, April 28, 1970, Box 41, White House Special Files: Haldeman.

26. President Nixon's Address to the Nation, April 30, 1970, White House Communications Agency, Audio Recording, P-700429.

27. Notes, Lawrence Higby, undated, Box 252; and Notes of Meeting with the President, H. R. Haldeman, May 2, 1970, Box 41. Both in White House Special Files: Haldeman.

28. Memo, Bryce Harlow to Richard Nixon, June 9, 1970, Box 81, President's Office Files: Memoranda to the President.

29. Memo, Herb Klein to Richard Nixon, May 1, 1970, Box 3, White House Special Files: Klein Papers.

30. Notes of Meeting with the President, H. R. Haldeman, May 1, 1970, Box 41, White House Special Files: Haldeman.

31. W. Safire, *Before the Fall: An Inside View of the Pre-Watergate White House* (Garden City, N.Y.: Doubleday, 1975), 188; Memo on White House Communication, undated, Box 60, White House Special Files/White House Central Files: Subject Files—Confidential Files.

32. Memo, H. R. Haldeman to Herb Klein and Jeb Magruder, May 12, 1970, Box 60, White House Special Files: Haldeman.

33. Memo, Richard Nixon to H. R. Haldeman, May 14, 1970, Box 2, President's Personal Files: Memos From the President.

34. Notes of Meeting with the President, H. R. Haldeman, May 11, 1970, and April 30, 1970. Both in Box 41, White House Special Files: Haldeman.

35. Notes of Meeting with the President, H. R. Haldeman, May 11, May 17, May 18, May 28, May 31, and June 4, 1970, Box 41, White House Special Files: Haldeman.

36. Notes of Meeting with the President, H. R. Haldeman, April 30, 1970, Box 41; Memo, Jeb Magruder to H. R. Haldeman, May 6, 1970, Box 60. Both in White House Special Files: Haldeman.

37. Notes of Meeting with the President, H. R. Haldeman, June 3, 1970, Box 41, White House Special Files: Haldeman.

38. Notes of Meeting with the President, H. R. Haldeman, May 2, 1970, Box 41; Memo, Jeb Magruder to H. R. Haldeman, June 10, 1970, Box 60. Both in White House Special Files: Haldeman.

39. Notes of Meeting with the President, H. R. Haldeman, May 20, 1970, Box 41, White House Special Files: Haldeman.

40. Memo, H. R. Haldeman to Herb Klein and Jeb Magruder, May 12, 1970, Box 60, White House Special Files: Haldeman.

41. Shawcross, 135–136.

42. Notes of Meeting with the President, H. R. Haldeman, May 4, 1970, Box 41, White House Special Files: Haldeman.

43. "Kent State: Martyrdom That Shook the Country," *Time,* May 18, 1970, 14; "Jackson Police," A1.

44. M. Marder, "U.S. Aids Viet Raid in Cambodia," *Washington Post,* April 30, 1970, A1, A14; R. Nixon, *RN: The Memoirs of Richard Nixon,* (1978; rpt., New York: Warner, 1979), 1: 559; Karnow, 608.

45. C. Kilpatrick, "Nixon Sends GIs Into Cambodia to Destroy Enemy Sanctuaries," *Washington Post,* May 1, 1970, A1; A. M. Schlesinger, Jr., *The Imperial Presidency* (1973; rpt., New York: Popular Library, 1974), 189.

46. "At War with War," *Time,* May 18, 1970, 11; Shawcross, 144–145; Rich, "Senators Denounce," A15.

47. R. Evans, Jr., and R. D. Novak, *Nixon in the White House: The Frustration of Power* (New York: Random House, 1971), 292–296.

48. Notes of Meeting with the President, H. R. Haldeman, May 8, 1970, Box 41, White House Special Files: Haldeman; H. Kissinger, *White House Years* (Boston: Little, Brown, 1979), 513–514, 497; Karnow, 610.

49. Memo, Daniel Moynihan to Richard Nixon, May 9, 1970, Box 6, President's Office Files: President's Handwriting.

50. D. N. Freeman, "Freedom of Speech Within the Nixon Administration," *Communication Quarterly* 24 (1976), 3–10.

51. Notes of Meeting with the President, H. R. Haldeman, May 10 and May 7, 1970, Box 41, White House Special Files: Haldeman.

52. H. G. Klein, *Making It Perfectly Clear* (Garden City, N.Y.: Doubleday, 1980), 340.

53. Marder, "U.S. Aids Viet Raid," A14.

54. R. M. Nixon, *Six Crises* (Garden City, N.Y.: Doubleday, 1962), xiii, xiv, xvi.

55. W. Kayser, *The Grotesque in Art and Literature,* trans. U. Weisstein (1957; rpt., Bloomington: Indiana UP, 1963), 19–20.

56. G. G. Harpham, *On the Grotesque: Strategies of Contradiction in Art and Literature* (Princeton: Princeton UP, 1982), 81–86; Kayser, 18, 34–37, 169, 171–173.

57. K. Burke, *Attitudes Toward History,* 3d ed. (Berkeley: U of California P, 1984), 62–63.

58. Kayser, 185, 161.

59. Burke, *Attitudes Toward History,* 64.

60. R. H. Brown, *A Poetic for Sociology* (Cambridge: Cambridge UP, 1977), 177.

61. Thomson, 21; Harpham, 178.

62. Thomson, 24, 59.

63. Kayser, 184–185; Harpham, 3–22.

64. Burke, *Attitudes Toward History,* 59–60.

65. Nationwide Address, April 30, 1970, *WCPD,* 597, 600.

66. News Conference, May 8, 1970, *WCPD*, 616; Nationwide Address, April 30, 1970, *WCPD*, 597, 600, 598–599.

67. Nationwide Address, April 30, 1970, *WCPD*, 597.

68. Ibid.

69. Ibid., 600.

70. Ibid., 601.

71. Ibid., 600.

72. Interview, July 1, 1970, *WCPD*, 869, 865.

73. Discussion with College Students, May 9, 1970, *WCPD*, 622.

74. Report to the Nation, June 3, 1970, *WCPD*, 721.

75. Nationwide Address, April 30, 1970, *WCPD*, 597; Report to the Nation, June 3, 1970, *WCPD*, 723.

76. Nationwide Address, April 30, 1970, *WCPD*, 601, 600.

77. Report to the Nation, June 3, 1970, *WCPD*, 724; Nationwide Address, April 30, 1970, *WCPD*, 599, 600.

78. Report to the Nation, June 3, 1970, *WCPD*, 725.

79. Nationwide Address, April 30, 1970, *WCPD*, 601, 600 (emphasis added).

80. Ibid., 597.

81. Newman, 211.

82. Nationwide Address, April 30, 1970, *WCPD*, 599.

83. Report, June 30, 1970, *WCPD*, 843. Newman (214) noted this contradiction, as well.

84. Notes of Meeting with the President, H. R. Haldeman, May 3, 1970, Box 41, White House Special Files: Haldeman; Briefing Book Back-up, Patrick Buchanan to Richard Nixon, May 6, 1970, Box 14, White House Special Files: Patrick J. Buchanan.

85. Nationwide Address, April 30, 1970, *WCPD*, 599.

86. News Conference, May 8, 1970, *WCPD*, 616.

87. Nationwide Address, April 30, 1970, *WCPD*, 598.

88. Report to the Nation, June 3, 1970, *WCPD*, 723.

89. Memo, Richard Nixon to H. R. Haldeman, May 14, 1970, Box 2, President's Personal Files: Memos From the President.

90. "The President: Cambodian Report," *Newsweek*, June 15, 1970, 29; Report to the Nation, June 3, 1970, *WCPD*, 722, 724.

91. Nationwide Address, April 30, 1970, *WCPD*, 598.

92. News Conference, May 8, 1970, *WCPD*, 619.

93. Nationwide Address, April 30, 1970, *WCPD*, 597–598.

94. Ibid., 599, 601.

95. Ibid., 601.

96. News Conference, May 8, 1970, *WCPD*, 617; Report to the Nation, June 3, 1970, *WCPD*, 724.

97. L. Hinds and C. Smith, "Rhetoric of Opposites," *Nation*, Feb. 16, 1970, 173. Gonchar and Hahn studied a number of Nixon's early speeches as president and made this same observation. See R. M. Gonchar and D. F. Hahn, "The Rhetorical Predictability of Richard Nixon," *Today's Speech* 19 (1971), 7.

98. Nationwide Address, April 30, 1970, *WCPD*, 601.

99. Ibid., 598.

100. Interview, July 1, 1970, *WCPD*, 868.

101. R. P. Hart, *Verbal Style and the Presidency: A Computer-Based Analysis* (Orlando, Fla.: Academic, 1984), 280.

102. Gonchar and Hahn, 3.

103. Draft #3, undated; Draft #3, April 30, 1970; and President's Reading Copy of Radio/TV Statement, April 30, 1970; all located in Box 58, President's Personal Files: Speech File. Draft, June 3, 1970, and Final Working Draft, June 3, 1970; both located in Box 59, President's Personal Files: Speech File.

104. For example, Nationwide Address, April 30, 1970, *WCPD*, 600; News Conference, May 8, 1970, *WCPD*, 620.

105. Report to the Nation, June 3, 1970, *WCPD*, 724.

106. Interview, July 1, 1970, *WCPD*, 863, 867.

107. News Conference, May 8, 1970, *WCPD*, 620.

108. Nationwide Address, April 30, 1970, *WCPD*, 600, 597.

109. News Conference, May 8, 1970, *WCPD*, 617; Report to the Nation, June 3, 1970, *WCPD*, 724.

110. Nationwide Address, April 30, 1970, *WCPD*, 599, 600; Draft #3, April 30, 1970, Box 58, President's Personal Files: Speech File.

111. Report to the Nation, June 3, 1970, *WCPD*, 722.

112. News Conference, May 8, 1970, *WCPD*, 619.

113. Nationwide Address, April 30, 1970, *WCPD*, 601; Draft #3, April 30, 1970, Box 58, President's Personal Files: Speech File.

114. Gonchar and Hahn, 7.

115. "Vietnam: Mr. Nixon's Quick Fix," A12.

116. Kissinger, *White House Years*, 504–505; Safire, 187; Summary Memo on Cliff Miller Report, Dwight Chapin, April 30, 1970, Box 116, White House Special Files/Staff Member Office Files.

117. Nixon, *Six Crises*, xiv.

118. Nationwide Address, April 30, 1970, *WCPD*, 601.

119. News Conference, May 8, 1970, *WCPD*, 617.

120. Interview, July 1, 1970, *WCPD*, 863.

121. Report to the Nation, June 3, 1970, *WCPD*, 724 (emphasis added).

122. Notes for June 3 Speech and Untitled Notes, Richard Nixon, June 1970, Box 59, President's Personal Files: Speech File.

123. "Nixon's Gamble," 23.

124. Windt, "The Presidency," 10.

125. Nationwide Address, April 30, 1970, *WCPD*, 600, 601; Report to the Nation, June 3, 1970, *WCPD*, 721.

126. Nationwide Address, April 30, 1970, *WCPD*, 597; Nixon, *RN*, 1: 472.

127. Nationwide Address, April 30, 1970, *WCPD*, 599.

128. Ibid., 601; Tape#3-RN, Memo, Richard Nixon to Patrick Buchanan, April 29, 1970, Box 58, President's Personal Files: Speech File.

129. Nationwide Address, April 30, 1970, *WCPD*, 600.

130. J. de Onis, "Nixon Puts 'Bums' Label on Some College Radicals," *New York Times,* May 2, 1970, A1.

131. Presidential Statement, May 4, 1970, *WCPD,* 613.

132. T. O. Windt, Jr., *Presidents and Protesters: Political Rhetoric in the 1960s* (Tuscaloosa: U of Alabama P, 1990), 125.

133. News Conference, May 8, 1970, *WCPD,* 619.

134. Nationwide Address, April 30, 1970, *WCPD,* 600.

135. Report to the Nation, June 3, 1970, *WCPD,* 724.

136. Ibid.

137. Nationwide Address, April 30, 1970, *WCPD,* 599.

138. Interview, July 1, 1970, *WCPD,* 867.

139. Charles W. Colson Oral History Interview with Frederick J. Graboske, June 15, 1988, 43–44; R. B. Semple, Jr., "Nixon Meets Heads of 2 City Unions; Hails War Support," *New York Times,* May 27, 1970, A1, A18.

140. Memo, Tom Charles Huston to Richard Nixon, John Ehrlichman, H. R. Haldeman, Murray Chotiner, Lyn Nofziger, Harry Dent, and Bryce Harlow, undated, Box 139, White House Special Files: Haldeman.

141. Report to the Nation, June 3, 1970, *WCPD,* 722.

142. News Conference, May 8, 1970, *WCPD,* 616.

143. Ibid., Memo, Edward L. Morgan to Richard Nixon, May 8, 1970, Box 81, President's Office Files: Memoranda for the President.

144. Discussion with College Students, May 9, 1970, *WCPD,* 621–624; Memo on the Trip to Lincoln Memorial, Richard Nixon, Undated, Box 2, President's Personal Files: Memoranda From the President.

145. Ibid.

146. Memo, John L. Campbell, Chester E. Finn, Jr., William E. Casselman II, Lee W. Huebner, Christopher C. DeMuth, Donald Murdoch, Jeffrey Donfeld, Hugh W. Sloan, Jr., to Richard Nixon, June 5, 1970, Box 6, President's Office Files: President's Handwriting.

147. Notes of Meeting with the President, H. R. Haldeman, May 3 and May 2, 1970, Box 41, White House Special Files: Haldeman.

148. Notes of Meeting with the President, H. R. Haldeman, May 2, 1970, Box 41, White House Special Files: Haldeman.

149. Notes of Meeting with the President, H. R. Haldeman, May 4, 1970, and May 6, 1970. Both located in Box 41, White House Special Files: Haldeman.

150. Notes of Meeting with the President, H. R. Haldeman, May 12, 1970, Box 41, White House Special Files: Haldeman; Memo, Chuck Colson to Patrick Buchanan, Murray Chotiner, Ken Cole, Harry Dent, John Ehrlichman, Tom Huston, Herb Klein, Ed Morgan, Jeb Magruder, Lyn Nofziger, and Bill Safire, Oct. 6, 1970, Box 44, White House Special Files: Colson.

151. Notes of Meeting with the President, H. R. Haldeman, May 20, 1970, Box 41, White House Special Files: Haldeman.

152. Notes of Meeting with the President, H. R. Haldeman, May 12, 1970, Box 41, White House Special Files: Haldeman.

153. Notes of Meeting with the President, H. R. Haldeman, May 11, 1970, Box 41, White House Special Files: Haldeman.

154. Notes of Meeting with the President, H. R. Haldeman, May 3, 1970, Box 41, White House Special Files: Haldeman.

155. Hinds and Smith, 172–174.

156. G. Wills, *Nixon Agonistes* (Boston: Houghton Mifflin, 1970), 413–416.

157. R. L. Scott, "Rhetoric That Postures: An Intrinsic Reading of Richard M. Nixon's Inaugural Address," *Western Speech Communication Journal* 34 (1970), 49; K. K. Campbell, *Critiques of Contemporary Rhetoric* (Belmont, Calif.: Wadsworth, 1972), 52–56; W. L. Benoit, "Richard M. Nixon's Rhetorical Strategies in His Public Statements on Watergate," *Southern Speech Communication Journal* 47 (1982), 202–203.

158. C. Jablonski, "Richard Nixon's Irish Wake: A Case of Generic Transference," *Central States Speech Journal* 31 (1980), 282–289.

159. E. Black, "Electing Time," *Quarterly Journal of Speech* 59 (1973), 129; Windt, *Presidents and Protesters,* 106.

160. R. P. Hart, "Absolutism and Situation: *Prolegomena* to a Rhetorical Biography of Richard M. Nixon," *Communication Monographs* 43 (1976), 208.

161. K. Burke, *Permanence and Change,* 3d ed. (Berkeley: U of California P, 1984), 113.

162. Hart, *Verbal Style and the Presidency,* 147.

163. Thomson, 40–41, 63.

164. Karnow, 44–45.

165. Henry Kissinger, *Years of Upheaval* (Boston: Little, Brown, 1982), 336, 337.

166. Shawcross, 395–396.

167. Rich, "Congress Reacts," A10; J. W. Finney, "Senate Unit Votes to Restrict Funds in Cambodia War," *New York Times,* May 12, 1970, A1, A17.

168. A. Austin, *The President's War* (New York: New York Times, 1971), 328–329; 84 Stat. (1971), 2055; R. M. Pious, *The American Presidency* (New York: Basic Books, 1979), 397.

169. P. D. Carter, "Final Tally in Senate Is 58–37," *Washington Post,* July 1, 1970, A1; 84 Stat. (1971), 1942–1943.

170. Shawcross, 214.

171. Pious, 401.

172. Karnow, 592, 612.

CHAPTER FIVE—THE QUIET MAN: FORD'S PORTRAYAL OF LEADERSHIP DURING THE *MAYAGUEZ* CRISIS

1. S. Karnow, *Vietnam: A History* (1983; rpt., New York: Penguin Books, 1984), 654, 11, 24; "Phnom Penh Surrenders to Rebel Forces After Offer of a Cease-Fire Is Rejected," *New York Times,* April 17, 1975, A1; "Minh Surrenders, Vietcong in Saigon," *New York Times,* April 30, 1975, A1, A16.

2. Remarks at Tulane University, April 23, 1975, *WCPD,* 431; Statement by the President, April 29, 1975, *WCPD,* 458.

3. Statement by the Press Secretary, May 12, 1975, *WCPD,* 510.

4. L. Cannon, "Ford Action Applauded by Friends, Foes," *Washington Post,* May 16, 1975, A1, A16; "Public Reaction Favors Bombings to Free Ship," *Washington Post,* May 15, 1975, A17.

5. J. D. Bass, "The Appeal to Efficiency as Narrative Closure: Lyndon Johnson and the Dominican Crisis, 1965," *Southern Speech Communication Journal* 50 (1985), 104, 118–119; G. A. Hauser, "Administrative Rhetoric and Public Opinion: Discussing the Iranian Hostages in the Public Sphere," *American Rhetoric: Context and Criticism,* ed. T. W. Benson (Carbondale: Southern Illinois, UP, 1989), 354–356.

6. R. L. Scott, "Rhetoric and Silence," *Western Journal of Speech Communication* 36 (1972), 146.

7. "A Strong But Risky Show of Force," *Time,* May 26, 1975, 17; S. Rich, "Congress Rallies Behind President," *Washington Post,* May 15, 1975, A16.

8. T. O. Windt, ed., *Presidential Rhetoric: 1961 to the Present,* 3d ed. (1978; Dubuque, Iowa: Kendall/Hunt, 1983), 221.

9. "Nixon's Crisis—and Ford's," *Newsweek,* Sept. 23, 1974, 32.

10. G. R. Ford, *A Time to Heal* (1979; rpt., New York: Berkley Books, 1980), 199, 190–191.

11. Karnow, 20–23; Remarks at Tulane University, April 23, 1975, *WCPD,* 431.

12. "Strong But Risky," 10; R. G. Head, F. W. Short, and R. C. McFarlane, *Crisis Resolution: Presidential Decision Making in the Mayaguez and Korean Confrontations* (Boulder, Colo.: Westview Press, 1978), 104–105; M. Getler and C. Kilpatrick, "Cambodia Seizes U.S. Merchant Ship," *Washington Post,* May 13, 1975, A1.

13. Head, Short, and McFarlane, 107.

14. Informal Briefing, Ron Nessen, May 16, 1975, Box 14, Ron Nessen Papers.

15. R. Rowan, *The Four Days of Mayaguez* (New York: W. W. Norton, 1975), 68–69, 175.

16. Ibid., 83, 145–152, 158–159.

17. Ford, *A Time to Heal,* 268, 271–272.

18. R. Nessen, *It Sure Looks Different From the Inside* (Chicago: Playboy, 1978), 123–124.

19. M. Getler, "Last Marines Lifted Off Isle; Toll Unknown," *Washington Post,* May 16, 1975, A1, A10; Head, Short, and McFarlane, 138, 140.

20. News Conference #222, May 15, 1975, Box 14, Ron Nessen Papers; Summary of Harris Poll, Louis Harris, June 9, 1975, Box 36, Presidential Handwriting File; Cannon, "Ford Action Applauded," A1, A16.

21. "New Test for U.S.," *U.S. News and World Report,* May 26, 1975, 19.

22. Cannon, "Ford Action Applauded," A16; H. Sidey, "An Old-Fashioned Kind of Crisis," editorial, *Time,* May 26, 1975, 18; R. Morris, "What to Make of *Mayaguez,*" editorial, *New Republic,* June 14, 1975, 9.

23. Ford, *A Time to Heal,* 267.

24. Pindar, "Nemean Odes," *The Odes of Pindar,* trans. J. Sandys (1915; rpt., London: William Heinemann, 1946), 361.

25. R. P. Hart, *The Sound of Leadership: Presidential Communication in the Modern Age* (Chicago: U of Chicago P, 1987), 59–60.

26. Memos, Bob Orben to Robert Hartmann, April 29, 1975, Nov. 5, 1975, and Jan. 1976. All found in Box 39, Counsellors to the President: Robert T. Hartmann.

27. Note, Gerald Ford to Robert Hartmann, undated; Memo, Bob Orben, undated. Both found in Box 39, Counsellors to the President: Robert T. Hartmann.

28. Memos, Bob Orben to Robert Hartmann, April 29, 1975, Nov. 5, 1975, and Oct. 17, 1975. All found in Box 39, Counsellors to the President: Robert T. Hartmann.

29. Memo, Bob Orben, undated, Box 39, Counsellors to the President: Robert T. Hartmann.

30. Hart, *The Sound of Leadership,* 60.

31. Nessen, 119.

32. K. V. Erickson and W. V. Schmidt, "Presidential Political Silence and the Rose Garden Strategy," *Southern Speech Communication Journal* 47 (1982), 403–404, 410. Although Erickson and Schmidt deal with the rose garden strategy, a president's announced refrain from campaigning for reelection, their observations about the benefits of surrogates and the protection silence yields seem equally pertinent to Ford and the *Mayaguez.*

33. Statement by the Press Secretary, May 12, 1975, *WCPD,* 510.

34. Statement by the Press Secretary, May 13, 1975, *WCPD,* 510; Statement by the Press Secretary, May 14, 1975, *WCPD,* 512.

35. News Conference #214, May 13, 1975, Box 90, Ron Nessen Papers.

36. R. T. Hartmann, *Palace Politics: An Inside Account of the Ford Years* (New York: McGraw-Hill, 1980), 326.

37. "Strong But Risky," 12; Rowan, 70.

38. Hartmann, 328; Nessen, 128; The President's Statement on the *Mayaguez* Seizure, May 15, 1975, White House Communications Agency, Video Recording, F307 Pt. I.

39. R. P. Hart, *Verbal Style and the Presidency: A Computer-Based Analysis* (Orlando, Fla.: Academic, 1984), 163.

40. R. Reeves, *A Ford, Not a Lincoln* (New York: Harcourt Brace Jovanovich, 1975), 199–200.

41. Nationwide Remarks, May 15, 1975, *WCPD,* 514.

42. Ibid.

43. Campaign Debate, Oct. 6, 1976, *WCPD,* 1457.

44. Interview of President Ford by Hugh Sidey, May 16, 1975, Box 14, Ron Nessen Papers.

45. Nationwide Remarks, May 15, 1975, *WCPD,* 514.

46. News Conference, July 9, 1976, *WCPD,* 1145.

47. Remarks and a Question-and-Answer Session at West Bend High School in Wisconsin, April 2, 1976, *WCPD,* 554.

48. Campaign Debate, Oct. 6, 1976, *WCPD,* 1456.

49. News Conference #216, May 13, 1975, Box 90, Ron Nessen Papers.

50. Remarks and a Question-and-Answer Session at West Bend High School in Wisconsin, April 2, 1976, *WCPD,* 554; News Conference, July 9, 1976, *WCPD,* 1145; Campaign Debate, Oct. 6, 1976, *WCPD,* 1456.

51. Campaign Debate, Oct. 6, 1976, *WCPD,* 1457, 1456.

52. News Conference, June 25, 1975, *WCPD,* 677.

53. Remarks and a Question-and-Answer Session at West Bend High School in Wisconsin, April 2, 1976, *WCPD*, 554.

54. Remarks to Reporters Outside the Palace of Fine Arts Theatre, Oct. 6, 1976, *WCPD*, 1465.

55. Remarks and a Question-and-Answer Session in Evansville, Indiana, April 23, 1976, *WCPD*, 686–687.

56. News Conference, July 9, 1976, *WCPD*, 1145.

57. Interview of President Ford by Hugh Sidey, May 16, 1975, Box 14, Ron Nessen Papers.

58. Remarks to Reporters Outside the Palace of Fine Arts Theatre, Oct. 6, 1976, *WCPD*, 1465; Campaign Debate, Oct. 6, 1976, *WCPD*, 1456.

59. Interview, May 23, 1975, *WCPD*, 545.

60. Campaign Debate, Oct. 6, 1976, *WCPD*, 1457.

61. Remarks with Capt. Charles T. Miller and Crew Members of the USNS *Greenville*, July 24, 1975, *WCPD*, 775–776.

62. Campaign Debate, Oct. 6, 1976, *WCPD*, 1456.

63. R. L. Lyons, "Congress Overrides Veto, Enacts War Curbs," *Washington Post*, Nov. 8, 1973, A1, A9; W. T. Reveley, III, *War Powers of the President and Congress* (Charlottesville: UP of Virginia, 1981), 233.

64. P. M. Holt, *The War Powers Resolution: The Role of Congress in U.S. Armed Intervention* (Washington, D.C.: American Enterprise Institute for Public Policy Research, 1978), 3.

65. 87 Stat. (1973), 555, 556; Reveley, 246.

66. Holt, 26.

67. 87 Stat. (1973), 555–556.

68. Holt, 12–19.

69. B. Gwertzman, "Ford Asks $972-Million in Aid for Saigon and Right to Use Troops for Evacuation," *New York Times*, April 11, 1975, A1, A11.

70. Reveley, 251; Holt, 15.

71. G. R. Ford, "Appendix," *War Powers and the Constitution* (Washington, D.C.: American Enterprise Institute for Public Policy Research, 1984), 28.

72. See, for example: T. F. Eagleton, "Congress's 'Inaction' on War," editorial, *New York Times*, May 6, 1975, A39.

73. Holt, 18, 31.

74. Notes, no author, undated, Box 14, Ron Nessen Papers (spelling and grammar corrected).

75. R. M. Pious, *The American Presidency* (New York: Basic Books, 1979), 406.

76. 87 Stat. (1973), 556–557.

77. Reveley, 242.

78. Letter to the Speaker of the House and the President Pro Tempore of the Senate, May 15, 1975, *WCPD*, 515.

79. Holt, 39.

80. H. D. S. Greenway, "Marines Depart Thailand," *Washington Post*, May 15, 1975, A1, A12; D. F. Hahn, "Corrupt Rhetoric: President Ford and the *Mayaguez* Affair," *Communication Quarterly* 28 (1980), 38–43; C. J. Lamb, *Belief Systems and Decision*

Making in the Mayaguez Crisis (Gainesville: U of Florida P, 1989), 30–32; W. Shawcross, *Sideshow: Kissinger, Nixon, and the Destruction of Cambodia* (New York: Pocket Books, 1979), 432–434.

81. Plaintiffs' Opening Brief in Support of the Court's Jurisdiction of Plaintiffs' Claims for Relief Against the United States, Jan. 18, 1980, Case of Francis Patrano [Plaintiff], Alfred J. Rappenecker, Albert Minichiello, Darryl Kastl, Frank Conway, Raymond Paul Friedler, Jr. [Plaintiffs], Carol A. Schmidt, Administratix of the Estate of Earl C. Gilbert [Plaintiff], Juan P. Sanchez and Wilbert N. Bock [Plaintiffs] vs. United States of America, Defendant, U.S. District Court, Northern District of California, Vertical File, The Gerald R. Ford Library.

82. Memo, William J. Baroody, Jr., to Robert Hartmann, May 30, 1975, Box 36, Counsellors to the President: Robert T. Hartmann.

83. Summary of Harris Poll, Louis Harris, June 9, 1975, Box 36, Presidential Handwriting File.

84. *The Ford Presidency: A Portrait of the First Two Years,* White House Office of Communications, Aug. 1976, Box 21: Ron Nessen Papers.

85. Ford, *A Time to Heal,* 121–122.

CHAPTER SIX—IDEALISM HELD HOSTAGE: JIMMY CARTER AND THE CRISIS IN IRAN

1. B. Gwertzman, "Government in Iran Vows Help in Siege," *New York Times,* Nov. 5, 1979, A1, A10; "Teheran Students Seize U.S. Embassy and Hold Hostages," *New York Times,* Nov. 5, 1979, A1, A10.

2. Remarks at Briefing for State Governors, Nov. 16, 1979, *WCPD,* 2132; Presidential Statement, Nov. 17, 1979, *WCPD,* 2141; Proclamation 4709, Dec. 16, 1979, *WCPD,* 2252–2253; Remarks on Lighting the National Christmas Tree, Dec. 13, 1979, *WCPD,* 2245.

3. Internal Transcript of Remarks at Meeting with Selected Members of Congress, Dec. 5, 1979, Box 61, White House Press Office—Powell.

4. Remarks Concerning Candidacy, Dec. 2, 1979, *WCPD,* 2194.

5. R. Carter, *First Lady From Plains* (Boston: Houghton Mifflin, 1984), 321.

6. G. A. Hauser, "Administrative Rhetoric and Public Opinion: Discussing the Iranian Hostages in the Public Sphere," *American Rhetoric: Context and Criticism,* ed. T. W. Benson (Carbondale: Southern Illinois UP, 1989), 331, 354.

7. News Conference, Nov. 28, 1979, *WCPD,* 2168; News Conference, Sept. 18, 1980, *WCPD,* 1828.

8. C. Vance, *Hard Choices: Critical Years in America's Foreign Policy* (New York: Simon and Schuster, 1983), 375–376; J. Carter, *Keeping Faith* (New York: Bantam, 1982), 457–458; "Iran: The Test of Wills," *Time,* Nov. 26, 1979, 20.

9. Memo, Jerry Rafshoon to Jimmy Carter, undated, "Memoranda from Jerry Rafshoon—June, July, & August 1979," Box 28, Rafshoon Papers.

10. Remarks on Discontinuance of Imports, Nov. 12, 1979, *WCPD,* 2107.

11. H. H. Saunders, "Diplomacy and Pressure, November 1979–May 1980," 93–94, and R. Carswell and R. J. Davis, "The Economic and Financial Pressures: Freeze and

Sanctions," 173–200. Both in *American Hostages in Iran: The Conduct of a Crisis,* ed. P. H. Kreisberg (Yale: Yale UP, 1985).

12. Presidential Statement, Nov. 17, 1979, *WCPD,* 2141; Memo, Jody Powell to Jimmy Carter, Nov. 13, 1979, Box 61, White House Press Office—Powell.

13. Letter, Jody Powell to editors and news directors nationwide, Nov. 27, 1979, Box 38, White House Press Office: Powell Files; Memo, Ray Jenkins to Fran Voorde, Nov. 29, 1979, Box CO-32, White House Central Files: Countries.

14. Memo, Anne Wexler to Jody Powell, Nov. 28, 1979, and Report, Bob Maddox, undated; both in Box 61, White House Press Office—Powell.

15. Remarks on Lighting the National Christmas Tree, Dec. 13, 1979, *WCPD,* 2245.

16. Proclamation 4709, Dec. 16, 1979, *WCPD,* 2253, 2252.

17. Remarks Concerning Candidacy, Dec. 2, 1979, *WCPD,* 2194.

18. Internal Transcript of Remarks at Meeting with Selected Members of Congress, Dec. 5, 1979, and Internal Transcript of Informal Session with Members of the Press, Dec. 8, 1979. Both in Box 61, White House Press Office—Powell.

19. Hauser, 346. Glad argues that a major factor in Carter's inflation of the hostage issue was his own "narcissistic, expansionistic personality structure." See B. Glad, "Personality, Political and Group Process Variables in Foreign Policy Decision-Making: Jimmy Carter's Handling of the Iranian Hostage Crisis," *International Political Science Review* 10 (1989), 35–61.

20. T. Mathews, "America Closes Ranks," *Newsweek,* Dec. 17, 1979, 42; Memo, William D. Blair to Acting Secretary of State, Dec. 13, 1979, Box 61, White House Press Office—Powell.

21. T. Mathews, "A Daring Escape From Iran," *Newsweek,* Feb. 11, 1980, 26–29.

22. Saunders, 72–143.

23. H. Jordan, *Crisis: The Last Year of the Carter Presidency* (1982; rpt., New York: Berkley Books, 1983), 86–87, 206–208; "A Game Without End," *Time,* Mar. 31, 1980, 29.

24. Remarks to Reporters, April 1, 1980, *WCPD,* 576; D. Broder, L. Cannon, H. Johnson, M. Schram, R. Harwood, and the Staff of the *Washington Post, The Pursuit of the Presidency 1980,* ed. R. Harwood (New York: Berkley Books, 1980), 114. Jody Powell maintains that no political motive lay behind the announcement. See J. Powell, *The Other Side of the Story* (New York: William Morrow, 1984), 215–222.

25. Remarks on U.S. Actions, April 7, 1980, *WCPD,* 611–612.

26. Daily Diary, April 24 and 25, 1980, Box PD-79, Appointments/Scheduling/Advance/Presidential Diary Office; Letter to the Speaker of the House and the President Pro Tempore of the Senate, April 26, 1980, *WCPD,* 779.

27. Talking Points, Undated, Box 92, Staff Offices, Counsel—Cutler.

28. P. Salinger, *America Held Hostage* (Garden City, N.Y.: Doubleday, 1981), 237–238. I first learned of this report by way of Hauser, 359–360.

29. Nationwide Address, April 25, 1980, *WCPD,* 772.

30. A. J. Mayer, "A Mission Comes to Grief in Iran," *Newsweek,* May 5, 1980, 26.

31. Vance, 409–411; "Debacle in the Desert," *Time,* May 5, 1980, 25.

32. Memo, Hamilton Jordan to Jimmy Carter, April 8, 1980, Box 79, Chief of Staff Jordan.

33. Broder et al, 119; Remarks and a Question-and-Answer Session, April 30, 1980, *WCPD,* 804.

34. Hauser, 361, makes this same observation.

35. A. Deming, "A Hostage Returns," *Newsweek,* July 28, 1980, 45–46; Jordan, 295.

36. Z. Brzezinski, *Power and Principle: Memoirs of the National Security Advisor, 1977–1981* (New York: Farrar, Straus, Giroux, 1983), 504–506.

37. R. Carswell and R. J. Davis, "Crafting the Financial Settlement," *American Hostages in Iran: The Conduct of a Crisis,* ed. P. H. Kreisberg (New Haven: Yale UP, 1985), 201–234.

38. J. Kifner, "Reagan Takes Oath as 40th President; Promises an 'Era of National Renewal'; Minutes Later, 52 U.S. Hostages in Iran Fly to Freedom After 444-Day Ordeal," *New York Times,* Jan. 21, 1981, A1, A8.

39. Brzezinski, 508–509.

40. C. Hitchens, "Minority Report," *Nation,* July 4/11, 1987, 7; C. Hitchens, "Minority Report," *Nation,* Nov. 21, 1987, 582.

41. Exit Interview, Jody Powell by David Alsobrook, Dec. 2, 1980, the White House, Washington, D.C.

42. Hauser, 330.

43. Vance, 380.

44. Notes of Staff Meeting with the President, Ray Jenkins, Jan. 16, 1980, Box 5, White House Press Office—Jenkins.

45. Memo, Al McDonald to Jody Powell, Nov. 26, 1979, Box 38, White House Press Office—Powell.

46. Memo, Anne Wexler to Jody Powell and Hamilton Jordan, Nov. 7, 1979, Box 62, White House Press Office—Powell.

47. Memo, Al McDonald to Hamilton Jordan, Nov. 8, 1979, and Memo, Al McDonald to Hamilton Jordan, Nov. 13, 1979. Both in Box 61, White House Press Office—Powell.

48. Memo, Jody Powell to Jimmy Carter, Jan. 16, 1980, Box 40, White House Press Office—Powell.

49. Memo, Jody Powell to Jimmy Carter, undated, Box 40, White House Press Office—Powell.

50. Broder et al, 108.

51. Notes of Senior Staff Meeting, Jan. 12, 1980, Ray Jenkins, Box 5, White House Press Office—Jenkins; Memo, Mike Chanin to Phil Wise and Jane Fenderson, Jan. 28, 1980, Box 38, White House Press Office: Powell.

52. Memo, Hedley Donovan to Jimmy Carter, Jan. 28, 1980, Box 40, White House Press Office—Powell.

53. Draft Announcement on Iran, April 7, 1980, Box 62, White House Press Office—Powell.

54. Outline of Possible Speech on Iran in Appendix Attached to Memo, Christine Dodson to Robert Hunter, Gary Sick, Linc Bloomfield, Roger Molander, Jerry Oplinger, Marshall Brement, Tom Thornton, Jaspar Welch, Donn Gregg, Roger Sullivan, Bob Blackwill, Jim Rentschler, Bill Odom, Jerry Funk, and Bill Pastor, July 22, 1980, Box 1, White House Central Files, Subject File: Speeches.

55. Cambridge Survey Research Report, Undated, Box 77, Chief of Staff—Jordan.

56. Hauser, 365.

57. R. M. Weaver, *The Ethics of Rhetoric* (Chicago: Henry Regnery Company, 1953), 56; R. L. Johannesen, R. Strickland, and R. T. Eubanks, "Richard M. Weaver on the Nature of Rhetoric: An Interpretation," *Language Is Sermonic,* ed. R. L. Johannesen, R. Strickland, and R. T. Eubanks (Baton Rouge: Louisiana State UP, 1970), 21. This chapter, I would like to emphasize, deals with *rhetorical* idealism and pragmatism, rather than these philosophies per se. For writings about the philosophy of idealism in the United States, I refer the reader to: J. Royce, *The Philosophy of Josiah Royce,* ed. J. K. Roth (New York: Thomas Y. Crowell, 1971) and *Contemporary Idealism in America,* ed. C. Barrett (1932; rpt., New York: Russell and Russell, 1964). For sources on the philosophy of pragmatism, see W. James, *Pragmatism* (1955; rpt., Cleveland: Meridian Books, 1967); J. Dewey, *Philosophy and Civilization* (New York: Minton, Balch, 1931); J. Dewey, *Theory of Valuation* (1939; rpt., Chicago: U of Chicago P, 1950).

58. Johannesen, Strickland, and Eubanks, 21–22; Weaver, *The Ethics of Rhetoric,* 56; R. M. Weaver, "Language Is Sermonic," *Language Is Sermonic,* ed. R. L. Johannesen, R. Strickland, and R. T. Eubanks (Baton Rouge: Louisiana State UP, 1970), 212–213.

59. K. Burke, *A Grammar of Motives* (1945; rpt., Berkeley: U of California P, 1969), 171.

60. Weaver, *The Ethics of Rhetoric,* 86–87; Johannesen, Strickland, and Eubanks, 22.

61. Burke, 178–181, 190, 193, 310.

62. Weaver, "Language Is Sermonic," 209.

63. Burke, 277, 276.

64. Weaver, "Language Is Sermonic," 214–215.

65. Cicero, *De Inventione,* trans. H. M. Hubbell (1949; rpt., Cambridge: Harvard UP, 1960), 2.4, 12; Aristotle, *The "Art" of Rhetoric,* trans. J. H. Freese (1926; rpt., Cambridge: Harvard UP, 1959), 1.3, 1.6, 3.17.

66. E. G. Bormann, *The Force of Fantasy: Restoring the American Dream* (Carbondale: Southern Illinois UP, 1985), 18–19, 44–52.

67. R. P. Hart, "The Functions of Human Communication in the Maintenance of Public Values," *Handbook of Rhetorical and Communication Theory,* ed. C. C. Arnold and J. W. Bowers (Boston: Allyn and Bacon, 1984), 759.

68. C. C. Arnold, "Reflections on American Public Discourse," *Central States Speech Journal* 28 (1977), 74, 73.

69. J. D. Bass, "The Appeal to Efficiency as Narrative Closure: Lyndon Johnson and the Dominican Crisis, 1965," *Southern Speech Communication Journal* 50 (1985), 116–117.

70. C. V. Crabb, Jr., *American Diplomacy and the Pragmatic Tradition* (Baton Rouge: Louisiana State UP, 1989), 183.

71. Interview, May 23, 1975, *WCPD,* 545.

72. Remarks at Briefing for State Governors, Nov. 16, 1979, *WCPD,* 2133.

73. Session with Reporters, April 18, 1980, *WCPD,* 745.

74. Burke, 344.

75. Remarks on Discontinuance of Imports, Nov. 12, 1979, *WCPD,* 2107; State of the Union, Jan. 23, 1980, *WCPD,* 194.

76. Remarks to State Department Employees, Dec. 7, 1979, *WCPD,* 2205. See also Remarks in Corpus Christi, Texas, Sept. 15, 1980, *WCPD,* 1731.

77. Session with Editors and Broadcasters of Harte-Hanks Communications, April 23, 1980, *WCPD,* 765.

78. News Conference, Nov. 28, 1979, *WCPD,* 2168; State of the Union, Jan. 23, 1980, *WCPD,* 195.

79. Draft Announcement on Iran, April 7, 1980, Box 62, White House Press Office— Powell; Remarks on U.S. Actions, April 7, 1980, *WCPD,* 611.

80. R. P. Hart, *Verbal Style and the Presidency: A Computer-Based Analysis* (Orlando, Fla.: Academic, 1984), 280, 16.

81. News Conference, Nov. 28, 1979, *WCPD,* 2173.

82. Remarks to State Department Employees, Dec. 7, 1979, *WCPD,* 2205.

83. Remarks at Briefing for State Governors, Nov. 16, 1979, *WCPD,* 2131.

84. *Meet the Press,* Jan. 20, 1980, *WCPD,* 112.

85. Remarks in Merced, California, July 4, 1980, *WCPD,* 1311; Remarks in Corpus Christi, Texas, Sept. 15, 1980, *WCPD,* 1731.

86. News Conference, April 17, 1980, *WCPD,* 706.

87. Remarks in Lyndhurst, New Jersey, Oct. 15, 1980, *WCPD,* 2265; Remarks in Flint, Michigan, Oct. 1, 1980, *WCPD,* 1992.

88. Burke, 344–345.

89. Remarks on Discontinuance of Imports, Nov. 12, 1979, *WCPD,* 2107; Session with Foreign Correspondents, April 12, 1980, *WCPD,* 669; Remarks on U.S. Actions, April 7, 1980, *WCPD,* 611, 612.

90. Nationwide Address, April 25, 1980, *WCPD,* 773, 772; News Conference, April 29, 1980, *WCPD,* 794, 793.

91. Mayer, 26.

92. Remarks in Merced, California, July 4, 1980, *WCPD,* 1311; Exchange with Reporters, Dec. 24, 1980, *WCPD,* 2833.

93. Burke, 310.

94. News Conference, Nov. 28, 1979, *WCPD,* 2173; News Conference, Feb. 13, 1980, *WCPD,* 307.

95. News Conference, Nov. 28, 1979, *WCPD,* 2167; Remarks on U.S. Actions, April 7, 1980, *WCPD,* 612; Remarks in Flint, Michigan, Oct. 1, 1980, *WCPD,* 1992; Session with Foreign Correspondents, April 12, 1980, *WCPD,* 671; Nationwide Address, Jan. 4, 1980, *WCPD,* 25.

96. Exchange with Reporters, April 28, 1980, *WCPD,* 786; Session with Foreign Correspondents, April 12, 1980, *WCPD,* 671; Remarks in Flint, Michigan, Oct. 1, 1980, *WCPD,* 1992; Remarks to American Society of Newspaper Editors, April 10, 1980, *WCPD,* 633.

97. Exchange with Reporters, Nov. 4, 1980, *WCPD,* 2683.

98. Session with Reporters, April 18, 1980, *WCPD,* 745.

99. Remarks on the Election, Nov. 4, 1980, *WCPD,* 2690.

100. Remarks at Briefing for State Governors, Nov. 16, 1979, *WCPD,* 2131.

101. Exchange with Reporters, Dec. 26, 1980, *WCPD,* 2841.

102. Burke, 201.

103. Interview, Oct. 1, 1980, *WCPD,* 2013.

104. Remarks on Discontinuance of Imports, Nov. 12, 1979, *WCPD,* 2107; News Conference, Nov. 28, 1979, *WCPD,* 2167; Session with Editors and Broadcasters of Harte-Hanks Communications, April 23, 1980, *WCPD,* 765; Remarks to State Department Employees, Dec. 7, 1979, *WCPD,* 2205; Remarks on U.S. Actions, April 7, 1980, *WCPD,* 612; Exchange with Reporters, Nov. 4, 1980, *WCPD,* 2683; Remarks in Lyndhurst, New Jersey, Oct. 15, 1980, *WCPD,* 2265.

105. Mailgram, Hedley Donovan to Islamic Scholars, Jan. 29, 1980, Box 2, Staff Offices, Hedley Donovan.

106. Session with Reporters from Westinghouse Broadcasting Company, April 18, 1980, *WCPD,* 742.

107. D. F. Hahn, "The Rhetoric of Jimmy Carter, 1976–1980," *Presidential Studies Quarterly* 14 (1984), 272.

108. M. J. Rozell, "President Carter and the Press: Perspectives from White House Communications Advisers," *Political Science Quarterly* 105 (1990), 426.

109. Memo, Rick Hertzberg to Jody Powell, Sept. 29, 1980, Box 11, Staff Offices—Powell; Broder et al, 304–305.

110. Hauser, 364–365.

111. Memo, Jerry Rafshoon to Jimmy Carter, undated, "Memoranda from Jerry Rafshoon—June, July, & August 1979," Box 28, Rafshoon Papers.

112. J. Carter, *Why Not the Best?* (Nashville: Broadman, 1975), 11.

113. M. A. Martin, "Ideologues, Ideographs, and 'The Best Men': From Carter to Reagan," *Southern Speech Communication Journal* 49 (1983), 13.

114. J. H. Patton, "A Government as Good as Its People: Jimmy Carter and the Restoration of Transcendence to Politics," *Quarterly Journal of Speech* 63 (1977), 255.

115. K. V. Erickson, "Jimmy Carter: The Rhetoric of Private and Civic Piety," *Western Journal of Speech Communication* 44 (1980), 224–225.

116. T. Szulc, "Our Most Ineffectual Postwar President," *Saturday Review,* April 29, 1978, 10, 14.

117. L. Altenberg and R. Cathcart, "Jimmy Carter on Human Rights: A Thematic Analysis," *Central States Speech Journal* 33 (1982), 447.

118. J. Fallows, "The Passionless Presidency," *Atlantic Monthly,* May 1979, 42.

119. Ibid., 34.

120. Altenberg and Cathcart, 446.

CHAPTER SEVEN—MISSION AND MANIFEST DESTINY IN GRENADA: RONALD REAGAN RALLIES THE AMERICAN FAITHFUL

1. Radio Address, Oct. 26, 1985, *WCPD,* 1303.

2. W. Isaacson, "A Rallying Round for Reagan," *Time,* Nov. 14, 1983, 39.

3. Nationwide Address, Oct. 27, 1983, *WCPD,* 1500; L. Speakes with R. Pack, *Speaking Out: The Reagan Presidency from Inside the White House* (New York: Charles Scribner's Sons, 1988), 159.

4. Statement by the Principal Deputy Press Secretary, Mar. 2, 1984, *WCPD,* 289.

5. J. K. Black, "The Selling of the Invasion of Grenada," *USA Today,* May 1984, 20;

H. O'Shaughnessy, *Grenada: An Eyewitness Account of the U.S. Invasion and the Caribbean History That Provoked It* (New York: Dodd, Mead, 1984), 166–167; A. Payne, P. Sutton, and T. Thorndike, *Grenada: Revolution and Invasion* (New York: St. Martin's Press, 1984), 155; Speakes, 161–162.

6. D. R. Heisey, "Reagan and Mitterand Respond to International Crisis: Creating Versus Transcending Appearances," *Western Journal of Speech Communication* 50 (1986), 326–328.

7. D. E. Procter, "The Rescue Mission: Assigning Guilt to a Chaotic Scene," *Western Journal of Speech Communication* 51 (1987), 248–250, 253.

8. B. J. Dow, "The Function of Epideictic and Deliberative Strategies in Presidential Crisis Rhetoric," *Western Journal of Speech Communication* 53 (1989), 303–304.

9. D. C. Klope, "Defusing a Foreign Policy Crisis: Myth and Victimage in Reagan's 1983 Lebanon/Grenada Address," *Western Journal of Speech Communication* 50 (1986), 343–345, 338.

10. D. S. Birdsell, "Ronald Reagan on Lebanon and Grenada: Flexibility and Interpretation in the Application of Kenneth Burke's Pentad," *Quarterly Journal of Speech* 73 (1987), 271.

11. M. Eliade, "Myths—Sacred History, Time, and Intercommunication," *Myths, Rites, Symbols: A Mircea Eliade Reader,* ed. W. C. Beane and W. G. Doty, (1975; rpt., New York: Harper Colophon Books, 1976), 1, 2–3; M. Eliade, *The Sacred and the Profane* (1957; rpt., New York: Harcourt Brace Jovanovich, 1959), 95.

12. R. Wellek and A. Warren, *Theory of Literature,* 3d rev. ed. (London: Jonathan Cape, 1966), 191.

13. K. Burke, *Language as Symbolic Action* (Berkeley: U of California P, 1966), 390; J. Campbell, *Myths to Live By* (1972; rpt., New York: Bantam, 1988), 9; E. Cassirer, *Language and Myth,* trans. S. K. Langer (1946; rpt., New York: Dover Publications, 1953), 44; G. M. Cuthbertson, *Political Myth and Epic* (Lansing: Michigan State UP, 1975), 221.

14. W. Lance Bennett, "Myth, Ritual, and Political Control," *Journal of Communication* 30 (1980), 167.

15. L. Baritz, *Backfire: A History of How American Culture Led Us Into Vietnam and Made Us Fight the Way We Did* (New York: William Morrow, 1985), F. Merk with L. B. Merk, *Manifest Destiny and Mission in American History* (New York: Alfred A. Knopf, 1963), 262–263.

16. Merk, 29, 24.

17. See Baritz, 27–34.

18. Remarks to Reporters, Aug. 20, 1982, *WCPD,* 1048.

19. F. D. Wormuth and E. B. Firmage with F. P. Butler, *To Chain the Dog of War: The War Power of Congress in History and Law* (Dallas: Southern Methodist UP, 1986), 261.

20. Nationwide Address, Sept. 20, 1982, *WCPD,* 1183.

21. Letter to the Speaker of the House and the President Pro Tempore of the Senate, Sept. 29, 1982, *WCPD,* 1232.

22. 87 Stat. (1973), 555–556.

23. Letter to the Speaker of the House and the President Pro Tempore of the Senate, May 15, 1975, *WCPD,* 515.

24. Letter to the Speaker of the House and the President Pro Tempore of the Senate, April 26, 1980, *WCPD,* 777–778.

25. Letter to the Speaker of the House and the President Pro Tempore of the Senate, Sept. 29, 1982, *WCPD,* 1232.

26. Wormuth and Firmage, 262.

27. I. M. Destler, "Dateline Washington: Life After the Veto," *Foreign Policy* 52 (1983), 181–182; M. J. Glennon, "The War Powers Resolution Ten Years Later: More Politics Than Law," *American Journal of International Law* 78 (1984), 577.

28. Letter to the Speaker of the House and the President Pro Tempore of the Senate, Aug. 30, 1983, *WCPD,* 1187.

29. Wormuth and Firmage, 262.

30. Ibid., 263.

31. Presidential Statement, Oct. 12, 1983, *WCPD,* 1422–1423.

32. L. Cannon, *President Reagan: The Role of a Lifetime* (New York: Simon and Schuster, 1991), 445.

33. S. V. Roberts, "Legislators Say Reagan Must Reassess U.S. Role," *New York Times,* Oct. 24, 1983, A8.

34. "America Held Hostage," editorial, *New York Times,* Oct. 24, 1983, A18.

35. Session with Editors and Broadcasters, Oct. 24, 1983, *WCPD,* 1483.

36. "Operation Urgent Fury," prod. M. Obenhaus, *Frontline,* PBS, Feb. 2, 1988.

37. Remarks to National Association of Manufacturers, Mar. 10, 1983, WCPD, 377–378; Nationwide Address, Mar. 23, 1983, *WCPD,* 445.

38. K. W. Banta, "Spice Island Power Play," *Time,* Oct. 31, 1983, 78; Session with Reporters, Oct. 25, 1983, *WCPD,* 1487.

39. H. Smith, "1,900 U.S. Troops, With Caribbean Allies, Invade Grenada and Fight Leftist Units; Moscow Protests; British Are Critical," *New York Times,* Oct. 26, 1983, A16.

40. Letter to the Speaker of the House and the President Pro Tempore of the Senate, Oct. 25, 1983, *WCPD,* 1493–1494.

41. M. Rubner, "The Reagan Administration, the 1973 War Powers Resolution, and the Invasion of Grenada," *Political Science Quarterly* 100 (1985–1986), 638–639; Wormuth and Firmage, 260–261.

42. O'Shaughnessy, 206; K. P. Schoenhals and R. A. Melanson, *Revolution and Intervention in Grenada* (Boulder, Colo.: Westview Press, 1985), 156; C. Kaiser, "An Off-the-Record War," *Newsweek,* Nov. 7, 1983, 83; Speakes, 158.

43. Kaiser, 83.

44. Baritz, 26, 27.

45. Merk, 262–263.

46. C. H. Brown, *Agents of Manifest Destiny* (Chapel Hill: U of North Carolina P, 1980), 16, 24.

47. Merk, 24, 29.

48. J. D. Bass and R. Cherwitz, "Imperial Mission and Manifest Destiny: A Case Study of Political Myth in Rhetorical Discourse," *Southern Speech Communication Journal* 43 (1978), 228.

49. C. V. Crabb, Jr., *Policy-Makers and Critics: Conflicting Theories of American Foreign Policy,* 2d ed. (New York: Praeger, 1986), 190–191.

50. K. W. Ritter and J. R. Andrews, *The American Ideology: Reflections of the Revolution in American Rhetoric* (Annandale, Va.: Speech Communication Association, 1978), 85, 82.

51. Baritz, 30, 33–34.

52. Cuthbertson, 157, 221.

53. Nationwide Address, Oct. 22, 1962, *PPP,* 809.

54. Nationwide Address, Oct. 7, 1964, *PPP,* 2: 1242; Nationwide Address, April 30, 1970, *WCPD,* 601.

55. Interview, May 23, 1975, *WCPD,* 545.

56. Proclamation 4709, Dec. 16, 1979, *WCPD,* 2252–2253.

57. R. E. Crable and S. L. Vibbert, "Argumentative Stance and Political Faith Healing: 'The Dream Will Come True,'" *Quarterly Journal of Speech* 69 (1983), 294–295; W. R. Fisher, *Human Communication as Narration* (Columbia: U of South Carolina P, 1987), 148–150; G. T. Goodnight, "Ronald Reagan's Re-formulation of the Rhetoric of War: Analysis of the 'Zero Option,' 'Evil Empire,' and 'Star Wars' Addresses," *Quarterly Journal of Speech* 72 (1986), 401; Klope, 336–349; W. F. Lewis, "Telling America's Story: Narrative Form and the Reagan Presidency," *Quarterly Journal of Speech* 73 (1987), 282; K. W. Ritter and D. Henry, *Ronald Reagan: The Great Communicator* (Westport, Conn.: Greenwood, 1992); J. H. Rushing, "Ronald Reagan's 'Star Wars' Address: Mythic Containment of Technical Reasoning," *Quarterly Journal of Speech* 72 (1986), 415–433; C. A. Smith, "MisteReagan's Neighborhood: Rhetoric and National Unity," *Southern Speech Communication Journal* 52 (1987), 221; P. D. Erickson, *Reagan Speaks: The Making of an American Myth* (New York: New York UP, 1985). Of special interest here is Ritter and Henry's book that traces the religious themes in Reagan's rhetoric over the course of his political career, including his presidential role as "America's pastor."

58. Session with Reporters, Oct. 25, 1983, *WCPD,* 1487; Remarks at Campaign Reunion, Nov. 3, 1983, *WCPD,* 1520; Remarks to Military in Cherry Point, N.C., Nov. 4, 1983, *WCPD,* 1522.

59. W. R. Fisher, "Romantic Democracy, Ronald Reagan, and Presidential Heroes," *Western Journal of Speech Communication* 46 (1982), 301–303.

60. Session with Reporters, Oct. 25, 1983, *WCPD,* 1487; Remarks to Military in Cherry Point, N.C., Nov. 4, 1983, *WCPD,* 1522; Acceptance Speech, Aug. 23, 1984, *WCPD,* 1170; Remarks to Veterans of Foreign Wars, Aug. 24, 1984, *WCPD,* 1178.

61. Session with Reporters, Oct. 25, 1983, *WCPD,* 1487; Ceremony for Medical Students and U.S. Military Personnel, Nov. 7, 1983, *WCPD,* 1537.

62. Nationwide Address, Oct. 27, 1983, *WCPD,* 1500–1501.

63. Session with Reporters, Oct. 25, 1983, *WCPD,* 1487, 1489; Nationwide Address, Oct. 27, 1983, *WCPD,* 1501; Remarks to Military in Cherry Point, N.C., Nov. 4, 1983, *WCPD,* 1522; Remarks at Summit Conference of Caribbean Heads of State, July 19, 1984, *WCPD,* 1044.

64. Session with Reporters, Oct. 25, 1983, *WCPD,* 1487.

65. Remarks to Military in Cherry Point, N.C., Nov. 4, 1983, *WCPD,* 1522; Nationwide Address, Oct. 27, 1983, *WCPD,* 1501.

66. Radio Address, Oct. 26, 1985, *WCPD,* 1303.

67. Remarks at Campaign Reunion, Nov. 3, 1983, *WCPD,* 1520.

68. Remarks to Military Personnel in Cherry Point, N.C., Nov. 4, 1983, *WCPD,* 1521.

69. Remarks to Congressional Medal of Honor Society, Dec. 12, 1983, *WCPD,* 1683; Remarks at Rally in Elizabeth, New Jersey, July 26, 1984, *WCPD,* 1080.

70. Erickson, 93; Goodnight, 401; Klope, 344; Lewis, 282; C. A. Smith, 227–228.

71. Remarks in St. George's, Grenada, Feb. 20, 1986, *WCPD,* 251.

72. Remarks at Campaign Reunion, Nov. 3, 1983, *WCPD,* 1520.

73. Remarks to Military in Cherry Point, N.C., Nov. 4, 1983, *WCPD,* 1522.

74. State of the Union, Jan. 25, 1984, *WCPD,* 93.

75. Burke, *Language as Symbolic Action,* 391; J. T. Marcus, "The World Impact of the West: The Mystique and the Sense of Participation in History," *Myth and Mythmaking,* ed. H. A. Murray (1959; rpt., Boston: Beacon, 1968), 226–227.

76. Remarks at Campaign Reunion, Nov. 3, 1983, *WCPD,* 1520.

77. Rushing, "Ronald Reagan's 'Star Wars' Address," 420.

78. Remarks to Military in Cherry Point, N.C., Nov. 4, 1983, *WCPD,* 1522; Remarks to Congressional Medal of Honor Society, Dec. 12, 1983, *WCPD,* 1683.

79. Remarks at Campaign Reunion, Nov. 3, 1983, *WCPD,* 1520; Remarks to Military in Cherry Point, N.C., Nov. 4, 1983, *WCPD,* 1521.

80. Acceptance Speech, Aug. 23, 1984, *WCPD,* 1170.

81. Nationwide Address, Oct. 27, 1983, *WCPD,* 1502; Ceremony for Medical Students and U.S. Military Personnel, Nov. 7, 1983, *WCPD,* 1536, 1537; Remarks to Military in Cherry Point, N.C., Nov. 4, 1983, *WCPD,* 1522.

82. Remarks to Military in Cherry Point, N.C., Nov. 4, 1983, *WCPD,* 1522; Remarks to Veterans of Foreign Wars, Aug. 24, 1984, *WCPD,* 1178; Radio Address, Feb. 22, 1986, *WCPD,* 260; Remarks at Rally in Elizabeth, New Jersey, July 26, 1984, *WCPD,* 1079.

83. Remarks at Campaign Reunion, Nov. 3, 1983, *WCPD,* 1520.

84. State of the Union, Jan. 25, 1984, *WCPD,* 93.

85. Remarks to Congressional Medal of Honor Society, Dec. 12, 1983, *WCPD,* 1681.

86. Remarks to Military in Cherry Point, N.C., Nov. 4, 1983, *WCPD,* 1522.

87. Remarks at Rally in Elizabeth, New Jersey, July 26, 1984, *WCPD,* 1080.

88. Radio Address, Nov. 5, 1983, *WCPD,* 1535.

89. Remarks to Veterans of Foreign Wars, Aug. 24, 1984, *WCPD,* 1178.

90. Acceptance Speech, Aug. 23, 1984, *WCPD,* 1170.

91. State of the Union, Jan. 25, 1984, *WCPD,* 93.

92. Remarks to Congressional Medal of Honor Society, Dec. 12, 1983, *WCPD,* 1682.

93. R. P. Hart, *Verbal Style and the Presidency: A Computer-Based Analysis* (Orlando, Fla.: Academic, 1984), 280.

94. Nationwide Address, Oct. 27, 1983, *WCPD,* 1502. Klope also observed this theme of progress. Klope, 343–344.

95. Eliade, *The Sacred and the Profane,* 47–49, 34.

96. S. Bercovitch, *The American Jeremiad* (Madison: U of Wisconsin P, 1978), 163–

164; Bass and Cherwitz, 225–231; Rushing, "Ronald Reagan's 'Star Wars' Address," 424.

97. C. A. Smith, 236.

98. Session with Reporters, Oct. 25, 1983, *WCPD*, 1487, 1488; Nationwide Address, Oct. 27, 1983, *WCPD*, 1501.

99. Interview, Dec. 23, 1983, *WCPD*, 1742.

100. K. Burke, *The Rhetoric of Religion* (1961; rpt., Berkeley: U of California P, 1970), 258.

101. Cassirer, 32.

102. Eliade, "Myths—Sacred History," 33.

103. Written Responses to Questions Submitted by Radio Marti, June 9, 1986, *WCPD*, 842.

104. Nationwide Address, Oct. 27, 1983, *WCPD*, 1502.

105. Remarks to Military in Cherry Point, N.C., Nov. 4, 1983, *WCPD*, 1521.

106. Burke, *The Rhetoric of Religion*, 195; Burke, *Language as Symbolic Action*, 395; Bercovitch, 178; Eliade, *The Sacred and the Profane*, 47–49.

107. Nationwide Address, Oct. 27, 1983, *WCPD*, 1502, 1501.

108. Ibid., 1501–1502.

109. Remarks to Congressional Medal of Honor Society, Dec. 12, 1983, *WCPD*, 1682.

110. Remarks to Military in Cherry Point, N.C., Nov. 4, 1983, *WCPD*, 1522. Klope (346–347) and Heisey (327–328) also observe Reagan's use of victimage in his televised address about Grenada.

111. Remarks to Military in Cherry Point, N.C., Nov. 4, 1983, *WCPD*, 1522.

112. Remarks at Campaign Reunion, Nov. 3, 1983, *WCPD*, 1520.

113. Eliade, *The Sacred and the Profane*, 47–49.

114. Radio Address, Feb. 22, 1986, *WCPD*, 260.

115. Session with Editors of Gannett Newspapers, Dec. 14, 1983, *WCPD*, 1694.

116. Acceptance Speech, Aug. 23, 1984, *WCPD*, 1170.

117. Radio Address, Oct. 26, 1985, *WCPD*, 1303.

118. Ceremony for Medical Students and U.S. Military Personnel, Nov. 7, 1983, *WCPD*, 1537; Remarks at Campaign Reunion, Nov. 3, 1983, *WCPD*, 1520; Radio Address, Oct. 26, 1985, *WCPD*, 1303.

119. Marcus, 223, 233.

120. K. H. Jamieson, *Eloquence in an Electronic Age* (New York: Oxford UP, 1988), 121–123; Ritter and Henry, 105–107.

121. Lewis, 291; C. A. Smith, 238.

122. Jamieson, 160; Lewis, 287.

123. Crable and Vibbert, 293–294, 297, 299–300. Interestingly, Crable and Vibbert could not find these lines in any of Sandburg's poetry.

124. Nationwide Address, Oct. 27, 1983, *WCPD*, 1502.

125. Radio Address, Feb. 22, 1986, *WCPD*, 260.

126. State of the Union, Jan. 25, 1984, *WCPD*, 93, 94.

127. E. Magnuson, "Getting Back to Normal," *Time,* Nov. 21, 1983, 17; Schoenhals and Melanson, 153.

128. E. Magnuson, "The Heat of the Kitchen," *Time,* Oct. 8, 1984, 18, 23–24.

129. Remarks in St. George's, Grenada, Feb. 20, 1986, *WCPD,* 249, 250; R. Stengel, "In Grenada, Apocalypso Now," *Time,* Mar. 3, 1986, 18.

130. Eliade, *The Sacred and the Profane,* 51.

131. Bercovitch, 23, 62.

CHAPTER EIGHT—"AN ENDLESS SERIES OF HOBGOBLINS": THE RHETORIC AND POLITICS OF CRISIS FROM JOHN KENNEDY TO GEORGE BUSH AND BEYOND

1. "Crisis," *The Compact Edition of the Oxford English Dictionary* (New York: Oxford UP, 1971); "κρίσις," *Liddell and Scott's Greek-English Lexicon,* 1977 abridged ed.

2. "καιρός," *Liddell and Scott's Greek-English Lexicon,* 1977 abridged ed.

3. Nationwide Address, Dec. 20, 1989, *WCPD,* 1974.

4. Ibid.

5. D. E. Procter, "The Rescue Mission: Assigning Guilt to a Chaotic Scene," *Western Journal of Speech Communication* 51 (1987), 247–248.

6. J. D. Barber, "The Presidency: What Americans Want," *Perspectives on the Presidency,* ed. S. Bach and G. T. Sulzner (Lexington, Mass.: D.C. Heath, 1974), 145.

7. M. Edelman, *Political Language: Words That Succeed and Policies That Fail* (New York: Academic, 1977), 49.

8. Nationwide Address, Dec. 20, 1989, *WCPD,* 1974.

9. Ibid.; Session with Reporters, Dec. 30, 1989, *WCPD,* 2005; Remarks on Surrender of Noriega, Jan. 3, 1990, *WCPD,* 8; State of the Union, Jan. 31, 1990, *WCPD,* 146.

10. Nationwide Address, Oct. 22, 1962, *PPP,* 809.

11. Remarks on Surrender of Noriega, Jan. 3, 1990, *WCPD,* 8–9.

12. J. D. Bass, "The Appeal to Efficiency as Narrative Closure: Lyndon Johnson and the Dominican Crisis, 1965," *Southern Speech Communication Journal* 50 (1985), 119; D. C. Klope, "Defusing a Foreign Policy Crisis: Myth and Victimage in Reagan's 1983 Lebanon/Grenada Address," *Western Journal of Speech Communication* 50 (1986), 338, 343.

13. Interview, May 23, 1975, *WCPD,* 545.

14. A. J. Mayer, "A Mission Comes to Grief in Iran," *Newsweek,* May 5, 1980, 26.

15. W. Safire, "Not Oil Nor Jobs," Editorial, *New York Times,* Nov. 19, 1990, A19.

16. G. Buffon, "Discours sur le Style," *The Art of the Writer,* ed. L. Cooper (Ithaca: Cornell UP, 1952), 153–154.

17. Session with Reporters, Dec. 30, 1989, *WCPD,* 2004, 2005.

18. R. A. Cherwitz and K. S. Zagacki, "Consummatory Versus Justificatory Crisis Rhetoric," *Western Journal of Speech Communication* 50 (1986), 318–319; W. Brockriede and R. L. Scott, *Moments in the Rhetoric of the Cold War* (New York: Random House, 1970), 82–84; Klope, 343; D. R. Heisey, "Reagan and Mitterand Respond to International Crisis: Creating Versus Transcending Appearances," *Western Journal of Speech Communication* 50 (1986), 328.

19. Nationwide Address, Dec. 20, 1989, *WCPD,* 1974–1975; News Conference, Dec. 21, 1989, *WCPD,* 1980–1982.

20. Nationwide Address, April 30, 1970, *WCPD*, 600.

21. News Conference, Dec. 21, 1989, *WCPD*, 1979; Remarks on Surrender of Noriega, Jan. 3, 1990, *WCPD*, 9.

22. Remarks at Campaign Reunion, Nov. 3, 1983, *WCPD*, 1520; Remarks to Military in Cherry Point, N.C., Nov. 4, 1983, *WCPD*, 1521; Remarks to Congressional Medal of Honor Society, Dec. 12, 1983, *WCPD*, 1682.

23. "Nixon's Gamble: Operation Total Victory?" *Newsweek*, May 11, 1970, 23; H. Kissinger, *White House Years* (Boston: Little, Brown, 1979), 504–505.

24. T. O. Windt, Jr., "The Presidency and Speeches on International Crises: Repeating the Rhetorical Past," *Speaker and Gavel* 11 (1973), 11; T. O. Windt, Jr., *Presidents and Protesters: Political Rhetoric in the 1960s* (Tuscaloosa: U of Alabama P, 1990), 55; R. B. Gregg and G. A. Hauser, "Richard Nixon's April 30, 1970 Address on Cambodia: The 'Ceremony' of Confrontation," *Speech Monographs* 40 (1973), 171–172; D. S. Birdsell, "Ronald Reagan on Lebanon and Grenada: Flexibility and Interpretation in the Application of Kenneth Burke's Pentad," *Quarterly Journal of Speech* 73 (1987), 272.

25. Nationwide Address, Oct. 22, 1962, *PPP*, 807.

26. Nationwide Address, April 30, 1970, *WCPD*, 600.

27. Nationwide Address, Dec. 20, 1989, *WCPD*, 1974; News Conference, Jan. 5, 1990, *WCPD*, 14; Remarks at Bush Administration Executive Forum, Jan. 18, 1990, *WCPD*, 62.

28. News Conference, Jan. 5, 1990, *WCPD*, 19; News Conference, Dec. 21, 1989, *WCPD*, 1983; Remarks at Ceremony for the Panama Campaign Streamer, Mar. 8, 1990, *WCPD*, 382.

29. R. Slotkin, *Regeneration Through Violence* (Middletown, Conn.: Wesleyan UP, 1973).

30. M. Q. Hale, "Presidential Influence, Authority, and Power and Economic Policy," *Toward a Humanistic Science of Politics: Essays in Honor of Francis D. Wormuth*, ed. D. H. Nelson and R. L. Sklar (Lanham, Md.: UP of America, 1983), 420.

31. Cherwitz and Zagacki, 313–314; R. P. Newman, "Pity the Helpless Giant: Nixon on Cambodia," *Essays in Presidential Rhetoric*, rev. ed., ed. T. Windt with B. Ingold (1983; Dubuque, Iowa: Kendall/Hunt, 1984), 209; Heisey, 327; Klope, 346–347; Brockriede and Scott, 82–84; Windt, "The Presidency," 10–11; Windt, *Presidents and Protesters*, 27, 39–40, 55; Gregg and Hauser, 173, 178; R. A. Cherwitz, "Lyndon Johnson and the 'Crisis' of Tonkin Gulf: A President's Justification of War," *Western Journal of Speech Communication* 42 (1978), 99; Bass, 115; Birdsell, 272.

32. Nationwide Address, Oct. 22, 1962, *PPP*, 809.

33. J. Cramer, "Noriega on Ice," *Time*, Jan. 15, 1990, 24–25.

34. Remarks at Summit Conference of Caribbean Heads of State, July 19, 1984, *WCPD*, 1044; Nationwide Address, Oct. 27, 1983, *WCPD*, 1501.

35. News Conference, Dec. 21, 1989, *WCPD*, 1979–1982; Nationwide Address, Dec. 20, 1989, *WCPD*, 1974; News Conference, Jan. 5, 1990, *WCPD*, 16.

36. P. Wander, "The Rhetoric of American Foreign Policy," *Quarterly Journal of Speech* 70 (1984), 353, 354.

37. R. L. Ivie, "Images of Savagery in American Justifications for War," *Communication Monographs* 47 (1980), 280.

38. D. J. Finlay, O. R. Holsti, and R. R. Fagen, *Enemies in Politics* (Chicago: Rand McNally, 1967), 8.

39. News Conference, Dec. 21, 1989, *WCPD,* 1983; Nationwide Address, Dec. 20, 1989, *WCPD,* 1974.

40. Nationwide Address, Dec. 20, 1989, *WCPD,* 1974.

41. Session with Reporters, Dec. 31, 1989, *WCPD,* 2005; Remarks to American Farm Bureau Federation, Jan. 8, 1990, *WCPD,* 30.

42. Nationwide Address, Dec. 20, 1989, *WCPD,* 1974; Session with Reporters, Dec. 31, 1989, *WCPD,* 2005; Remarks on Surrender of Noriega, Jan. 3, 1990, *WCPD,* 9.

43. M. W. Warner, "Bush Battles the 'Wimp Factor,'" *Newsweek,* Oct. 19, 1987, 29; R. W. Apple, Jr., "War: Bush's Presidential Rite of Passage," *New York Times,* Dec. 21, 1989, A1.

44. According to E. Noelle-Neumann, a "spiral of silence" may occur when supporters of one point of view become vocal and their position is widely disseminated by the media. That is, individuals who disagree with the publicized perspective may remain silent because of a fear of social isolation. Salmon and Kline point out, quite rightly I believe, that Noelle-Neumann ignores the importance of reference groups as individuals may not care if they hold opinions different from the majority so long as their friends are in agreement with them. Nonetheless, Noelle-Neumann's work provides insight into one of the factors at work in public opinion. See E. Noelle-Neumann, *The Spiral of Silence: Public Opinion—Our Social Skin* (Chicago: U of Chicago P, 1984); C. T. Salmon and F. G. Kline, "The Spiral of Silence Ten Years Later," *Political Communication Yearbook 1984,* ed. K. R. Sanders, L. L. Kaid, and D. Nimmo (Carbondale: Southern Illinois UP, 1985), 6–8. For more on the functions that identification with a common purpose may serve, see R. N. Lebow, *Between Peace and War: The Nature of International Crisis* (Baltimore: Johns Hopkins UP, 1981), 197–198.

45. P. Hernadi, *Beyond Genre: New Directions in Literary Classification* (Ithaca: Cornell UP, 1972), 58.

46. Letter to the Speaker of the House and the President Pro Tempore of the Senate, April 16, 1986, *WCPD,* 499–500; R. Clark, "Libyan Epilogue," *Nation,* July 5/12, 1986, 5; R. Manning, "The Raid: Was It Worth It?" *U.S. News and World Report,* May 5, 1986, 18.

47. For a good synopsis of the evidence, see "High Crimes and Misdemeanors," prods. S. Jones and E. Sams, *Frontline,* PBS, Nov. 27, 1990.

48. Statement by Press Secretary, Dec. 20, 1989, *WCPD,* 1975; M. Dowd, "A Sense of Inevitability in Bush's Decision to Act," *New York Times,* Dec. 24, 1989, A9; Letter to the Speaker of the House and the President Pro Tempore of the Senate, Dec. 21, 1989, *WCPD,* 1985.

49. T. L. Friedman, "Congress Generally Supports Attack, But Many Fear Consequences," *New York Times,* Dec. 21, 1989, A21.

50. J. K. Javits, "War Powers Reconsidered," *Foreign Affairs,* 64 (1985), 137, 139–140.

51. R. E. Denton, Jr., and D. F. Hahn, *Presidential Communication: Description and Analysis* (New York: Praeger, 1986), 127.

52. L. L. Kaid and J. Foote, "How Network Television Coverage of the President and Congress Compare," *Journalism Quarterly* 62 (1985), 59; also M. B. Grossman and M. J. Kumar, *Portraying the Presidency* (Baltimore: Johns Hopkins UP, 1981), 259.

53. "Democrats' Lawsuit Against Bush Rejected," *Lafayette Journal and Courier,* Dec. 14, 1990, A8.

54. A. Clymer, "Congress Acts to Authorize War in Gulf," *New York Times,* Jan. 13, 1991, A1; A. Rosenthal, "Bush Sends Mixed Signals to Iraq About When a War Might Begin," *New York Times,* Jan. 13, 1991, A6.

55. "Excerpts of Resolutions Debated by Congress," *New York Times,* Jan. 13, 1991, A8; Clymer, A1.

56. M. Oreskes, "Selling of a Military Strike: Coffins Arriving as Bush Speaks," news analysis, *New York Times,* Dec. 22, 1989, A18.

57. J. B. Treaster, "Military Command Belittles General," *New York Times,* Dec. 27, 1989, A14; S. Komarow, "Pooling Around in Panama," *Washington Journalism Review,* Mar. 1990, 49.

58. Statement by Press Secretary, Dec. 20, 1989, *WCPD,* 1975.

59. S. W. Cloud, "How Reporters Missed the War," *Time,* Jan. 8, 1990, 61; Komarow, 52, 49.

60. "Atrocities in Panama Charged," *Lafayette Journal and Courier,* Nov. 14, 1990, A6; " 'Panama Invasion Above Board,' " *Lafayette Journal and Courier,* Nov. 28, 1990, A3.

61. C. D. Jaco, "Military to Journalists: NOW HEAR THIS," *Washington Journalism Review,* Mar. 1990, 53; R. Suro, "Vatican Is Blaming U.S. for Impasse on Noriega's Fate," *New York Times,* Dec. 30, 1989, A7.

62. G. Cranberg, "A Flimsy Story and a Compliant Press," *Washington Journalism Review,* Mar. 1990, 48; L. H. Lapham, "Deja Vu," *Harper's,* Mar. 1990, 12, 15, 17.

63. Oreskes, "Selling," A18.

64. M. K. Deaver with M. Herskowitz, *Behind the Scenes* (New York: William Morrow, 1987), 147.

65. R. W. Apple, "Men Plan; Battle Has a Mind of Its Own," *New York Times,* Jan. 13, 1991, D1; W. A. Henry, III, "Fencing in the Messengers," *Time,* Jan. 14, 1991, 17.

66. M. Oreskes, "President Wins Bipartisan Praise for Solution of Crisis Over Noriega," *New York Times,* Jan. 5, 1990, A1.

67. H. L. Mencken, *In Defense of Women* (1918; rpt., New York: Alfred A. Knopf, 1924), 53.

68. Friedman, A21.

69. "Panama Invasion Tab: $27 Million," *Lafayette Journal and Courier,* May 29, 1990, C3.

70. "Panama Struggles to Recover," *Lafayette Journal and Courier,* Dec. 16, 1990, A15.

71. R. P. Hart, *The Sound of Leadership: Presidential Communication in the Modern Age* (Chicago: U of Chicago P, 1987), 46, 15.

72. A. L. George, *Managing U.S.–Soviet Rivalry* (Boulder, Colo.: Westview Press, 1983), 1.

73. M. Edelman, *The Symbolic Uses of Politics* (1964; rpt., Urbana: U of Illinois P, 1967), 14.

74. Nationwide Address, Aug. 8, 1990, *WCPD,* 1216–1218.

SELECTED BIBLIOGRAPHY

PRESIDENTIAL ARCHIVES:

The following repositories are all part of the National Archives and Records Administration's Office of Presidential Libraries.

I. Holdings of the John F. Kennedy Library,
Boston, Massachusetts

Meeting Recordings and Audiotape Transcripts
    Executive Committee. Oct. 16, 1962.
National Security Files
    Countries: Cuba (3.25 linear ft.)
President's Office Files
    Countries: Cuba (.76 linear ft.)
    Speech Files (6.3 linear ft.)
White House Staff Files
    Pierre E.G. Salinger. Press Secretary. (111 linear ft.)
    Theodore C. Sorensen. Staff Assistant and Speechwriter. (45 linear ft.)

II. Holdings of the Lyndon Baines Johnson Library,
Austin, Texas

National Security Files
    Countries: Vietnam (98 linear ft.)
    Memos to President (17 linear ft.)
    NSC History (21 linear ft.)
    Speech File (3 linear ft.)
Oral Histories
    Douglass Cater. Special Assistant. May 8, 1969.
    George Reedy. Press Secretary. Dec. 20, 1983.
Statements of Lyndon Baines Johnson (124 linear ft.)
White House Central Files
    Confidential Files (72 linear ft.)
    EX FG 1 or Federal Government-Organizations: The President (4.54 linear ft.)
    Name File: Frank Stanton. President of CBS. (.083 linear ft.)
White House Communications Agency: Audio Recordings
    Radio and Television Report to the American People. Aug. 4, 1964.
    Remarks of the President at the State Capitol. Des Moines, Iowa. Oct. 7, 1964.

III. Holdings of the Nixon Presidential Materials, Alexandria, Virginia

Oral Histories
    Charles W. Colson. Special Counsel. June 15, 1988.
President's Office Files (38 cubic ft.)
President's Personal Files (69 cubic ft.)
White House Communications Agency: Audio Recordings
    Radio and Television Address to the Nation. April 30, 1970.
White House Special Files
    Patrick J. Buchanan. Special Assistant. (9 cubic ft.)
    Dwight Chapin. President's Appointments Secretary. (14 cubic ft.)
    Charles W. Colson. Special Counsel. (43 cubic ft.)
    H.R. Haldeman. Chief of Staff. (136 cubic ft.)
    Herbert Klein. Director of Communications. (2 cubic ft.)
White House Special Files/White House Central Files: Subject Files—Confidential
    Files (14 cubic ft)

IV. Holdings of the Gerald R. Ford Library, Ann Arbor, Michigan

Vertical File
White House Communications Agency: Video Recordings
    Nationwide Remarks. May 15, 1975.
White House Staff Files
    Robert T. Hartmann. Counsellor to the President. (38 linear ft.)
    Ron Nessen. Press Secretary. (33 linear ft.)
    Staff Secretary's Office: Presidential Handwriting File. (24 linear ft.)

V. Holdings of the Jimmy Carter Library, Atlanta, Georgia

Appointments/Scheduling/Advance/Presidential Diary Office. (46.25 linear ft.)
Gerald M. Rafshoon Collection (4 linear ft.)
Oral Histories
    Jody Powell. Press Secretary. Exit Interview. Dec. 2, 1980.
White House Central Files
    Countries: Iran (9 linear ft.)
    Speeches (12.5 linear ft.)
White House Staff Files
    Lloyd Cutler. Presidential Counsel. (27.5 linear ft.)
    Hedley Donovan. Senior Adviser. (3 linear ft.)
    Ray Jenkins. Special Assistant. (2.5 linear ft.)
    Hamilton Jordan. White House Chief of Staff. (33 linear ft.)
    Jody Powell. Press Secretary. (76.25 linear ft.)

GOVERNMENT PUBLICATIONS

Constitution of the United States.

Dept. of Defense. *United States-Vietnam Relations, 1945–67: 4.* Washington, D.C.: U.S. Government Printing Office, 1971.

Public Papers of the Presidents. Washington, D.C.: Government Printing Office, 1955, 1961–1965.

United States Statutes at Large. Washington, D.C.: United States Government Printing Office, 1947, 1955, 1957, 1962, 1964, 1971, 1973.

Weekly Compilation of Presidential Documents. Washington, D.C.: Office of the Federal Register, National Archives and Records Service, General Services Administration. 1970–1990.

BOOKS

Allison, G. T. *Essence of Decision.* Boston: Little, Brown, 1971.

Altschuler, B. E. *LBJ and the Polls.* Gainesville: U of Florida P, 1990.

Ambrose, S. E. *Eisenhower: 2.* New York: Simon and Schuster, 1984.

Aristotle. *The "Art" of Rhetoric.* Trans. J. H. Freese. 1926. Rpt. Cambridge: Harvard UP, 1959.

Austin, A. *The President's War.* New York: New York Times, 1971.

Barber, J. D. *The Presidential Character.* 3d ed. Englewood Cliffs, N.J.: Prentice-Hall, 1985.

Baritz, L. *Backfire: A History of How American Culture Led Us Into Vietnam and Made Us Fight the Way We Did.* New York: William Morrow, 1985.

Barrett, C., ed. *Contemporary Idealism in America.* 1932. Rpt. New York: Russell and Russell, 1964.

Bercovitch, S. *The American Jeremiad.* Madison: U of Wisconsin P, 1978.

Black, E. *Rhetorical Criticism: A Study in Method.* 1965. Rpt. Madison: U of Wisconsin P, 1978.

Blair, H. *Lectures on Rhetoric and Belles Lettres: 1.* Ed. H. F. Harding. Carbondale: Southern Illinois UP, 1965.

Blight, J. G., and D. A. Welch. *On the Brink: Americans and Soviets Reexamine the Cuban Missile Crisis.* New York: Hill and Wang, 1989.

Bormann, E. G. *The Force of Fantasy: Restoring the American Dream.* Carbondale: Southern Illinois UP, 1985.

Bradlee, B. C. *Conversations with Kennedy.* 1975. Rpt. New York: Pocket Books, 1976.

Brockriede, W., and R. L. Scott. *Moments in the Rhetoric of the Cold War.* New York: Random House, 1970.

Broder, D., L. Cannon, H. Johnson, M. Schram, R. Harwood, and the Staff of the *Washington Post. The Pursuit of the Presidency 1980.* Ed. R. Harwood. New York: Berkley Books,1980.

Brown, C. H. *Agents of Manifest Destiny.* Chapel Hill: U of North Carolina P, 1980.

Brown, R. H. *A Poetic for Sociology.* Cambridge: Cambridge UP, 1977.

Brzezinski, Z. *Power and Principle: Memoirs of the National Security Advisor, 1977–1981.* New York: Farrar, Straus, Giroux, 1983.

Bundy, M. *Danger and Survival: Choices About the Bomb in the First Fifty Years*. New York: Random House, 1988.

Burke, K. *Attitudes Toward History*. 3d ed. Berkeley: U of California P, 1984.

———. *Dramatism and Development*. Barre, Mass.: Clark UP, 1972.

———. *A Grammar of Motives*. 1945. Rpt. Berkeley: U of California P, 1969.

———. *Language as Symbolic Action*. Berkeley: U of California P, 1966.

———. *Permanence and Change*. 3d ed. Berkeley: U of California P, 1984.

———. *The Philosophy of Literary Form*. 3d ed. Berkeley: U of California P, 1973.

———. *A Rhetoric of Motives*. 1950. Rpt. Berkeley: U of California P, 1969.

———. *The Rhetoric of Religion*. 1961. Rpt. Berkeley: U of California P, 1970.

Campbell, J. *Myths to Live By*. 1972. Rpt. New York: Bantam, 1988.

Campbell, K. K. *Critiques of Contemporary Rhetoric*. Belmont, Cal.: Wadsworth, 1972.

Cannon, L. *President Reagan: The Role of a Lifetime*. New York: Simon and Schuster, 1991.

Carter, J. *Keeping Faith*. New York: Bantam, 1982.

———. *Why Not the Best?* Nashville: Broadman, 1975.

Carter, R. *First Lady From Plains*. Boston: Houghton Mifflin, 1984.

Cassirer, E. *Language and Myth*. Trans. S. K. Langer. 1946. Rpt. New York: Dover Publications, 1953.

Cicero. *De Inventione*. Trans. H. M. Hubbell. 1949. Rpt. Cambridge: Harvard UP, 1960.

———. *De Oratore*. Trans. E. W. Sutton. Rev. ed. London: William Heinemann, 1959.

Clark, K. C., and L. J. Legere. *The President and the Management of National Security*. New York: Frederick A. Praeger, 1969.

The Compact Edition of the Oxford English Dictionary. New York: Oxford UP, 1971.

Cormier, F. *LBJ the Way He Was*. New York: Doubleday, 1977.

Crabb, C. V., Jr. *American Diplomacy and the Pragmatic Tradition*. Baton Rouge: Louisiana State UP, 1989.

———. *Policy-Makers and Critics: Conflicting Theories of American Foreign Policy*. 2d ed. New York: Praeger, 1986.

Cuthbertson, G. M. *Political Myth and Epic*. Lansing: Michigan State UP, 1975.

Deaver, M. K., with M. Herskowitz. *Behind the Scenes*. New York: William Morrow, 1987.

Denton, R. E., Jr. *The Symbolic Dimensions of the American Presidency: Description and Analysis*. Prospect Heights, Ill.: Waveland, 1982.

Denton, R. E., Jr., and D. F. Hahn. *Presidential Communication: Description and Analysis*. New York: Praeger, 1986.

Dewey, J. *Philosophy and Civilization*. New York: Minton, Balch, 1931.

———. *Theory of Valuation*. 1939. Rpt. Chicago: U of Chicago P, 1950.

Edelman, M. *Constructing the Political Spectacle*. Chicago: U of Chicago P, 1988.

———. *Political Language: Words That Succeed and Policies That Fail*. New York: Academic, 1977.

———. *The Symbolic Uses of Politics*. 1964. Rpt. Urbana: U of Illinois P, 1967.

Eisenhower, D. D. *Mandate for Change, 1953–1956*. Garden City, N.Y.: Doubleday, 1963.

Eliade, M. *The Sacred and the Profane*. 1957. Rpt. New York: Harcourt Brace Jovanovich, 1959.

Erickson, P. D. *Reagan Speaks: The Making of an American Myth.* New York: New York UP, 1985.

Evans, R., and R. Novak. *Lyndon B. Johnson: The Exercise of Power.* New York: New American Library, 1966.

———. *Nixon in the White House: The Frustration of Power.* New York: Random House, 1971.

Finlay, D. J., O. R. Holsti, and R. R. Fagen. *Enemies in Politics.* Chicago: Rand McNally, 1967.

Fisher, W. R. *Human Communication as Narration.* Columbia: U of South Carolina P, 1987.

Ford, G. R. *A Time to Heal.* 1979. Rpt. New York: Berkley Books, 1980.

George, A. L. *Managing U.S.-Soviet Rivalry.* Boulder, Colo.: Westview Press, 1983.

Goldman, E. F. *The Tragedy of Lyndon Johnson.* New York: Alfred A. Knopf, 1969.

Goodwin, R. N. *Remembering America: A Voice from the Sixties.* Boston: Little, Brown, 1988.

Goulden, J. C. *Truth Is the First Casualty.* New York: James B. Adler, 1969.

Graber, D. A. *Verbal Behavior and Politics.* Urbana: U of Illinois P, 1976.

Grossman, M. B., and M. J. Kumar. *Portraying the Presidency.* Baltimore: Johns Hopkins UP, 1981.

Hamilton, A., J. Madison, and J. Jay. *The Federalist Papers.* New York: New American Library, 1961.

Harpham, G. G. *On the Grotesque: Strategies of Contradiction in Art and Literature.* Princeton: Princeton UP, 1982.

Hart, R. P. *The Sound of Leadership: Presidential Communication in the Modern Age.* Chicago: U of Chicago P, 1987.

———. *Verbal Style and the Presidency: A Computer-Based Analysis.* Orlando, Fla.: Academic, 1984.

Hartmann, R. T. *Palace Politics: An Inside Account of the Ford Years.* New York: McGraw-Hill, 1980.

Head, R. G., F. W. Short, and R. C. McFarlane. *Crisis Resolution: Presidential Decision Making in the Mayaguez and Korean Confrontations.* Boulder, Colo.: Westview Press, 1978.

Hermann, C. F., ed. *International Crises: Insights From Behavioral Research.* New York: The Free Press, 1972.

Hernadi, P. *Beyond Genre: New Directions in Literary Classification.* Ithaca: Cornell UP, 1972.

Hinds, L. B., and T. O. Windt, Jr. *The Cold War as Rhetoric: The Beginnings, 1945–1950.* New York: Praeger, 1991.

Holt, P. M. *The War Powers Resolution: The Role of Congress in U.S. Armed Intervention.* Washington, D.C.: American Enterprise Institute for Public Policy Research, 1978.

Isaacs, A. R. *Without Honor: Defeat in Vietnam and Cambodia.* Baltimore: Johns Hopkins UP, 1983.

James, W. *Pragmatism.* 1955. Rpt. Cleveland: Meridian Books, 1967.

Jamieson, K. H. *Eloquence in an Electronic Age.* New York: Oxford UP, 1988.

———. *Packaging the Presidency: A History and Criticism of Presidential Campaign Advertising.* New York: Oxford UP, 1984.

Johnson, L. B. *The Vantage Point.* New York: Holt, Rinehart and Winston, 1971.

Jordan, H. *Crisis: The Last Year of the Carter Presidency.* 1982. Rpt. New York: Berkley Books, 1983.

Karnow, S. *Vietnam: A History.* 1983. Rpt. New York: Penguin Books, 1984.

Kayser, W. *The Grotesque in Art and Literature.* Trans. U. Weisstein. 1957. Rpt. Bloomington: Indiana UP, 1963.

Kearns, D. *Lyndon Johnson and the American Dream.* 1976. Rpt. New York: New American Library, 1977.

Kennedy, J. F. *Profiles in Courage.* 1955. Rpt. New York: Harper and Row, 1964.

Kennedy, R. F. *Thirteen Days.* 1968. Rpt. New York: New American Library, 1969.

Kern, M., P. W. Levering, and R. B. Levering. *The Kennedy Crises: The Press, the Presidency, and Foreign Policy.* Chapel Hill: U of North Carolina P, 1983.

Kissinger, H. *White House Years.* Boston: Little, Brown, 1979.

———. *Years of Upheaval.* Boston: Little, Brown, 1982.

Klein, H. G. *Making It Perfectly Clear.* Garden City, N.Y.: Doubleday, 1980.

Lamb, C. J. *Belief Systems and Decision Making in the Mayaguez Crisis.* Gainesville: U of Florida P, 1989.

Lasswell, H. D. *Propaganda Technique in World War I.* 1927. Rpt. Cambridge: M.I.T., 1971.

Lebow, R. N. *Between Peace and War: The Nature of International Crisis.* Baltimore: Johns Hopkins UP, 1981.

Liddell and Scott's Greek-English Lexicon. Abridged ed. Oxford: Oxford UP, 1977.

Light, P. C. *The President's Agenda.* Baltimore: Johns Hopkins UP, 1982.

Longinus. *On the Sublime.* Trans. G. M. A. Grube. New York: Library of Liberal Arts, 1957.

Medhurst, M. J., R. L. Ivie, P. Wander, and R. L. Scott. *Cold War Rhetoric: Strategy, Metaphor, and Ideology.* New York: Greenwood, 1990.

Mencken, H. L. *In Defense of Women.* 1918. Rpt. New York: Alfred A. Knopf, 1924.

Merk, F., with L. B. Merk. *Manifest Destiny and Mission in American History.* New York: Alfred A. Knopf, 1963.

Miller, M. *Lyndon: An Oral Biography.* New York: G.P. Putnam's Sons, 1980.

Mueller, J. E. *Wars, Presidents and Public Opinion.* New York: John Wiley and Sons, 1973.

Nessen, R. *It Sure Looks Different From the Inside.* Chicago: Playboy, 1978.

Neustadt, R. E. *Presidential Power: The Politics of Leadership From FDR to Carter.* 2d ed. New York: Macmillan, 1986.

Nixon, R. *RN: The Memoirs of Richard Nixon: 1.* 1978. Rpt. New York: Warner, 1979.

———. *Six Crises.* Garden City, N.Y.: Doubleday, 1962.

Noelle-Neumann, E. *The Spiral of Silence: Public Opinion—Our Social Skin.* Chicago: U of Chicago P, 1984.

O'Donnell, K. P., and D. F. Powers with J. McCarthy. *"Johnny, We Hardly Knew Ye."* 1972. Rpt. New York: Pocket Books, 1973.

O'Shaughnessy, H. *Grenada: An Eyewitness Account of the U.S. Invasion and the Caribbean History That Provoked It.* New York: Dodd, Mead, 1984.

Payne, A., P. Sutton, and T. Thorndike. *Grenada: Revolution and Invasion.* New York: St. Martin's Press, 1984.

Peacham, H. *The Garden of Eloquence*. Ed. R. C. Alston. 1577. Rpt. Menston, England: Scolar, 1971.

Perelman, C., and L. Olbrechts-Tyteca. *The New Rhetoric: A Treatise on Argumentation*. Trans. J. Wilkinson and P. Weaver. 1969. Rpt. Notre Dame: U of Notre Dame P, 1971.

Pindar. *The Odes of Pindar*. Trans. J. Sandys. 1915. Rpt. London: William Heinemann, 1946.

Pious, R. M. *The American Presidency*. New York: Basic Books, 1979.

Powell, J. *The Other Side of the Story*. New York: William Morrow, 1984.

Pradhan, P. C. *Foreign Policy of Kampuchea*. New Delhi: Radiant, 1985.

Reeves, R. *A Ford, Not a Lincoln*. New York: Harcourt Brace Jovanovich, 1975.

Reveley, W. T., III. *War Powers of the President and Congress*. Charlottesville: UP of Virginia, 1981.

Ritter, K. W., and J. R. Andrews. *The American Ideology: Reflections of the Revolution in American Rhetoric*. Annandale, Va.: Speech Communication Association, 1978.

Ritter, K. W., and D. Henry. *Ronald Reagan: The Great Communicator*. Westport, Conn.: Greenwood, 1992.

Rowan, R. *The Four Days of Mayaguez*. New York: W.W. Norton, 1975.

Royce, J. *The Philosophy of Josiah Royce*. Ed. J. K. Roth. New York: Thomas Y. Crowell, 1971.

Safire, W. *Before the Fall: An Inside View of the Pre-Watergate White House*. Garden City, N.Y.: Doubleday, 1975.

Salinger, P. *America Held Hostage*. Garden City, N.Y.: Doubleday, 1981.

———. *With Kennedy*. Garden City, N.Y. : Doubleday, 1966.

Schell, J. *The Time of Illusion*. 1975. Rpt. New York: Vintage Books, 1976.

Schlesinger, A. M., Jr. *The Imperial Presidency*. 1973. Rpt. New York: Popular Library, 1974.

———. *A Thousand Days*. 1965. Rpt. Greenwich, Conn.: Fawcett, 1967.

Schoenhals, K. P., and R. A. Melanson. *Revolution and Intervention in Grenada*. Boulder, Colo.: Westview Press, 1985.

Shawcross, W. *Sideshow: Kissinger, Nixon, and the Destruction of Cambodia*. New York: Pocket Books, 1979.

Sherry, R. *A Treatise of Schemes and Tropes*. 1550. Rpt. Gainesville, Fla.: Scholars' Facsimiles and Reprints, 1961.

Slotkin, R. *Regeneration Through Violence*. Middletown, Conn.: Wesleyan UP, 1973.

Sorensen, T. C. *Kennedy*. New York: Harper and Row, 1965.

Speakes, L., with R. Pack. *Speaking Out: The Reagan Presidency from Inside the White House*. New York: Charles Scribner's Sons, 1988.

Stone, I. F. *In a Time of Torment*. New York: Random House, 1967.

Stuckey, M. E. *The President as Interpreter-in-Chief*. Chatham, N.J.: Chatham House Publishers, 1991.

Stueck, W. W., Jr. *The Road to Confrontation: American Policy Toward China and Korea, 1947–1950*. Chapel Hill: U of North Carolina P, 1981.

Tebbel, J., and S. M. Watts. *The Press and the Presidency: From George Washington to Ronald Reagan*. New York: Oxford UP, 1985.

Thompson, K. W. *Ten Presidents and the Press*. Lanham, Md.: UP of America, 1983.

Thomson, P. *The Grotesque.* London: Methuen, 1972.

Tulis, J. K. *The Rhetorical Presidency.* Princeton: Princeton UP, 1987.

Turner, K. J. *Lyndon Johnson's Dual War: Vietnam and the Press.* Chicago: U of Chicago P, 1985.

Vance, C. *Hard Choices: Critical Years in America's Foreign Policy.* New York: Simon and Schuster, 1983.

Walton, R. J. *Cold War and Counterrevolution.* New York: Viking, 1972.

War Powers and the Constitution. Washington, D.C.: American Enterprise Institute for Public Policy Research, 1984.

Weaver, R. M. *The Ethics of Rhetoric.* Chicago: Henry Regnery Company, 1953.

Wellek, R., and A. Warren. *Theory of Literature.* 3d rev. ed. London: Jonathan Cape, 1966.

White, T. H. *The Making of the President 1964.* New York: Atheneum Publishers, 1965.

Wills, G. *The Kennedy Imprisonment.* 1981. Rpt. New York: Pocket Books, 1983.

————. *Nixon Agonistes.* Boston: Houghton Mifflin, 1970.

Windchy, E. G. *Tonkin Gulf.* Garden City, N.Y.: Doubleday, 1971.

Windt, T. O., Jr., ed. *Presidential Rhetoric: 1961 to the Present.* 3d ed. 1978. Dubuque, Iowa: Kendall/Hunt, 1983.

————. *Presidents and Protesters: Political Rhetoric in the 1960s.* Tuscaloosa: U of Alabama P, 1990.

Wormuth, F. D., and E. B. Firmage with F. P. Butler. *To Chain the Dog of War: The War Power of Congress in History and Law.* Dallas: Southern Methodist UP, 1986.

Zarefsky, D. *President Johnson's War on Poverty: Rhetoric and History.* Tuscaloosa: U of Alabama P, 1986.

ARTICLES AND CHAPTERS

Altenberg, L., and R. Cathcart. "Jimmy Carter on Human Rights: A Thematic Analysis." *Central States Speech Journal* 33 (1982), 446–457.

Arnold, C. C. "Reflections on American Public Discourse." *Central States Speech Journal* 28 (1977), 73–85.

Barber, J. D. "The Presidency: What Americans Want." *Perspectives on the Presidency.* Eds. S. Bach and G. T. Sulzner. Lexington, Mass.: D. C. Heath, 1974. 144–151.

Bass, J. D. "The Appeal to Efficiency as Narrative Closure: Lyndon Johnson and the Dominican Crisis, 1965." *Southern Speech Communication Journal* 50 (1985), 103–120.

Bass, J. D., and R. Cherwitz. "Imperial Mission and Manifest Destiny: A Case Study of Political Myth in Rhetorical Discourse." *Southern Speech Communication Journal* 43 (1978), 213–232.

Benham, T. W. "Polling for a Presidential Candidate: Some Observations on the 1964 Campaign." *Public Opinion Quarterly* 24 (1965), 185–199.

Bennett, W. L. "Myth, Ritual, and Political Control." *Journal of Communication* 30 (1980), 166–179.

Bennett, W. L., P. Dempsey Harris, J. K. Laskey, A. H. Levitch, and S. E. Monrad. "Deep and Surface Images in the Construction of Political Issues: The Case of Amnesty." *Quarterly Journal of Speech* 62 (1976), 109–126.

Benoit, W. L. "Richard M. Nixon's Rhetorical Strategies in His Public Statements on Watergate." *Southern Speech Communication Journal* 47 (1982), 192–211.

Benson, T. W. "Rhetoric as a Way of Being." *American Rhetoric: Context and Criticism.* Ed. T. W. Benson. Carbondale: Southern Illinois UP, 1989. 293–322.

Bernstein, B. J. "Courage and Commitment: The Missiles of October." *Foreign Service Journal.* Dec. 1975. 9–11, 24–27.

———. "The Cuban Missile Crisis." *Reflections on the Cold War.* Eds. L. H. Miller and R. W. Pruessen. Philadelphia: Temple UP, 1974. 108–142.

Berthold, C. A. "Kenneth Burke's Cluster-Agon Method: Its Development and an Application." *Central States Speech Journal* 27 (1976), 302–309.

Birdsell, D. S. "Ronald Reagan on Lebanon and Grenada: Flexibility and Interpretation in the Application of Kenneth Burke's Pentad." *Quarterly Journal of Speech* 73 (1987), 267–279.

Black, E. "Electing Time." *Quarterly Journal of Speech* 59 (1973), 125–129.

Brummett, B. "The Representative Anecdote as a Burkean Method, Applied to Evangelical Rhetoric." *Southern Speech Communication Journal* 50 (1984), 1–23.

Buffon, G. "Discours sur le Style." *The Art of the Writer.* Ed. L. Cooper. Ithaca: Cornell UP, 1952. 146–155.

Burke, K. "Dramatism." *International Encyclopedia of the Social Sciences: 7.* Ed. D. L. Sills. New York: Macmillan/Free Press, 1968. 445–452.

———. "Rhetoric, Poetics, and Philosophy." *Rhetoric, Philosophy, and Literature: An Exploration.* Ed. D. M. Burks. West Lafayette, Ind.: Purdue UP, 1978. 15–33.

———. "The Rhetorical Situation." *Communication: Ethical and Moral Issues.* Ed. L. Thayer. New York: Gordon and Breach Science Publishers, 1973. 263–275.

Carswell, R., and R. J. Davis. "Crafting the Financial Settlement." *American Hostages in Iran: The Conduct of a Crisis.* Ed. P. H. Kreisberg. New Haven: Yale UP, 1985. 201–234.

———. "The Economic and Financial Pressures: Freeze and Sanctions." *American Hostages in Iran: The Conduct of a Crisis.* Ed. P. H. Kreisberg. New Haven: Yale UP, 1985. 173–200.

Cherwitz, R. A. "Lyndon Johnson and the 'Crisis' of Tonkin Gulf: A President's Justification of War." *Western Journal of Speech Communication* 42 (1978), 93–104.

———. "Masking Inconsistency: The Tonkin Gulf Crisis." *Communication Quarterly* 28 (1980), 27–37.

Cherwitz, R. A., and K. S. Zagacki. "Consummatory Versus Justificatory Crisis Rhetoric." *Western Journal of Speech Communication* 50 (1986), 307–324.

Chomsky, N. "Cambodia in Conflict." *Cambodia: The Widening War in Indochina.* Eds. J. S. Grant, L. A. G. Moss, and J. Unger. New York: Washington Square, 1971. 34–51.

Crable, R. E., and S. L. Vibbert. "Argumentative Stance and Political Faith Healing: 'The Dream Will Come True.'" *Quarterly Journal of Speech* 69 (1983), 290–301.

————. "Managing Issues and Influencing Public Policy." *Public Relations Review* 11 (1985), 3–16.

Destler, I. M. "Dateline Washington: Life After the Veto." *Foreign Policy* 52 (1983), 181–186.

————. "National Security Management: What Presidents Have Wrought." *Political Science Quarterly* 95 (1980–81), 573–588.

Dow, B. J. "The Function of Epideictic and Deliberative Strategies in Presidential Crisis Rhetoric." *Western Journal of Speech Communication* 53 (1989), 294–310.

Dowling, R. E., and G. Marraro. "Grenada and the Great Communicator: A Study in Democratic Ethics." *Western Journal of Speech Communication* 50 (1986), 350–367.

Eliade, M. "Myths—Sacred History, Time, and Intercommunication." *Myths, Rites, Symbols: A Mircea Eliade Reader.* Eds. W. C. Beane and W. G. Doty. 1975. Rpt. New York: Harper Colophon Books, 1976. 1–129.

Erickson, K. V. "Jimmy Carter: The Rhetoric of Private and Civic Piety." *Western Journal of Speech Communication* 44 (1980), 221–235.

Erickson, K. V., and W. V. Schmidt. "Presidential Political Silence and the Rose Garden Strategy." *Southern Speech Communication Journal* 47 (1982), 402–421.

Fisher, W. R. "Romantic Democracy, Ronald Reagan, and Presidential Heroes." *Western Journal of Speech Communication* 46 (1982), 299–310.

Freeman, D. N. "Freedom of Speech Within the Nixon Administration." *Communication Quarterly* 24 (1976), 3–10.

Glad, B. "Personality, Political and Group Process Variables in Foreign Policy Decision-Making: Jimmy Carter's Handling of the Iranian Hostage Crisis." *International Political Science Review* 10 (1989), 35–61.

Glennon, M. J. "The War Powers Resolution Ten Years Later: More Politics Than Law." *American Journal of International Law* 78 (1984), 571–581.

Gonchar, R. M., and D. F. Hahn. "The Rhetorical Predictability of Richard Nixon." *Today's Speech* 19 (1971), 3–13.

Goodnight, G. T. "Ronald Reagan's Re-formulation of the Rhetoric of War: Analysis of the 'Zero Option,' 'Evil Empire,' and 'Star Wars' Addresses." *Quarterly Journal of Speech* 72 (1986), 390–414.

Greenstein, F. I. "Popular Images of the President." *The Presidency.* Ed. A. Wildavsky. Boston: Little, Brown, 1969. 287–296.

Gregg, R. B., and G. A. Hauser. "Richard Nixon's April 30, 1970 Address on Cambodia: The 'Ceremony' of Confrontation." *Speech Monographs* 40 (1973), 167–181.

Hahn, D. F. "Corrupt Rhetoric: President Ford and the *Mayaguez* Affair." *Communication Quarterly* 28 (1980), 38–43.

————. "The Media and the Presidency: Ten Propositions." *Communication Quarterly* 35 (1987), 254–266.

————. "The Rhetoric of Jimmy Carter, 1976–1980." *Presidential Studies Quarterly* 14 (1984), 265–288.

Hale, M. Q. "Presidential Influence, Authority, and Power and Economic Policy." *Toward a Humanistic Science of Politics: Essays in Honor of Francis D. Wormuth.* Eds. D. H. Nelson and R. L. Sklar. Lanham, Md.: UP of America, 1983. 399–437.

Hart, R. P. "Absolutism and Situation: *Prolegomena* to a Rhetorical Biography of Richard M. Nixon." *Communication Monographs* 43 (1976), 204–228.

———. "A Commentary on Popular Assumptions About Political Communication." *Human Communication Research* 8 (1982), 366–382.

———. "The Functions of Human Communication in the Maintenance of Public Values." *Handbook of Rhetorical and Communication Theory.* Eds. C. C. Arnold and J. W. Bowers. Boston: Allyn and Bacon, 1984. 749–791.

Hauser, G. A. "Administrative Rhetoric and Public Opinion: Discussing the Iranian Hostages in the Public Sphere." *American Rhetoric: Context and Criticism.* Ed. T. W. Benson. Carbondale: Southern Illinois UP, 1989. 323–383.

Heisey, D. R. "Reagan and Mitterand Respond to International Crisis: Creating Versus Transcending Appearances." *Western Journal of Speech Communication* 50 (1986), 325–335.

Henderson, P. G. "Organizing the Presidency for Effective Leadership: Lessons from the Eisenhower Years." *Presidential Studies Quarterly* 17 (1987), 43–69.

Herek, G. M., I. L. Janis, and P. Huth. "Decision Making During International Crises." *Journal of Conflict Resolution* 31 (1987), 203–226.

Ivie, R. L. "Images of Savagery in American Justifications for War." *Communication Monographs* 47 (1980), 279–294.

Jablonski, C. "Richard Nixon's Irish Wake: A Case of Generic Transference." *Central States Speech Journal* 31 (1980), 164–173.

Javits, J. K. "War Powers Reconsidered." *Foreign Affairs* 64 (1985), 130–140.

Johannesen, R. L., R. Strickland, and R. T. Eubanks. "Richard M. Weaver on the Nature of Rhetoric: An Interpretation." *Language Is Sermonic.* Eds. R. L. Johannesen, R. Strickland, and R. T. Eubanks. Baton Rouge: Louisiana State UP, 1970. 7–32.

Kaid, L. L., and J. Foote. "How Network Television Coverage of the President and Congress Compare." *Journalism Quarterly* 62 (1985), 59–65.

Klope, D. C. "Defusing a Foreign Policy Crisis: Myth and Victimage in Reagan's 1983 Lebanon/Grenada Address." *Western Journal of Speech Communication* 50 (1986), 336–349.

Lebow, R. N. "The Cuban Missile Crisis: Reading the Lessons Correctly." *Political Science Quarterly* 98 (1983), 431–458.

Leng, R. J. "Reagan and the Russians: Crisis Bargaining Beliefs and the Historical Record." *The American Political Science Review* 78 (1984), 338–355.

Lewis, W. F. "Telling America's Story: Narrative Form and the Reagan Presidency." *Quarterly Journal of Speech* 73 (1987), 280–302.

Marcus, J. T. "The World Impact of the West: The Mystique and the Sense of Participation in History." *Myth and Mythmaking.* Ed. H. A. Murray. 1959. Rpt. Boston: Beacon, 1968. 221–239.

Martin, M. A. "Ideologues, Ideographs, and 'The Best Men': From Carter to Reagan." *Southern Speech Communication Journal* 49 (1983), 12–25.

Newman, R. P. "Pity the Helpless Giant: Nixon on Cambodia." *Essays in Presidential Rhetoric.* Rev. ed. Ed. T. Windt with B. Ingold. 1983. Dubuque, Iowa: Kendall/ Hunt, 1984. 204–223.

Patton, J. H. "A Government as Good as Its People: Jimmy Carter and the Restoration of Transcendence to Politics." *Quarterly Journal of Speech* 63 (1977), 249–257.

Pollard, J. E. "The Kennedy Administration and the Press." *Journalism Quarterly* 41 (1964), 3–14.

Pratt, J. W. "An Analysis of Three Crisis Speeches." *Western Journal of Speech Communication* 34 (1970), 194–203.

Procter, D. E. "The Rescue Mission: Assigning Guilt to a Chaotic Scene." *Western Journal of Speech Communication* 51 (1987), 245–255.

Rozell, M. J. "President Carter and the Press: Perspectives from White House Communications Advisors." *Political Science Quarterly* 105 (1990), 419–434.

Rubner, M. "The Reagan Administration, the 1973 War Powers Resolution, and the Invasion of Grenada." *Political Science Quarterly* 100 (1985–1986), 627–647.

Rushing, J. H. "Ronald Reagan's 'Star Wars' Address: Mythic Containment of Technical Reasoning." *Quarterly Journal of Speech* 72 (1986), 415–433.

Salmon, C. T., and F. G. Kline. "The Spiral of Silence Ten Years Later." *Political Communication Yearbook 1984.* Eds. K. R. Sanders, L. L. Kaid, and D. Nimmo. Carbondale: Southern Illinois UP, 1985. 3–30.

Saunders, H. H. "Diplomacy and Pressure, November 1979-May 1980." *American Hostages in Iran: The Conduct of a Crisis.* Ed. P. H. Kreisberg. New Haven: Yale UP, 1985. 72–143.

Scott, R. L. "Rhetoric That Postures: An Intrinsic Reading of Richard M. Nixon's Inaugural Address." *Western Speech Communication Journal* 34 (1970), 46–52.

———. "Rhetoric and Silence." *Western Journal of Speech Communication* 36 (1972), 146–158.

Small, W. J. "Crisis News Management in the Kennedy Years." *Media Power in Politics.* Ed. D. A. Graber. Washington, D.C.: CQ Press, 1984. 325–330.

Smith, C. A. "MisteReagan's Neighborhood: Rhetoric and National Unity." *Southern Speech Communication Journal* 52 (1987), 219–239.

Stelzner, H. G. "Ford's War on Inflation: A Metaphor That Did Not Cross." *Communication Monographs* 44 (1977), 284–297.

Vibbert, S. L., and D. M. Bostdorff. "Issue Management in the 'Lawsuit Crisis.'" *The Ethical Nexus.* Ed. C. Conrad. Norwood, N.J.: Ablex, 1993. 103–120.

Walker, S. G. "Bargaining Over Berlin: A Re-Analysis of the First and Second Berlin Crises." *Journal of Politics* 44 (1982), 152–164.

Wander, P. "The Rhetoric of American Foreign Policy." *Quarterly Journal of Speech* 70 (1984), 339–361.

Weaver, R. M. "Language Is Sermonic." *Language Is Sermonic.* Eds. R. L. Johannesen, R. Strickland, and R. T. Eubanks. Baton Rouge: Louisiana State UP, 1970. 201–225.

Welch, D. A. "Cuban Decision Making Reconsidered." *Journal of Conflict Resolution* 33 (1989), 430–445.

Windt, T. O., Jr. "The Presidency and Speeches on International Crises: Repeating the Rhetorical Past." *Speaker and Gavel* 11 (1973), 6–14.

Winfield, B. H. "The New Deal Publicity Operation: Foundations for the Modern Presidency." *Journalism Quarterly* 61 (1984), 40–48, 218.

CONTEMPORARY MEDIA ACCOUNTS

Albright, R. C. "Key Legislators of Both Parties Back Blockade." *Washington Post.* Oct. 23, 1962. A14.

"America Held Hostage." Editorial. *New York Times.* Oct. 24, 1983. A18.

Apple, R. W., Jr. "Men Plan; Battle Has a Mind of Its Own." *New York Times.* Jan. 13, 1991. D1.

———. "War: Bush's Presidential Rite of Passage." *New York Times.* Dec. 21, 1989. A1, A21.

"At War With War." *Time.* May 18, 1970. 6–12.

"Atrocities in Panama Charged." *Lafayette Journal and Courier.* Nov. 14, 1990. A6.

Banta, K. W. "Spice Island Power Play." *Time.* Oct. 31, 1983. 78.

Barnet, R. J. "Bush's Splendid Little War." *Nation.* Jan. 22, 1990. 73, 76–77.

Berke, R. L. "Noriega Arraigned in Miami in a Drug-Trafficking Case; He Refuses to Enter a Plea." *New York Times.* Jan. 5, 1990. A1, A10.

Black, J. K. "The Selling of the Invasion of Grenada." *USA Today.* May 1984. 19–21.

Cannon, L. "Ford Action Applauded by Friends, Foes." *Washington Post.* May 16, 1975. A1, A16.

Carter, P. D. "Final Tally in Senate Is 58–37." *Washington Post.* July 1, 1970. A1, A12.

Clark, R. "Libyan Epilogue." *Nation.* July 5/12, 1986. 5.

Cloud, S. W. "How Reporters Missed the War." *Time.* Jan. 8, 1990. 61.

Clymer, A. "Congress Acts to Authorize War in Gulf." *New York Times.* Jan. 13, 1991. A1, A8.

"Congressmen and Editors Choose Cuba as the Main Campaign Issue." *Washington Post.* Oct. 18, 1962. A2.

Cramer, J. "Noriega on Ice." *Time.* Jan. 15, 1990. 24–27.

Cranberg, G. "A Flimsy Story and a Compliant Press." *Washington Journalism Review.* Mar. 1990. 48.

"Debacle in the Desert." *Time.* May 5, 1980. 12–17, 19–20, 25.

Deming, A. "A Hostage Returns." *Newsweek.* July 28, 1980. 45–46.

"Democrats' Lawsuit Against Bush Rejected." *Lafayette Journal and Courier.* Dec. 14, 1990. A8.

"Dirksen and Halleck Say G.O.P. Must Make Vietnam an Issue." *New York Times.* July 3, 1964. A7.

Dowd, M. "A Sense of Inevitability in Bush's Decision to Act." *New York Times.* Dec. 24, 1989. A9.

Eagleton, T. F. "Congress's 'Inaction' on War." Editorial. *New York Times.* May 6, 1975. A39.

"Excerpts of Resolutions Debated by Congress." *New York Times.* Jan. 13, 1991. A8.

Fallows, J. "The Passionless Presidency." *Atlantic Monthly.* May 1979. 33–46, 48.

Finney, J. W. "Senate Unit Votes to Restrict Funds in Cambodia War." *New York Times.* May 12, 1970. A1, A17.

Friedman, T. L. "Congress Generally Supports Attack, But Many Fear Consequences." *New York Times.* Dec. 21, 1989. A21.

"A Game Without End." *Time.* Mar. 31, 1980. 28–29.

Getler, M. "Last Marines Lifted Off Isle; Toll Unknown." *Washington Post.* May 16, 1975. A1, A10.

Getler, M., and C. Kilpatrick. "Cambodia Seizes U.S. Merchant Ship." *Washington Post.* May 13, 1975. A1, A13.

"Goldwater, Congressional Leaders Support President in SE Asia Action." *Washington Post.* Aug. 5, 1964. A1.

Greenway, H. D. S. "Marines Depart Thailand." *Washington Post.* May 15, 1975. A1, A12.

Gwertzman, B. "Ford Asks $972-Million in Aid for Saigon and Right to Use Troops for Evacuation." *New York Times.* April 11, 1975. A1, A11.

———. "Government in Iran Vows Help in Siege." *New York Times.* Nov. 5, 1979. A1, A10.

Henry, W. A., III. "Fencing in the Messengers." *Time.* Jan. 14, 1991. 17.

"High Crimes and Misdemeanors." Prods. S. Jones and E. Sams. *Frontline.* PBS. Nov. 27, 1990.

Hinds, L., and C. Smith. "Rhetoric of Opposites." *Nation.* Feb. 16, 1970. 172–174.

Hitchens, C. "Minority Report." Editorial. *Nation.* July 4/11, 1987. 7.

———. "Minority Report." Editorial. *Nation.* Nov. 21, 1987. 582.

"The 'In' Party's Dramatic Triumph." *Newsweek.* Nov. 19, 1962, 31.

"Iran: The Test of Wills." *Time.* Nov. 26, 1979. 20–24, 26, 31–32.

"Is Castro's Cuba a Soviet Base?" *U.S. News and World Report.* Sept. 10, 1962. 43–46.

Isaacson, W. "A Rallying Round for Reagan." *Time.* Nov. 14, 1983. 37, 39.

"Jackson Police Fire on Students." *New York Times.* May 15, 1970. A1, A21.

Jaco, C. D. "Military to Journalists: NOW HEAR THIS." *Washington Journalism Review.* Mar. 1990. 53.

Kaiser, C. "An Off-the-Record War." *Newsweek.* Nov. 7, 1983. 83.

Keller, B. "Soviets Say Nuclear Warheads Were Deployed in Cuba in '62." *New York Times.* Jan. 29, 1989. A1, A10.

"Kennedy Pledges Free News Access." *New York Times.* May 10, 1961. A3.

"Kent State: Martyrdom That Shook the Country." *Time.* May 18, 1970. 12–14.

Kifner, J. "4 Kent State Students Killed by Troops." *New York Times.* May 5, 1970, A1, A17.

———. "Reagan Takes Oath as 40th President; Promises an 'Era of National Renewal'; Minutes Later, 52 U.S. Hostages in Iran Fly to Freedom After 444-Day Ordeal." *New York Times.* Jan 21, 1981. A1, A8.

Kilpatrick, C. "Nixon Sends GIs Into Cambodia to Destroy Enemy Sanctuaries." *Washington Post.* May 1, 1970. A1, A18.

Komarow, S. "Pooling Around in Panama." *Washington Journalism Review.* Mar. 1990. 45, 49, 52–53.

Krock, A. "Mr. Kennedy's Management of the News." *Fortune.* Mar. 1963. 82, 199, 201–202.

Lapham, L. H. "Deja Vu." *Harper's.* Mar. 1990. 12–15, 17.

Lyons, R. L. "Congress Overrides Veto, Enacts War Curbs." *Washington Post.* Nov. 8, 1973. A1, A9.

Magnuson, E. "Getting Back to Normal." *Time.* Nov. 21, 1983. 16–17.

———. "The Heat of the Kitchen." *Time.* Oct. 8, 1984. 18, 23–24.

Manning, R. "The Raid: Was It Worth It?" *U.S. News and World Report.* May 5, 1986. 18–19.

Marder, M. "American Planes Hit North Viet-Nam After 2d Attack on Our Destroyers; Move Taken to Halt New Aggression." *Washington Post.* Aug. 5, 1964. A1, A9.

———. "U.S. Aids Viet Raid in Cambodia." *Washington Post.* April 30, 1970. A1, A14.

———. "U.S. Destroyer Fights Off 3 PT Boats in Attack Off Coast of North Viet-Nam." *Washington Post.* Aug. 3, 1964. A1, A13.

Mathews, T. "America Closes Ranks." *Newsweek.* Dec. 17, 1979. 42, 45.

———. "A Daring Escape From Iran." *Newsweek.* Feb. 11, 1980. 26–29.

Mayer, A. J. "A Mission Comes to Grief in Iran." *Newsweek.* May 5, 1980. 24–27.

"Minh Surrenders, Vietcong in Saigon." *New York Times.* April 30, 1975. A1, A16.

Mohr, C. "Goldwater and Scranton Clash on Military's Role." *New York Times.* July 10, 1964. A1, A12.

Morris, R. "What to Make of *Mayaguez.*" Editorial. *New Republic.* June 14, 1975. 9–12.

"New Test for U.S." *U.S. News and World Report.* May 26, 1975. 19–22.

"A *Newsweek* Poll: Mr. Nixon Holds Up." *Newsweek.* May 25, 1970. 30.

"Nixon's Crisis—and Ford's." *Newsweek.* Sept. 23, 1974. 30–34.

"Nixon's Gamble: Operation Total Victory?" *Newsweek.* May 11, 1970. 22–26, 28.

Norris, J. G. "USS *Maddox* on Patrol as Attack Came." *Washington Post.* Aug. 3, 1964. A1.

Onis, J. de. "Nixon Puts 'Bums' Label on Some College Radicals." *New York Times.* May 2, 1970. A1, A10.

"Operation Urgent Fury." Prod. M. Obenhaus. *Frontline.* PBS. Feb. 2, 1988.

Oreskes, M. "President Wins Bipartisan Praise For Solution of Crisis Over Noriega." *New York Times.* Jan. 5, 1990. A1, A12.

———. "Selling of a Military Strike: Coffins Arriving as Bush Speaks." News Analysis. *New York Times.* Dec. 22, 1989. A18.

"'Panama Invasion Above Board.'" *Lafayette Journal and Courier.* Nov. 28, 1990. A3.

"Panama Invasion Tab: $27 Million." *Lafayette Journal and Courier.* May 29, 1990. C3.

"Panama Struggles to Recover." *Lafayette Journal and Courier.* Dec. 16, 1990. A15.

"The 'Phantom Battle' That Led to War." *U.S. News and World Report.* July 23, 1984. 56–67.

"Phnom Penh Surrenders to Rebel Forces After Offer of a Cease-Fire Is Rejected." *New York Times.* April 17, 1975. A1, A18.

"The President: Cambodian Report." *Newsweek.* June 15, 1970. 29–30.

"Public Reaction Favors Bombings to Free Ship." *Washington Post.* May 15, 1975. A17.

Rich, S. "Congress Rallies Behind President." *Washington Post.* May 15, 1975. A1, A16.

———. "Congress Reacts." *Washington Post.* May 2, 1970. A1, A10.

———. "Senators Denounce Nixon Move." *Washington Post.* April 30, 1970. A1, A15.

Roberts, S. V. "Legislators Say Reagan Must Reassess U.S. Role." *New York Times.* Oct. 24, 1983. A8

Rosenthal, A. "Bush Sends Mixed Signals to Iraq About When a War Might Begin." *New York Times.* Jan. 13, 1991. A6.

Safire, W. "Not Oil Nor Jobs." Editorial. *New York Times.* Nov. 19, 1990. A19.

Semple, R. B., Jr. "Nixon Meets Heads of 2 City Unions; Hails War Support." *New York Times*. May 27, 1970, A1, A18.

Sidey, H. "An Old-Fashioned Kind of Crisis." Editorial. *Time*. May 26, 1975. 18.

Smith, H. "1,900 U.S. Troops, With Caribbean Allies, Invade Grenada and Fight Leftist Units; Moscow Protests; British Are Critical." *New York Times*. Oct. 26, 1983. A1, A16.

Stengel, R. "In Grenada, Apocalypso Now." *Time*. Mar. 3, 1986. 17–18.

"A Strong But Risky Show of Force." *Time*. May 26, 1975. 9–14, 17–18.

Suro, R. "Vatican Is Blaming U.S. for Impasse on Noriega's Fate." *New York Times*. Dec. 30, 1989. A1, A7.

Szulc, T. "Our Most Ineffectual Postwar President." *Saturday Review*. April 29, 1978. 10–15.

"Teheran Students Seize U.S. Embassy and Hold Hostages." *New York Times*. Nov. 5, 1979. A1, A10.

"Transcript of Goldwater's Speech Accepting Republican Presidential Nomination." *New York Times*. July 17, 1964. A10.

Treaster, J. B. "Military Command Belittles General." *New York Times*. Dec. 27, 1989. A14.

"Vietnam: Mr. Nixon's Quick Fix. . . ." Editorial. *Washington Post*. May 2, 1970. A12.

"Vietnam: 'We Seek No Wider War.'" *Newsweek*. Aug. 17, 1964. 17–18.

Warner, M. W. "Bush Battles the 'Wimp Factor.'" *Newsweek*. Oct. 19, 1987. 28–30, 32, 35–36.

INDEX